THE PLAYS OF NATHAN FIELD

PLATE I—NATHAN FIELD, the DULWICH COLLEGE PORTRAIT

THE PLAYS
of
NATHAN FIELD

Edited from the Original Quartos
with Introductions and Notes

by

WILLIAM PEERY

THE UNIVERSITY OF TEXAS PRESS
AUSTIN
1950

PRINTED IN THE UNITED STATES OF AMERICA

To
the memory of my
FATHER *and* MOTHER

PREFACE

A significant figure in Renaissance literary history, the actor-playwright, represented not only by players such as Samuel Rowley and Robert Wilson but also by Heywood, Jonson, and Shakespeare, can be studied to advantage in the comedies of Nathan Field. The plays here presented have been uniformly praised for certain good qualities, are interesting pieces from the point of view of the social as well as that of the literary historian, and seem technically adroit and I think genuinely humorous to the reader of today. As yet they have not been satisfactorily edited.

That no edition of an early dramatist can be suitable for all classes of readers is obvious. This edition I have designed to fill a need lying somewhere between that of the bibliographical specialist, to whom even microfilm and photostatic copies are unsatisfactory, and that of him who desires to meet few obstacles to the interest of a general reader. The late Ronald B. McKerrow describes an ideal scholarly edition as "one which, on the positive side, should approach as closely as the extant material allows to a fair copy, made by the author himself, of his plays in the form which he intended finally to give them, and, on the negative side, should not in any way be coloured by the preconceived ideas or interpretations of later times" (*Prolegomena for the Oxford Shakespeare*, 6). McKerrow admitted that his ideal is generally unattainable, but the editor will come near it who makes a scrupulously accurate copy of the most authoritative text, corrects its obvious misprints, frees it of irregularities resulting from the conventions and limitations of early printing, and faithfully acknowledges his departures from the copy-text. Such has been my attempt in this edition. It is freely admitted, however, that as Greg says, "we cannot hope to achieve a certainly correct text, not so much on account of the uncertainties of transmission . . . as because the author may never have produced a definitive text for us to recover. All textual criticism, I suppose, is in a manner tentative" (*EP*, ix).

Although my main object has been to establish the text of Field's comedies and to purify it of the numerous metrical, grammatical, and miscellaneous improvements to which it was subjected by nineteenth-century editors, I have tried in the introductions and commentary to furnish the serious student of Jacobean drama the related information he is likely to need as he reads Field's plays, and to summarize what scholars have contributed to our knowledge of them.

In this edition of the plays of which Field was sole author, to the question of Field's collaboration with other dramatists I make no contribution other than providing for Field's undoubted work the first critical text, a prerequisite to sound investigation of the subject. Principal discussions of the question are listed in the Bibliography, Sec. 2. There is external evidence for Field's collaboration in the plays I list in the Bibliography, 1, *ii, 1*. Dean R. Florence Brinkley concludes (p. 147) that the internal evidence is satisfactory for Field's having collaborated, also, in those plays which I list in the Bibliography, 1, *ii, 2*. I have quoted or cited in explanatory notes all passages in these plays which I regard as significantly parallel to passages in Field's undoubted work.

Since the authorities consulted in the preparation of this edition have wide diversity and for the most part pertain more to other subjects than to Field, it has seemed undesirable to list them in a formal bibliography. The Bibliography here offered, therefore, is concerned only with works by and works about Field. Of the former it usually gives the first edition and one or more modern editions. Of the latter, it attempts to include specialized studies but not all mentions of Field in general histories of the drama and literature, such as Ward, say, and Baugh and others, *A Literary History of England*. Sufficient bibliographical information for the location of the many other works cited in introductions and commentary is given in footnotes on the first reference to each work, which can be located through the Index. Unless otherwise stated, an author is regularly cited in the edition first mentioned, which may be located through the Index under the author's name. Abbreviated references used for authorities most fre-

quently cited are given in a table preceding the Index; bibliographical information for works listed there does not appear
in the footnotes.

It is a pleasure to acknowledge my indebtedness to the many
institutions and persons who have assisted me in this under-
taking. For permission to use as copy-texts the Folger quarto
editions of these plays I am grateful to the officials of the
Folger Shakespeare Library and the Trustees of Amherst College. For permission to reproduce the title pages which appear
herein and the Dulwich portrait of Field, I am indebted to
the Folger and Huntington Libraries and the Governors of
Dulwich College. For the loan or use of material on Field and
for facilitating my investigation in many ways, I thank the
authorities and staffs of the libraries of Amherst, Mount
Holyyoke, and Smith Colleges; of Duke, Harvard, McGill,
North Carolina, Texas, and Yale Universities; and of the
British Museum, the Huntington Library, the Library of
Congress, the Peabody Institute Library, the Rosenbach Company, and the Victoria and Albert Museum. I gratefully
acknowledge grants from the Smith Research Fund of the
University of North Carolina, which helped make available
to me the copy-texts for this edition, and from the Research
Institute of The University of Texas, which made possible its
publication. All who have been concerned with this book at
The University of Texas Press have been most helpful, kind,
and patient.

Individuals to whom I am indebted for generous services
of many sorts are George R. Coffman, Hardin Craig, Giles E.
Dawson, Waldo H. Dunn, C. K. Edmonds, Georgia Faison,
F. C. Francis, R. H. Griffith, W. W. Greg, Alfred Harbage,
T. P. Harrison, Jr., Robert H. Haynes, William A. Jackson,
Percy Lawler, Howard F. Lowry, R. M. Lumiansky, J. G.
McManaway, Dougald MacMillan, T. O. Mabbott, Frank I.
Mapes, Frederick W. Moore, T. M. Parrott, Anne S. Pratt,
Harry H. Ransom, Fannie Ratchford, DeWitt T. Starnes,
George C. Taylor, Emma Va. Unger, William Wells, Arnold
Williams, and Gertrude L. Woodward. Though I disagree
with some of her observations on Field, I am pleased to acknowl-
edge my indebtedness, one shared by all students of Jacobean

drama, to Dean Brinkley for her significant contribution to the scholarship on my subject. She has read this book in manuscript and made suggestions which improved it. I am particularly indebted to Professor Robert B. Sharpe, of the University of North Carolina, and to the late Professor C. F. Tucker Brooke, of Yale University, my directors during the post-doctoral year in which this version of my edition was largely prepared; and to Professor Robert A. Law, of The University of Texas, who volunteered to read the page proofs. Finally I would express my indebtedness to Beverley Hamer Peery, my wife, for clerical, scholarly, and hortatory services without which this edition would have been more imperfect than it is.

AUSTIN, TEXAS

January, 1950

TABLE OF CONTENTS

LIST OF PLATES

I. GENERAL INTRODUCTION

I. GENERAL INTRODUCTION

1. NATHAN FIELD[1]

At four o'clock on the afternoon of Sunday, 13 January 1583,[2] while the Paris Garden "dogs and Bear were in the chiefest Battel,"[3] the overloaded galleries crashed to the ground. John Field, the Puritan divine, promptly pronounced the disaster "an extraordinary iudgement of God" upon the seven known dead and over one hundred fifty "prophaners of the Lordes day" who there were "sore hurt and maimed."[4] O Tempora! O Mores! Such is to be expected of the wicked Bankside, of that city in which

there is no Dicing house, Bowling alley, Cock pit, or Theater, that can be found empty. Those flagges of defiance against God, & trumpets that are blown to gather together such company, will sooner preuail to fil those places, then the preaching of the holy worde of God . . . to fill Churches.[5]

"Heathenishe *Enterludes* and *Playes*" must be banished, not only upon the Sabbath, but "vtterly rid and taken away."[6] But John Field's youngest son, as fate would have it, was one day to draw throngs back to that very spot[7] to hear, in the new Hope Theatre erected on the Paris Garden site, the most learned

---

[1] The only extended treatments of Field's life and works are Brinkley and Verhasselt. Earlier writers are often incorrect as to Field's given name, the date of his death, and his personal and professional life. For reviews of Brinkley and for accounts of Field's life by others, see Bibliography, Sec. 2. Having known Brinkley's 1927 *MLN* article but not her book, Verhasselt appears to claim credit which must be given to Brinkley. Verhasselt fails in the attempt to "give a clearer biography than has been given up [*sic*] so far" (p. 489; cf. p. 508), and seems not to know of any recent Field studies in American or British journals. Of the short lives, the best are Nungezer (pp. 135–141) and Bentley (pp. 434–436).

[2] John Stowe and E. Howes, *Annales, or, a General Chronicle of England* (London, 1615), 695.

[3] John Field, *A Godly exhortation* (London, 1583); from abstract by Chambers, IV, 220.

[4] *Ibid.*

[5] *Ibid.*, 219.

[6] *Ibid.*, 221.

[7] A point previously made by Brinkley, 7.

dramatist of England in one of his plays pay public tribute to Field's greatness as an actor.[8]

When John Field was buried, 26 March 1588,[9] the crochety but worthy preacher left in the world manuscripts without which the Marprelate Controversy might not have been;[10] some worldly goods;[11] and seven children for whom he assured himself of his widow Joan's "uprighte and motherly care."[12] Two were girls. At the age of twenty, one, Dorcas, married; the other, Elizabeth, died.[13] Perhaps it is well that the father did not live to follow the career of his son Theophilus, who by not very admirable means became successively Bishop of Llandaff, Bishop of St. David's, and Bishop of Hereford.[14] The other four boys, named John, Jonathan, Nathaniel,[15] and Nathan,[16] make perhaps not such an "odd quartette" of sons as they have been supposed[17] for a man and wife named John and Joan. John Field would have been more than disappointed in Nathan.

Nathan Field was baptized at St. Giles, Cripplegate, 17 October 1587.[18] Of his earliest childhood we know nothing. He

[8]Jonson, *Bartholomew Fair*, 5.3.86ff.; *Ben Jonson*, ed. C. H. Herford and Percy Simpson (Oxford, 1925—).
[9]Brinkley, 5; Verhasselt, 490.
[10]J. Dover Wilson, *CHEL*, III, 430.
[11]His will is transcribed by Brinkley, 149f.
[12]*Ibid.*, 149.
[13]*Ibid.*, 7.
[14]*Ibid.*, 8–10.
[15]Nathaniel, the stationer, was apprenticed to Ralph Jackson 29 September 1596 [*SR*, II, 215]; took up his freedom 3 June 1611 [*SR*, III, 683]; and was buried 20 February 1632 (1633) [Collier, *HEDP*, III, 438]. Most of the few works registered as to be published by him were written by his brother Theophilus [*SR*, IV, 133, 137, 167; 188, 191].
[16]It is hard to see why scholars who read in the registers of baptism and burial at St. Giles, Cripplegate, about John and Jonathan, continued until very recently to identify Nathan with Nathaniel. Brinkley traces and unravels the confusion of names in *MLN*, XLII (1927), 10–15 and in her book, 10–15. Her research added final proof to the argument of Chambers [II, 316–318] and W. W. Greg [*TLS*, 15 April 1926, p. 283; 3 June 1926, p. 374] against T. W. Baldwin [*TLS*, 27 May 1926, p. 355, and *MLN*, XLI (1926), 32–34] by producing letters of administration to Dorcas Field Rice and to Nathaniel's widow Anne, from which we know that the married Nathaniel and the single Nathan both lived to maturity, as stationer and actor-playwright. The confusion of names, however, continues to exist in works by reputable scholars; see *SP*, XLIV (1947), 301, 439; *NQ*, CXC (1946), 121. In this edition I shall not attempt to call attention to all the erroneous views which this confusion made possible.
[17]Brinkley, 11.
[18]Baptismal register; Collier, *HEDP*, III, 425.

was probably less than six months old when his father died. That loss to his family and the Puritan cause was a gain to episcopacy and the stage; for it is hard to believe that John Field would have allowed sons of his to become bishop and actor. How it felt to be the youngest of seven fatherless "preacher's kids" in Elizabethan England we do not hear. Nathan probably emerged into the world, if we may judge from contemporary practice,[19] about the age of nine, or in 1596; the next record shows him as "a scholler of a gramer schole in London, kepte by one M[r] Monkaster,"[20] i. e., St. Paul's School and Richard Mulcaster, under whom Field's dramatic training possibly began.[21] How long Field attended St. Paul's we do not know. Probably sometime late in 1600, almost certainly before 6 January 1601,[22] if we may borrow words written of another schoolboy, Field was "moste wrongfully, vnduly & vniustly taken"[23] by Nathaniel Giles, Henry Evans, and James Robinson or their agents and carried to the Black-friars Theatre,

there to sorte him wth mercynary players & such other chil-deren as by the abuse aforesaid they had there placed, and by lyke force & vyolence him there to deteyne & compell to exercyse the base trade of a mercynary enterlude player, to his vtter losse of tyme, ruyne & disparagment.[24]

Likewise impressed for the company were:

one John Chappell a gramer schole scholler of one M[r] Spykes schole neere Criplegate, London; John Motteram, a gramer scholler in the free schole at Westmister; . . . Alvery Trus-sell, an apprentice to one Thomas Gyles; one Phillipp Pykman

[19]Brinkley, 15.

[20]Star Chamber Proceedings, Elizabeth, Bundle C 46, No. 39; *Clifton vs. Robinson and others*; Fleay, *LS*, 128.

[21]Dramatic activities were considerably less important, however, in Field's time at St. Paul's under Mulcaster than they were at Merchant Taylors' under him [T. H. Vail Motter, *The School Drama in England* (New York, 1929), 151f., 105–124].

[22]The new company performed at Court 6 January 1600 (1601) [Steele, 121]. On 2 September 1600 Richard Burbage leased the 1596 Blackfriars Theatre to Henry Evans [Chambers, II, 41f.], who according to Burbage seems there to have *intended* to establish a company of boys.

[23]Fleay, *LS*, 127f.

[24]*Ibid.*, 129.

and Thomas Grymes, apprentices to Richard and Georg Chambers; Salmon Pavey, apprentice to one Peerce. . .[25]

The irate Henry Clifton was able to secure his son's release after a day and a night.[26] Field's father was dead, and we know not why Joan Field's "motherly care," if exerted, was unavailing. Field remained at Blackfriars, immediately to become the leading actor of the company.[27] The boys with whom he was associated were, according to Clifton, "noe way able or fitt for singing, nor by anie the sayd confederates endevoured to be taught to singe, but . . . abusively employed, as aforesayd, only in playes & enterludes."[28] Clifton, however, was not a disinterested witness. Frederick Gerschow referred to the Blackfriars boys as "junger Knaben, die sich der Singekunst mit Ernst befleissigen müssen und auf allen Instrumenten lernen, auch dabenebenst studieren;"[29] yet evidence that adequate provision was made for the academic education of the Blackfriars children seems slight.[30] Brinkley assigns to this period of Field's life Jonson's reading of Latin with him.[31]

In addition to those named by Clifton, Field's associates at this time included Thomas Day, John Underwood, Robert Baxter, and John Frost;[32] and William Ostler and Thomas Marton.[33] Brinkley's description of the life of the boys at Blackfriars seems rather idyllic: "No doubt these boys were very congenial;"[34] "The relation between the young actors and their poets was a very friendly one."[35] Unless human nature has

[25]*Ibid.*, 128.
[26]Chambers, II, 44.
[27]If we may judge from his name's appearing first in the actor-lists and from indications later to be pointed out.
[28]Fleay, *LS*, 128.
[29]*Transactions of the Royal Historical Society*, n. s., VI, (1892), 26. Chambers [II, 47f.] discounts Gerschow on the Blackfriars.
[30]Cf. Hillebrand, 186.
[31]P. 22, also exp. n. to *W*, To the Reader, 14. The evidence [*Ben Jonson*, ed. Herford and Simpson, I, 137] is discussed in *SAB*, XXI (1946), 80–86.
[32]Actor list to *Cynthia's Revels* (1601); *Ben Jonson*, IV, 184. Throughout the present edition dates in parentheses after the titles of dramatic works are probable dates of first production as given by Harbage. Despite criticism [*MP*, XL (1942), 201–212], this authority seems sufficiently reliable for my purpose. When necessary I depart from Harbage and cite authority or discuss the evidence.
[33]Actor list to *Poetaster* (1601); *Ben Jonson*, IV, 325.
[34]P. 21.
[35]P. 22. Brinkley speaks also on the other side, however; p. 23.

greatly deteriorated, it seems at least as likely that the boys of grammar-school background—Chappell, Clifton, Motteram, and Field—had frequent difficulties with the former apprentices—Trussell, Pykman, Grymes, and Pavy. Apparently the boys slept in the apartment of seven rooms made from the old Parliament Chamber above the Great Hall.[36] If we may believe Clifton, they were kept at Blackfriars "againste the wills of the said childeren;"[37] young Clifton with "vyolence, threats & terrour"[38] was ordered to learn his lines and handed over to Henry Evans with the injunction "that yf he did not obey the sayd Evans, he should be surely whipped."[39]

Yet life at the Blackfriars Theatre must have offered splendid compensations. As part of the Christmas festivities of 1600–1601, the Chapel boys had the opportunity of playing, 6 January 1601, before the Queen.[40] This "show wth musycke and speciall songs"[41] is to be identified with Jonson's *Cynthia's Revels*,[42] in which Field probably had the leading role.[43] They played before the Queen again on Shrove Sunday, 22 February.[44] The next season they entertained royalty 6 January, 10 January, and 14 February.[45] Life at St. Paul's or any other school is hardly likely to have been so exciting, to a boy under fifteen, as life at the Blackfriars must have been. "Do the boys carry it away?" Hamlet asks Rosencrantz on being told of "the late innovation." "Ay, that they do, my lord," is the reply. By what was essentially a fad,[46] one of the stranger fads in English literary history, this "eyrie of children, little eyases, that cry out on the top of question," were "most tyrannically clapp'd for 't."[47] The Children of the Chapel soon became, and for some time remained, rivals of the great adult companies.

[36]Adams, 192.
[37]Fleay, *LS*, 128.
[38]*Ibid.*, 129.
[39]*Ibid.*, 131.
[40]Steele, 121.
[41]*Ibid.*
[42]Chambers, III, 364.
[43]*Ben Jonson*, IV, 184.
[44]Steele, 122.
[45]*Ibid.*, 124.
[46]Wallace, 177; Hillebrand, 274f.
[47]*Hamlet* 2.2.377f., 347f., 354ff.; *The Complete Works of Shakespeare*, ed. George Lyman Kittredge (Boston, 1936).

For the next dozen years Field's life is intricately inter-woven with the stories of the various Queen's Revels companies. These complicated histories, filled as they are with lawsuits among the managers and skirmishes and breaks with authori-ties over the satirical content of the plays the boys were called upon to present, have already been told in detail by a number of authorities.[48] Let us concern ourselves here only with those events which seem most likely to have concerned Field.

During 1603 the theatres were closed for the illness of Eliza-beth, 19 March, and again for the plague, which broke out seriously in April.[49] Like the men's companies, the boys were given royal protection 4 February 1604 by a patent[50] to Ed-ward Kirkham, Alexander Hawkins, Thomas Kendall, and Robert Payne; a licenser in Samuel Daniel; and a new name, Children of the Revels to the Queen. The new company ap-peared at Court 21 February.[51] Before turning seventeen, Field had played principal roles before two monarchs.

But the life of a boy actor, like that of a chorister, is short. Was Field troubled by uncertainty as to what lay ahead for him? The boy who specialized in women's roles must have faced the hazard of being dropped from the company when his voice changed; this natural cause likely accounts for many boy actors' not being heard from as adults.[52] We do not know whether Field played women's parts or, like Pavy, men's.[53] In the renewal of Giles' commission to take up singing children, 7 November 1606,[54] provision was made that "after the chaunge

[48]e. g., Chambers, II, 23–61; Murray, I, 354–366; Wallace, passim; Hillebrand, esp. 171–252; and Adams, 213–225, 317–321, and 342–347.
[49]Chambers, IV, 349.
[50]Ibid., II, 49.
[51]Steele, 138.
[52]e. g., in the Chapel company, Chappell, Motteram, Trussell, Pykman, Grymes, Day, Baxter, Frost, and Marton. Of the thirteen known Chapel children, only three—Field, Ostler, and Underwood—seem to have become adult actors.
[53]Authority for Field's having acted women's parts is Malone Var., III, 213, which gives no evidence. Malone may not have kept in mind the distinction between an adult company, in which boys played women (or boys), and a children's company, like the Chapel, in which many boys must have played men. The roles generally attributed to Field [mentioned chronologically below] are all male. Malone's probably erro-neous view persists in Schelling [I, 473, 519] and even Nungezer [141].
[54]MSC, I, 362f.

of voice and service spente of anye the Children soe taken as aforesaide that . . . good order shalbe taken for there p'ferment."[55] But we do not know that any such provision was made for child actors. If Field expected to continue his career as an adult, was he perhaps troubled by Hamlet's scruple,

Will they not say afterwards, if they should grow themselves to common players (as it is most like, if their means are no better), their writers do them wrong to make them exclaim against their own succession?[56]

Difficulties lay ahead, moreover, for Field's particular company. As Heywood complains, those in charge of the boy companies assigned

bitternesse, and liberall inuectiues against all estates, to the mouthes of Children, supposing their iuniority to be a priuiledge for any rayling, be it neuer so violent. . .[57]

For the next few years the Queen's Revels company was repeatedly in trouble with authorities on this count. Chambers speaks of a "first trouble, the nature of which is unknown,"[58] over Marston's *Dutch Courtesan* (1604). Then the boys acted their licenser's *Philotas* (1604), which because of a supposed relation to Essex brought Daniel before the Privy Council.[59] Even more serious was the affair of *Eastward Ho!* (1605)[60] in which satire on the Scots, on the new knights,[61] and on the King himself exceeded the privilege of railing accorded even to "fine enghles." Chapman and Jonson were imprisoned and threatened with the loss of their ears.[62] According to Murray, "the authors, and some of the actors, were imprisoned and the company temporarily prohibited from acting."[63] "Since Field was the leading actor," Brinkley adds, "we may safely assume

---

[55]*Ibid.*, 363.
[56]*Hamlet* 2.2.364ff.
[57]*Apology for Actors* (ed. Richard H. Perkinson; New York, 1941), G3v.
[58]II, 51. Chambers assigns the play to 1603–4 [III, 430] but also to 1605 [II, 50].
[59]Chambers, III, 275f.; Adams, 216. Brinkley implies [25] that the company suffered a loss of royal favor, but Hillebrand [193] terms the outcome for the company "no serious discomfort."
[60]Chambers, III, 254–256; Hillebrand, 193f.
[61]Cf. *W* 1.2.165 and exp. n., 3.4.14f.; and *A* 5.2.218.
[62]Chambers, III, 254.
[63]I, 355; cf. Fleay, *LS*, 245.

that at the age of seventeen he was experiencing life in an
Elizabethan prison,[64] in company with his older friends, Jonson and Chapman."[65] That the company lost the direct patronage of Queen Anne for this affair is implied by the title-pages
of its subsequent plays;[66] for a time it is referred to as Children of the Revels, without reference to Anne. "It is indeed
strange," writes Hillebrand, "that after so many misadventures
with the censorship, the directors and playwrights of the company should have taken the warnings so little to heart."[67] For
the production in February 1606 of Day's *Isle of Gulls,* in
which, "from the highest to the lowest, all men's parts were
acted of two divers nations . . ., sundry were committed to
Bridewell."[68] Field "was, doubtless, among the 'sundry.' "[69]

It was about this time that Kirkham left the Revels company
to become manager of the Paul's boys,[70] and Robert Keysar
entered the Revels syndicate.[71] Having Keysar as "interest w[th]
them," the Revels children now began to pay their own rent
at Blackfriars and to be "Masters themselues"[72] under the name
Children of the Blackfriars.[73] Probably at this time Field wrote
what may be his earliest verse,[74] the commendatory lines to
Volpone, which was published early in 1607. Appearing beside Beaumont, Chapman, Donne, and Fletcher, Field at the
age of nineteen shows a becoming modesty: his is a "weake
flame" and a "lame-blind Muse."[75]

[64]If this assumption be correct, this prison rather than the Blackfriars
Theatre could be the scene of the readings from Martial with Jonson; see
SAB, XXI (1946), 82.
    [65]Brinkley, 26.
    [66]Marston, *Sophonisba* (1605); Sharpham, *The Fleir* (1606); Day,
Isle of Gulls (1606); cf. Chambers, II, 51, and n. 3.
    [67]P. 194.
    [68]James Birch, *The Court and Times of James the First* (London, 1848),
I, 61f. On the satire in the play see Chambers, III, 286 and Hillebrand,
194f.
    [69]Brinkley, 26. Hillebrand says [195] that some actors may "possibly"
have been among them.
    [70]Murray, I, 353; Hillebrand, 195.
    [71]Hillebrand, 201f.
    [72]*Evans vs. Kirkham;* Fleay, *LS,* 249.
    [73]Chambers, II, 53.
    [74]Percy Simpson, *NQ,* 8th series, VIII (1895), 301.
    [75]For an estimate of what this poem means to Field-Jonson relations,
see *SAB,* XXI (1946), 83.

Under Keysar the Revels company soon resumed its playing of satire, with the greatest indiscretions of its career. One was a play concerning the domestic affairs of the French king, usually identified as one of Chapman's Byron plays,[76] against which the French ambassador made formal protest which resulted in the imprisonment of three persons; "mais le principal qui est le compositeur eschapa."[77] The other indiscretion was the performance of a play no longer extant, possibly by Marston.[78]

Un jour ou deux devant, ilz avoient dépêché leur Roy, sa mine d'Escosse et tous ses Favorits d'une estrange sorte; [*in cipher* car apres luy avoir fait dépiter le ciel sur le vol d'un oyseau, et faict battre un gentilhomme pour avoir rompu ses chiens, ilz le dépeignoient ivre pour le moins une fois le jour. . .][79]

Away at Thetford on a hunting journey,[80] James on hearing of this attack angrily vowed that the Children of the Blackfriars "should neuer play more but should first begg their bred, and he wold haue his vow performed."[81] From the French ambassador we learn of the consequent closing of the theatres and an effort on the part of four companies to avoid a threatened permanent ban by payment of a hundred thousand francs—an effort which La Boderie thought might be successful if they should agree never to present contemporary history or living persons again.[82]

James, however, seems not to have kept his vow; for at the Christmas season of 1608–1609 the Children of the Blackfriars presented three plays at Court,[83] their first appearance there since 1 and 3 January 1605.[84] To explain this rather surprising Court appearance, Hillebrand offers the hypothesis that the royal anger had not extended to the boys themselves, who under their new manager Keysar, who had not been involved in the troubles over *Philotas* and *Eastward Ho!*, could still be

[76]Hillebrand, 199.
[77]La Boderie to the Marquis de Sillery, 8 April 1608; Chambers, III, 257.
[78]Chambers, II, 54.
[79]*Ibid.*, III, 257.
[80]*MSC*, II, 148.
[81]Sir Thomas Lake to Lord Salisbury, 11 March 1608; *MSC*, II, 149.
[82]Chambers, I, 304; III, 258.
[83]Steele, 159f.
[84]*Ibid.*, 141f.

welcomed. On the other side of the question we have, however, besides the testimony of Lake already quoted, the direct
word of Evans that "some of the boyes" had been "committed
to prison by his Maties commaund" and that when the King
"had prohibited that no plaies should be more vsed"[85] at the
Blackfriars, Kirkham had distributed the property of the company. How long the theatre remained closed on this occasion
is uncertain,[86] for from July 1608 to December 1609 London
dramatic performances were interrupted or discontinued on
account of the raging plague.[87] In February 1610 Keysar
stated that he had "kept boyes theise Two yeares to his ex-
ceedinge Charge of purpose to have Continewed playes in the
said howse vpon the ceasing of the generall sicknes."[88] Finally,
however, his "Companye of the moste exparte and skillfull
acto^rs w^thin the Realme of England" was necessarily "dispersed
and turned awaye to the abundante hurte of the said young
men."[89] The breaking of the company evidently did not hurt
John Underwood and William Ostler, who probably at this
time went over to the King's men.[90] Contrary to former belief,[91] it is now thought that Field did not join the King's men
until later.[92]

Keysar's breaking of the company seems neither to have
hurt Field. It was in these troubled days that the actor first
appears to have shown a desire to become a playwright. Perhaps like many people connected with theatrical production
then and now he was aware, in one of the moments when
the insubstantial pageant had faded, of the transitoriness of

[85]*Evans vs. Kirkham*, Fleay, *LS*, 222, 221; cf. Hillebrand, 201.
[86]But see Hillebrand, 203.
[87]Chambers, IV, 351; Adams, 316.
[88]*Keysar vs. Burbage et al.*, Wallace, *Shakespeare and His London Associates as Revealed in Recently Discovered Documents* (Lincoln, 1910), 83.
[89]*Ibid.*, 90; cf. Hillebrand, 201f.
[90]Chambers, II, 348, 331.
[91]e. g., Murray, I, 357.
[92]Baldwin, 51, and n. 29; Chambers, II, 59; III, 228; Brinkley, 28; Verhasselt, 498, 504. The former view was based on the testimony of Cuthbert Burbage in 1635, which has been misread. For the evidence see *Sharer's Papers*;
J. O. Halliwell-Phillipps, *Outlines of the Life of Shakespeare* (London, 1890),
I, 317. Burbage does not speak of Field as having joined the King's in
1608 or 1609. The boys were taken, not all at one time, but when they
grew up to be men, in process of time.

theatre values. That peculiar empathic group magic evoked by the actor is soon broken by the cries of the watermen or the taxi-drivers, but the playwright has another book he can put on his shelf. No doubt acquainted with a number of dramatists, Field may have been influenced by the greater opportunity of gathering the "commodity" afforded by a career such as Shakespeare's. At this time Beaumont and Fletcher, Brinkley points out, "had just begun to write plays, and it may be that it was their success that stirred Field's ambition."[93] This was a slack season for his company;[94] and, the playwrights having been dismissed, a new playwright, Field may have reasoned, might have an open road. Whatever the immediate source of his ambition, we find it first expressed in his verses contributed to Fletcher's *Faithful Shepherdess* (1608),[95] which show Field happy in the association his position afforded him with leading playwrights.

Let us pause to take stock of Field's potential resources as a playwright. His unsettled life had cut him off from any deep roots such as love of the country, the home, or conventional domestic virtues; it had not given him the schooling of a man of letters. On the other hand, he must have had a thorough knowledge of life in Jacobean London. Reared on the stage itself, he probably had, moreover, an excellent knowledge of stagecraft; he knew from experience what would "play" in the theatre and how other dramatists had presented things, successfully and unsuccessfully. As associates he had practicing dramatists who could assist him and perhaps use their influence for him.[96] And, finally, he had the ear of Henslowe. It may be well here to list the plays in which Field is known to have acted, or in which as a member of the company which

[93]P. 45.

[94]Brinkley, 45f.

[95]*The Works of Francis Beaumont and John Fletcher*, ed. A. Glover and A. R. Waller (Cambridge, 1905–1912), II, 519. For discussion of the bearing of this poem on Field's relations with contemporaries, see *SAB*, XXI (1946), 83f. Chambers dates *Faithful Shepherdess* 1608–1609 [III, 221] and 1609–1610 [III, 313]. My references to the plays included by Glover and Waller are by volume and page.

[96]For an examination of the traditional view that Jonson taught Field playwriting as well as Latin see *SAB*, XXI (1946), 80–86.

produced them he probably had acted, by the time at which he wrote his own plays.[97]

1600	Love's Metamorphosis, 1590, rev.	Q1601
1601	Cynthia's Revels	AL, Q1601
	The Spanish Tragedy, 1587, rev.	Hillebrand, 293
	Contention between Liberality and Prodigality, 1567, rev.	Chambers, IV, 26
	Poetaster	AL, Q1602
1602	Gentleman Usher	Chambers, III, 251
	May Day	Q1611; Chambers, III, 256
1603	Sir Giles Goosecap	Q1606
1604	All Fools	Q1605
	Bussy D'Ambois	Hillebrand, 205, 304f.; but see Chambers, III, 254
	Monsieur D'Olive	Q1606
	Philotas	Chambers, III, 276
	Dutch Courtesan	Q1605
	The Malcontent	Chambers, III, 432
1605	The Widow's Tears	Q1612; Chambers, III, 256; Hillebrand, 205
	Eastward Ho!	Q1605
	Parasitaster	Q1606
	Wonder of Women	Q1606; Chambers, III, 433
	Trick to Catch the Old One	Chambers, III, 439
1606	Isle of Gulls	Q1606
	The Fleir	Q1607
1607	Law Tricks	Q1608
	Knight of the Burning Pestle	Chambers, III, 220f.[98]
	Your Five Gallants	SR, III, 372
1608	1 or 2 Byron	Q1608
	The Faithful Shepherdess	Chambers, III, 222
	Cupid's Revenge	Q1615
	The Case Is Altered, 1597, rev.	Q1609
1609	The Coxcomb	AL; Chambers, III, 223
	Epicoene	AL; 1616 Folio
1610	Revenge of Bussy	Q1613
	Insatiate Countess	Q1613

[97]Of original productions, the dates are Harbage's; and since my purpose here is only to indicate that the productions preceded the writing of Field's plays, I here pass over in silence differences in scholarly opinion as to the dating of these plays. I place revivals in their proper chronological position without regard to the order of their initial productions. In the column at right, *AL* stands for actors' lists; a date preceded by *Q* indicates that my attribution to Field's company is based upon the title-page of a quarto published in that year; in some instances I cite a modern authority. From this list I purposely omit some doubtful items such as Chapman's *Chabot* and the Beaumont-Fletcher *Four Plays or Moral Representations in One*. The last two or three items included may have followed the writing of *W* but probably preceded that of *A*.

[98]Field presumably played the doltish Humphrey: "Were you never none of Mr. Moncasters scholars" (VI, 169). Cf. Chambers, II, 316; Baldwin, 204. See also exp. n. to *W*, Dram. pers., 3.

If a first-hand knowledge of the drama from the point of view of the actor can aid a playwright, Field's experience had equipped him well.

When a new syndicate of King's men took over the Black-friars, probably in the fall of 1609,[99] Keysar, Philip Rosseter, and others reorganized the Revels boys and established[100] them at the Whitefriars Theatre, recently vacated by the short-lived boy company of which Drayton was one of the managers.[101] Field is said to have become the manager of the new company.[102] It was at the Whitefriars that Field's first play, *A Woman is a Weather-cocke*, was performed "diuers times Priuately," probably in December 1609.[103] Under Keysar the Whitefriars Revels boys appeared at Court five times during the Christmas season of 1609–1610.[104] One of the plays there presented must have been *Weather-cocke*, and Field probably played his usual important role.

On 4 January 1610 Rosseter secured for the company a patent entitling the boys once more to be called "Children of the Revells to the Queene."[105] The principal members of this, the Second Queen's Revels company, are given in the actor-list to *Epicoene* (1609). Of the boys who had entered Black-friars in 1600, Field alone remained.[106] The company is occa-sionally traceable during 1610–1613 in the provinces, appear-ing at Maidstone, Norwich, and Coventry.[107]

Whether or not prompted by the success of his first play, as evidenced by its being taken to Court, in 1610 or 1611 Field

[99]Chambers, II, 55, 510. Adams (pp. 224f.) would date earlier.
[100]Adams (p. 317) dates earlier: "probably in February."
[101]Chambers, II, 55; Hillebrand, *JEGP*, XXI (1922), 327.
[102]Fleay, *LS*, 185.
[103]See below, *W* Intro., i.
[104]Steele, 162; Hillebrand, 238.
[105]*MSC*, I, 272. One may not infer that this return to royal favor was a reward for pleasing performances at Court since the warrant for it was obtained in December, probably before the Christmas appearances, *MSC*, I, 271.
[106]Brinkley, 29, regards Richard Baxter, named in the actor-list to *Epicoene*, as one of Field's early associates. She evidently confuses Richard Baxter with Will Barksted, with whom Robert but not Richard Baxter is possibly to be identified [Nungezer, 28–30, 33; Chambers, II, 301]. Richard Baxter seems never to have been one of the Blackfriars children [Nungezer, 32f.; Bentley, 360–362].
[107]Murray, I, 364.

must have written *Amends for Ladies*, which was probably acted by 10 October 1611.[108] Again Field probably but not certainly had a role in the production. However the play fared, Field seems never again to have written a play without one or more collaborators. Why he gave up individual authorship is unknown.[109] As his company's dark, handsome,[110] and probably dashing leading actor, whose name must have been on many lips and whose presence must often have been sought out, a high-spirited unacademic youth such as Field, like successful young literati in later periods, may have found life in Jacobean London so full that writing about it seemed less important than merely living it. The collaboration on which Field was shortly to embark may have been more or less required by his position in the company.[111] About this time Field must have done whatever work he did on *Four Plays in One* (1612) and *The Honest Man's Fortune* (1613).[112] Also in the year of the death of Prince Henry, *A Woman is a Weather-cocke* was published in quarto. From the nature of the corrections during impression,[113] it would seem likely that Field himself saw the volume through the press.

In March 1613 Rosseter united the Second Queen's Revels company with Henslowe's Lady Elizabeth's company,[114] under a rather peculiar arrangement. At times it amounted to an amalgamation;[115] at other times the companies seem to have maintained their individualities.[116] The combination, which

---

[108]See below, *A* Intro., i.

[109]"Since he was greater as a practical playwright than as a creative genius, he gave up individual composition after writing two plays and was satisfied to collaborate with Beaumont, Fletcher, and Massinger, placing his technical skill at the service of those with greater genius than he possessed" [Brinkley, 46]. The record does not make this evident. We do not know how satisfied Field was; and scholars hardly agree that to Field should be attributed those parts of the collaborate plays which show most technical skill.

[110]See the Dulwich portrait, Frontispiece.

[111]From Field's letters to Henslowe [see below] one would infer that a short time later he was more or less regularly engaged in collaboration. Cf. Verhasselt, 503.

[112]Chambers, III, 227; Brinkley, 101–110, 131–136.

[113]See below, *W* Intro., iii.

[114]Fleay, *LS*, 186.

[115]Chambers, II, 60.

[116]Cf. the patent authorizing the building of Rosseter's Blackfriars; *MSC*, I, 278.

was sometimes called by the name of Henslowe's group, may have acted at Whitefriars for a time;[117] possibly at the Swan;[118] and probably at the Rose.[119] One of its plays, *The Honest Man's Fortune* (1613), names Field first among its principal actors.[120]

In the clutches of the shrewd Henslowe,[121] Field and the company fared ill. To this time one must assign Field's undated letters to Henslowe.[122] One reveals that Field was in some kind of collaboration with Daborne on a plot which promises to "make as beneficiall a play as hath Come these seauen yeares."[123] From what follows one would judge that Daborne had control of the script and that Field was trying to secure it for the company. The letter is subscribed "yo[r] louing and obedient Son." Another letter[124] reflects Field's personal financial condition. "Unluckily taken on an execution of 30 *l*," Field is canny in the handling of the crochety Henslowe; the proper admixture of flattery and shrewdness in Field's request very likely produced the desired result. The third letter, written by Field but signed also by Daborne and Massinger, may indicate collaboration of the three and definitely requests £5 as bail for them:

you vnderstand o[r] vnfortunate extremitie and J doe not thincke you so void of christianitie, but that you would throw so much money into the Thames as wee request now of you; rather then endanger so many innocent liues; you know there is x*l·* more at least to be receaued of you, for the play, wee desire you to lend vs v*l.* of that, w[ch] shall be allowed to you w[t]hout w[ch] wee cannot be bayled, nor J play any more till this be dispatch'd, it will loose you xx*l.* ere the end of the next weeke, beside the hinderance of the next new play, pray

[117]Fleay, *LS*, 187; Brinkley, 29.
[118]Chambers, II, 257.
[119]*Ibid.*
[120]*Beaumont and Fletcher*, X, 202. Verhasselt (p. 500) dates 1616.
[121]*Articles of Grievance, Articles of Oppression;* Chambers, II, 248f., 250 and Collier, *The Alleyn Papers* (London, 1843), 78–81.
[122]*Dulwich MS 1, Articles 100, 69, 68;* Greg, *HP*, 65–67, 84. The order of mention is Greg's order of probable date, which is "reasonable" [Chambers, II, 251, n. 3].
[123]Greg, *HP*, 84.
[124]*Ibid.*

S^r. Consider our Cases w^{t}h humanitie, and now giue vs cause to acknowledge you our true freind in time of neede. . .[125]

With its appeal first to profit and then to an ideal, this letter was entirely effective with Henslowe, who sent the money back by Field's messenger.[126] Field's appeals were based on the sound principle of showing Henslowe that to grant them would be to Henslowe's real advantage.

Probably to this period also must be assigned two episodes which may have brought on Field more discredit than he deserves. When Henslowe did not make good on his agreement to compensate the company for lying idle one day a fortnight while the theatre was used for bear baiting, Field asserted himself and secured from Henslowe "soe much as his share out of 50^{ll} would have Come vnto."[127] Field was similarly selfish in obtaining even more compensation after the addition of Robert Pallant and Robert Dawes to the company. These players were offered small sums from Henslowe's part of the gallery receipts; "and because Mr Field was thought not to bee drawne therevnto,"[128] Henslowe included him in the arrangement. In these affairs, Field did place his own interest above that of the company. But his fellow players, it should be noted, make no complaint against him in either business. They object, rather, to the conduct of Henslowe:

in one moneth after vnwilling to beare soe greate a Charge, he Called the Companie together, and told them that this 24^s [for Pallant, Dawes, and Field] was to be Charged vppon them, threatninge those which would not Consent therevnto to breake the Companie and make vpp a newe without the[m]. . .[129]

This device seems to have been resorted to by Henslowe on other occasions. "Should these fellowes Come out of my debt," they quote him as saying, "I should have noe rule with

[125]*Ibid.*, 65f. Creizenach [p. 67] finds this letter "very sad reading."
[126]As we know from the receipt to the messenger, Robert Davison, on the manuscript.
[127]Chambers, II, 249. Chambers [II, 253; I, 366] calls this bribery. Note that Field's fellows do not object to his part in this business; they take exception only to Henslowe's.
[128]Chambers, II, 249.
[129]*Ibid.*

them."[130] His rule was evidently threatened in the spring of 1614, for then observing that "the Companie drewe out of his debt and Called vppon him for his accompts hee brooke the Companie againe·"[131] Following this reorganization, probably in March 1614,[132] Field, at the age of twenty-six, became leader and official representative of his company.[133]

By the fall of 1614 the Lady Elizabeth's men were acting at the newly erected Hope Theatre, on the site of the old Paris Garden, where what Field's father declared an "extraordinary iudgement of God" had been visited upon the Sabbath-breakers. There on 31 October they presented *Bartholomew Fair*, in which Field, who it is agreed played the role of John Littlewit, had the pleasure of hearing lines in which the great Jonson places him on a level with Burbage, greatest actor of King's:

> COK. . . . which is your *Burbage* now?
> LAN. What meane you by that, Sir?
> COK. Your best *Actor*. Your *Field*?
> IOH. Good ifaith! You are euen with me, Sir.[134]

On the following day Field heard the same praises sung in royal ears when the company took *Bartholomew Fair* to Court for a performance at which Field was payee.[135]

In 1614 or 1615,[136] the Lady Elizabeth's men were strengthened by a union with the Prince's players.[137] Like that between the Revels boys and the Lady Elizabeth's men, it seems to have permitted the companies to maintain separate identities.[138] It must have been this union of companies which offered the performance of Field's *Amends for Ladies* described on the

[130]*Ibid.*, 250.
[131]*Ibid.*, 249f.
[132]*Ibid.*, 253.
[133]Agreement between Henslowe and Meade; Chambers, II, 254f.
[134]5.3.86–89.
[135]Steele, 189.
[136]Bentley, 198. Fleay [*LS*, 187] and Greg [*HD*, II, 138] say 1614; Chambers [II, 259] and Brinkley [p. 31], 1615.
[137]Chambers, II, 259.
[138]*Ibid.*; Bentley, 176, 198.

title-page of the 1618 quarto.[139] It seems unlikely that Field went over to the King's men before this performance.[140]

It was in the year of Shakespeare's death that the Puritan attack upon the stage struck directly at Field. His new minister at St. Mary Overies, the Reverend Mr. Thomas Sutton, had evidently pronounced all actors, and Field in particular, damned, directly to Field's face before the congregation. In *Feild the Players Letter to Mr Sutton, Preacher att St. Mary Overs*[141] Field rises as the controversial champion of the quality in a calm, forceful argument which reminds that he came of ministerial forbears and which is in marked contrast to the conception of him one might form from his plays alone. "Beare wittnes with me," he cries,

O my Conscience, and reward me, O Lord, according to the truth of my lipps, how I love the Sanctuary of my God and worship towardes his holy alter; how I have, according to my poore talent, indeavoured to study Christ and make sure my eleccion; how I reverence the feete of those that bring glad tidings of the Gospell, and that I beare in my soule the badge of a Christian practise to live the lief of the faithfull, wish to dye the death of the righteous, and hope to meete my Saviour in the Cloudes.[142]

Christ, according to Field, instead of pronouncing "uncharitable and unlimitted curses of condemnacions," gently brought the strayed lamb home upon His shoulders; for Christ "suffred for all mens sinnes not excepting the player, thoughe in his tyme there were some." Interesting from the standpoint of Field's reading is a reference to the Bible, "Godes whole volume—which I haue studied as my best parte."[143] This dispute may have been one such as could not amicably be settled; for the commission[144] to Dorcas Field Rice shows that at his death Field was a parishioner of St. Giles in the Fields.

---

[139]See below, *A* Intro., i.
[140]Chambers [II, 259] dates Field's going 1615, but elsewhere [S, I, 80] implies a different date. Baldwin [p. 51] says "Field came into the company [King's] about the middle of 1616." The first indisputable evidence, however, dates the connection 1617, as will be pointed out.
[141]Ed. J. O. Halliwell-Phillipps (London, 1865) and reprinted in *Illustrations of the Life of Shakespeare* (London, 1874), 115–117.
[142]*Illustrations*, 115.
[143]*Ibid.*, 116.
[144]Brinkley, 153.

Field's name does not appear among those of players who stayed with Henslowe after the Lady Elizabeth's-Prince's combination of 1614 or 1615; and it has been thought that he and others for a time travelled with Rosseter in the provinces under their old patent as Children of the Revels.[145] By 19 March 1616, however, that company seems to have performed *The Scornful Lady* "in the Blacke Fryers,"[146] which Chambers identifies with Rosseter's new, only partially completed Porter's Hall theatre.[147] When this structure "was sufficiently completed for the production of plays," according to Brinkley, "Field and his associates had a great reunion under the kindly care of Rosseter and produced Field's *Amends for Ladies*, which had belonged to the Whitefriars company of the Children."[148]

Sometime in 1617, I take it, Field must have gone over to the King's men,[149] for his name then begins to appear in the actor-lists of the King's company Beaumont-Fletcher plays.[150] Assigned to Field are younger lover roles in double leads with Burbage.[151] If, as is believed,[152] Field had a hand in *The Queen of Corinth* and *The Knight of Malta*, these collaborations must be assigned to the early days of Field's short connection with the King's men. That with Massinger and Fletcher in *The Jeweler of Amsterdam* (1617) may have followed. In 1618 Field published *Amends for Ladies*, of which he or his agent made considerable correction while the book was at press.[153]

[145]*Ibid.*, 33.
[146]The play was entered *SR* [III, 585] on that date, and the title-page of the 1616 quarto locates the performance there.
[147]III, 230. On the theatre see exp. n. to *A* t.-p. 4.
[148]P. 34. On this performance see below, *A* Intro., i.
[149]In giving 1616, Baldwin [p. 51] is giving the earliest possible date from the point of view of the Shakespearean company. We are bound to consider also the earliest possible date from the point of view of Field biography. Verhasselt (p. 504) like Baldwin dates the connection 1616.
[150]*Mad Lover* (1617), *Queen of Corinth* (1617), *Knight of Malta* (1618), *Loyal Subject* (1618); Bentley, 72. These plays are hard to date; Bentley gives 1616 for *Mad Lover*; Baldwin gives 1616 for *Mad Lover* and for *Queen of Corinth*.
[151]Baldwin [pp. 204f.] gives him Euphanes in *Queen of Corinth*, Miranda in *Knight of Malta*, Polydore in *Mad Lover*, Thierry in *Thierry and Theodoret*, and Young Archas in *Loyal Subject*.
[152]Brinkley, 147.
[153]See below, *A* Intro., iii.

The collaboration with Massinger in *The Fatal Dowry* (1619) probably represents Field's last writing for the stage.[154]

On 27 March 1619 Field is named seventh in a list including Heminges, Burbage, and Condell in the Signet Bill[155] preparatory to the issuance of new letters patent, which the sharers probably desired as a means of making sure their right to act in the Blackfriars.[156] Field was first described as a housekeeper[157] in the suit of *Witter vs. Heminges and Condell,*[158] 28 April 1619. On 19 May 1619 he was named fourth among the King's men to receive new livery.[159] On 24 May 1619, writing of the promotion of Theophilus Field to the bishopric of Llandaff, Thomas Lorkin identified Theophilus as "Field, the player's brother."[160] Between 5 and 15 June 1619 Sir William Trumbull wrote to James Hay:

> I am told he [the Earl of Argyll] was privy to the payment of 15 or 16 poundes sterling to one of your lordships Trayne called Wisedome for the nourseing of a childe which the world sayes is daughter to my lady [Argyll] and N[at] Feild the Player.[161]

On 2 August 1620 Field's sister, Dorcas Field Rice, was commissioned administrator of the estate of "Nathan Feild late of the parish of Saint Giles in the Fields."[162] The date of Field's death is not known; but since the name of his successor, John Rice, appears among the names of actors in the stage directions of *Sir John von Olden Barnavelt,* August 1619,[163] Miss Brinkley I think quite justifiably surmises that by that date "he had withdrawn from the theatre and may already have died."[164] A further plausible conjecture might be offered that

---

[154]Brinkley, 81.
[155]*MSC,* I, 280–282.
[156]Chambers, II, 218.
[157]Probably coming into Shakespeare's share; Baldwin, 51.
[158]Wallace, *Shakespeare and His London Associates,* 63.
[159]*Hist. MSS Com., Report IV, Part I* (London, 1874), 299.
[160]Birch, *op. cit.,* II, 167.
[161]Edward J. L. Scott, *The Athenaeum, 1882, Part I,* 103.
[162]Brinkley, 153.
[163]Bentley, 74.
[164]Brinkley, 44. Verhasselt (p. 505) dates "19 or perhaps 20." It is no longer necessary to refute such views as that Field failed to complete his alternation of contributions to *The Fatal Dowry* because of his retirement from the stage [C. L. Lockert, *MLN,* XXXV (1920), 293, n. 1], that Field retired to become a stationer [Bayne, *CHEL,* VI, 251], or that he left the King's in a huff because Taylor was imported as successor to Burbage [Fleay, *BC,* I, 173].

Field probably was alive as late as 5 June 1619.[165] If so, his
death most likely occurred in June, July, or August 1619.

The fame which Field had enjoyed through most of his days
did not pass with his death. One meets quite a number of
allusions to him throughout the century, though usually to his
acting rather than to his authorship. While still living, he
may have been satirized by Henry Parrot in *Laqueia ridiculosi,
or springes for woodcocks*, 1613.[166] Ashmolean MS 47[167] contains an epigram which Collier prints under the title, "Field,
the Player, on His Mistress, the Lady May."[168]

> It is the fair and merry month of May,
> That clothes the Field in all his rich array,
> Adorning him with colours better dyed
> Than any king can wear, or any bride.
> But May is almost spent, the Field grows dun
> With too much gazing on that May's hot sun;
> And if mild Zephirus, with gentle wind,
> Vouchsafe not his calm breath, and the clouds kind
> Distil their honey-drops, his heat to 'lay,
> Poor Field will burn e'en in the midst of May.[169]

This epigram seems slender grounds for Chambers' generaliza-
tion that Field's "moral character was hardly becoming to the
son of a preacher."[170] The epigram titled "De Agello et Othello"
is probably a forgery.[171]

---

[165]Had an event in Field's career so important as his death been recent
and known to the gossiping Trumbull, it is not unlikely that he would
have taken cognizance of it in his letter to Hay.

[166]Bk. II, Ep. 45.

[167]Folio 49.

[168]*MPA*, 217. Collier states that this poem appears in other commonplace books of the period and Chambers [II, 317] says as much; but so
far as I know only the Ashmolean version has been named.

[169]Collier, *MPA*, 217.

[170]II, 317. On the basis of this epigram and of the Trumbull letter,
Baldwin [p. 206, n. 18] incautiously concludes that such roles as Euphanes
in *The Queen of Corinth* and young Archas in *The Loyal Subject* likely
"give us not only Field's physical but his moral portrait as well."

[171]Chambers, *S*, II, 391. Brinkley [p. 43] points out that the lines "have
a strangely non-Elizabethan sound" and, the "fundamental error," that
Field was a bachelor. Without giving evidence, Verhasselt seems to think,
however, that Field may have married (p. 505). For the epigram see
Collier, *MPA*, 220 and n. 1.

Either before or very soon after Field's death, Jonson told Drummond of having read Latin with Field.[172] In 1623 Field was mentioned seventeenth among the principal actors in Shakespeare's plays in the First Folio.[173] The jest of John Taylor, in *Wit and Mirth*,[174] 1629, seems unauthentic and is known to have been applied to others than Field.[175] *The Fatal Dowry: A Tragedy, As it hath been often Acted at the Private House in Blackfriars, by his Majesties Servants. Written by P. M. and N. F.*, was published in 1632.[176] On 7 April 1634 Chapman's *Bussy D'Ambois* was revived and played at Court by the King's men.[177] The prologue, probably intended for this performance and printed in the quarto of 1641, refers to the play as one

> still believed in Court to be our own.
> To quit our claim, doubting our right or merit,
> Would argue in us poverty of spirit
> Which we must not subscribe to: FIELD is gone,
> Whose action first did give it name. . . .[178]

In 1639 was published the second quarto of *Amends for Ladies*.[179] In 1651 Henry Vaughan refers to Field as a well known actor, in his poem "Upon Mr. *Fletchers* Playes, published, 1647."[180]

Field's fame survived the Restoration. In 1664 Richard Flecknoe in *A Short Discourse of the English Stage* wrote:

In this time were Poets and Actors in their greatest flourish, Johnson, Shakespear, with Beaumont and Fletcher, their Poets, and Field and Burbidge their Actors.[181]

[172]*Ben Jonson*, I, 137; *SAB*, XXI (1946), 81f.
[173]Little should be inferred about Field's importance in the King's from the position of the name. The order of names in the Folio is "a little puzzling" [Chambers, II, 219f.].
[174]W. C. Hazlitt, *Shakespeare Jest-Books* (London, 1864), III, 24f.
[175]Dodsley⁴, XI, 6, n. 1; Brinkley, 41.
[176]Ed. C. L. Lockert, Jr. (Lancaster, 1918).
[177]Chambers, III, 253.
[178]*The Plays and Poems of George Chapman*, ed. Thomas Marc Parrott (New York, 1910–1914), I, 3. As to whether Field created the role of Bussy, see Hillebrand, 304f., and Chambers, III, 254.
[179]See below, *A* Intro., iii.
[180]*The Works of Henry Vaughan*, ed. Leonard C. Martin (Oxford, 1914), I, 54.
[181]W. C. Hazlitt, *The English Drama and Stage under the Tudor and Stuart Princes* (London, 1869), 277.

And, later,

It was the happiness of the Actors of those times to have such Poets as these to instruct them, and write for them; and no less of those Poets to have such docile[182] and excellent Actors to Act their Playes, as a Field and Burbidge. . . .[183]

In *Epigrams of All Sorts*, 1670, after inveighing against the mutilation of one of his plays, Flecknoe pronounces a curse upon the companies of his day:

> May, never *Poet* write for them agen:
> But they be forc'd to Act *old Plays* like those
> For want of new, are forc'd to wear *old Cloathes;*
> And come o' th' *Stage* all tattered and poor,
> In old cast sutes, which *Field* and *Burbadge* woar.[184]

A Woman is a Weather-cocke, but not *Amends for Ladies*, was among the old plays revived by the Duke's company at Lincoln's Inn Fields.[185]

In *Historia Histrionica*, attributed to James Wright, we read: "Since the Reformation, in Queen Elizabeth's time, plays were frequently acted by quiristers and singing-boys," among which the Children of the Chapel are said to have been "at that time famous for good action."[186] After quoting Jonson on Pavy, the author states:

Some of these chapel-boys, when they grew men, became actors at the Blackfriars; such were Nathan. Field and John Underwood. Now I can hardly imagine that such plays and players as these are included in the severe censure of the councils and fathers.[187]

This account of Field and his works through the seventeenth century may be concluded with the mention of Gerard Langbaine, who lists both Field's comedies in *Momus Triumphans*[188] and begins the scholarly study of them in *An Account of the English Dramatick Poets*.[189]

---

[182]From Field's unwillingness to be browbeaten by Henslowe, as indicated in the letters [Greg, *HP*, 65–67, 84], one would hardly call Field a docile actor; but then, neither was Henslowe a poet.
[183]Hazlitt, *English Drama and Stage*, 279.
[184]Pp. 73f.
[185]See below, *W* Intro., i.
[186]Dodsley⁴, XV, 416.
[187]*Ibid.*, 416f.
[188]London, 1688, p. 9.
[189]Oxford, 1691. See below, *A* Intro., ii.

2. FIELD'S RELATION TO SOME CONTEMPORARIES

When he wrote *A Woman is a Weather-cocke* and *Amends for Ladies*, Field had acted in plays by Beaumont, Chapman, Fletcher, Jonson, and Marston. There is insufficient evidence for saying, as has been said, that Field, "naturally enough, established friendly relations with all of them."[190] There is evidence connecting Field with several leading dramatists, and his plays are rightly to be estimated in connection with the work of these and others of his contemporaries. Let us consider briefly Field's relations, both biographical and literary, to Jonson, Shakespeare, Fletcher, Chapman, and Middleton.

In addition to association with the same dramatic company, three types of external evidence connect Field with Jonson: Jonson's own statement to Drummond,[191] Field's having acted in certain of Jonson's plays,[192] and Field's commendatory verses to *Volpone* and *Catiline*.[193] From this evidence and from that found in the plays, it has been customary[194] to say that Field was influenced by Jonson directly and demonstrably, more or less as was Brome.

Recent studies, however, have shown that this view, resting primarily upon external rather than internal evidence, needs to be modified. Jonson's remark to Drummond, which probably does indicate that Jonson and Field read Latin together, has been romantically embellished in a tradition that Jonson and Field were especially close friends.[195] This tradition seems to have resulted in the extension of Field's "curriculum" under

[190]Brinkley, 39.
[191]"Nid field was his Schollar," etc., *Conversations, Ben Jonson*, I, 137.
[192]*Cynthia's Revels, Poetaster, Eastward Ho!*, and *Epicoene*.
[193]And possibly to Fletcher's *The Faithful Shepherdess* [cf. Verhasselt, 497], though the reference there, as I show, is not necessarily to Jonson.
[194]Cf. Bayne, *CHEL*, VI, 237; Schelling, *English Literature during the Lifetime of Shakespeare* (New York, 1927), 231; Mina Kerr, *Influence of Ben Jonson on English Comedy* (Philadelphia, 1912), 52–54; Brinkley, 72–77; Thorndike, 190.
[195]Bayne, *CHEL*, VI, 237, 248; Kerr, *op. cit.*, 53; Brinkley, 15f., 22.

Jonson to include playwriting as well as Latin.[196] As a consequence traditional descriptions of Jonson's influence on Field
are highly colored and untrustworthy.[197] Re-examination of
the internal evidence justifies the following conclusions:[198]

Jonson did not, as has been maintained,[199] necessarily influence Field in his choice of subjects for satire, Field having
chosen subjects[200] common in the period and treated by others
who also may have influenced him. The non-judicial tone of
Field's satire, indeed, sharply differentiates his satire from
Jonson's, which is judicial; Jonson seems not to have influenced
Field, as has been said,[201] in satirical attitude. Jonson did not,
as has been claimed,[202] necessarily influence Field in the
realistic portrayal of contemporary life, which may have had
another literary source and may well have come from life
rather than from literature. Whether Jonson influenced Field
in plot[203] is doubtful since Field's plots are unlike Jonson's in
conception, in execution, and in their emphasis on serious
romantic motives more than on intrigue. Field's humour
characterization is neither, as has been said,[204] necessarily Jon-
sonian nor very similar to Jonson's. The absence of noteworthy verbal borrowings,[205] imitations of scenes,[206] or comic
devices,[207] and consideration of the other internal evidence
taken separately and as a whole, point to the conclusion that
the influence of Jonson on Field has been exaggerated. On
the positive side, Field may have drawn from Jonson hints

[196]Kerr, op. cit., 52–54; Schelling, I, 473, 519.
[197]SAB, XXI (1946), 80–86.
[198]SP, XLIII (1946), 496f.
[199]Brinkley, 77.
[200]Law, religion, the new nobility, pride in pedigree, use of cosmetics
and tobacco.
[201]Schelling, I, 520; Kerr, op. cit., 54, 57.
[202]Kerr, op. cit., 55.
[203]Kerr, op. cit., 56; Brinkley, 73.
[204]Schelling, I, 520; Kerr, op. cit., 56; Brinkley, 74.
[205]See exp. n. to W 1.2.340ff. and 4.2.120 for two which seem genuine.
Two in two plays, however, are indeed few.
[206]See exp. n. to W 1.1.s. div. for one claimed by Brinkley.
[207]Brinkley claims for Jonson the device of having a character recognize
quoted verses (W 1.2.340ff.), compose verses (W 3.3.13ff.), give instructions
on the art of wooing (A 3.1.11ff.), and marry a "boy bride" (A 3.2.41ff.,
5.2.266). See exp. nn. to these lines.

for certain of his characters[208] and two or three of his speeches. Certainly Field is not in comedy the derivative of Jonson that the Brome of *The Weeding of Covent Garden* and *The Sparagus Garden* is.

As a leading member of the various Queen's Revels companies, Field is not likely to have known Shakespeare so well, say, as he probably knew Jonson and Chapman—if, indeed, he knew Shakespeare personally at all. The boy Field seems not to have acted with the King's men.[209] By the time Field had attained distinction as an adult actor,[210] Shakespeare had virtually retired to Stratford.[211] When Field began to act for the King's[212] Shakespeare was no longer living.

This is not to say, however, that Field, man or boy, did not know Shakespeare's plays and draw upon them in his own writing. Little need be said for the tradition[213] that Field played Othello since that playing if it occurred would likely have followed the writing of *Weather-cocke* and *Amends*. One passage in the latter play,[214] however, establishes beyond doubt that Field knew *1 Henry IV* (1597) by 1618 and probably by 1611. Scholars have seen a Shakespearean influence in a number of other passages in Field's comedies, in imitated scenes, comic dialogue, and in miscellaneous verbal echoes.

Act III, Scene 2, of *Weather-cocke* has been regarded[215] as an imitation of Act III, Scene 4, of *Hamlet*. Act III, Scene 3, of *Amends* is thought[216] to have been influenced by Act I, Scene 2, of *The Merchant of Venice*, but beyond the cataloguing of a lady's suitors the scenes have little resemblance.

---

[208]See exp. nn. to *W*, dram. pers. 7 and 9, *A*, dram. pers. 2 and 9.

[209]See above, n. 92.

[210]The first indisputable evidence is Jonson's tribute in *Bartholomew Fair*, 31 October 1614 (see above); but from Henslowe's including Field with Pallant and Dawes in special financial considerations, one might argue that his adult reputation began somewhat earlier.

[211]Chambers, *S*, I, 86f.

[212]As has been seen above, the first positive evidence is Field's name in Beaumont-Fletcher King's plays most probably to be dated after Shakespeare's death.

[213]Collier, *MPA*, 220; cf. Brinkley, 43; Chambers, *S*, II, 391; Verhasselt, 505f.

[214]*A* 4.3.24ff. See exp. n.

[215]E. Koeppel, 76; D. J. McGinn, 108, calls it a "possible" imitation. See exp. n. to *W* 3.2.71ff.

[216]Fischer, 38; Brinkley, 78. See exp. n. to *A* 3.3.83ff.

For the development of several passages of comic dialogue there is clearer evidence that Field may have taken hints from Shakespeare. On the simplest level, the hint may be for mere wordplay.[217] The coward Feesimple's comic boasting in *Amends* has reminded scholars[218] of Falstaff's. A clearcut instance of Field's following Shakespeare not only in the device of doubling an extravagant salutation but also in wittily commenting thereon is seen in *Amends*.[219] Of Field's verbal echoes of Shakespeare which have been pointed out, most are not entirely convincing. Only four seem to me worthy of discussion.[220] The rest are commonplace figures,[221] proverbial expressions,[222] and the like. From such evidence Field's direct debt to Shakespeare is seen to be, though small, demonstrable.

Beyond their collaboration, which followed the writing of *Weather-cocke* and *Amends,* little evidence connects the younger Field biographically with Fletcher. That which we have, however, is of some importance—though I think to Field's connection with another than Fletcher. Field's first expression of literary ambition, as we saw, is to be found in verses[223] he contributed to *The Faithful Shepherdess* (1608). They are perhaps even more important for the following reference:

> Opinion, that great foole, makes fooles of all,
> And (once) I feard her till I met a minde
> Whose grave instructions philosophicall,
> Toss'd it like dust upon a march strong winde,
> He shall for ever my example be,
> And his embraced doctrine grow in me.

The grave, philosophical mind has been thought[224] to be Jonson's, and this identification may be the correct one. It was recently proposed,[225] however, that the reference may be to

---

[217]See exp. n. to *W* 4.2.109.
[218]Fischer, 38; Brinkley, 78; and see exp. n. to *A* 4.2.88ff.
[219]See exp. n. to 1.1.191ff.
[220]See exp. nn. to *W*, To the Reader, 8f., *W* 1.2.2f., 5.2.117, and *A* 1.1.192f.
[221]e. g., *A* 3.2.7ff. and exp. n.
[222]e. g., *W* 1.2.15 and exp. n.
[223]*Beaumont and Fletcher*, II, 519.
[224]*Ben Jonson*, V, 6; Brinkley, 72; Verhasselt, 497.
[225]*SAB*, XXI (1946), 84.

Chapman, for whom such a strong case exists that one must at least say the question has not been settled.

It would be appropriate at this point to amass echoes of Chapman by Field, not only to bear out what I think is the fact, that Chapman influenced Field perhaps as much as, or more than, did Jonson, but also to strengthen the case for Chapman rather than Jonson as the grave mind of this poem. A number of such parallel passages might be cited. The symbolic use of the willow,[226] satire on the newly created knights,[227] satire on pedigree,[228] a catalogue of the functions of a waiting-woman,[229] would seem to furnish considerable evidence for Chapman's having influenced Field. All of these elements, however, are open to the objection which must be raised against alleged verbal echoes by Field of Jonson and Shakespeare, that they are often found elsewhere in Renaissance drama.[230] The same objection would have to be advanced to parallels which might be urged between Field and Beaumont and Fletcher.[231] If *The Scornful Lady*[232] preceded *Amends*, Field may, however, have borrowed from its authors the business of making a woman jealous by her lover's interesting himself in another man disguised as a woman.[233] This is the only suggestion of direct, specific literary influence I have found of Beaumont or Fletcher on Field.

In general tone, however, Field's plays strongly resemble the comedies among the Beaumont-Fletcher plays. Like the latter, they tend to present characters differentiated by types rather than fully individualized; and with apparent cheerful-

[226]*W* 1.2.233, 2.1.68; *A* 5.2.8; *All Fools*, 1.1.40.
[227]*W* 1.2.165, 3.4.14f., *Bussy D'Ambois*, 1.2.124; *Monsieur D'Olive*, 1.1.264ff., 4.2.76ff.; and *Widow's Tears*, 4.1.28. These are plays in which Field probably had acted.
[228]*W* 1.2.201f.; *Humorous Day's Mirth*, Sc. 5, 88f.
[229]*A* 1.1.360ff.; *All Fools*, 2.1.282ff.; cf. *Monsieur D'Olive*, 5.1.190ff., *Bussy D'Ambois*, 2.2.58ff.
[230]See exp. nn. to these lines.
[231]e. g., see exp. nn. to *W* 3.3.27 and *A* 1.1.425. There are a number of others.
[232]The date is debatable. Harbage gives 1613 with a query, "Written c. 1610? Rev. c. 1613?" Baldwin Maxwell presents the older views and argues for 1610 [*Studies in Beaumont, Fletcher, and Massinger* (Chapel Hill, 1939), 17–28].
[233]See exp. n. to *A* 2.3.76.

ness, when the plot requires they sacrifice integrity[234] in this superficial characterization. They are sensational in their use of novel situation and surprise. Their action is always brisk. They unite sophisticated farce with rather witty repartee of a post-Elizabethan variety. They emphasize the relations, often the combat, between the sexes. They are based upon the view[235] that "no woman in the world," despite the lip service they pay to woman's virtue,

> Can hould out in the end, if youth, shape, wit,
> Met in one subiect, doe assault her aptlie.[236]

They are brilliantly theatrical, rather than authentic, readings of the life of those for whom they were written and originally acted. For Field as for Fletcher, comedy was "neither a means of reforming society nor of idealizing life, it was only an entertainment."[237] In this respect the comedy of Field is a good deal more like that of Fletcher than like that of Jonson. From his contribution to *The Faithful Shepherdess* we may infer, however, that Field thought Fletcher something more than a talented commercial playwright. Yet if Field imitated Fletcher in the sweet morality of *The Faithful Shepherdess,* in the misty profitableness beyond the filmed reason of the crowd,[238] he must have done so in other than his individually written plays.

Field's relations, both biographical and literary, with Chapman were close. It is not necessary to repeat that part of the evidence which has already been given in connection with Field's life and his relation to other contemporaries. When he wrote his plays, Field probably had acted in *The Gentleman Usher, May Day, Sir Giles Goosecap, All Fools, Bussy D'Ambois, Monsieur D'Olive, The Widow's Tears, I and II Charles*

[234]e. g., see *W* 3.2.135ff.; 5.2.81f., 123, 157f.; *A* 5.2.159 and exp. nn. to these lines.
[235]Field presents also the opposite view, and whether his plays are anti-feminist as they have usually been called or whether they are feminist is not an easy question. See *SP,* XLIII (1946), 485.
[236]*A,* 3.1.5f. and exp. n. This is one of the aspects of Field's plays which render them "a link in the chain of plays leading toward Restoration drama" (Brinkley, 79). *Weather-cocke,* which probably exhibits this doctrine the more forcefully, was among the old plays revived after the Restoration [John Downes, *Roscius Anglicanus,* ed. Montague Summers (London, 1928), 27].
[237]Thorndike, 216.
[238]*Beaumont and Fletcher,* II, 519.

Duke of Byron, and *The Revenge of Bussy D'Ambois.* Field
may have known Chapman almost from the beginning of his
career as leading actor for the Chapel children.[239] Chapman
wrote the rather tortured verse prefaced to *A Woman is a
Weather-cocke.* Field's literary relations with Chapman, however, are more significant. Chapman as well as Jonson could
have provided Field with models both for his satire[240] and for his
humour characterization.[241] Perhaps more important is Chapman's influence on Field's effective if somewhat bombastic
rhetoric in passages representing what Bayne calls "Field's
natural bent," the portrayal of "ideal heroes, headstrong and
indomitable."[242] Bayne finds it "highly probable that Field,
quite as much as Massinger, was responsible for the romantic
side" of *The Fatal Dowry,* "and especially for the uncompro-
mising honesty of Romont. In this respect, Chapman was his
master. . ."[243] Brinkley speaks of Field's "imitation of Chapman's rhetoric and aphoristic sentences" and of the similarity
between Field's and Chapman's attitude toward women.[244] In
addition to these general evidences of influence, I find one instance of Field's specific indebtedness to Chapman for an
imitated scene.[245] Considering all of the kinds of evidence, one
may safely say that Chapman probably exerted much more
influence on Field than has generally been realized.

So far as I have been able to determine, there are only two
biographical connections between Field and him whom Jonson called "but a base fellow,"[246] Thomas Middleton. Field
probably had acted in *Your Five Gallants* (1607) and *A Trick
to Catch the Old One* (1605). The other connection is considerably less certain. Chambers states that Field's introduction of Moll Cutpurse in *Amends for Ladies*[247] suggests that
Field was in rivalry with Middleton and Dekker in their play,

[239]See *SAB,* XXI (1946), 84.
[240]*SP,* XLIII (1946), 383–386.
[241]*Ibid.,* 493.
[242]*CHEL,* VI, 250.
[243]*Ibid.,* 251.
[244]Pp. 77f. I can not agree with Brinkley that "Chapman was Field's
master in the matter of equipping plays with full stage directions" (p. 78)
for a reason to be pointed out below, Intro., 3.
[245]See exp. n. to *W* 1.1. s. div.
[246]*Conversations, Ben Jonson,* I, 137.
[247]*A* 2.1.16–57.

The Roaring Girl (1610) at the Fortune.[248] The episodic nature of Moll's single appearance perhaps bears out this view. The most important evidence for the literary relation between Field and Middleton, however, is the long line of bright comedies in which Middleton had presented London life realistically, apparently rather for amusement than for judicial satire.[249] Field's connection with them is not so much a debt for words, characters, or incidents as a general resemblance in the tone which distinguishes them from other Jacobean comedies. Like Field's, their plots[250] involve intrigues and disguisings and are quite rapid in their movement.[251] Indeed, a number of the standard descriptions of the work of Middleton, as they pertain to plot construction, moral tone, and facility of invention and expression, are almost as applicable to Field.[252] Field's comedies, I think, are as like those of Middleton as those of any other playwright.

From a study of Field's relations with some of his contemporaries one should emerge with three generalizations. First, scholars have exaggerated Field's debt to Jonson, to whom Field may owe no more than he owes to Chapman and Middleton. Second, Field's plays ought to be compared, in general tone and in plot, with those of Middleton, with which they have not been traditionally connected. Finally, the nature of

---

[248]III, 314.
[249]*SP*, XLIII (1946), 486, 487.
[250]*Ibid.*, 489f.
[251]Ward, II, 538.
[252]"It was his usual practice to combine two plots into a single play; and this he ordinarily effected with much constructive skill, although he worked too hurriedly to attend to minor unevennesses, and here and there forgot in his haste to carry out fully the moral lesson which he intended to convey" [Ward, II, 538]; "The early comedy of Middleton is as light, rancid and entertaining as anything in Elizabethan drama. It is irresponsible rather than immoral, and does not exactly recommend, or approve of, the trickeries and debaucheries which it represents in a lifelike way, under improbable conditions. Yet the writer is no more careful of his ethical than of his other probabilities, and takes little trouble to keep up any consistency in the minds or morals of his agile puppets. His aim is at effect, and he rarely fails in his aim" [Arthur Symons, *CHEL*, VI, 71.]; "It was easy for him to set these people talking as they would really talk, or with just that heightening which his sense of pungent and appropriate words gave him; and he could set scene after scene galloping across the stage, without taking more trouble than his public demanded as to making his plots consistent or probable, so long as they went at full speed along familiar ways" [*ibid.*, 73]. Cf. also Thorndike, 153ff.

Field's comedy is probably best explained, not by the influence upon him of one or another dramatist, but by his being a resident of Jacobean London and a shrewd Jacobean actor-playwright. Apparently he was not so possessed of "hopes and love to Poesie" or of exacting intellectual integrity such as some have found in Shakespeare, that he could not appropriate from the successful plays of his day as he knew them from acting in them, whatever ingredients he needed in his own excellent recipe for satisfying the tastes, as he had observed them at first hand, of Jacobean audiences.

3. FIELD'S COMEDIES, A CRITICAL ESTIMATE

It is perhaps surprising to find that plays no better known than those of Field, plays which make so many concessions as his do to the seventeenth-century audience, should consistently have been held in high critical regard. Langbaine declared Field to be "not only a Lover of the Muses, but belov'd by them, and the Poets his Contemporaries,"[253] and was of the opinion that Field's comedies "still bear Reading."[254] "*A Woman is a Weathercock*, and its sequel, *Amends for Ladies*," according to J. P. Collier, "are the productions of no ordinary poet: in comic scenes Field excels Massinger, . . . and in those of a serious character he may be frequently placed on a footing of equality."[255] *Amends* Collier terms an "excellent old comedy" which "seems to have been deservedly popular. . . .

It is not easy to decide whether the comic or the serious scenes are the best; although the first are not without some of the coarseness which belonged to the manners of the age. The language is generally well chosen: some passages are of the higher order of poetry. . . . The characters are numerous, varied, and well distinguished. . . . The plot is threefold, . . . but the incidents are interwoven with ingenuity, and concluded without confusion.[256]

[253]P. 198.
[254]*Ibid.*
[255]*Weathercock* (London, 1829), 3.
[256]*Amends* (London, 1829), 3.

John Genest calls *Amends for Ladies* "a good C.—"[257] Joseph
Knight regards Field's plays as "excellent comedies in their
class. The comic scenes are above the level of Massinger and
Shirley, and the serious passages need not shame those poets."[258]
Weather-cocke, according to Ward, "bespeaks the confidence
of youth"; and both plays "are alike characterised by a curious
combination of recklessness and *aplomb*"[259] for which Ward
would account by the remark that Field "knew his audience
as well as he knew his stage, and could safely indulge in the
freedom permitted to an acknowledged favourite."[260] Ward
acknowledges Field's "easy and effective" plot construction and
adds that "the wit of the writing is frequently very pointed
and fresh."[261] The treble plot of *Amends*, Ward finds, "is
managed with considerable skill; and apart from objections on
which there is no necessity for dwelling, the comedy merits
high praise as an effective and in its design healthy work."[262]
Both of the comedies, according to A. W. Verity, "are excellent
pieces of work . . . singularly clever in the easy manipulation of plot and underplot, and touched throughout with the
vivacity and *verve* of true, though somewhat boisterous, comedy."[263] Verity finds Field's merits to have been "happily hit
off in Mr. Swinburne's lines,"[264]

> Field, bright and loud with laughing flower and bird
> And keen alternate notes of laud and gird.[265]

Felix E. Schelling finds Field's comedies imitative of Jonson's.
"But when all has been said," he concludes,

[257]*Some Account of the English Stage, from the Restoration in 1660 to
1830* (Bath, 1832), X, 22.
[258]*DNB*, XVIII, 409.
[259]III, 49.
[260]*Ibid.*
[261]*Ibid.*
[262]*Ibid.*, 50. One suspects that Ward's "objections" are not unlike those
of Tucker Brooke, who dismisses the plays here edited as "two lewd London comedies"; *A Literary History of England*, ed. Albert C. Baugh (New
York, 1948), p. 583.
[263]P. 336.
[264]*Ibid.*
[265]"Sonnets on the English Dramatic Poets," *Works*, ed. Edmund Gosse
and T. J. Wise (London, 1925–27), V, 190. Smart, realistic comedy of
London life, however, is an unlikely setting for birds and flowers; and
one who looks for them in Field will be disappointed.

both remain singularly fresh if somewhat boisterous specimens
of the comedy of London life, and bespeak the dramatic apti-
tude born of practical conversance with the stage. Field was
clearly a favorite who could presume on his popularity and
thrive in his presumption.[266]

Schelling considers each of the three leading women in *Amends*
"an admirable type of her class and, what is more, a living
woman."[267] Though Ronald Bayne has a somewhat lower
opinion of Field than most critics, he finds *Weather-cocke* "full
both of matter and of varied promise of dramatic ability."[268]
Dean Brinkley, finally, apparently anxious not to claim too
much for her subject,[269] praises Field's "great skill in plot-
ting,"[270] sprightliness of style,[271] and knowledge of "stage technique—how to arrange effective scenes, how to group characters on the stage, and how to manage entrances and exits."[272]

If critics have been in virtual agreement over Field's merits,
they have been less certain as to which of the comedies is the
better. Koeppel speaks of Field's "ersten und besten schau-
spiel."[273] Bayne believes *Amends* to be, on the whole, "a more
hasty piece of work than the first; it has the drawbacks of
an after-thought."[274] Its comic scenes he considers "less original
and less amusing than those of the first."[275] He notices, however, "a distinct maturity and strengthening"[276] in the style
of *Amends*. Collier states that *"Amends for Ladies* will be
found, on the whole, a superior performance to *A Woman is
a Weathercock."*[277] Verity holds the same opinion, finding
Amends "less extravagant in the lighter scenes, and less rhetorical where the dramatist would strike a serious note."[278] Such

[266]I, 520f.
[267]*Ibid.*
[268]*CHEL,* VI, 250.
[269]Cf. *RES,* V (1929), 110.
[270]Pp. 49f.
[271]Pp. 60f.
[272]Pp. 80; 66–69.
[273]P. 76.
[274]*CHEL,* VI, 250.
[275]*Ibid.,* 251.
[276]*Ibid.,* 250. Rather remarkable in view of the comparatively short
time between the composition of the two; see below, *W* and *A* Intro., i.
[277]*Weathercock,* 1829, 5.
[278]P. 336.

differences of critical preference are perhaps less important
than recognition of the nature of Field's plays and, consequently, Field's position in the history of dramatic literature.

Field in his plays, Dean Brinkley states,

put together a clever assortment of situations, phrases, and
words, taken over from the plays in which he had played,
combined with these some of the popular sentiments and characters of the day, added his personal animus toward women,[279]
and threw over all of this his own exuberant personality.[280]

Playwriting is not so simple as this recipe makes it seem, as
anyone who has attempted it will agree; and the recipe does
not adequately represent the facts in Field's case. No editor
has yet found any source for the plot of *A Woman is a Weather-
cocke*, and Field's debt to sources in *Amends for Ladies* has
been exaggerated.[281] The evaluation of Field's individually
written comedies is an illustration of a fault in modern scholarship, a tendency to be so cautious as not to give one's conclusions the importance they deserve. Field's plays, Dean Brinkley concludes, "furnish a unique example of the work of the
clever actor-playwright, who is without any real creative
genius."[282]

There would certainly be insufficient justification for claiming for Field genius of the first or second order. But his
comedies do reveal genius of a sort, and we will do well to
recognize it for what it is. Technically, *Weather-cocke* is a
remarkable achievement for a boy not over twenty-two.[283] By
the age of twenty-four, Field had written *Amends*;[284] and the
two plays exhibit a mastery of dramatic technique, at least,

[279]Based upon the "Othello" epigram and the tradition that Field was
inordinately jealous, the view that Field held a personal animus toward
women should have been abandoned when the unmarried Nathan was
distinguished from the married Nathaniel. Field's portrayal of women
seems to be conventional and derived from previous dramatic tradition as
illustrated in Chapman and Fletcher. See the discussion of Field's relations to these writers, above, and *SP*, XLIII (1946), 489f.

[280]P. 46.

[281]See below, *A* Intro., ii.

[282]P. 80.

[283]*Weather-cocke* was probably composed in 1609; see below, *W* Intro., i.

[284]Probably composed by October 1611; see below, *A* Intro., i.

hardly to be matched at the same age by most of his contemporaries.[285] If we disregard age, Field's comedies compare
very favorably in technical dexterity with other first plays by
greater writers than he.[286] Within their limitations Field's
plays from a strictly technical point of view are rather distinguished.

And this, I suppose, is only what one would expect from
the gifted actor-playwright. Field, as Dean Brinkley says,

commands our attention as the product of external circumstances. As an actor he learned playmaking in a practical
school. He knew his audience and what scenes pleased them;
he knew the charm of music and the pleasure of sprightly
dialogue; and he knew stage technique. . . .[287]

Attributable to Field's having been an actor, according to
Brinkley, is his portrayal of character. It "is external and
reveals the author's visualization of the characters rather than
his omniscience as to their inner being."[288] Of his outspoken
speech, Brinkley writes, "it seems almost as though the young
actor were taking advantage of his popularity in seeing how
far he could go."[289] Field's "longer speeches are rhetorical and
afford an opportunity for the display of histrionic talent."[290]
Brinkley points out that Field caters to audience taste by staging wedding processions in both plays[291] and a mask in *Weather-*

[285]By the age of twenty-four, Chapman, Chettle, Day, Dekker, Fletcher,
Ford, Gascoigne, Greene, Jonson, Kyd, Lodge, Lyly, Middleton, Munday,
Nashe, Peele, Shakespeare, Sharpham, and Whetstone had, so far as is
known, written no plays. By that age Beaumont may have written his
part of *The Woman Hater* and *The Knight of the Burning Pestle;* Heywood, *The Four Prentices of London;* Marlowe, *Tamburlaine* and *Dr.
Faustus;* and Marston, *Antonio and Mellida.* These generalizations are
based upon the dates or probable dates of birth and production of earliest
play as given by Chambers.
[286]Critics have done a good deal of apologizing for the lack of this
quality in Chapman's *Blind Beggar of Alexandria* and *An Humorous Day's
Mirth;* see Parrott, *Chapman,* II, 674f., 687f. Either of Field's plays seems
the equal, both in structure and in characterization, of Jonson's *The Case
Is Altered;* cf. Ward II, 351 and Herford and Simpson, *Ben Jonson,* I,
313, on these aspects of the Jonson play. Either seems the equal in
structure of *Every Man in His Humour;* see Elisabeth Woodbridge, *Studies
in Jonson's Comedy* (Boston, 1898), 47f.
[287]P. 80.
[288]P. 53.
[289]P. 57.
[290]P. 60.
[291]*W* 2.1.116ff. and exp. n.; *A* 5.2. has a wedding in the offing but
hardly stages the procession.

cocke,[292] and by making much use of music, stage fights, rowdy scenes, and the antics of characters whose function is primarily comic.[293] His dialogue, it is asserted, "shows that Field realized that both actor and audience found pleasure in quick repartee";[294] and the frequent use of pithy sayings[295] is said to be "partly due, no doubt, to his knowledge that they gave mental pleasure because they could so easily be remembered and carried away by the audience."[296] The completeness of Field's stage directions is connected with Field's having been an actor in the company that produced his plays.[297] Since Field obtained his knowledge of drama primarily, so far as we know, as an actor,[298] his having been an actor might be said to have given him his conception of what drama is. "The type of play in which Field had taken part as a boy-actor," Brinkley writes, "naturally influenced him tremendously when he began to write. . . . It was very natural, then, for Field to write satire and to introduce the element of music into his plays, for he had grown up with the idea that a successful play must contain both."[299] Brinkley quotes Boyle, finally, to the effect that actor-playwrights "are apt to repeat themselves, and to borrow unconsciously from other writers in whose plays they had acted."[300]

A tabulation, in terms of traits objectively ascertainable and subject to count, of the characteristics of technique and style peculiar to the actor-playwright would doubtless be a very

---

[292]*W* 5.2.

[293]Brinkley, 66f.

[294]*Ibid.*, 67.

[295]I find in Field's plays fifteen proverbs, seventeen apothegms, five proverbial comparisons, and seventeen other proverbial expressions, or fifty-four instances of indebtedness to proverbial matter. They can be located through the exp. nn. in this edition, but they have been collected and studied; see *SFQ*, X (1946), 1–16. Field is there found to have used proverbial matter for individual and group characterization, to obtain credence for the arguments advanced by characters in support of their actions as the play progresses, and for stylistic embellishment.

[296]Brinkley, 68.

[297]*Ibid.*

[298]From *W*, To the Reader, 15f., one can not be sure whether Field means "hearing many" as actor or as spectator, but he undoubtedly saw plays in which he did not act.

[299]Pp. 71f.

[300]*ES*, VII (1882), 74.

useful tool to students of the drama; but unfortunately it can hardly be demonstrated that a given characteristic results from first-hand experience with and on the stage.[301] The argument from the completeness of the writer's stage directions, though as good perhaps as any, is tricky.[302] Little confidence may be placed in evidence from length of speeches[303] or self-repetition.[304] There may be a difference in the nature of the borrowings of actor and non-actor playwrights, but I think it is not as Boyle implies[305] one of quantity.[306] Whether or not characters are quickly and economically identified on their first

[301]Without success, I have tried out twenty-one tests. This conclusion is interesting in the light of theory underlying modern instruction in dramatic technique. The late Professors George Pierce Baker and Frederick H. Koch believed that a playwright would be the better playwright for a first-hand knowledge of acting and theatre arts; and sometimes the curriculum in dramatic art is arranged on this principle. Perhaps it is correct; but if so, the contribution of a knowledge of acting to the plays of the actor-playwright seems extremely difficult if not impossible to isolate and measure objectively.

[302]Perhaps the actor is more likely than the non-actor to visualize business and stage groupings and therefore might be thought to be more inclined than the non-actor to write complete directions. The actor in his own production, however, would have less need than the non-actor to write full directions since he could orally explain precisely what he intended. Jonson provided full explanations when publishing his masks. In one place [p. 68] Brinkley attributes Field's complete directions to his acting; in another [p. 78], to the example of Chapman, who, however, according to Parrott, as a rule "is very sparing of stage directions" [I, 656]. Parrott takes the full stage directions of *The Blind Beggar of Alexandria* and *The Gentleman Usher* to indicate that the quartos of these plays were printed from playhouse manuscripts [II, 673, 753]. Field's very careful stage directions, full but distinctly non-literary [e. g., those at W 2.1. 116ff., 222ff., 5.2.1ff.; A 5.2.180ff.] seem to offer one of the clearest evidences of the possible influence on his writing of his acting and, perhaps, directing.

[303]If any conclusions may be drawn from the plays of modern student writers, the non-actors seem to write longer speeches than the actors. In the Jacobean theatre, however, the long speech, perhaps owing to the convention of the soliloquy, seems to have been less difficult to tolerate than in the modern theatre.

[304]I see no reason why an actor-playwright should repeat previous writing more often than the non-actor. Certainly Boyle does not offer sufficient evidence to establish such a view.

[305]*Loc. cit.*

[306]The exp. nn. to this edition show comparatively few borrowings, outside of commonplaces, of extended passages reflective of contemporary thought, such as the non-actor might borrow out of interest in the subjects. What borrowings they show, rather, are in clever situations, comic turns, and devices for characterization. See exp. nn. to W 1.1. s. div., A 3.3. 83ff., 1.1.191ff.

entrance[307] and whether or not exits are motivated are not
conclusive tests because these aspects of dramatic technique,
being perhaps the most objective, are also among the more
obvious points in dramaturgy; they are those which a clever
person who had never acted would be likely at once to recognize and employ of his own accord. Other factors than an
author's previous connection with the stage come into play:
the extent to which he is intelligent, able to imitate, and
willing to imitate. This last factor, and what Miss Brinkley
says of Field's characterization and his various concessions to
the audience, involve the important question of the writer's
motive in and attitude toward his writing. It may be felt that
the actor, presumably in a better position than the non-actor
to know what has been proved theatrically effective, is under
greater compulsion than the non-actor both to imitate and to
depart for the sake of audience appeal from an honest effort
to record or interpret human life. But one is confronted with
imitativeness and insincerity also in the ranks of the non-
actors. For all these reasons one must remain skeptical of
attempts to differentiate, by any of the standards yet proposed,
between the styles and techniques of actor and non-actor playwrights.[308]

Perhaps confusion may be avoided, and the place of Field in
dramatic history be more descriptively evaluated, if we here
borrow some wise words from a modern critic. On the occasion of another actor-playwright's being awarded the Nobel
Prize, Bernard DeVoto made a workable if not etymologically
justifiable distinction between the playwright and the dramatist:

. . . workable theatricality is the measure of successful playwriting. In the theater the test is not: Is this true to the

[307]For Field's varied practice in this respect see *SP*, XLIII (1946), 491f.,
and n. 59.
[308]This is not to say that the actor-playwright may not show more
keen interest than other playwrights in the theatre and theatrical affairs.
I do not doubt that Field's life as an actor has something to do with the
number of allusions in his plays to theatres, other plays, and playgoing.
A denizen of the theatre world, writing for those attracted to that world,
Field often refers to playhouses, actors, and the things which interest those
attracted to the world of the theatre. See *W* 1.1.44f., 1.2.340ff., 2.1.275ff.,
2.2.118, 3.2.149ff., 3.3.27, 3.4.23, 5.2.187f., 5.2.230f.; *A* 2.1.152f., 2.2.107,
2.4.34ff., 3.4.25f., 3.4.106f., 4.3.24, 5.2.15ff., 5.2.48f.

realities of human experience? Instead the test is: Is this fictitious representation satisfactory to the artificial conditions of the theater? With luck—or with genius—a play may pass both tests, but it must pass the second, and if they are in conflict, the first must yield. The theater is under many limitations: the exigencies of space and time; the dictation of the literal . . . ; and especially the necessary conditions of people meeting together as an audience, the lowered intelligence, the lulled critical faculty, the enhanced emotionalism and suggestibility of a group, the substitution of emotional accord for the desire to experience and understand that is fed by other forms of literature. Under all these limitations, the theater succeeds in its own terms. They are terms of the momentarily effective, not the permanently true or the permanently illuminating. . . . Where honest and thorough presentation of life makes available material, the theater will use it; where it does not, the theater must and cheerfully will depart from it for the sake of the theatrical values. . . .

A great dramatist, I take it, is one who has somehow managed to transcend the limitations of the theater and, while preserving the theatrical values that pass the second test, to add to them some profundity of human experience, human understanding, or human enlightenment that brings the art of the theater into the same area as the highest art of fiction or poetry [309]

DeVoto's distinction, by which Eugene O'Neill is held to be "a fine playwright" but no great dramatist, is a happy one in accounting for a difference, which would prove embarrassing to whoever believes that insincerity is a characteristic of actor-playwrights, between Robert Wilson, say, and Ben Jonson, or between Field and Shakespeare. It helps us, moreover, to understand Field's merits and his place in the history of the drama.

Field's plays conform to the limitations of the theatre, meet "the exigencies of space and time; the dictation of the literal." His stories are told in terms of the existing stage, terms which have been peculiarly effective in the theatre. I have already spoken of his identification of characters on their first appear-

[309]*Saturday Review of Literature*, XV (21 November 1936), 3f. Quoted by permission of the author and publishers.

ance. His skillful motivation of exits,[310] too, reveals his merit as a practical playwright. Numerous other points of excellence in his dramaturgy, such as economy in dialogue,[311] preparation for a scene to be emphasized,[312] and full use of the various physical resources of his stage[313] might be mentioned; but perhaps enough has been said in illustration of Field's technical merits, which will be apparent to the reader of the plays. His "fictitious representations" meet DeVoto's second test: they are satisfactory to the artificial conditions of the theatre.

But Field too often fails to pass the other test, and his failure gives the key to a sound evaluation of his work. I do not refer to his probable concessions to audience taste in such matters as his frequent allusions to contemporary events, manners, and customs,[314] which give Field's plays a part of their sophistication and much of their value to the student of the seventeenth century. I do not refer, either, to what is probably insincerity in Field's portrayal of woman,[315] in which, like others, he seems to have made literary capital out of a contemporary—indeed, perennial—interest. I refer to the more basic insincerity: that too often Field is content, apparently, where "honest and thorough presentation of life" will not make

[310]Of Field's seventy-two exits within scenes, eleven are motivated by the completion of business the characters came on the stage to effect [e.g., in W 1.2.26 the Taylor leaves when he has finished trussing Count Frederick], thirty-five are motivated by a previous statement of the person leaving the stage, fourteen are motivated by a previous statement of a person remaining, and one is motivated by a subsequent statement of a person remaining. Various other types of motivation are used. Only two of the seventy-two exits within scenes are unmotivated. The Renaissance stage seems not to have required motivation for exits at the ends of scenes since, usually, all characters left the stage then; but Field motivates eleven of his fifteen exits of this type.

[311]e.g., W 5.1.118ff. and exp. n., 5.2.13–17.

[312]See exp. n. to A 3.4. s. div.

[313]In this edition staging is tentatively suggested in exp. nn. following the headings of the scenes.

[314]These are mentioned in exp. nn. and discussed consecutively by Fischer, 52–54 and Brinkley, 53–57. See also SP, XLIII (1946), 486, nn. 34, 35f.

[315]Field seems to have had no strong convictions on the feminist question. He indicts woman and man in both plays. His writing of Amends was not necessary on grounds of intellectual equity since Weather-cocke shows woman accused of inconstancy but found not guilty. The antithesis which writers [Langbaine, 198; Collier, A 3; Verity, 334] have seen between Weather-cocke and Amends is a specious one. See SP, XLIII (1946), 485 and SAB, XXI (1946), 129–141.

good theatre, to depart from such presentation for the sake of
theatrical values. Sometimes he sacrifices consistency or prob-
ability for a play on words.[316] Sometimes he lessens convinc-
ingness by failing to make adequate preparation for forthcoming events.[317] Far more serious, in my opinion, is Field's
violation of character for the sake of farcical or other theatrical
effect. In *Amends,* for example, when the Maid, whom all
believe to be suddenly ill on the day of her marriage to the
old Count, is led out, her prospective husband *"sits in a chaire
and fals a sleepe."*[318] This comic business is not convincing,
but it probably brought a laugh and served to motivate a
laugh line at 148. After these pleasantries Proudly, apparently
for no reason other than to evoke a humorously callous line
from the Count, though he has had no word from the sickroom
falsely reports the news that his sister and the Count's bride
is dead.[319] In *Weather-cocke* Nevill, instead of sharing with
the troubled Scudmore his plan for the latter's relief, dis-
guises himself from his friend as well as from the others, for
the flimsiest of excuses, that

> Good deeds shew double, that are timely done,
> And ioy that comes past expectation.[320]

The real reason, of course, is to provide us with sufficient com-
plications for a full-length play. Outside the theatre such a
friend as Nevill would probably have taken Scudmore into
his confidence. A similar violation of character is seen in
Worldly, who seems to have been conceived as an affable self-
made man of wealth, and who takes the defeat of his plan to
marry his daughter Bellafront off to Count Frederick with
the genial remark, "It boots not to be angry."[321] Field gives
us virtually nothing to support Bellafront's charges that she
was compelled to marry the Count

> by the threats
> Of a seuere Father, that in his hand
> Did gripe my fortunes;[322]

---

[316]e.g., *W* 5.2.203, *A* 1.1.336f.
[317]See *W* 3.2.135f., 5.2.223, *A* 4.4.120 and exp. nn. thereto.
[318]5.2.84 and see exp. n.
[319]See 5.2.159 and exp. n.
[320]2.1.23f.; and see exp. n.
[321]*W* 5.2.85; and see exp. n. to 81f.
[322]*W* 3.2.135ff.; and see exp. n.

or Worldly's violent behavior when Strange falsely accuses
himself and Katherine of murder. Without investigating the
charges, Worldly bursts out,

> To New-gate with him hence, take her along,
> Out Murtherers, whoore thou art no child of mine,
> Fetch Constable and Officers, Away.[323]

The character whom Field violates most flagrantly, however,
is Strange.[324] In the final scene of the play, when the audience
presumably has been thrilled by the abduction of Bellafront
in the mask and the removal of Nevill's double disguise, Field
has Strange act more like a playwright than a sensible young
merchant, apparently for the sake of extracting the last ounce
of theatrical value from the situation.[325] Field either deliberately conceived of the merchant as an incredibly eccentric
farce character, or, finding that theatrical compulsions required that the merchant do incredible things, attempted to
conceal the weaknesses in his motivation by stressing them and
calling him Strange. In either case, without apparent regret
Field departs from the "honest and thorough presentation of
life."

What then is Field's place in the history of dramatic literature? Dean Brinkley calls him a "clever actor-playwright . . .
without any real creative genius."[326] Ready to write the final

[323]5.2.159ff.
[324]See exp. n. to W dram. pers., 5.
[325]Having wounded and captured Pouts and forced his recantation of
the slanderous charge against Kate, Strange in disguise as a soldier brings
Pouts before the company with the witty comment, referring to the
slander, "You see he cannot stand to't" [5.2.96]. When Pouts has apolo-
gized to Kate, instead of revealing his identity Strange remains silent
while Pouts accuses the supposed soldier and Katherine of having mur-
dered the supposedly missing Strange. Strange has no motive for his
violent effort [123] to silence this accusation, which he can readily prove
ridiculous merely by unmasking, except the theatrically telling if rather
whimsical one of fulfilling the conditions of Pouts' oath [4.2.67ff.]. Field,
however, has the motive of sustaining the perplexity and final surprise of
the audience as long as possible. He makes Strange as soldier falsely
confess this crime which has never been committed [5.2.157f.] and prevents the dire consequences of his confession by revealing his identity
as it were in the nick of time. See exp. nn.
[326]P. 80.

sentence in her book, however, she is less conservative and I
think more nearly correct:

Although the body of his work is fairly small, the quality is
good enough to make Field a dramatist of more distinction than
has previously been recognized and to make us feel that his
early death was a misfortune to drama as well as to the stage.[327]

Emend "dramatist" to "practical, journalistic playwright," and
the conclusion reached by Brinkley twenty-two years ago still
holds good—particularly if one adds that though Field mort-
gaged his integrity as a writer, if he had any, that quality is
perhaps hardly to be expected in one who was, like Field, the
darling of the public stage.

4. FIELD'S EDITORS

The descent of the text of Field's plays has been studied in
detail elsewhere.[328] Here it will suffice to characterize briefly
the several editions.

Weather-cocke and *Amends* were first edited by John Payne
Collier,[329] who by his citation of quarto readings implies that
he is reprinting the first edition of each play when notice to
the contrary is not given. The textual notes to this edition
show that Collier is guilty of errors of both commission and
omission. Along with most editors of his time, Collier prac-
tices more or less consistent modernization in spelling and
punctuation, departing from his copy-texts in hundreds of
minutiae not ordinarily visible in the textual notes to this
edition and therefore left out of count. In addition to these,
Collier has introduced two hundred seventy departures from
his copy-texts:[330] substitutions, additions, deletions, "improvements" in grammar, and regularizations of metre. Yet Collier cites his copy-texts in notes only thirty-four times, of

[327]P. 147.
[328]The University of Texas *Studies in English*, 1947, 5–17.
[329]London, 1829.
[330]Textual notes contain abundant illustrations; for discussion see Texas
Studies, 1947, 6f., 9–11.

which only fifteen acknowledge departures. Without indicating that he is so doing, Collier prints *Amends* from a defective copy of the unauthoritative quarto of 1639.[331] Collier, finally, was evidently unaware that both *Weather-cocke* and *Amends* underwent correction during impression.[332] Yet Collier's edition is clearly the best text of Field until now available.

The plays were next[333] edited, in 1875, by W. Carew Hazlitt.[334] This edition introduces into the text of the two plays one hundred twenty-two new readings, of which only twenty-six are acknowledged; all are conjectural, and all are made at points where the copy-text reading seems closer than Hazlitt or Collier to Field's probable intention. Of the two hundred seventy readings Collier introduces, Hazlitt adopts two hundred fifty-four. It seems, therefore, that Hazlitt set up his text from Collier's, without reference to the quartos except in the few difficult passages where he cites them in textual notes.[335] Hazlitt's edition is a more accurate reproduction of Collier's text than of the Field quartos.

Field's plays were next edited by A. W. Verity in 1888.[336] This edition introduces into the text seventy-six readings found neither in the copy-texts nor in Collier or Hazlitt. Only four of these departures are acknowledged. Verity's text shows no evidence of having been prepared from the quartos. Of the hundred twenty-two readings introduced by Hazlitt, Verity adopts one hundred four. Of Collier's two hundred seventy new departures, Verity follows every one of the two hundred fifty-four adopted by Hazlitt. Since he follows none of the sixteen which Hazlitt rejects, it is almost certain that Verity set up his text from Hazlitt's.[337] The present edition takes no reading from Verity.

[331]*Ibid.*, 7f.

[332]See below, *W* and *A* Introductions, iii.

[333]The version in *The Old English Drama* [London, 1830, II] is a reprint of *C*, differing from it only in occasional misprints and less frequent corrections of *C*'s obvious misprints. That in *Five Old Plays, Forming a Supplement to the Collections of Dodsley and Others* [London, 1833] seems to be a rebinding with other plays of remainders of *C*; see Texas *Studies*, 1947, p. 11, n. 20.

[334]*Dodsley*⁴, XI, 1–86, 87–172.

[335]Texas *Studies*, 1947, 11–14.

[336]*Nero and Other Plays*, 333–411, 413–488.

[337]For further description of Verity's practice, see Texas *Studies*, 1947, 14–16.

Such is the descent of Field's text through the nineteenth century, and such is the provenance of Verity's edition, which has been that cited by most scholars who have studied Field or, in studying other subjects, have had occasion to draw upon his plays for evidence. Hundreds of readings illustrate increasingly large departure from the copy-texts with each successive edition. One line of descent among the nineteenth-century editions makes very clear the continued degeneration which the text of Field has suffered. It shows Hazlitt altering lines to improve metre and acknowledging his alterations with brackets; it shows Verity accepting Hazlitt's departures from the copy-texts and Collier, but destroying the evidence of Hazlitt's departure by omitting his editorial brackets. The quarto of *Weather-cocke* at 1.1.41f. reads:

> *Neu.* What, vp already *Scudmore,* neare a Wench with thee? Not thy Laundresse?

Collier prints these lines:

> *Nevill.* What, up already, Scudmore! Ne're a wench With thee? Not thy laundresse?

Written as verse, Collier's new second line is too short and irregular. Possibly not looking at the quarto, in which he would have seen that the passage is prose, Hazlitt prints:

> NEV. What, up already, Scudmore! Ne're a wench With thee? Not [e'en] thy laundress?

The degeneration is completed by Verity:

> *Nev.* What, up already, Scudmore! Ne'er a wench With thee? Not e'en thy laundress?[338]

The importance of such degeneration is seen when we remember that arguments from metrics and vocabulary are among the more frequently offered reasons for finding Field's hand in collaborate plays.[339]

---

[338]Seven other examples of this type are at *W* 2.1.290, 305, 4.1.30; *A* 5.1.78, 107, 5.2.201f., 215.

[339]Brinkley's conclusions on Field's versification, the most reliable we have, are based upon only eight hundred twelve lines of Verity's edition.

5. THE PRESENT EDITION

For each of the plays which follow, the copy-text chosen is the copy of the first quarto edition in the Folger Shakespeare Library. The collation of six copies[340] of each first edition shows that while the quartos were being run off, alterations were made in several printing forms,[341] which therefore exist in more than one state. When not present in the copy-text, the corrected state of a given form was obtained from another than the Folger copy.[342]

The general intent of this edition has been stated in the Preface. It remains to apply that intent to some problems met with in these texts and to illustrate the solutions of the present editor.

Obvious verbal misprints, such as "towatd" for "toward,"[343] or "reckoniug" for "reckoning"[344] are here corrected, with acknowledgment in the textual notes. The seventeenth-century compositor seems often to have erred, too, in punctuation. Without committing himself to any hypothetical "system" of Elizabethan punctuation, an editor may and should correct simple misprints in pointing.[345] This edition corrects punctuation where the copy-texts make such errors and, moreover, where it is apparent that the compositor's convenience rather than

[340]See "Key to Sigla" preceding text. nn. to each play.
[341]See *W* Intro. iii and *A* Intro. iii.
[342]The corrected state of outer G and inner I of *W* 1612 was obtained from the copy in the Library of Congress. The corrected state of outer A and E of *A* 1618 was obtained from British Museum 11773. C. 3; the corrected state of inner C and the most corrected state of inner G of *A* were obtained from the Huntington Library copy bearing the common title-page.
[343]*W* 1.1.148.
[344]*A* 3.4.150.
[345]It is obvious that a period after *visitation* in
   "You were not wont to make your visitation
   So short and carelesse"   [*W* 1.1.78f.]
is a typographical error.

fidelity to his copy or to his own practice elsewhere has led to the omission of punctuation at the ends of crowded lines.[346]

When it does not correct such errors or make up such deficiencies, the punctuation of this edition is that of the copy-text where the copy-text does not depart from early seventeenth-century punctuation as this editor understands that controversial subject; but all such departures have been acknowledged. In general, the counsel of Percy Simpson[347] has been followed; but in punctuation as in most other editorial questions this edition owes a debt to McKerrow[348] and Greg.[349] A frequent punctuation with Elizabethan authors and compositors, that which teachers of composition call the comma splice, has generally been retained.[350] In most instances, altering the punctuation of the copy-text does not require one to be excessively subjective, for contemporary practice in the pointing of many frequently recurring constructions is known. Capitals have been supplied to uncapitalized verse lines, but these departures are recorded. To make such alterations as the foregoing is not to apply a modern standard to a work of another period; and those who prefer the exact punctuation of the quartos will find it in the textual notes.[351]

Very often to mechanical considerations are due, also, variations in the wording, spelling, typography, and position of stage directions, the variant spellings of speakers' names, and indeed variant spellings within the lines themselves. Usually,

[346]On A 2[r] of W 1612, a page divided by a panel compartment, the names Sir Innocent Ninnie and Sir Abraham Ninny are not followed by periods, probably because these lines, unlike the others on the page, contain insufficient room for periods. This phenomenon occurs also in the lines of the plays; see text. nn. to W 1.2.9 and A 4.2.44, for but two examples.

[347]Simpson, passim.

[348]Bibl. and Prolegomena for the Oxford Shakespeare: A Study in Editorial Method (Oxford, 1939).

[349]EP.

[350]Such commas, however, sometimes appear to link a phrase or clause to another to which it does not logically belong. Where serious ambiguity might have resulted from retaining the comma, this edition sacrifices consistency to clarity, records the quarto reading, and prints a heavier stop. For examples see W 2.2.65, A 3.1.6.

[351]This policy seems less exceptionable than that of a recent editor of Shakespeare who bases his punctuation on a set of "rules that Shakespeare would presumably observe if he were writing to-day" [Works, ed. Kittredge, iv].

moreover, the lineation and position of prose and sometimes even of verse were determined in part by the necessity of fitting a given amount of copy into a given space. There is variation, too, in the spelling, abbreviation, and punctuation of scene-division headings. Since the copy-texts of Field's plays are reasonably consistent in most of these matters, the present editor attempts to approach more nearly to the author's "fair copy" by bringing such irregularities into conformity with a standard based upon the consistency of the quartos. This edition usually retains abbreviations occurring in prose passage and stage directions; it expands abbreviations in verse passages so as to avoid perplexing the reader as to scansion; but such expansions are noted. It has not seemed worthwhile to retain ornamental and large-font initial letters; they are here replaced by ordinary capitals, and the capital which follows them is reduced and the lines are respaced. These departures are acknowledged.

Unless an edition is to carry impedimenta of hundreds of textual notes which have only mechanical significance, it must admit certain kinds of departures from its copy-texts with only a general acknowledgment. In this edition the following departures are made silently:

All indentations for paragraphs, the spacing after punctuation points, and the abbreviation of speakers' names preceding speeches have been normalized.

VV, vv, and long s, wrong font letters, swash capitals, and inverted commas for apostrophes have been replaced by appropriate equivalents.

Head and foot pieces and lace ornaments are omitted from both copy-texts. They may, however, be readily located through the collations in W and A Introductions, iii.

Rules are omitted from the text of A where in the copy-text they provide display on A3^r and separate scenes on C1^v, D3^v, F1^r, G3^r, and H1^r.

In the same play, names of characters in centered stage directions appear in large and small caps; those in marginal directions, in upper and lower case italics. Preserving this distinction, I have normalized a few typographical exceptions.

Since this edition is not intended to be a facsimile and since the texts contain no instance in which it has significance, I do not preserve the distinction between n and u when turned.

The pagination of the copy-texts is here preserved by the retention of the original signatures and by the addition in brackets of signatures for unsigned quarto pages. When regular, catchwords have been omitted; when irregular, included in textual notes.

This edition is the first to number the lines of Field's plays. The method is by typographical rather than metrical units within the acts and scenes of this edition. Except in a few instances noted, the verse preserves the lineation of the copy-texts. I have not thought it necessary, however, to note turned lines of verse which I handle in the modern fashion whether the copy-text placed the runover at left or at right, or crowded it in. Scene divisions not in the quartos, most of them first supplied by Collier, have been added whenever a change of locality is clearly indicated in the lines or whenever all the characters leave the stage before the entrance of another group of characters come about new business.[352] Such additions are, of course, bracketed and noted.

In addition to acknowledging departures from the copy-texts, the textual notes record all variants in the copies of the first quartos collated for this edition. It has seemed inadvisable to record in detail the misprints and other insignificant variants in the second quarto of *Amends for Ladies,* neither an authoritative text nor a reproduction by an editor. For the convenience of the reader the collation in the textual notes includes, also, whatever readings from the editions of Collier, Hazlitt, and Verity seemed likely to assist him in his own solution of textual problems. A few readings relatively insignificant from a textual point of view have been admitted so as to make readily available material which it has been necessary to discuss in introductions and notes. Since this edition is not designed to enable the reader to construct from its textual notes the editions of the later editors, it does not ordinarily record their modernization of the spelling and punctuation of the quartos unless it suggests an interpretation that would not likely occur to the reader from the copy-text spelling and punctuation. It does not record as those of the later editors corrections of purely

[352]Fleay, *BC,* II, 199; Greg,, *EP,* 137.

typographical errors, which it has been thought better for the present editor to correct of his own authority since his is the first edition to preserve the old spelling.

Textual notes, finally, discuss questions of reading, leaving for the explanatory notes questions of interpretation. Where necessary, cross references are provided. In the explanatory notes, following each scene division I have included tentative discussions of the probable staging of the scene. In such notes I bravely use the modern terms, upstage and downstage.

The method of citation used in the textual notes is to print variants opposite a lemma from this edition. Lemmas are meant to give the exact readings of the copy-texts unless they are otherwise signed or unless they are followed by readings marked *QQ*, *Qa*, *Qb*, etc. For example,

$$W \ 1.2.84 \ \text{Morrow}] \ \text{morning} \ HV$$

means that in *Weather-cocke*, Act I, Scene 2, Line 84, the quarto reads "Morrow" and that Hazlitt and Verity print for that word the word "morning." Further,

$$A \ 3.4.122 \ Fees. \ \text{CHV}] \ Tear. \ \text{QQ, Q2}$$

means that the present edition follows Collier, Hazlitt, and Verity in giving a speech to Feesimple, rather than the quartos, which give it to Tearchops. The note

$$W \ 5.2.173 \ \text{woman-Citizen} \ Qbce, \ CHV] \ \text{Roman-Citizen} \ Qadf$$

means that this edition follows the corrected state of this printing form, represented by the copies in the Huntington and Congressional Libraries and the copy belonging to the Rosenbach Company, as did Collier, Hazlitt, and Verity.

A sigla of a nineteenth-century edition after a reading of this edition means that the previous editor gave essentially but not literally the same reading as this edition. For example,

$$W \ 2.1.95 \ \text{vs} \ CHV] \ \text{vp} \ QQ$$

means that Collier, Hazlitt, and Verity read "us" as does the present editor. It does not mean that they print "v" for "u." This limitation upon the accuracy of its readings from previous editions was necessary if the textual notes to this edition were not to occupy perhaps double their present room.

Alternation between roman and italic type in that part of
the textual notes which contains the collation, as illustrated
in the notes quoted above, has made possible in most instances
the accurate representation of the practice in italicization of
all the editions quoted—an end more desirable than consistency
of typography within the textual notes themselves. In textual
notes which discuss readings, such alternation would have
served no purpose and is not practiced.

II. A WOMAN IS A WEATHER-COCKE

II. A WOMAN IS A WEATHER-COCKE

1. INTRODUCTION

i. Date and Performance

Under date of 23 November 1611 the *Stationers' Register* contains the following entry:

John Budge. Entred for his Copy vnder th' [h]andes of Sir GEORGE BUC[KE] knighte and master *Lounes* warden, A booke called, *A woman is a weathercocke*, beinge a Comedye[1]

The quarto resulting from this registration did not appear until 1612.

The date of composition of *Weather-cocke*, however, must be placed earlier. An anterior limit of date may be set shortly after 25 March 1609, when John William, Duke of Cleves, died;[2] for the play contains two allusions[3] to the wars over the succession of Cleves. The posterior limit is afforded by the known date of performance. *Weather-cocke* was "acted before the King in WHITE-HALL."[4] before its publication in 1612. After the Christmas season of 1609–1610, the Revels company did not appear at Court until it presented *Cupid's Revenge*

---

[1]III, 471.

[2]Thorndike, *The Influence of Beaumont and Fletcher on Shakspere* (Worcester, 1901), 86.

[3]*W* 1.2.123f. and 313. For the meaning of these allusions see exp. nn. Taken together, the two, if they are not interpolations, suggest that the play was written after English aid to Cleves was expected, but before the war was over. Unfortunately, however, we may not be sure what period is thus defined. Samuel R. Gardiner [*History of England from the Accession of James I to the Outbreak of the Civil War* (4th ed.; London, 1894–1896), II, 100], Thorndike [*Influence of Beaumont and Fletcher*, 86], and Chambers [III, 229] state that English troops first took part in 1610. From the evidence of Barberigo, Venetian ambassador to Savoy [*Calendar of State Papers*, Venetian, ed. Rawdon Brown *et al.* (London, 1865—), XI, 407] we know that one English regiment was committed in the war sometime prior to 9 January 1610. I think it unlikely that these allusions are interpolations; they seem to be insufficiently pointed to justify their being subsequently added.

[4]T.-p., 5f.

there, 5 January 1611–1612.[5] It is clear that *Weather-cocke* must have been one of the five plays presented by the White-friars children at Court before the King and Prince Henry at Christmas, 1609–1610.[6]

The title-page of *Weather-cocke* specifies also private per-formances at the Whitefriars theatre. If the usual policy of taking to Court plays which had proved themselves before commercial audiences[7] was followed, *Weather-cocke* was per-formed in the Whitefriars before Christmas 1609–1610. Since in 1609 the plague deaths exceeded forty per week, the cri-terion for closing the theatres,[8] up to 30 November,[9] it seems probable that the original Whitefriars production of *Weather-cocke* occurred between 1 December 1609 and the performance at Court that Christmas.[10]

Exactly where *Weather-cocke* was staged at Court can not be determined. It may have been presented in the Cockpit, which according to Prince Henry's Privy Purse Accounts for 1610–1612 was occasionally used for dramatic productions as well as for cocking.[11] More probably it was performed in

[5]Steele, 162–169; Chambers, IV, 125.

[6]Steele, 162; Chambers, III, 313 and IV, 175. All other known per-formances of the company at Court between 25 March 1609 and 1612 are identifiable by title. The fact that the company was not entitled to use the name "Children of her Maisties Reuels" until 4 January 1610 seems to be irrelevant since title-pages were likely to call a company by the name it bore when the play was last on the stage prior to publication [Steele, *ibid.*; Chambers, II, 51, n. 3]. The warrant for the patent authorizing the company again to bear the Queen's name, moreover, was obtained in December 1609, most likely before Christmas and the Court performances [*MSC*, I, 271f.].

[7]Fleay, *BC*, I, 185; Chambers, I, 223. Brinkley evidently does not think this policy was followed with *W* since she dates the Whitefriars perform-ances "1610 and 1611" [p. 47]. Her date, however, is based on the title-page designation of the company, which, for reasons pointed out in n. 6, seems to me inadequate grounds for so late a date.

[8]Chambers, I, 331.

[9]*Ibid.*, IV, 351.

[10]Most scholars date the play 1609–1610. Cf. Verity, 333; Hillebrand, 321. Harbage dates 1609 but allows limits, 1609–1610 [p. 80]. Chambers dates 1609? [III, 313] as does Verhasselt [p. 501]. Thorndike [*Influence of Beaumont and Fletcher*, 87], following Fleay [*BC*, I, 185], dates "be-tween Jan. 1610 and Nov. 1611." Though the play may have been revived during 1610 and 1611, the original production seems more likely to have come in December 1609.

[11]Peter Cunningham, *Extracts from the Accounts of the Revels at Court, in the Reigns of Queen Elizabeth and King James I* (London, 1842), xiiif.

the Great Hall, the usual place for Court dramatics.[12] Whether in Cockpit or Hall, we have almost no evidence as to the physical resources of the stage on which this performance was given.[13] Nor have we sufficiently detailed specifications for the Whitefriars theatre[14] to enable us to speak definitely of the physical resources of the stage on which the initial performance of *Weather-cocke* was given.

Of the reception accorded *Weather-cocke* by its first audiences there are no contemporary records. That it was favorably received on perhaps more than one showing one may probably infer from its being selected for the Court performance already noted. How often it may have been acted we do not know. It was among the Jacobean plays revived by the Duke's company at Lincoln's Inn Fields in 1667,[15] a production Collier does not mention.[16] Listed by John Downes in a column and without author's name immediately after *"Three Comedies of Mr. Sherly's, viz. / The Grateful Servant. / The Witty Fair One. / The School of Complements."*[17], it was not identified as Field's by F. G. Waldron, who in his edition of *Roscius Anglicanus*, 1789, emended *"Three Comedies of Mr. Sherly's"* to read *"Four Comedies of Mr. Sherly's,"*[18] thus depriving Field of the authorship.

ii. Sources

"Da diese Komödie," writes Heinrich Fischer, "der Quellenforschung keinerlei Anhaltspunkte bietet, so darf wohl angenommen werden, dass sie ganz auf eigener Erfindung des Dichters beruht."[19] Neither previous editors nor historians of

---

[12]Adams, 388.
[13]The Great Hall was about forty feet wide by ninety feet long; the Cockpit was smaller [Adams, 387, 392f.].
[14]See exp. n. to *W*, t.-p., 8.
[15]Allardyce Nicoll, *A History of Restoration Drama: 1660–1700* (Cambridge, 1928), 168.
[16]As, in Genest's opinion, "he certainly ought to have done" [*op. cit.*, X, 22].
[17]*Roscius Anglicanus*, 27.
[18]*Ibid.*, 192.
[19]P. 13.

the drama have pointed out any sources for *Weather-cocke*, and the present editor's search for sources has availed little. The explanatory notes to this edition show instances in which Field seems to have availed himself of suggestions from others for some of his characters, situations, and, rarely, lines.

Characters for whom it has been suggested that Field is in debt include Pouts, who may owe something to Master Stephen in *Every Man in his Humour*, and Sir Abraham Ninny, who may owe something to Sir Amorous La-Foole and Master Matthew.[20] Situations for which Field may have received the suggestion from other writers are the opening of the play, which has been declared similar to *Every Man in his Humour*, 1.5[21] but which seems to resemble more closely the opening of *The Widow's Tears*.[22] *Weather-cocke* 3.2.71ff. may contain suggestions from the Closet Scene in *Hamlet*.[23] A few passages have been cited as parallel to passages in the work of other playwrights.[24] The only parallels sufficiently close to be acceptable to the present editor are at 1.2.52f., which I think is an echo of Shakespeare's Sonnet 20; at 4.2.109, which shows Field using an old pun used by Shakespeare; and at 4.2.120, which seems to show Field improving on a passage in *Eastward Ho!*[25] *The Spanish Tragedy* is alluded to at 1.1.44f. and burlesqued at 1.2.340ff. Persius is alluded to and translated at 1.1.93ff. The play contains, finally, a number of rather common classical allusions and proverbs. To point out such possible borrowings, however, is not the same as to offer bona fide sources of story. One's inability to discover more extensive source material than has yet been found renders the conventional view of how Field wrote his plays[26] inadequate. When the scholars have finished, *Weather-cocke* remains substantially an original invention, and Field in this play a dramatist less dependent on literary sources than most of his fellows.

[20]See exp. nn. to these characters, *W* dram. pers.
[21]Brinkley, 75.
[22]See *SP*, XLIII (1946), 495.
[23]See exp. n. to the lines.
[24]See exp. nn. to To the Reader, 8f., and 5.2.117.
[25]See exp. nn. to these lines.
[26]See above, p. 37.

iii. The Edition of 1612

The only seventeenth-century edition of *Weather-cocke* is the quarto of 1612,[27] *STC* 10854 and Greg 299.[28] It has the following title-page:

A / Woman is a Wea- / ther-cocke. / *A New Comedy,* / As it was acted before the King in / WHITE-HALL. / *And diuers times Priuately at the* / White-Friers, By the Children of her / Maiesties Reuels. / [*rule*] / *Written by* NAT: FIELD. / [*rule*] / *Si natura negat faciat Indagnatio versnm.* / [*device*] / Printed at London, for *Iohn Budge,* and are to be sold at / the gteat South doore of *Panles,* and at Brittaines / Bursse. I6I2.

This edition has the following collation:

4⁰; A–H⁴, I²; 34 unnumbered leaves.

A1ʳ: *title-page;* A1ᵛ *blank;* A2ʳ: *Dramatis personae* (lace ornament head and foot pieces, columns separated by panel compartment); A2ᵛ: *blank;* A3ʳ: To any Woman that hath beene no Weather-Cocke, *in italics, signed* N. F. (lace ornament headpiece); A3ᵛ: To the Reader, *signed N. F.* (lace ornament headpiece); A4ʳ: To his Loued Sonne, Nat. Field, and his Weather-cocke Woman, *verses in italics, signed* George Chapman (lace ornament headpiece); A4ᵛ: *blank;* B1ʳ *head-title* A Woman's a Weather-cocke *and text* (lace ornament headpiece); B2ᵛ—I2ᵛ: *text. Running title:* A Woman's a Wether-cocke.

Lace ornaments separate acts on C4ᵛ, G, and H1ᵛ. Blanks[29] occur on F2ᵛ and F3. The signature H2 is misprinted G2. Catchwords: *B1* To, *C1* It, *D1* And, *E1 Stran., F1* Periurd, *G1* With, *H1* uing, *I1 Kate.*

[27]Copies are comparatively numerous and well distributed. This edition was based upon a collation of six copies as follows: Folger, Huntington, Congressional, and Harvard libraries; the Rosenbach Company, and the Dyce Collection, Victoria and Albert Museum. I used microfilm copies of the second and last named. Other copies are in the British Museum, the Bodleian, at Eton, in the Newberry library, and in the collections of Mr. Carl H. Pforzheimer and Dr. A. S. W. Rosenbach.

[28]*Bibl. Dram.,* I, 438.

[29]For explanations see text. nn. to 3.2.223 and 3.3.40.

A
Woman is a Wea
ther-cocke.

A New Comedy,
As it was acted before the King in
WHITE-HALL,

And diuers times Priuately at the
White Friers, By the Children of her
Maiesties Reuels.

Written by NAT:FIELD.

Si natura negat faciat Indagnatio versum.

Printed at London, for *Iohn Budge,* and are to be sold at
the gteat South doore of *Paules,* and at Brittaines
Burffe. 1612.

PLATE II—TITLE-PAGE OF *A Woman is a Weather-cocke,* 1612,
FROM THE COPY IN THE FOLGER SHAKESPEARE LIBRARY

The printer of the 1612 quarto of *Weather-cocke*, according to Greg,[30] "appears from the device to have been William Jaggard." Since the ownership of the device in 1612, however, is uncertain, the identity of the printer is not fully established. Neither are we sure of the nature of the copy from which he printed, though there are evidences that it may have been of playhouse origin.[31] A number of the stage directions[32] seem to be descriptive of a well directed performance; but since the author was also a leading performer, this fact may be of small weight in determining the nature of the copy. More convinc-. ing evidence, perhaps, is the repetition in stage directions at 2.1.225f.[33] I attach little significance to the permissive stage direction at 5.2.1f., from which some might argue that the quarto was not set up from playhouse copy. The sort of vagueness in *"Enter 2. or 3. setting 3. or 4. Chaires, & 4. or 5. stooles"* is as much that of the practical theatre man as that of the literary author.

Whoever printed *Weather-cocke*, he did the job carelessly. In addition to leaving the two blanks and misprinting one signature, previously mentioned, he made numerous other errors, some of trivial and some of more grave nature. The quarto contains a few turned letters and a considerable number of typographical errors due to similarity between certain characters in this font. In eight words *t* is printed for *r*; in nine, *r* for *t*. *E* is once printed for *F*; *e* is three times printed for *c*; *s* is twice printed for *e*; *l* and *r* are each once printed for *i*. In one instance letters are transposed, and there are eight other misspellings. Three pairs of adjacent words are printed with-

---

[30]*Bibl. Dram.*, I, 438. But see exp. n. to t.-p., 14.

[31]In the case of work by a non-literary actor-playwright like Field, perhaps the source of the copy is not very important. He is unlikely to have prepared a "literary" fair copy that might be expected to differ from a producible book as a beginning playwright without theatrical experience often does.

[32]e. g., those at 2.1.116ff., 222ff., and 5.2.1ff.

[33]See text. n. to the line.

out intervening space. Lack of room in the line doubtless caused the sixteen failures to punctuate at the end of a line concluding a sentence or speech. The initial letters of sixty verse lines are not capitalized.[34] In seven instances periods are used at points which are not full stops, and there are a few other obvious errors in punctuation.

Somewhat more important errors and inconsistencies of the quarto are the repetition of speakers' names[35] and the inconsistency in logic of failing to indicate scene divisions required by the lines, beyond the first scene division, in four of the five acts,[36] but the latter phenomenon is of course quite often encountered. Necessary names of characters have been omitted from two stage directions;[37] and others are confused in various ways.[38] One speech is unassigned;[39] two speeches are wrongly assigned;[40] and two passages appear to be corruptions.[41]

Although *Weather-cocke* 1612 is poorly printed, there is ample evidence that some effort at correctness was made in four of its eighteen printing forms. The inner forms of Signatures F and I and the outer forms of Signatures G and H were corrected during impression.[42] The consequent significant variants, which seem not to have been known to previous editors of Field, have not been embodied in the previous editions. Corrections are as follows:

---

[34]A peculiarity of *Weather-cocke* 1612 is that fifty-eight of these sixty begin with the same letter, *a*. Their distribution in the forms indicates that this phenomenon must be charged to some other cause than the exhaustion of the compositor's supply of capital *A*'s toward the end of each form.

[35]See text. nn. to 3.2.71 and 4.3.27. The repetition at 1.1.26 is of a different order; see text. n.

[36]i.e., in all except Act 4, which contains *no* scene divisions.

[37]At 3.3.85 and 5.1.91.

[38]See text. nn. to 1.2.197, 2.1.225ff.

[39]1.2.93.

[40]4.1.13ff. and 5.1.53f.

[41]2.1.216 and 4.1.71.

[42]See *The Library*, 5th Series, I (1946), 62–64.

PAGE	LINE	STATE X (UNCORRECTED)[43]	STATE Y (CORRECTED)[44]
INNER F			
1ᵛ	3.2.138	liberall tongue	liberall talking tongue
	151	glad my	my glad
	153	contented	counented
	154	I had a Mistris free of all	The Mistris that I had free of
	155	her, deare	her, so deare
2ʳ	168	redeeme from	redeeme me from
	197	all that	all can
3ᵛ	3.3.48	right Worthy and	Worthy and right
	67	efaith	Ifaith
	70	as	tis
4ʳ	84	Truth	Troth
	87	my	mine
OUTER G			
2ᵛ	4.1.102	it	wit
		all	al
3ʳ	4.2.31	Was	Twas
4ᵛ	4.3.27	doost loue	doost thou loue
	28	sworn neuer	sworn it neuer
	30	Because is	Because he is
		that is	is it
	34	Morgley	Morglay
OUTER H			
1ʳ	4.3.54	laugh'd	smil'd
	56	His	In
	59	rheumaticke	rheumatickly
2ᵛ	5.1.50	there, go	there, Sirrha go
INNER I			
2ʳ	5.2.173	Roman-Citizen	woman-Citizen

[43]Represented, in inner F, by the Huntington copy; in outer G, by the Folger and Harvard copies; in outer H, by the Congressional, Dyce, Harvard, and Rosenbach copies; and in inner I, by the Dyce, Folger, and Harvard copies.

[44]Represented, in inner F, by the Congressional, Dyce, Folger, Harvard, and Rosenbach copies; in outer G, by the Congressional, Dyce, Huntington, and Rosenbach copies; in outer H, by the Folger and Huntington copies; and in inner I, by the Congressional, Huntington, and Rosenbach copies.

A
Woman is a Wea-
ther-cocke.

A New Comedy,
As it was acted before the King in   5
WHITE-HALL.

And diuers times Priuately at the
White-Friers, By the Children of her
Maiesties Reuels.

Written by NAT: FIELD.   11

Si natura negat facit Indignatio versum.

ᴵDeviceᴵ

Printed at London, for *Iohn Budge,* and are to be sold at   15
the great South doore of *Paules,* and at Brittaines
Bursse. 1612

[A1ʳ]

Dramatis personæ

Count Fredericke.	Bellafront.
Sir Iohn Worldly.	Katherine.
Neuill.	Lucida.
Scudmore.	Lady Ninnie.
Strange.	Mistris Wagtayle. 5
Pendant.	*A* Parson.
Captaine Powts.	*A* Page.
Sir Innocent Ninnie.	Seruants.
Sir Abraham Ninny.	⌈*A* Tailor.⌉ A2

To any Woman that hath beene no Weather-Cocke.

I did determine, not to haue Dedicated my Play to any Body, because forty shillings I care not for, and aboue, few or none will bestowe on these matters, especially falling from so famelesse a pen as mine is yet. And now I looke vp, and finde to whom my Dedication is, I   5 *feare I am as good as my determination: notwithstanding I leaue a libertie to any Lady or woman, that dares say she hath beene no weather-Cocke, to assume the Title of Patronesse to this my Booke. If she haue beene constant, and be so, all I will expect from her for my paynes, is,*   10 *that she will continue so, but till my next Play be printed, wherein she shall see what amendes I haue made to her, and all the sex, and so I end my Epistle, without a Latine sentence.*

                                    N.F.

                                      A3

To the Reader.

Reader, the Sale-man sweares, youle take it very ill, if
I say not somewhat to you too. Introth you are a stranger
to me; why should I Write to you? you neuer writ to mee,
nor I thinke will not answere my Epistle. I send a
Comedie to you heer, as good as I could then make; nor   5
sleight my presentation, because it is a play: For I tell
thee Reader, if thou bee'st ignoraunt, a Play is not so
ydle a thing as thou art, but a Mirrour of mens liues and
actions: now, be it perfect or imperfect, true or false, is
the Vice or Vertue of the Maker. This is yet, as well, as   10
I can, *Quales ego vel Cluuienus.* Thou must needs haue
some other Language then thy Mother tong, for thou
thinkst it impossible for me to write a Play that did not
vse a word of Latine, though he had enough in him. I
haue beene vexed with vile playes my selfe, a great   15
while, hearing many, nowe I thought to be euen with
some, and they shoulde heare mine too. Fare thee well,
if thou hast any thing to say to me, thou know'st where
to heare of me for a yeare or two, and no more I assure
thee   20

                                        N.F.

                                        [A3ᵛ]

To his Loued Sonne,
Nat. Field, and his We-
ther-cocke Woman.

To many formes, as well as many waies,
  Thy Actiue Muse, turnes like thy Acted woman:
In which, disprais'd inconstancie, turnes praise;
  Th' Addition being, and grace of Homers *Sea-man,*
In this life's rough Seas tost, yet still the same: 5
  So turns thy wit, Inconstancy to stay,
And stay t' Inconstancy: And as swift Fame
  Growes as she goes, in Fame so thriue thy Play,
And thus to standing, turne thy womans fall,
Wit turn'd to euerie thing, prooues stay in all.   10

                                George Chapman.

                                          [A4ʳ]

A Woman's a Weather-cocke.

Actus primus, Scena prima.

Enter Scudmore, as in his Chamber in a morning, halfe
ready, reading a Letter.

Scud. *Legit.* Whereas you write, my fortunes and my
    birth
Made aboue yours, may be a reall cause   5
That I must leaue you, know thou worthiest man,
Thou hast a soule, whose plenteous wealth supplies
All the leane wants blinde Chance hath dealt to thee.
Yet could I thinke, the Goddes from all their store,
Who ne're knew indigence vnto their will,   10
Would (out of all their stocke of Vertue left,
Or out of all new graces they can make)
Make such another peece as *Scudmore* is,
Then might he iustly feare; but otherwise,
Sooner the Masculine Element of Fire,   15
Shall flame his *Pyramids* downe to the Earth;
Sooner her Mountaines shall swell vp to Heauen,
Or softest Aprill showers quench fires in Hell;
Sooner shall Starres from this Circumference,
Drop like false fierie exhalation,   20
Then I be false to vowes made vnto thee;
In whom, ought ne're a fault: I ne're could see,
But that you doubted once my constancie.
    Yours through the world, and to the end of Time.
                           Bellafront.   25

Scud. Loqui, vt raptus. If (what I feele) I could ex-
presse in words,
Methinkes I could speake ioy enough to men,   B
To banish sadnesse from all loue, for euer:
Oh thou that reconcil'st the faults of all   30
That froathy sex, and in thy single selfe
Confin'st, nay hast engrost Vertue enough
To frame a spacious world of vertuous women;
Hadst thou bin the Beginning of thy sex,
I thinke the Deuill in the Serpents skin,   35
Had wanted Cunning to orecome thy goodnesse,
And all had liu'd and dy'de in Innocency
The white Originall Creation.   *Knockes within.*
Whose there? Come in.
              Enter Neuill.   40
Neu. What, vp already *Scudmore*, neare a Wench with
thee? Not thy Laundresse?
Scud. Good-morrow my deare *Neuill*.
Neu. What's this? A Letter; Sure it is not so,
A Letter written to *Hieronimo*!   45
Scud. By Heauen you must excuse me; Come, I know
You will not wrong my friendship and your manners
To tempt me so.
Neu. Not for the world my friend,
Farewell, Good-morrow.   *Exiturus.*   50
Scud. Nay Sir, Neither must you
Depart in anger from this friendly hand:
I sweare, I loue you better then all men,
Equally with all Vertue in the world:
Yet this would be a Key to lead you to   55
A prize of that importance.
Neu. Worthy friend,
I leaue you not in anger: What de'e meane?
Nor am I of that inquisitiue Nature fram'd,

To thirst to know your priuate businesses: 60
Why, they concerne not me; If they be ill
And dangerous, t'would greeue me much to know em.
If good; they be so, though I know em not:
Nor would I do your loue so grosse a wrong,
To Couet, to participate affaires   [B1ᵛ]
Of that neere touch, which your assured loue
Doth thinke not fit, or dares not trust me with.
    Scud. How sweetly does your friendship play with
       mine,
And with a simple subtilty, steales my heart   70
Out of my bosome. By the holiest Loue
That euer made a Story, y'are a man
With all good so repleate, that I durst trust you
Euen with this secret, were it singly mine.
    Neu. I do beleeue you, farewell worthy friend.   75
    Scud. Nay looke you, this same fashion does not please
       me,
You were not wont to make your visitation
So short and carelesse.
    Neu. Tis your Iealousie   80
That makes you thinke it so, for by my soule
You haue giuen me no distast, in keeping from me
All things that might be burthenous, and oppresse me.
Introth I am inuited to a wedding,
And the Morne faster goes away from me,   85
Then I go toward it: and so Good-morrow.
    Scud. God-morrow Sir, thinke I durst shew it you.
    Neu. Now by my life I not desire it Sir,
Nor euer lou'd these prying listening men,
That aske of other states and passages,   90
Not one among a hundered but proues false,
Enuious and slanderous, and wil cut that throat
He twines his armes about. I loue that Poet

That gaue vs reading, not to seeke our selues
Beyond our selues, Farewell.   95
   Scud. You shall not go,
I cannot now redeeme the fault I haue made
To such a friend, but in disclosing all.
   Neu. Now if you loue me, do not wrong me so,
I see you labour with some serious thing.   100
And thinke (like Fayries Treasure) to reueale it,
Will cause it vanish; and yet to conceale it
Will burst your breast, tis so delicious,
And so much greater then the Continent.
   Scud. Oh, you haue pierc't my entrails with your   105
       words   B2
And I must now explaine all to your eies,
Read, and be happy in my happinesse.
   Neu. Yet thinke on't, keepe thy secret, and thy friend
Sure and entire; Oh! giue not me the meanes   110
To become false heereafter; or thy selfe
A probable reason to distrust thy friend,
Though he be neare so true, I will not see't.
   Scud. I die by Heauen, if you denie againe,
I starue for Counsell; take it, looke vpon it;   115
If you do not, it is an æquall plague,
As if it had beene knowne and published:
For God-sake read, but with this Caution,
By this right hand, by this yet vnstain'd sword,
Were you my father flowing in these waues,   120
Or a dear sonne exhausted out of them,
Should you betray this soule of all my hopes,
Like the two brethren (though loue made em Starres)
We must be neuer more seene both againe.
   Neu. I read it fearlesse of the forfeiture,   125
Yet warne you, be as *Cautelous,* not to wound
My integritie, with doubt, on likelyhoods,

From misreport, but first exquire the Truth.
          Legit Neu., Scud. aliquando respiciens.
  Scud. Read, whilst I tell the Storie of my loue,   130
And sound the Truth of her heroicke Spirit,
Whom eloquence could neuer flatter yet,
Nor the best tongue of praises reach vnto.
The Maide there nam'd, I met once on a Greene
Neere to her Fathers house; me thought she show'd,   135
For I did looke on her, indeed no eie
That ow'd a sensible member, but must dwell
Awhile on such an obiect.
The passing Horses, and the feeding Kine
Stood still, and left their iournies and their food,   140
The singing Birds were in contention
Which should light neerest her; for her cleare eies
Deceiu'd euen men, they were so like bright skies.   [B2ᵛ]
Neere in a Riuolet, swum two beauteous Swans,
Whiter then any thing, but her necke and hands,   145
Which they left straight to comfort her: A Bull
Being baiting on the Greene for the Swaines sport,
She walking toward it, the vex'd sauage beast
Ceast bellowing; the snarling Dogges were mute,
And had enough to do to looke on her,   150
Whose face brought Concord, and an end of iarres,
Though Nature made em euer to haue warres.
Had there bin Beares and Lyons, when she spake
They had bin charmed too: For Græcians Lute
Was rusticke Musicke to her heauenly tongue,   155
Whose sweetnesse e'ne cast slumbers on mine eies,
Soft as Content, yet would not let me sleepe.
  Neu. Yours through the world, and to the end of time.
                                Bellafront.
Which *Bellafront?* Rich Sir *Iohn Worldlies* Daughter?   160

Scud. She is the food, the sleepe, the aire I liue by.

Neu. Oh heauen! we speake like Goddes, and do like
  Dogges.

Scud. What meanes my

Neu. This day, this *Bellafront* the Rich Heire,   165
Is married vnto Count *Fredericke,*
And that's the wedding I was going to.

Scud. I prethie do not mocke me, Married?

Neu. It is no matter to be plaid withall,
But euen as true as women all are false.   170

Scud. Oh! that this stroake were Thunder to my brest,
For *Neuill* thou hast spoake my heart in twaine,
And with the sudden whirlewind of thy breath,
Hast rauisht me out of a temperate soile,
And set me vnder the red burning Zone.   175

Neu. For shame returne thy blood into thy face,
Knowst not how slight a thing a woman is?

Scud. Yes, and how serious too: Come Ile t'the
  Temple,
She shall not damne her selfe for want of Counsell.   180

Neu. Oh! prethee run not thus into the streets,
Come dresse you better, so: Ah! as thy cloaths   B3
Are like thy mind, too much disorder'd.
How strangely is this Tide turn'd? For a world
I would not but haue cal'd heere, as I went.   185
Collect thy Spirits, we will vse all meanes
To checke this blacke fate, flying toward thee; Come,
If thou miscarriest, tis my day of doome.

Scud. Yes, now I'me fine, Married? It may be so,
But women looke too't, for if she proue vntrue,   190
The Diuell take you all, that are his due.   ⌈*Exeunt.*⌉

[Actus primus, Scena secunda.]

Enter Count Fredericke, a Taylor trussing him, attended by a Page.

Count. Is Sir *Iohn Worldly* vp, Boy?
Page. No my Lord.
Count. Is my Bride vp yet?   5
Page. No.
Count. No, and the Morne so faire.
    Enter Pendant.
Pen. Good morrow my thrice honor'd & heroick Lord.
Page. Good morrow your Lord and Maister you might   10
say, for breuitie sake.
 Count. Thou 'ast a good Taylor, and art verie fine.
Pen. I thanke your Lordship.
Page. I you may thanke his Lordship indeed.
Pen. Foregod this Dublet sits in print my Lord.   15
And the Hose excellent; the Pickadell rare.
 Page. Heele praise himselfe in trust with my Lords
taylor, for the next S. *Georges* sute.
 Count. Oh, Good-morrow Taylour, I abhorre billes in
a Morning.   20
 Pen. Your Honor sayes true; their Knauerie will be
discern'd by day-light,
But thou maist watch at night with bill in hand,
And no man dares finde fault with it.
 Tay. A good iest Efaith, Good-morrow to your Lord-   25
ship, a verie good iest.   *Exit Taylor.*
 Count. I wonder my inuited guests are so tardie,
What's a clocke?   [B3ᵛ]

Pen. Scarse seauen my Lord.

Count. And what newes *Pendant?*   30
What think'st thou of my present marriage?
How shewes the Beautie to thee I shall wed?

Pen. Why to all women, like *Diana* among hir
   Nimphs.

Page. There's all his reading.   35

Pen. A beautie of that purenesse and delight,
That none is worthy of her but my Lord,
My honorable Lord.

Count. But then her fortune
Matcht with her beautie, makes her vp a match.   40

Pen. By Heauen vnmatcheable, for none fit but Lords,
And yet for no Lord fit, but my good Lord.

Count. And that her Sister then should loue me to,
Is it not strange?

Pen. Strange: No, not strange at all,   45
By *Cupid,* there's no woman in the world
But must needs loue you, doate, go madde for you;
If you vouchsafe reflection; Tis a thing
That does it home: thus much reflection
Catches em vp by Dozens, like wilde foule.   50

Page. Now ye shall tast the meanes by which he eates.

Pen. Nature her selfe hauing made you, fell sicke
In loue with her owne worke, and can no more
Make man so louelie, being diseasd with loue.
You are the worlds Minion, of a little man;   55
Ile say no more, I would not be a woman,
For all has beene got by them.

Count. Why man, why?

Pen. Hart, I should follow you like a young rank
   whore,   60
That runs proud for her loue, plucke you by 'th sleeue,
Who ere were with you, in the open streete,

With the impudencie of a drunken Oyster-wife,
Put on my fighting wastcoate, and the Ruffe
That feares no tearing, batter downe the windowes   65
Where I suspected you might lie all night,
Scratch faces, like a Wilde-Cat of *Pict-hatch*.   [B4ʳ]
    Count. *Pendant* thou't make me dote vpon my selfe.
    Pen. *Narcissus* by this hand, had farre lesse cause.
    Count. How knowst thou that?   70
    Page. They were all one my Lord.
    Pen How do I know, I speake my Conscience.
His beauties were but shaddowes to my Lord,
Why Boy his presence would enkindle sin,
And longing thoughts in a deuoted Nun: 75
Oh foote, oh Legge, oh Hand, oh body, face,
By *Ioue* it is a little man of wax.
    Count. Th' art a rare Rascall; Tis not for nothing
That men call thee my Commendations.
    Page. For nothing, no, he would be loath it should.   80
              Enter Captaine Poutes.
    Count. Good Morrow, and good welcome Captaine
    Poutes.
    Cap. Good Morrow to your honour, and all ioy
Spring from this match, and the first yeare a Boy,   85
I commend these two verses a purpose, to salute your
Honor.
    Count. But how haps it Captaine, that your intended
marriage with my Father in Lawes third daughter, is not
solemnized to day?   90
    Pen. My Lorde tells you true Captaine, it woulde haue
sau'd meat.
    ˡ*Cap.*˩ Faith I know not, Mistris *Kate* likes me not,
shee sayes I speake as if I had a pudding in my mouth,
and I aunswered her, if I had it was a white pudding,   95
and then I was the better arm'd for a woman; for I had a

case about mee: so one laught, and the other cried fie: the
third saide I was a Bawdy Captaine, and there was all I
could get of them.

Count. See Boy, if they bee vp yet, Maids are long   100
lyers I perceiue.

Page. How if they will not admit me my Lord?

Count. Why should not they admit you my Lorde, you
cannot Commit with em my Lord.

Page. Marry therefore my Lord.   *Exit Page.* [B4ᵛ]

Count. But what should be the reason of her sodain
alteration, she listned to thee once: Ha.

Pen. Haue you not heard my Lord, or de'e not know?

Count. Not I, I sweare.

Pen. Then you know nothing that is worth the   110
knowing.

Cap. That's certaine, he knowes you.

Pen. There's a young Merchant, a late Sutor, that deals
by wholesale, and Heire to Land, well descended, of
worthy education, beholding to Nature.   115

Count. Oh, tis young *Strange.*

Cap. Ist he that lookes like an *Italian* Taylour? Out of
the lac'd wheele, that weares a Bucket on's head?

Count. That is the man, yet beleeue mee Captaine, it
is a noble sprightly Cittizen.   120

Cap. Has he money?

Count. Infinitely wealthy.

Cap. Then Captaine thou art cast, would I had gone
for *Cleeueland*; *Worldly* loues money better then I loue
his Daughter, Ile to some Company in Garrison: God   125
b'wy.

Count. Nay, ye shall dedicate this day to me,
We speake but by the way man, nere dispaire;
I can assure you, shee's yet as free as Ayre.

Pen. And you may kill the Merchant with a looke,   130

I'de threaten him to death: my honor'd Lord
Shall be your friend, goe too, I say he shall,
You shall haue his good word, shall he my Lord?
   Count. Sfut, he shall haue my bond to do him good.
   Pen. Law, Tis the worthiest Lord in Christendome: 135
Oh Captaine, for some fourescore braue Spirits, once
To follow such a Lord in some attempt.
   Cap. A hundred Sir were better.

   Enter old Sir Innocent Ninnie, my Lady Ninnie, Sir
        Abraham, and Mistris Wagtayle. 140
   Count. Heere's more Guesse.
   Cap. Is that Man and Wife?   C
   Pen. It is Sir *Innocent Ninne,* that's his Lady,
And that Maister *Abraham* their onely sonne.
   Count discoursing with In: La:, Abra: looking about. 145
   Cap. But did that little, old, dri'de Neats tongue, that
Eele-skin get him?
   Pen. So tis said Captaine.
   Cap. Methinkes, he in his Lady, should shew like a
Needle in a Bottle of Hay. 150
   Pen. One may see by her Nose, what Pottage shee
loues.
   Cap. Is your name *Abraham;* Pray who dwels in your
Mothers backside, at the signe of the Aqua-vitæ bottle.
   Pen. Gods precious: Saue you Mistris *Wagtaile.* 155
   Wag. Sweet M. Pendant.   *(Puls hir by the sleeue.*
   Abra. Gentlemen, I desire your better acquaintance,
you must pardon my Father, hee's somewhat rude, rude, &
my Mother grosly brought vp, as you may perceiue.
   Count. Yong Maister *Abraham,* cry ye mercie Sir. 160
   Abra. Your Lordships poor friend, & Sir *Abra: Ninny.*
The Dubadub of Honor, piping hot,
Doth lye vpon my Worships shoulder blade.

Inno. Indeed my Lord, with much cost and labour, wee haue got him Knighted; and being Knighted, vnder 165 fauor my Lord, let me tell ye, hee'le proue a sore Knight as ere run at Ring. He is the one and onely *Ninnie* of our house.

La. Nin. He has cost vs something ere he came to this: Hold vp your head Sir *Abraham.*   170

Abra. Pish, pish, pish, pish.

Count. De'e heare how.

Pen. Oh, my Lord.

Cap. I had well hop'd she could not haue spoke, she is so fat.   175

Count. Long maist thou wear thy Knights-hood, and
      thy spurs
Pricke thee to Honor on, and pricke off Curs.

Abra. Sir *Abraham* thankes your Honour; and I hope, your Lordship will consider the simplicity of Parents, a 180 couple of old fooles my Lord, and I pray so take em.

Om. Ha, ha, ha.   [C1ᵛ]

Abra. I must be faine to excuse you heere, you'le needs be comming abroad with mee; if I had no more wit then you now, we should be finely laugh'd at.   185

Inno. Berlady his worship saies well wife, wee'le troble him no longer; with your Honors leaue, Ile in and see my old friend Sir *Iohn,* your Father that shall be.

La. Nin. Ile in to, and see if your Bride need no dressing.   *Exit Inno.* 190

Count. Sfut as much as a Tripe I thinke, hast them I pray. Captain, what think'st thou of such a woman in a long Sea Voyage, where there were a dearth of Victuals?

Cap. Venison my Lord, Venison.

Pen. I faith my Lord, such Venison as a Beare is.   195

Cap. Hart, she lookes like a blacke Bumbard, with a pint pot waiting vpon it.   *Exeunt Lady, Wag.*

Count. What Countrimen were your Ancestors S.
Abra.?

Abra. Countrimen, they were no Countrimen, I scorne   200
it, they were Gentlemen all, My Father is a *Ninnie,* and
my Mother was a Hammer.

Cap. You should be a Knocker then by the Mothers
side.

Abra. I pray my Lord, what is yon Gent. he looks so   205
like a Sarazen, that as I am a Christian I cannot endure
him.

Count. Take heed what you say Sir, hee's a Soldier.

Pen. If you crosse him hee'l blow you vp with Gunpowder.   210

Abra. In good faith, he lookes as if he had had a hand
in the treason, Ile take my leaue.

Count. Nay good Sir *Abraham,* you shall not leaue vs.

Pen. My Lord shall be your warrant.

Abra. My Lord shall be my warrant: Troth I doo not   215
see that a Lords warrant is better then any other mans,
vnlesse it bee to lay one by the heeles. I shall stay heere,
and ha my head broake; and then I ha my mends in my
owne hands, and then my Lords warrant will helpe me to
a plaister, that's all.   220

Count. Come, come, Captaine, pray shake the hand of
acquaintance with this Gentleman, he is in bodily feare of
you.   C2

Cap. Sir, I vse not to bite any man.

Abra. Indeed Sir, that would shew you are no Gentle-   225
man, I would you would bid me be couer'd: I am a knight,
I was Knighted a purpose to come a wooing to Mistris
Lucida, the middle Sister, Sir *Iohn Worldlyes* second
daughter; and she saide she would haue mee, if I could
make her a Ladie, and I can doo't now; Oh heere she   230
comes.

Enter Sir Iohn Worldly, Maister Strange, Kate, and
Lucida, with a Willow Garland.

Count. My Bride will neuer be readie I thinke: heer
are the other Sisters.   235

Pen. Looke you my Lorde; There's *Lucida* weares the
Willow Garland, for you; and will so go to Church I
hear: and looke you Captaine, that's the Merchant.

Abra. Now doth the pot of Loue boile in my bosome;
Cupid doth blow the fire; and I cannot Rime to bosome,   240
but Ile go reason with her.

World. Youle make her ioynture of that fiue hundred
you say, that is your inheritance, M. *Strange?*

Stra. Sir I will.

World. Kate, you do loue him?   245

Kate. Yes faith Father, with all my heart.

World. Take hands, kisse him, her portion is foure
thousand. Good-morrow my sonne *Count,* you stay long
for your Bride; but this is the day that sels her, and shee
must come forth like my Daughter, and your Wife.   250
I pray salute this Gentleman as your Brother,
This morne shall make him so; and though his habit
But speake him Cittizen, I know his worth
To be gentile in all parts. Captaine,

Cap. Sir.   255

World. Captaine, I could haue been contented well
You should haue married *Kate.*

Kate. So could not *Kate.*

World. You haue an honourable Title; a Souldier is
a ve-   [C2ᵛ]   rie honourable Title: A Captaine is a   260
Commander of Soldiers; But look you Captaine, Captaines
haue no money, therefore the *Worldlies* must not match
with Captaines.

Cap. So Sir, so.

World. There are braue warres.   265

Cap. Where?

World. Finde them out braue Captaine,
Win honor, and get monie; by that time
Ile get a Daughter for my Noble Captaine.

Cap. Good Sir, good.   270

World. Honor is Honor, but it is no money, *Aspiciens*
This is the Tumbler then must catch the Coney.   *Strange.*

Cap. Thou'rt an old fellow: Are you a Marchant Sir?

Stra. I shame not to say yes. Are you a Souldier Sir?

Abra. A Soldier Sir; Oh God I, he is a Captaine.   275

Stra. He may be so, and yet no Souldier Sir: For as
many are Soldiers, that are no Captaines; so manie are
Captaines that are no Soldiers.

Cap. Right Sir: and as manie are Cittizens that are no
Cuckolds.   280

Stra. So, many are Cuckolds, that are no Cittizens.
What ayle you Sir, with your robustious lookes?

Cap. I would be glad to see for my money, I haue
payde for my standing.

Stra. You are the Nobler Captaine Sir: 285
For I knowe manie that vsurpe that name,
Whose standings pay for them.

Cap. You are a Pedler.

Stra. You are a Pot-gun.

Cap. Merchant, I would thou hadst an Iron Tale like   290
me.

Count. Fie Captaine, you are too blame.

Pen. Nay, Gods will, you are too blame indeede, if my
Lord say so.

Cap. My Lord's an Asse, and you are another.   295

Abra. Sweete Mistris *Luce*; let you and I withdraw,
this is his humor.   C3   Send for the Constable.

Cap. Sirra, Ile beate you with a pudding on the change.

Stra. Thou dar'st as wel kisse the wide mouthed Canon

At his discharging, or performe as much   300
As thou dar'st speake: For Souldier you shall know,
Some can vse swords, that weare em not for show.

   Kate. Why Captaine, though ye be a man of warre,
you cannot subdue affection; you haue no alacritie in your
eie, and you speake as if you were in a Dreame, you are   305
of so melancholy and dull a disposition, that on my Conscience you would neuer get Children: Nay nor on my
bodie neither: and what a sinne were it in me, and a most
pregnant signe of Concupiscence, to marrie a man that
wantes the mettall of Generation; since that is the blessing   310
ordain'de for Marriage, procreation the onely end of it.
Besides, if I could loue you; I shall be heer at home, and
you in *Cleeueland* abroad; I among the bold Brittaines,
and you among the hot shots.

   World. No more puffing good Captaine; leaue bat-   315
teries with your breath, the short is this:
This worthy *Count,* this Morning makes my Son;
And with that happie Marriage this proceeds:
Worldly's my Name, *Worldly* must be my deeds.

   Cap. I will pray for Ciuill wars, to cut thy throat with-   320
out danger Marchant,
I will turne Pyrate, but Ile be reueng'd on thee.

   Stra. Do Captaine do, a halter will take vp our quarrel
then.

   Cap. Zoones, I will be reueng'd vpon ye all.   325
The strange aduenture th'art now to make
In that small Pinnace, is more perillous
Then any hazard thou could'st vndergo,
Remember a scorn'd Souldier tolde thee so. *Exit Captaine.*

   Stra. Go walke the Captaine good Sir *Abraham.*   330

   Abra. Good faith Sir, I had rather walke your horse,
I will not meddle with him, I would not keepe him Com- [C3ᵛ]
ᶜpaᴵnie in his drinke for a world.

World. But what good doo you Sir *Abraham* on my
     daughter,   335
I could be e'ne content, my *Lucida*
Would skip your wit, and looke vpon your wealth,
And this one day let *Hymen* Crowne ye all.
     Abra. Oh no, she laughes at me; and scornes my sute:
For she is wilder, and more hard withall,   340
Then Beast, or Bird, or Tree, or stonie wall.
     Kate. Ha, Godamercie old *Hieronimo.*
     Abra. Yet might she loue me for my louelie eies:
     Count. I but perhaps your nose she doth despise.
     Abra. Yet might she loue me for my dimpled chin: 345
     Pen. I but she sees your Beard is verie thin.
     Abra. Yet might she loue me for my proper bodie:
     Stra. I, but she thinkes you are an arrant Noddie.
     Abra. Yet might she loue me, cause I am an heire:
     World. I, but perhaps she does not like your ware.   350
     Abra. Yet might she loue me in despight of all:
     Luci. I, but indeed I cannot loue at all.
     World. Well *Luce,* respect Sir *Abraham* I charge you.
     Luci. Father, my vow is past: whilst the Earle liues
I neare will Marrie, nor will pine for him: 355
It is not him I loue now, but my humor.
But since my Sister he hath made his choise,
This wreath of Willow that begirts my browes,
Shall neuer leaue to be my Ornament
Till he be dead, or I be married to him.   360
     Pen. Life my Lord, you had best marrie em all three,
Theyle neuer be content else.
     Count. I thinke so to.
     World. These are impossibilities; Come, Sir *Abram.*
A little time will weare out this rash vow.   365
     Abra. Shall I but hope?

Luci. Oh, by no meanes. I cannot endure these round
Breeches, I am readie to sound at em.

Kate. The Hose are comely.   [C4ʳ]

Luci. And then his left Leg: I neuer see it, but I thinke   370
on a Plum-tree.

Abra. Indeed there's reason there should be some difference in my Legges, for one cost me twentie pound more
then the other.

Luci. Introth both are not worth halfe the mony.   375

Count. I hold my life one of them was broake, and cost
so much the healing.

Abra. Right hath your Lordship said, twas broke
     indeed,
At footeball in the Vniuersitie.   380

Pen. I know he is in loue, by his Verse vaine.

Stra. He cannot hold out on't: you shall heare.

Abra. Well since I am disdain'd; off Garters blew;
Which signifies Sir *Abrams* loue was true.
Off Cypresse blacke, for thou befits not me;   385
Thou art not Cypresse, of the Cypresse Tree,
Befitting Louers: Out greene Shoo-strings out,
Wither in pocket, since my *Luce* doth pout:
Gush eyes, thumpe hand, swell heart, Buttons flie open,
Thankes gentle Dublet; else my heart had broken.   390
Now to thy Fathers Countrey house at *Babram,*
Ride post; There pine and die, poore, poore Sir *Abram.*

Om. Oh dolefull dumpe.   *Musicke playes.*

World. Nay you shall stay the wedding, Hark the
     Musick,   395
Your Bride is readie.

Count. Put Spirit in your Fingers; Lowder still,
And the vast Ayre with your enchantments fill.

                              Exeunt Om.

Actus secundus, Scena prima.

Enter Neuill like a Parson.

ᴵ*Neu.*ᴵ Thus for my friends sake haue I taken orders,
And with my reasons and some hyre besides:
Won the knowne Priest, that was to Celebrate   [C4ᵛ]
This Marriage, to let me assume his place: 5
And heere's the Charracter of his face and beard.
By this means, when my friend confronts the Maide,
At the Church doore (where I appointed him
To meete him, like my selfe: for this strange shape
He altogether is vnwitting of)   10
If she (as one Vice in that sex alone
Were a great Vertue) to inconstancy past,
Ioyne impudency, and sleight him to his face,
Shewing a resolution to this match,
By this attempt it will be frustrate;   15
And so we haue more time, though but till night,
To worke to speake with her, or vse violence,
(For both my bloud and meanes are at his seruice.)
The reason too, I do this past his knowledge,
Is that his ioy may be the more compleat;   20
When being resolu'd shee's married and gone,
I can resolue him otherwise: Thus I know,
Good deeds shew double, that are timely done,
And ioy that comes past expectation.
                    Enter Scudmore in Tawny.   25
Yonder he comes, dead in his melancholy:
Ile question him, and see if I can raise
His Spirit from that, it restlesse rests vpon:

He cannot know me. Ho, Good-morrow Sir.

   Scud. Good-morrow to no liuing thing but one,   30
And that is *Neuill*: Oh, the Vowes, the Vowes,
The protestations and becomming Oaths
Which she has vtter'd to me, so sweet, so many,
As if she had beene couetous, not to leaue
One word for other Louers, which I pittied.   35
She saide indeede I did deserue em all;
Her lips made swearings sound of piety,
So sweet and prettily they came from her:
And yet this Morne shee's married to a Lord.
Lord, Lord, how often has she kist this hand,   40
Lost her selfe in my eyes, plaid with my haire,   D
And made me (a sinne I am not, subiect too)
Go away proud, emproued by her favors,
And yet this Morne shee's married to a Lord.
The Bels were ringing as I came along.   45
   Neu. Yes Sir, tis for the great Marriage twixt
   Scud. Pray hold there, I know it too well.
The Tokens and the Letters I haue still:
The dangers I haue past for her deere sake,
By day and night to satisfie her wishes;   50
That Letter I so lately did receiue,
And yet this Morne shee's married to a Lord:
Oh memory, thou blessing to all men,
Thou art my curse and cause of misery,
That tel'st me what I haue bin in her eyes,   55
And what I am: as it is impossible
To find one good in the whole word of women:
But how I loose my selfe, and the remembrance
Of my deere friend, who said he would meet me heere.
What is this Priest that walkes before the Church?   60
Why walke you heere so earely, Sir,
   Neu. I am appointed,

Heere to attend the comming of the Brides,
Old Sir *Iohn Worldlyes* Daughters.
  Scud. Are there two?   65
  Neu. Yes Sir, the eldest marries Count *Frederick.*
  Scud. Oh.
  Neu. The middlemost weares willow for his sake,
The youngest marries the rich Merchant *Strange.*
  Scud. He is right worthy, and my well knowne friend.   70
But Parson, if you marry *Bellafront,*
The horror of thy Conscience shall exceed
A Murtherers; Thou shalt not walke alone,
Nor eate, nor sleepe, but a sad Louers grones
And cursses, shall appeare and fright thy soule: 75
I tell thee Priest, they're sights, more terrible
Then Ghosts or Sprights, of which old wiues tell Tales,
Thou shalt run mad, thou shalt be damn'd indeed.
  Neu. Now God forefend, the reason Sir I pray?   [D1ᵛ]
  Scud. She is contracted Sir, nay married   80
Vnto another man, though it want forme:
And such strange passages and mutuall Vowes,
T'would make your short haire start through your blacke
    Cap,
Should you but heare it.   85
  Neu. Sir, Ile take no notice
Of things, I do not know: the iniur'd Gentleman,
May bring em after into the Spirituall Court,
And haue a faire pull on't, a poore Gentleman,
(For so I take him by his being deceiv'd)   90
Gainst a great Count, and an old wealthy Knight.
  Scud. Thou *Pancridge* Parson; Oh, for my frend
    Neuil,
Some wile or other might remoue this Priest,
And giue vs breathing to crosse their intent.   95
  Neu. Alas my deere friend.

Scud. Sir, do but you refuse to ioyne em.

Neu. Vpon what acquaintance Sir?

They are great persons, and I meane to rise,

I hope in time to haue three liuings man,   100

And this were not the way I take it Sir.

Scud. Why looke thee, there is Gold.

Neu. Oh by no meanes.

Scud. I seldome knew't refusd, yet by thy Coate;

But where it would haue bin a cause of good.   105

Neu. But looke ye, you shall see I'me a Deuine,

Of Conscience quite opposite to a Lawyer,

Ile giue you Counsell Sir without a fee:

This way they are to come, if you dare doo't,

Challenge her as your owne, at the Church doore,   110

I will not hinder you.   *Musicke playes.*

Scud. Oh harke they come,

Neuill my friend, well I must something do:

Oh, why should Musicke, which ioyes euerie part,

Strike such sharpe killing discords to my hart?   115

Musicke. Enter Sir Iohn Worldly, who meets the Parson, &
entertaines him. Count, Bellafront. Strange, Kath. Lucida,
with Willow. Pendant, Sir Inno: Ninnie, my Ladie Ninnie,
Mrs. Wagtayle, S. Abram Melancholy. W. P. walk grauely D2
afore all softly on. Scudmore stands before, and a Boy   120
singes to the tun'd Musicke.

The Song.

They that for Worldly wealth do wed,
That buy and sell the Marriage bed:
That come not warm'd with the true fire,   125
Resolu'd to keepe this Vow entire,
    To soone finde discontent,
    To soone shall they repent.
But Hymen *these are no such Louers,*

Which thy burning Torch discouers: 130
Though they liue then many a yeare,
Let each day as new appeare
    As this first; and delights
    Make of all Bridall Nights:
Io: Hymen *giue Consent,*   135
Blessed are the Marriages that nere repent.

Count. How now, who's this?
Pen. Young *Scudmore.*
Om. Tis young *Scudmore.*
Scud. Canst thou this holy Church enter a Bride,   140
And not a Coarse meeting these eyes of mine.
Bell. Yes, by my troth, what are your eies to me,
But gray ones, as they are to euerie body.
The Gentleman I do a little know:
Hee's franticke sure, forward a Gods name there.   145
  Luci. Sister, this is not well, and will be worse.
  Scud. Oh hold thy Thunder fast.
  Count. What is the matter?
  Pen. Ile aske my Lord: What is the matter Sir?
  World. Some ydle words my Lord, t'may be haue past   150
Twixt *Scudmo*re, and my Daughter heeretofore,
And he has dreamt em things of consequence.
  Pen. Pish, nothing else; set forward.
  Neu. By your leaue.   [D2ᵛ]
  Scud. Can there be such a soule in such a shape,   155
My Loue is subiect of such miserie,
Such strange impossibilities and mis-fortune,
That men will laugh at me, when I relate
The Storie of it, and conceiue I lye.
Why Madam that shall be, Lady *in Posse,* do Titles,   160
Honors, and Fortunes, make you so forgetfull?
  Bell. You are insolent, nay strangely sawcie Sir,

To wrong me in this publicke fashion.

World. Sirrha, go too, there's Law.

Scud. There is indeede,   165
And Conscience too, old *Worldly* thou hast one;
But for the other, wilde *Virginia,*
Blacke *Affricke,* or the shaggy *Scithia,*
Must send it ouer as a Merchandize,
Ere thou shew any heere.   170

Pen. My honor'd Lord,
Say but the word, Ile force him from the doore.

Count. I say the word, do it.

Scud. You my Lords fine foole?

Abra. I he Sir.   175

Scud. No, nor you my Lord fooles foole.

Inno. Ware Boy, come backe.

La. Nin. Come back I say Sir *Abraham.*

                                    Intrant Templum.

Stra. Tis such a forward child.   180

Scud. My passion and my cause of griefe's so great,
That it hath drownd all worthy parts in me:
As drinke makes Vertues vselesse in a man,
And with too much, kils naturall heat in him,
Or else I could not stand thus coldly tame,   185
And see them enter; but with my drawne sword
Should haile her by the haire vnto the Altar,
And Sacrifice her heart to wronged loue.

Kate. On my life tis so.

Stra. Worthy friend, I am exceeding sorrie to see this, 190
but cannot helpe it.   ⌈*Exeunt Kate, Strange.*⌉

Scud. Ile follow, and vnfold all in the Church: D3
Alas, to what end, since her mind is chang'd,
Had she bin loyall, all the earthly Lords
Could not haue borne her; so, what hainous sinne   195
Hath she committed, God should leaue her then:

I neuer dreamt of lying with my Mother,
Nor wisht my Fathers death, nor hated Brothers;
Nor did betray Trust, nor lou'd money better
Then an accepted friend; No such base thought,   200
Nor act vnnaturall, possest this breast:
Why am I thus rewarded women, women?
Hee's mad by Heauen, that thinkes you any thing
But sensuall Monsters, and is neuer wise
Nor good, but when he hates you, as I now,   205
Ile not come neere one, none of your base sex
Shall know me from this time, for all your Vertues
Are like the Buzzes, growing in the fields,
So Weakely fastned te'e, by Natures hand,
That thus much winde blowes all away at once,   210
Ye fillers of the world with Bastardy,
Worse then Diseases you are subiect too,
Know I do hate you all, will write against you,
And fight against you; I will eate no meate
Drest by a woman old or young, nor sleepe   215
Vpon a bed, made by their still giuen hands;
Yet once more must I see this Fœminine Diuell,
When I will looke her dead, speak her to hell;
Ile watch my time, this day to doo't, and then
Ile be in loue with death, and readier still   *Cornets.* 220
His mortall stroke to take, then he to kill.   *Exit Scud.*

*Loud Musicke. Enter as from the Church, Worldly, Neuill
like the Parson, Count, Bellafront, Strange, Katherine, Sir
Inno: Ninnie, Lady Ninnie, Sir Abra:, Lucida,
Wagtaile, Pendant; Poutes meetes   225
em.*
Count. Sweet is the loue purchast with difficulty.
Bell Then this Crosse accident doth rellish ours.   [D3ᵛ]
Stra. I rather thinke ours happier my faire *Kate,*

Where all is smooth, and no rub checkes our course.   230
    Cap. Are ye married?
    Count. Yes.
    Cap. The Deuill dance at your wedding: but for you
I haue something else to say, let me see, heere are rea-
sonable store of people, know all my beloued Brethren,   235
(I speak it in the face of the Congregation) this woman I
haue lyen with oftener.
    Om. How?
    La. Nin. Before God, you are a wicked fellow to speak
on't in this manner, if you haue.   240
    Stra. Lyen with her.
    Cap. Yes, Good-morrow, God giue ye ioy.   *Exit.*
    World. I am speachlesse with my anger, follow him,
If it be true, let her be prou'd a Whore;
If false, he shall abide the slander deerely.   245
    Abra. Follow that list, I will not meddle with him.
    World. Why speak'st thou not, to reconcile those looks
That fight sterne battels in thy husbands face.
    Kate. Thou art not so vnworthy to beleeue him,
If I did thinke thou didst, I would not open   250
My lips, to satisfie so base a thought,
Sprung from the slander of so base a Slaue.
    Stra. It cannot be, Ile tell you by to morrow;
I am no Foole *Kate.* I will finde some time
To talke with this same Captaine, *Pouts* de'e call him,   255
Ile lye we'e to night.
    Kate. Sir you shall not:
What staine my Honor hath receiu'd by this
Base Villaine, all the world takes notice of,
Marke what I Vow, and if I keepe it not,   260
May I be so giuen o're, to let this Rogue
Performe his slander; Thou that wert ordain'd,
And in thy Cradle markt to call me wife,

And in that Title made as my defense,
Yet suffered'st him to go away with life,   [D4ʳ]
Wounding my Honor dead before thy face,
Redeeme it on his head, and his owne way,
Euen by the sword his long profession,
And bring it on thy necke out of the field:
And set it cleere amidst the tongues of men,   270
That all eyes may discerne it slandered,
Or thou shalt neare enioy me as a wife:
By this bright Sun thou shalt not; Nay Ile thinke
As abiectly of thee, as any Mongrill
Bred in the Citty; Such a Cittizen   275
As the Playes flout still, and is made the subiect
Of all the stages. Be this true or no,
Tis thy best course to fight.
    World. Why *Kate* I say.
    Kate. Pray pardon me, none feeles the smart but I,   280
Tis thy best course to fight, if thou be'st still,
And like an honest Tradesman eat'st this wrong:
Oh, may thy Spirit and thy state so fall,
Thy first borne childe may come to the Hospitall.
    Stra. Heauen I desire thee heare her last request,   285
And graunt it to, if I do slacke the first;
By thy assured Innocencie I sweare,
Thou hast lost me halfe the Honor I shall win,
In speaking my intent, Come lets to dinner.
    Kate. I must not eate nor sleepe, weepe till't be done.   290
    Bell. Sister, this resolution is not good,
Ill thriues that Marriage that begins in blood.
    Kate. Sister, informe your selfe, I haue no Ladyship
To guild my infamie, or keepe tongues in awe:
If God loue Innocencie, I am sure he shall not   295
Loose in this action.
    Stra. Nor is't the others life,

Can giue her to the world my perfect wife,
But what I do conceiue. It is not blood then
Which she requires, but her good name againe,   300
And I will purchase it; for by heauen thou art
The excellent'st new fashion'd Maide in this,   [D4ᵛ]
That euer eare shall heare a Tale told off.
   Om. But heare ye.
   Stra. Good, saue your labors, for by Heauen Ile doo't.   305
If I doo't not, I shall be pointed at,
Proclaimd the Grand Rich Cuckold of the Towne;
Nay Wittall, euen by them are knowne for both.
   World. Take your reuenge by Law.
   Stra. It will be thought   310
Your greatnesse, and our money carries it:
For some say some men on the backe of Law,
May ride and rule it like a patient Asse,
And with a Golden Bridle in the mouth,
Direct it vnto any thing they please.   315
Others report, it is a Spiders web
Made to intangle the poore helplesse Flies,
Whilst the great Spiders that did make it first,
And rule it, sit i'th midst secure and laugh,
My Law in this shall onely be my sword,   320
But peraduenture not this month or two.
   Kate. This month or two.
   Count. Ile be your second then.
   Stra. You proffer too much honor, my good Lord.
   Pen. And I will be your third.   325
   Abra. Ile not be fourth, nor fift,
For the old Prouerbe's good, which long hath bin,
Sayes safest tis sleeping in a whole skin.
   Luci. Godamercy *Nab,* Ile ha thee, and bee but for thy
manhood.   330
   Inno. Wife, my Ladie *Ninnie,* do ye heare your Son,

he speakes seldome, but when he speakes.
    Luci. He speakes Prouerbes Efaith.
    La. Nin. Oh, tis a pestlence Knight Mistris *Lucida.*
    Luci. I and a pocky.   335
    Kate. This month or two, de'e loue me, not before,
It may be I will liue so longe Fames Whore.   *Exit Kate.*
    World. What lowring Starre rul'd my Natiuity,
Youle come to dinner?   **65253**   E
    Stra. Yes.   340
    Count. Good-morrow brother,
Come, let's be merry in despight of all,
And make this day (as t'should be) festiuall.
    World. This sowre thwart beginning may portend
Good, and be crown'd with a delicious end.   345
                             Exeunt all but Strange.
    Stra. So, Ile not see you till my taske be done,
So much false time I set to my intent,
Which instantly I meane to execute,
To cut off all meanes of preuention,   350
Which if they knew my day, they would assay:
Now for the Merchants honor, hit all right,
Kate, your yong *Strange* wil lie with you to night.   *Exit.*

[*Actus secundus, Scena secunda.*]

*Enter Wagtaile; the Page stealing after her, conceales
himselfe.*

    Wag. What a stir is heere made about lying with a
Gentlewoman, I haue beene lien with, a hundered and a
hundred times, and nothing has come on't, but haulke,   5

hum, haulke, hum, oh, oh. Thus haue I done for this
month or two, haulke, hum.

Page. Ah Gods will, are you at it, you haue acted your
Name too much, sweete Mistris *Wagtaile,* this was wittily,
though somewhat knauishly followed on me.   10

Wag. Umh, a my Conscience I am pepper'd, well thou
tumblest not for nothing, for hee Daunces as well that
got thee, and playes as well on the Violl, and yet hee
must not Father thee, I haue better men; let mee remember them, and heere in my Melancholy, choose out one   15
Rich enough, to rewarde this my stale Virginitie, or fitte
enough, to marrie my little Honestie; Haulke, hauke.

Page. Shee has a shrowde reach, I see that, what a casting shee keepes, marrie my Comfort is, wee shall heare by
and by, who has giuen her the Casting Bot- [E1ᵛ]   tle.   20

Wag. Hawk, hawke, hawke, bitter, bitter, pray God I
hurt not the Babe: Well, let me see, Ile beginne with
Knightes, *In primis,* Sir *Iohn Doot-well,* and Sir *William
Burnit.*

Page. A hot Knight by my Faith, *Dootwell* and *Burnit*   25
too.

Wag. For old Sir *Innocent Ninnie,* my Maister, if I
speak my Conscience looke yee, I cannot directly accuse
him, much has hee been about, but done nothing; marrie
for S. *Abraham,* I will not altogether quit him, let me see,   30
theres foure Knights, now for Gentlemen.

Page. And so shee'le come downe to the footmen.

Wag. Maister *Louall,* Maister *Liueby't,* and M. *Pendant,* huke, hi, vp, hi, vp.

Page. By this light I haue heard enough, shall I holde   35
your belly too, faire Maide of the fashion?

Wag. What say ye Iacke Sawce?

Page. Oh fie, ill Mutton, you are too angry; why look
ye, I am my Lordes Page, and you are my Ladies Gentle-

woman, wee should agree better, and I pray whether are   40
you riding with this burthen in your Dosser?

Wag. Why Sir, out of Towne, I hope tis not the firste
time you haue seene a child carried out of Town in a
Dosser, for feare of the Plague.

Page. You haue answer'd mee I promise you, but who   45
put it in I pray?

Wag. Not you Sir, I know by your asking.

Page. I, alas, I know that by my Talent; for I remember thus much Philosophie of my Schoole-Maisters, *Ex
nihilo nihil fit*; but come, setting this Duello of wit aside, I   50
haue ouer-hearde your Confession, and your casting about
for a Father, and introth in meere Charitie, came in to re-
lieue you. In the scrowle of Beasts, Horses, and Asses,
that haue fedde vpon this Common of yours, you named
one *Pendant,* Faith Wench let him bee the Father, hee is a   55
verie handsome Gentleman I can tell you, in my Lordes   E2
fauour, Ile be both secret and your friend, to my Lord, let
it be him, he shall either reward thee bountifully, or
marrie thee.

Wag. Sir you speake like an vnderstanding young   60
Gentleman, and I acknowledge my selfe much bounde to
you for your Counsell.

Pen. Will, Will. Within.

Page. My Lord has sent him to call mee, now I holde
a wager ont; if thou beest not a Foole, as most waighting   65
weomen are, thou'lt vse him in his kind.

Enter Pendant.

Pen. Why *Will* I say, go, my Lord cals extreamely.

Page. Did not I say so, Come this is but a trick to send
me off Sir.   *Exit Page.*   70

Pen. A notable little Rascall,
Prettie Mistris *Wagtayle*: why de'e walke so melancholy,
I sent him hence a purpose; Come shals do?

Wag. Do, what would you do, you haue done too
much alreadie.   75
Pen. What's the matter?
Wag. I am with childe by you.
Pen. By me? why by me? a good iest ifaith.
Wag. Youle finde it Sir in earnest.
Pen. Why, do you thinke I am such an Asse to beleeue   80
nobody has medled with you, but I.
Wag. Do you wrong me so much to thinke otherwise.
This tis for a poore Damsell like my selfe,
To yeeld her Honour and her youth to any,
Who straite conceaues she does so vnto many,   85
And as I haue a soule to saue, tis true.
Pen. Pray do not sweare, I do not vrge you too't,
Zoones, now I am vndone; you walke somewhat rounde,
Sweet-hart, has Nobody bin tampering with you els, think
ont, for by this light, I am not worth the estate of an   90
Apple wife, I do liue vpon commending my Lord, the
Lorde of hoasts knowes it; and all the world besides: for
mee to marrie thee, will vndo thee more,   [E2ᵛ]
And that thou maist keepe me, keepe thee in fashion,
Sell thee to English, French, to Scot, and all,   95
Till I haue brought thee to an Hospitall:
And there I leaue you, ha you not heard nor read,
Of some base slaue, that wagging his faire head,
Does whistling at one end of his shop walke,
Whilst some Gay-man doth vomit bawdy talke   100
In his wiues eares at the other; such a Rogue or woorse
shall I be: For looke ye Mistris *Wagtaile,* I doo liue like a
Chamelion vpon the ayre, and not like a Moale vppon the
earth, Land I haue none, I pray God send me a graue
when I am dead.   105
Wag. Its all one, Ile haue you for your qualities.
Pen. For my good ones, they are altogether vnknown,

because they haue not yet bin seene, nor euer will bee, for
they haue no being, in plaine tearmes, as God helpe me, I
haue none.   110

Wag. How came you by your good cloths?

Pen. By vndoing Taylors, and then my Lord (like a
Snake) casts a sute euerie quarter, which I slip into; ther-
fore, thou art worse then mad, if thou wilt cast away thy
self vpon me.   115

Wag. Why, what mends will you make me, can you
giue me some sum of money to marrie me to some Tradesman, as the play saies?

Pen. No by my troth: but tell mee this, has not Sir
Abraham bin familiar with you?   120

Wag. Faith, not enough to make vp a childe.

Pen. Couldst bee content to marrie him?

Wag. I by my troth, and thanke ye too.

Pen. Has he but kist thee?

Wag. Yes, and something more beside that.   125

Pen. Nay, and there ha beene any iot of the thing, be-
side that, Ile warrant thee, lay the child to him,
Stand stiffly to it, leaue the rest to me,
By that Foole thou shalt saue thy honestie.   *Exeunt.*   E3

Actus tertius, Scena prima.

Enter Strange, knocking at a doore. Enter a Seruingman.

Stra. Lyes Captaine *Powts* heere pray?

Ser. Sir he does.

Stra. I prethee tell him heere's a Gentleman
Would speake with him.   5

Ser. What may I call your name Sir?

Stra. No matter for my name.

Ser. Troth Sir, the Captaine is somewhat doubtfull of
strangers; and being as most Captaines are, a little in debt,
I know he will not speake with you, vnlesse you send your   10
Name.

Stra. Tell him my name is *Strange,* that I am come
About that businesse he spake off to day.   *Exit Seruant.*
To haue sent a formall Challenge by a Gentleman,
He being to choose his time, might peraduenture   15
Haue made him shift himselfe the sooner ouer.

                    Enter Powts aboue.

Cap. Sir, I know your businesse, you are come to serue
a warrant, or a Scitation, I will not speake with you: and
get you gone quickly too, or I may happen send a Bullet   20
through your Mazard.   *Exit.*

Stra. Strange Crosse, past expectation: well Ile try,
My other course may speed more hapily.   *Exit.*

[*Actus tertius, Scena secunda.*]

                    Musicke.

*Enter with Table Napkins: Count, Worldly, [Lucida,] Neuill,
Pendant, Sir Innocent, Lady, Sir Abra-
ham, Seruants with wine, Plate,
Tobacco and pipes.*   5

World. Sir, had you borne vs company to Church,
You had beene the better welcome.

Count. Faith you had, I must needs say so to.   [E3ᵛ]

Pen. And I must needs say as my Lord saies.

Neu. Sir *Iohn* I thanke you, and my honor'd Lord: 10

But I am sorrie for this other Newes
Concerning Mistris *Kate,* and my good friend.
   World. Tis certaine true: He keepes his word well too,
He saide he would come to dinner.
   La. Nin. All we cannot get M. *Katherine* out of hir   15
chamber.
   World. Oh good old woman, she is topshackeld.
   La. Nin. Tis pestlence Sacke, and cruell Clarret.
Knight, stand to me Knight I say, vp, a cold stomacke;
giue me my Aqua-vitæ bottle.   20
   Inno. Oh *Guiniuer,* as I am a Iustice of peace and
Coram, t'were a good deed to commit thee, Fie, fie, fie.
   Abra. Why alas, I cannot helpe this and I should bee
hang'd, shee'le bee as drunke as a Porter: Ile tell you
my Lorde, I haue seene her so bepisse the Rushes, as   25
shee has danc'd at a Wedding: Her bellie, and that
Aqua-vitæ bottle, haue almost vndone my Father: Well
I thinke in Conscience, shee is not my naturall begotten
Mother.
   Om. Ha, ha, ha.   30
   Luci. Well said my wise Sir *Abraham.*
   Count. Oh this Musicke
And good Wine is the soule of all the world.
   World. Come, wil your Lordship make one at Primero,
vntill your Bride come foorth.   35
   Neu. You can play well my Lord.
   Count. Who I?
   Pen. Who my Lord, the onelie player at Primero i'th
Court.
   Abra. I'de rather play at Bowles.   40
   Pen. My Lords for you for that too: the onely Bowler
in *London,* that is not a Churchwarden.
   Luci. Can he fence well too M. *Pendant?*
   Pen. Who my Lord? the only Fencer in Christendome,

hee'l hit you.   45
   Luci. He shall not hit me, I assure you now.
   Neu. Is he good at the exercise of drinking Sir?   [E4ʳ]
   Pen. Who my Lord; the onely Drunkard i'th World,
drinker I would say.
   Luci. Godamercie for that.   50
   Neu. I would he heard him.
   Abra. I know a better Whoremaister then he.
   Neu. Oh fie no, none so good as my Lord.
   Pen. Hardly, berlady, hardlie.
   Count. How now, whose this?   55
    Enter Scudmore like a Seruingman, with a Letter.
   World. What would you?
   Scud. I would speake with the Ladie *Bellafront,*
From the young Ladie *Lucie.*
   World. You had best send in your Letter, shee is with-   60
   drawne.
   Scud. My Ladie gaue me charge of the deliuery,
And I must doo't my selfe, or carrie it backe.
   World. A trustie seruant, that way leads you to her.
   Count. This trust in Seruants is a Iewell; Come,   65
Let vs to Bowles i'th Garden.   *Exeunt.*
   Scud. Blessed fate.
   Scudmore passeth one doore, and entereth the other, where
    Bellafront sits in a Chaire, vnder a Taffata
       Canopie.   70
Oh thou, whose words and actions seemd to me,
As innocent as this smooth sleepe, which hath
Lockt vp thy powers: would thou hadst slept, when first
Thou sent'st and profferedst me beautie and loue:
I had bin ignorant then of such a losse.   75
Happie's that wretch in my opinion,
That neuer ownd scarse Iewels, or bright Somes,
He can loose nothing but his constant wants:

But speaklesse is his plague, that once had store,
And from superfluous state fals to be poore: 80
Such is my hell-bred hap; could Nature make
So faire a superficies, to enclose
So false a heart; This is like gilded Tombes,
Compacted of Iet Pillars, Marble stones,   [E4ᵛ]
Which hide from's stinking Flesh, and rotten bones.   85
Pallas so sat (methinkes) in *Hectors* Tent;
But time so precious and so dangerous
Why do I loose thee? Madam, my Lady, Madam.
   Bell. Beleeue me my deare friend, I was enforcst: Ha,
I had a Dreame as strange as thou art fellow,   90
How cam'st thou hether? What's thy businesse?
   Scud. That Letter Madam tels you.
   Bell. Letter: Ha?
What doost thou mocke me? Here is nothing writ.
   Scud. Can you read any thing then in this face?   95
   Bell. Oh Basiliske, remooue thee from my sight,
Or thy harts bloud shall pay thy rash attempt.
Ho, Who attends vs there?
   Scud. Stirre not a foote,
And stop your clamorous acclamations,   100
Or by the bitternesse of my fresh wrongs,
Ile send your Ladiship to the Deuill quicke;
I know the hazard I do vndergo,
And whatsoere after becomes of me,
Ile make you sure first: I am come to speake,   105
And speake I will freely, and to bring backe
Your Letters, and such things you sent; and then,
Ile nere see those deceiuing eyes agen.
   Bell. Oh, I am sicke of my corruption,
For Godsake do not speake a word more to me.   110
   Scud. Not speake, yes woman, I will rore a lowd,
Call thee the falsest faire that euer breath'd,

Tell thee, that in this marriage, thou hast drown'd
All vertue, left to credit thy weake sex,
Which being (as t'were) committed to thy trust,   115
Thou traiterously hast betraid it thus.
Did I intice, or euer send thee guifts
To allure thee, to reflect a beame on me?
Nay, didst not thou thy selfe send and inuent
Past humaine wit, our meanes of intercourse?   120
Why dost thou then proue base vnto thy selfe,   F
Periur'd and impious, know the good thou hast lost
In my opinion, doth outvalue farre
The airy honors thou art married to.
   Bell. Oh peace, for you speake sharpnesse to my soule 125
More torturous, then hels plagues to the damn'd,
For loue sake hear me speake.
   Scud. For loues sake, no:
Loue is my surfet, and is turn'd in me
To a disease.   130
   Bell. Tyrant, my knees shall beg,
Till they get liberty for my tongue to speake,
Drown'd almost in the Riuers of mine eyes.
   Scud. What canst thou say, art thou not married?
   Bell. Alas I was enforst, first by the threats   135
Of a seuere Father, that in his hand
Did gripe my fortunes; next to that, the fame
Of your neglect, and liberall talking tongue,
Which bred my honour an eternall wrong.
   Scud. Pish, these are painted causes, till this Morne 140
He liu'd not in this land, that durst accuse
My intergritie, of such an ignorance.
But take your Letters heere, your paper Vowes,
Your Picture, and your Bracelets: and if euer
I build againe vpon a womans faith,   145
May sence forsake me: I will sooner trust

Dice, or a reconciled enemy: Oh God,
What an internall ioy my heart has felt,
Sitting at one of these same idle playes,
When I haue seene a Maids inconstancie   150
Presented to the life; how my glad eies
Haue stole about me, fearing least my lookes
Should tell the companie conuented there,
The Mistris that I had free of such faults.
    Bell. Oh! still retaine her, so deare *Scudmore* heare   155
      mee.
    Scud. Retaine thee so, it is impossible,
Art thou not married? Tis impossible,
Oh no! I do despise thee, and will flie   [F1ᵛ]
As far on earth as to the *Antipodes,*   160
And by some learn'd Magitian, whose deepe art
Can know thy residence on this Hemispheare;
There Ile be placst, my feete iust against thine,
To expresse the opposite Nature, which our harts
Must henceforth hold.   165
    Bell. Oh rather shoot me friend,
Then let me heare thee speake such bitternesse.
Oh pitty me, redeeme me from the hell
That in this Marriage I am like to feele,
Ile rather flye to barren wildernesses,   170
And suffer all wants with thee *Scudmore,* then
Liue with all plentie in this husbands armes,
Thou shalt perceiue I am not such a woman,
That is transported with vaine dignities,
Oh thy deare words haue knockt at my harts gates,   175
And entred: They haue pluckt the Diuels Vizard,
(That did deforme this face, and blinde my soule)
Off, and thy *Bellafront* presents her selfe,
(Lau'd in a Bath of contrite Virginall teares,)
Cloath'd in the Originall beautie that was thine: 180

Now for thy loue to God, count this not done,
Let time go backe, and be as when before it,
Or from thy memorie race it for euer.

    Scud. Ha, ha, hart was there euer such strange crea-
        tures fram'd,   185
Why dost thou speake such foolish sencelesse things?
Can thy forsaking him redeeme thy fault?
No, I will neuer mend an ill with worse.
Why thy example will make weomen false,
When they shall heare it, that before were true,   190
For after ill examples we do fly,
But must be vow'd to deeds of piety:
Oh woman, woman, woman, woman, woman,
The cause of future and Originall sinne,
How happy (had you not) should we haue beene,   195
False where you kisse, but murthering in your ire,
Loue all can woe, know all men you desire.   F2
Vngratefull, yet most impudent to craue,
Torturous as hell, insatiate as the graue:
Lustfull as Monkies, grinning in your ease,   200
Whom if we make not Idols, we neare please.
More vainly proud then fooles, as ignorant;
Baser then Parasites, Witches that enchant
And make vs sencelesse, to thinke death or life
Is yours to giue, when onely our beleefe   205
Doth make you able to deceiue vs so,
Begot by Drunkards, to breed sin and wo.
As many foule diseases hide your vaines,
As there are mischiefes coin'd in your quicke braines;
Not quicke in wit, fit to performe least good,   210
But to subuert whole States, shed Seas of blood;
Twice as deceitfull as are Crocodiles,
For you betray both waies; with teares and smiles,
Yet questionlesse there are as good, as bad:

Hence, let me go.   215
  Bell. Heare me, and thou shalt go:
I do confesse I do deserue all this,
Haue wounded all the Faith my sex doth owe,
But will recouer it, or pay my life:
Striue not to go, for you shall heare me first,   220
I charge thee *Scudmore,* thou hard-hearted man,
Vpon my knees: thou most implacable man,
                                          since penitence
And satisfaction to, gets not thy pardon,
I charge thee vse some meanes to set me free,   225
Before the Reuels of this night haue end,
Preuent my entering to this marriage bed;
Or by the memorie of *Lucretiaes* knife,
Ere Morne Ile die a Virgin, though a wife.   *Exit.*
  Scud. Pish do, the world will haue one mischiefe lesse.   230
                                                        Exit.

[Actus tertius, Scena tertia.]

Enter Sir Abraham throwing downe his Bowles.

  Abra. Bowle they that list, for I will Bowle no more,
Cupid that little Bowler in my brest   [F2ᵛ]
Rubs at my heart, and will not let me rest.
                    Rub, rub, within, flye, flye.   5
I, I, you may crie rub, flie to your Bowles,
For you are free, loue troubles not your iowles,
But from my head to heele; from heele to hart,
Behind, before, and round about I smart,
Then in this Arbor sitting all alone,   10

In dolefull Dittie, let me howle my mone.
Oh Boy, leaue pricking, for I vaile my Bonnet,
Giue me but breath while I do write a Sonnet.

Enter Pendant.

Pen. I haue lost my monie, and Sir *Abraham* too, yon-   15
der he sits at his Muse by heauen, drownd in the Ocean
of his loue, Lord how hee labours, like a hard bounde
Poet, whose braines had a frost in em, now it comes.

Abra. I die, I sigh.

Pen. What after you are dead? Verie good.   20

Abra. I die, I sigh, thou precious stonie Iewell.

Pen. Good: because she is hard-hearted.

Abra. I die.   *Write.*

Pen. He has di'de three times, and come againe.

Abra. I sigh thou precious stonie Iewell,   25
Wearing of silke, why art thou still so cruell.   *Write.*

Pen. Oh *Newington* conceit, and quieting eke.

Abra. Thy seruant *Abraham* sends this foolish Dittie.

Pen. You say true introth Sir.   29

Abra. Thy seruant *Abraham* sends this foolish Dit-   *Write.*
Tie vnto thee, pittie both him and it.   *Write.*

Pen. Tie vnto thee: well, if shee do not pittie both, tis
pittie she should liue.

Abra. But if thou still wilt poore Sir *Abraham* frump,
Come grim death come, heere giue thy mortall thumpe. *Write.*
So now Ile read it together.   36

I die, I sigh, thou precious stonie Iewell,
Oh wherefore wear'st thou Silke, yet art so cruell:
To thee thy *Ninnie* sends this foolish Dit————
Tie, and   pittie both him and it,   F3
If thou denie, and still Sir *Abraham* frumpe,
Come grim death come, heere giue thy mortall thumpe.
Let me see, who shall I get now, to set too a dumpish
Note?

Pen. In good faith I doo not know, but Nobody that is   45
wise, I am sure of that. It will be an excellent matter
sung to the knacking of the tongues. But to my businesse, God saue the Worthy and right Woorshipfull Sir
Abraham: what musing and writing: oh, this loue will
vndoo vs all, and that made me preuent loue, and vndoo   50
my selfe: but what newes of Mistris *Lucida,* ha, will shee
not come off, nor cannot you come on little *Abraham*?

Abra. Faith, I haue courted her, and courted her: and
she does as euerie bodie else does, laughes at all I can
doo or say.   55

Pen. Laughes, why that's a signe she is pleasd; doo
you not know when a woman laughes, shees pleasd.

Abra. I but she laughes most shamefully, & most scornfully.

Pen. Scornfully, hang her, shees but a bable.   60

Abra. Shees the fitter for my turne Sir, for they will
not sticke to say, I am a foole for all I am a Knight.

Pen. Loue has made you witty little *Nab,* but what a
mad villaine art thou, a striker, a fiftieth part of *Her-*
cules, to get one Wench with Childe, and go a wooing to   65
another.

Abra. With child, a good iest Ifaith, whom haue I got
with child?

Pen. Why Mistris *Wagtaile* is with childe, and will
bee deposd tis yours, she is my Kinswoman, and I wold be   70
loth our house should suffer any disgrace in her; if there
be law in *England,* which there should be, if wee may
iudge by their Consciences, or if I haue any friendes, the
Wench shall take no wrong: I cannot tell, I thinke my
Lorde will sticke to me.   75

Abra. De'e heare, talke not to me of Friends, Lawe, or
Conscience, if your Kinswoman say she is with Childe by
me, your Kinswoman is an arrant whore; Vds-will, haue   [F3ᵛ]

you nobodie to put your Guls vppon but Knights? That
Wagtaile is a whore, and Ile stand to it.   80

Pen. Nay, you haue stood to it alreadie; but to call my
Cozen whore, you haue not a minde to haue your throat
cut: ha you?

Abra. Troth no great minde Sir.

                    ⌈*Pendant*⌉ *drawes his sword.*   85

Pen. Recant your words, or die.

Abra. Recant, oh base; out sword, mine honor keepe,
Loue, thou hast made a Lyon of a Sheepe.

Pen. But will you fight in this quarrell?

Abra. I am resolu'd.   90

Pen. Hart, I haue puld an olde house ouer my heade;
heeres like to bee a tall fray, I perceiue a foole's vali-
anter then a Knaue at all times, would I were well ridde
of him, I had as liue meet *Hector* God knowes, if he dare
fight at all: they are all one to mee, or to speake more   95
modernly, with one of the Roaring Boyes.

Abra. Haue you done your prayers?

Pen. Pray giue me leaue Sir, put vp an't please you:
are you sure my Cossen *Wagtaile* is a Whore?

Abra. With sword in hand I do it not recant.   100

Pen. Well, it shall neuer bee saide *Iacke Pendant*
would venter his blood in a Whores quarrell: but Whore
or no Whore, she is most desperately in Loue with you,
praises your head, your face, your nose, your eies, your
mouth; the fire of her commendations, makes the potte   105
of your good parts runne ouer; and to conclude, if the
whore haue you not, I thinke the Pond at *Islington,* will
bee her Bathing-tubbe, and giue an ende to mortall
Miserie, but if shee belye you (pray put vppe Sir:) she
is an arrant whore, and so let her go.   110

Abra. Does she so loue me say you?

Pen. Yes, yes, out of all question the whore does loue

you abhominable.　　　　　　　　　　　　　　[F4ʳ]

Abra. No more of these foule termes if she do loue

me,　　　　　　　　　　　　　　　　　　　115

That goes by fate, I know it by my selfe,

Ile not denie but I haue dallied with her.

Pen. I, but hang her whoore, dallying will get no

Children.

Abra. Another whore, and draw; where is the Girle?　120

Pen. Condouling her misfortune in the Gallery,

Vpon the rushes, sitting all alone,

And for Sir *Abrahams* loue venting her mone.

Abra. I know not what to say, Fates aboue all,

Come lets go ouer-heare her, be this true,　　　　125

Welcome my *Wagtayle,* scornfull *Luce* adue.　　*Exit.*

Pen. One way it takes yet, tis a Fooles condition,

Whom none can loue: out of his penurie,

To catch most greedily at any wench

That giues way to his loue, or faignes her owne,　　130

First vnto him, and so Sir *Abraham* now

I hope will buy the poole where I will Fish,

Thus a quicke Knaue makes a fat foole his dish.　*Exit.*

⟨Actus tertius, Scena quarta.⟩

Enter Powts.

Cap. I haue plaide the melancholy Asse, and partlie

the Knaue, in this last businesse, but as the Parson said

that got the wench with child, Tis done now Sir, it cannot

bee vndone, and my purse or I must smart for it.　　5

Enter Seruant.

Ser. Your Trunks are shipt, and the Tide fals out
about twelue to night.

Cap. Ile away, this Law is like the Basiliske, to see it
first, is the death ont: This night and noble *London*   10
farewell, I will neuer see thee more, till I be knighted
for my Vertues. Let me see, when shall I returne; and
yet I doo not thinke but there are a great manie dubd for
their Vertues; otherwise how could there be so many poor
knights, what art thou? whats thy newes?   15

Enter Strange like a Souldier amazedly.

Stra. Zoones, a man is faine to breake open doores,
ere he can get in to you.   [F4ᵛ]   I would speake with
a Generall sooner.

Cap. Sir you may, hee owes lesse peraduenture: or if   20
more, he is more able to pay't: What ar't?

Stra. A Soldier, one that liues vpon this Buffe Ierkin,
t'was made of *Fortunatus* his pouch; and these are the
points I stand vpon, I am a Soldier.

Cap. A counterfeit Rogue you are.   25

Stra. As true a Rogue as thy selfe: Thou wrong'st me,
send your man away, go too, I haue strange and welcome
businesse to impart, the Merchant is deade, for shame;
let's walke into the fields, send away your man.

Cap. How?   30

Stra. Heere is a Letter from the lusty *Kate*
That tels you all, I must not giue it you
But vpon some conditions. Let vs walke,
And send away your man.

Cap. Go Sirrha, and bespeake Supper at the Beare, and   35
prouide Oares, Ile see *Graues-end* to night. *Exit* ⌐*Seruant*⌐.

Stra. The Gentlewoman will run mad after you then,
Ile tel! you more, let's walke.   *Exit.*

Actus quartus, [Scena prima.]

Enter Scudmore and Neuill.

[*Neu.*] I see great'st Spirits can serue to their owne
    ends,
Were you the seeming Seruing-man that past by?
    Scud. By my sad heart I was, and not a Tittle   5
Of my relation to thee wrong or faign'd.
    Neu. Introth you were too blame to venter so,
Mischiefes finde vs, we need not mischiefes seek;
I am not ti'de to that opinion,
They are like women, which do alwaies shun   10
Their louers and pursuers, and do follow   G
With most ranke appetites them that do flye:
    [*Scud.*] All mischiefe that I had is but one woman,
And that one woman all mischance to me,
Who speakes worst of them, then's the best of men,   15
They are like shaddowes, mischiefes are like them.
Death feares me, for introth I seeke him out;
The Sun is stale to me, to morrow Morne
As this, t'will rise, I see no difference;
The night doth visit me, but in one roabe,   20
She brings as many thoughts as she weares Starres
When she is pleasant, but no rest at all,
For what new strange thing should I couet life then?
Is not she false, whom onely I thought true?
Shall time to shew his strength make *Scudmore* liue,   25
Till (perish the vicious thought) I loue not thee,
Or thou deere friend, remoue thy heart from me.
    Neu. Time is as weake for that, as he is old,

Take comfort, and attend this counsell friend,
This match is neither Sacred nor sure,   30
Close Fate annihilates what Opinion makes,
And since she is resolu'd this night to die,
If you do not redeeme her, giue the meanes,
Or her bloud (credit me) will spring heauier greefes,
Sorer and stranger in thy oppressed hart   35
Then her false loue before. Besides, tis you
My *Scudmore* that are false, if you will not
Consent to let her make Vowes good, which were
But in a possibility to be broke,
This her Repentance casts her vice quite off: 40
And if you leaue her now, you take it on,
Nay you incurre a bloody mortall sinne,
You do become an actuall murtherer.
If you neglect her, she will kill her selfe
This night, by poyson, knife, or other meanes;   45
God giues you power to crosse her desperate will,
And if you saue not where you may, you kill.
    Scud. Why can my Noble and wise friend, thinke still
That what a woman saies, her heart doth meane?
Can you beleeue that she wil kil hir selfe.   [G1ᵛ]
Tis a full houre since she spake the word,
And God forbid, that any womans minde
Should not be chang'd and chang'd in a long houre.
She is by this time in her Lordly armes,
And like pleas'd *Iuno,* claspt by *Iupiter,*   55
Forgets the plaints of poore mortality,
Such state, such pride, as Poets shew her in,
Incenst with *Ioues* loose scapes vpon the earth,
She cast on me at our encountering;
As cold and heauie, as a Rocke of Ice   60
In her loue to me, which while I there staide,
My bitter and hot words resolu'd a little,

(Iust as the Sun doth Ice) I soften'd her,
And made her drowne her fault in her owne teares,
But thinke you she holds this flexible vaine: 65
No, I'me remou'd, and shee's congeal'd againe.
    Neu. How well does *Scudmore* speake, ill for him-
    selfe,
Wit's a disease, that fit employment wants,
Therefore we see, those happiest in best parts,   70
And vnder-borne fortunes vnder their merrits,
Grow to a sullen enuie, hate, and scorne
Of their Superiors; and at last, like winds
Breake forth into rebellious ciuil warres,
Or priuate Treasons; none so apt for these,   75
As melancholy wits fetter'd with neede.
How free's the Rusticke Swaine from these assaults,
He neuer feeles a passion all his life,
But when he cannot sleepe, or hunger gripes;
And though he want Reason, Wit, Art, nay Sence,   80
Is not so sencelesse to capitulate,
And aske God why he made not him as great
As that same foolish Lord, or that rich knaue:
His braines with nothing does Negotiate,
But his hard Husbandry, which makes him liue.   85
But haue we worthy gifts, as Iudgement, Learning,
Ingenious sharpnesse, which wise God indeed,
Doth seldome giue out of his equall hand,   G2
But ioyn'd with pouertie to make it euen
With Riches which he clogs with ignorance,   90
We vent our blessing in prophane conceits,
Or in strong Arguments against our selues,
Foule Bawdry, and starke blindly hold it best,
Rather to loose a soule, then loose a iest.
    Scud. Ill tearmes my friend, this wit in any man,   95
(For that but season'd with discretion)

Holds him in awe of all these blemishes,
Free's him of enuie, doth Phylosophize
His Spirit, that he makes no difference
Twixt man and man, twixt fortunes high and low,   100
But as the thicker they with vertues grow,
Freedome and bondage wit can make all one;
So t'would by being left, and being lou'd,
If I had any of it temper'd so:
But you haue spoke all this condemning me,   105
For hauing wit to speake against my selfe,
But Ile be rul'd by you in all.
    Neu.   Then thus:
To night by promise, I do giue a Maske,
As to congratulate the Bridall day,   110
In which the *Count, Pendant,* and the wise Knight,
Will be most worthy dancers, Sir you shall,
Learne but my part, which I will teach you to,
As nimbly as the Vsher did teach me,
And follow my further directions,   115
Though I i'th Morne were a prodigious wight,
Ile giue thee *Bellafront* in thine armes to night.
    Scud.   I am your property, my Enginer;
Prosper your purposes, shine thou eie of heauen,
And make thie lowring Morne, a smiling Eeuen.   *Exeunt.*   120

[*Actus quartus, Scena secunda.*]

Enter Cap. Powts with a Letter, and Strange like a Souldier.

    Stra.   Oh, these are *Lambeth* fields.
    Cap.   *Strange* murther'd on the wedding day by you,

At his owne Brides appointment, for my sake?
   Stra. As dead as Charity.   5
   Cap. This sounds not well.   [G2ᵛ]
   Stra. Zoones, you may say as well I am the man,
As doubt he liues, a plague of your beleefe,
De'e know this bloodie Ruffe which she has sent,
Least you should be incredulous, and this Ring   10
Which you haue seene her weare?
   Cap. I know the Ring,
And I haue seene the Ruffe about his necke,
This comes of enforc'd marriages; Where was't done?
And how escap't you?   15
   Stra. Sir receiue it briefly:
I am her Kinsman, and being newly come
Ouer, and not intending to stay long,
Tooke this day to go see my Cozen *Worldly*,
(For so my Name is) where I found all of them   20
So deepely drenched in the Bridall cup,
That sleepe had tane possession of their eies;
Bacchus had giuen them such an ouerthrow,
Their bodies lay like slaughtered carkasses;
One heere, one there, making such anticke faces,   25
As drunkennesse had mockt at drunkennesse,
Introth their postures and their sleepe like death,
(For their's, was liker death, then sober sleepe)
Remembred me of body-scattered fields,
After the bloudie battels I haue seene,   30
Twas such a season, to make short my tale,
As Fate had said, Now murthers may be done
And ne're reueal'd, approaching further, I
Lighted vpon a Chamber, where your Loue
Sat by this Merchant cast drunke on the bed,   35
Shee weeping and lamenting her mishap,
Assur'd both of my daring, and my trust,

Fell flat vpon the ground, then rais'd her selfe,
Hung on my necke, then sunke downe to my legs,
Told all things past to day, and neuer ceast   40
Till I had tane life from that halfe dead man
Before, whom straight I strangled with this Rope.
 Cap. You haue shew'd some kindnes to mee, I must
  loue you Sir,   G3
What did you with his bodie?   45
 Stra. Hauing first
By her direction put on these his Cloaths,
That like the Murther'd man, the safelyer
I might passe with her, being her Husbands shape,
If any of the Seruants had beene wak'd,   50
She shew'd me to a necessarie vault,
Within a Closset in the Chamber too,
And there I threw the bodie.
 Cap. Whence this bloud?
 Stra. That she her selfe first, let out of his vaines,   55
Wherein she dipt the Ruffe about his necke:
And said, Go beare this Ensigne of my loue,
To assure him what I dar'd for his deare sake.
 Cap. Where is the Maide?
 Stra. Captaine a Maide for you,   60
But well you know (I hope) she is no Maide,
But Maide or no Maide, she is at my Mothers,
Whence I will bring her whether you'le appoint
To night, and let this Tide conuey all hence,
For staying will be something perillous.   65
 Cap. Sir, I wil kill two men for you, till then
I owe my life to you, and if euer Rackes,
Strapadoes, wheele, or any torturous Engine,
Euen from the *Roman* Yoke, to the *Scotch* Boote,
Force me discouer you, or her, to Law,   70
Pray God the Merchant may re-spire againe,

But what a Villaine haue I beene to wrong her?
Did she not tell you how I iniur'd her?
   Stra. She said you challeng'd her, and publickly
Told you had lay'n with her, but Truths no wrong.   75
   Cap. Truth, t'was more false then Hell, and you shall
    see me,
(As Well, as I can repent of any sinne)
Aske her forgiuenesse for wounding of her Name,
And gainst the world recouer her lost fame.   80
Kind soule, would I could weepe, to make amends
Why I did slander her at the Church doore.   [G3ᵛ]
   Stra. The more base Villaine thou.   *Strike him.*
   Cap. Ha, what's the newes?
   Stra. Thou vnspeakeable Rascall, thou a Souldier,   85
A Captaine of the Suburbs, a poore foist,
That with thy Slops, and Cat a Mountaines face,
Thy blather chops, and thy robustious words,
Fright'st the poore whore, and terribly dost exact,
A weekely Subsidie, twelue pence a peece,   90
Whereon thou liu'st, and on my Conscience
Thou snapst besides, with cheats and Cut-purses.
   Cap. Hart, this is some rayling Poet, why you Rogue?
   Stra. Thou Rogue, far worse then Rogues, thou slan-
    derer.   95
   Cap. Thou worse then slanderous Rogues, thou mur-
    derer.
   Stra. Tis well remember'd, I will cut thy throat,
To appease that Merchants soule, which ne're will rest,
Till some reuenge be taken on thy tongue.   100
   Cap. Ile kill the first, and in thy vitall floud,   *Fight.*
Wash my hands cleane of that yong Merchants bloud.
   Stra. You fight as if you had fought afore,
I can still hold my sword, come on Sir.
   Cap. Zoones can you ward so well, I thinke you are one   105

Of the Noble science of Defence.

Stra. True, a' th Science of Noble Defence I am,
That fight in safegard of a vertuous name.   *Cadit Cap.*

Cap. Oh, now I vnderstand you, and you stand ouer
me, My hurts are not mortal, but you haue the better; if   110
your name be *Worldly,* be thankefull for your fortune.

Stra. Giue me thy sword, or I will kill thee.

Cap. Some wiser then some, I loue my reputation wel,
yet I am not so valiant an asse, but I loue my life better,
thers my sword.   115

Stra. Then get vpon my back, come al shalbe wel.
Ile carry thee vnto a Surgeon first,
And then vnto thy wench, Come we are friends.

Cap. Godamercy, zoones methinkes I see my selfe in
Moore-fields, vpon a wodden leg, begging three pence.   120

Stra. I thanke thee heauen for my successe in this,
To what perfection is my busines growne.
Seldom or neuer is right ouerthrowne.

                    Exit with Cap. on his backe.

                                   [G4ʳ]

[*Actus quartus, Scena tertia.*]

Enter Pendant, and Mistris Wagtaile, with worke
sowing a purse.

Pen. They say euerie woman has a Sprindge to catch a
Wood-cocke, remember my instructions, and let mee see
what a Paradice thou canst bring this foole into. 15. hun-   5
dered a yeare wench, wil make vs all merrie, but a foole to
boot; why we shall throw the house out at window; Let

mee see, there are two thinges in this foolish Transitorie
world, which should be altogether regarded, profite and
pleasure, or pleasure and profit, I know not which to　　10
place first, for indeed, they are Twinnes, and were borne
together; for Profit, this Marriage (God speed it) marries
you to it, and for pleasure, if I helpe you not to that as
cheape as any man in *England,* call me Cut; and so remember my instructions, for Ile go fetch Sir *Abraham. Exit.*　　15

Wag. Your instructions; Nay faith, you shall see I
haue as fruitfull a braine as a belly, you shall heare some
additions of my owne, my fantasie euen kickes like my
Bastard: well Boy, for I know thou art Masculine, neither
Thy Father nor thy Mother had any fœminine qualitie, but　　20
one, and that was to take a good thing when it was
proffer'd; when thou inherit'st Land, strange both to thy
Father and Grandfather, and rid'st in a Caroch, it may bee
thy Father an old Footeman, will be running by thy side,
but yonder comes the Gentle Knight, and my Squire.　　25

Enter Sir Abraham and Pendant stealing.

Vnfortunate Damsell, why doost thou loue
Where thou hast sworn it neuer to reueale?
May be he would vouchsafe to looke on thee:
Because he is a Knight, is it thy terror,　　30
Why peraduenture he is Knight-hoods Mirror.

Pen. De'e heare Sir *Abraham?*

Abra. Yes, with standing teares.

Wag. Beauis on *Arundell* with Morglay in hand,
Neere to my Knight in prowesse doth not stand;　　35
They say Sir *Beauis* slew both Bore and Draggon,
My Knight for that can drinke vp a whole Flaggon,　　[G4ᵛ]
A thing as famous now amongst our men,
As killing Monsters were accounted then,
Tis not thy legge, no, were it twice as good,　　40
Throws me into this melancholy mood,

Yet let me say and sweare, in a crosse Garter,
Poles neuer shew'd to eies a louelier quarter.

Abra. I, but all this while she does not name mee, shee
may meane Somebody else.   45

Pen. Meane Somebodie else, you shall heare her name
you by and by.

Wag. Courteous Sir Abraham.

Pen. Law ye there.

Wag. Oh, thy verie name,   50
Like to a Hatchet cleaues my heart in twaine,
When first I saw thee in those little Breeches,
I laugh'd for ioy, but when I heard thy speeches
I smil'd downe right, for I was almost franticke,
A moderne Knight should be so like an Anticke,   55
In words and deeds, those Pinkanies of thine,
For I shall ne're be blest to call them mine.

Abra. Say not so, Sweet-heart.

Wag. How they did run, not rheumatickly run,
But round about the roome, one ouer one,   60
That wide mouth no, small, no, but Middle-size,
That Nose Dominicall, that head, like ——————wise.

Pen. Very good, de'e marke that head like wise?

Abra. She has an excellent wit.

Pen. Ile now into her, Sir obserue what followes,   65
Now Turtle mourning still for the partie, for whome are
you working that purse?

Abra. For me I warrant her.

Wag. What newes good Cozen, I hope you haue not
reueal'd my Loue.   70

Pen. Yes faith, I haue acquainted the Knight withall,
and thou maist be asham'd to abuse a Gentleman so
slaunderously, he sweares he ne're lay with you.

Wag. Lay with mee, alas no, I say not so, not no man li- H
uing; but there was one night aboue the rest, that I   75

dreamt he lay with me, and did you ne're heare of a child
begot in a Dreame.

Abra. By this light, that very night I dreamt shee lay
with me.

Pen. I but Sir *Abra:* is no dreaming knight: in short,   80
he contemnes you, he scornes you at his heeles.

Abra. By God so he lyes, I haue the most adoo to forbeare, but that I would heare a little more.

Pen. And has sent this halter, you may hang your selfe,
or you may cut your throat, heere's a knife too.   85

Wag. Well, I will loue him in despight of all,
How ere he vses me, tis not the shame
Of being examin'd, or the feare of whipping.

Pen. Make as if thou would'st kill thy selfe.

Wag. Should moue me, wold but he vouchsafe his   90
    loue,
Beare him this purse fil'd with my latest breath,
                  Blowes in it.
I lou'd thee *Abraham Ninnie,* euen in death.
                  Offers to stab.   95

Abra. Hold, hold, thy Knight commands thee for to
    hold,
I sent no halter, poore soule how it pants,
Take Courage, looke vp.

Pen. Looke, Sir *Abraham* in person comes to see you.   100

Wag. Oh, let me die then in his worships armes.

Abra. Liue long and happy to produce thy Baby,
I am thy Knight, and thou shalt be my Lady:
Frowne Dad, fret Mother, so my loue looke chearely,
Thou hast my heart, and thou hast bought it dearely,   105
And for your paines, if *Abraham* liue to inherit,
He will not be vnmindfull of your merit;
Weare thou this Ring, whilst I thy labors Taske,
This Purse weare in my Cap, anon i'th Maske.

Wag. Oh happie woman.   110
Abra. To Supper let's, and merry be as may be.
Pen. Now God send euerie wise knight such a Lady.
                                                Exeunt.

Actus quintus, Scena prima.

                                                [H1ᵛ]

Enter Bellafront.

Bell. Titles and State de'e call it: Oh Content!
Thou art both beauty, meanes, and all in marriage:
Ioy dwels not in the Princes Pallaces,
They that enuie em do not know their cares,   5
Were I the Queene of Gold, it could not buy
An houres ease, for my oppressed heart.
Oh, were this Wedlocke knot to tie againe,
Not all the State and glorie it containes,
Ioyn'd with my Fathers fury, should enforce   10
My rash consent; but *Scudmore* thou shalt see,
This false heart (in my death) most true to thee.
          Shewes a Knife hanging by her side.
My Lord, my Father, all the Companie
Did note my sodaine sadnesse now at Supper,   15
Yet came I out, and put on faigned mirth,
And meane to sit out this nights Reuels too,
To auoide all suspect may grow in em,
Least my behauiour should my intent reueale:
Our greefes (like loue) we hardly can conceale,   20
Yon comes my Sisters: Are the Maskers ready?
Enter Lucida with her Willow Garland on, and Ka-
therine.

Luci. They are gone to dresse themselues, M. *Neuil's*
　come.　　　　　　　　　　　　　　　　　　　　　　25
I would I had not vow'd to liue a Maide,
I am a little taken with that Gentleman,
And yet if Marriage be so full of ill,
Let me be married to my Gyrlond still.
　Kate. Introth thy State is happier much then ours,　　　30
Were neuer two (like vs) vnfortunate.
　Luci. Thy case indeed, I needs must pitty much,
Because I thinke thy Vertue slander'd,
But for my Ladie Sister, if she reape
Sad discontent, tis nones but her owne fault,　　　　　35
I knew the passages twixt her and *Scudmore.*
　Bell. Sister, I wonder you will name a man,
I thinke not on, he was no match for mee,　　　　　H2
Why de'e blame me, that should rather blame
Your wandering eie, to loue a man lou'd me.　　　　　40
　Luci. Well tis too late now to expostulate.
But my poore little *Kate,* where is thy man?
　Kate. Lost, lost introth, to morrow I shall heare,
I make account hee's gone some fiue yeares voyage,
Till this disgrace of ours be ouer-blowne,　　　　　45
And for my Captaine *Powts,* by this time hee
Is ten mile on the Riuer toward *Graues-end.*
　　　Enter Sir Iohn Worldly, with two with
　　　　　Torches and Cudgels.
　World. Stand you two there, Sirrha go you with me.　　50
Why how now Girles heere still, what, & your Ladyship?
Away, away, I say, go take your places.
Some Torches for my Ladie. You Sirrha,
Is my Ladie *Ninnie* awake yet? *Exeunt Bell., Luci., Kate.*
　Ser. Yes Sir, she is awake, but she is scant sober, the　55
first thing she cal'd for, was her Aqua vitæ bottle.
　World. Who is with her?

Ser. The good Sir *Innocent,* and her Gentlewoman.

World. Go tell em I desire their Companie,

The Maske staies on em say, and de'e heare,   60

The sides of one a'th Chaire's must be let out,

For her great Ladyship.

Ser. Marrie shall it Sir.   *Exit Seruant.*

Enter Neuill, Count, Pendant, and Sir Abraham in

their Masking Robes, Sir Abra: knawing   65

on a Capons Legge

Neu. Soule man, leaue eating now, looke, looke, you

haue all dropt a your sute.

Abra. Oh Sir, I was in loue to day, and could not eate,

but heere's one knowes the case is alter'd, lend mee but a   70

Handkerchiefe to wipe my mouth, and I ha done.

Neu. Soule, how this Rascall staies with the rest of our

things.   [H2ᵛ]

World. How now son *Count,* what readie Maister

Neuill?   75

Neu. All readie, readie, onely we tarrie for our

Vizards & our Caps, I put em to a knaue to doing, because

I would haue em the better done.

Abra. If you put em to a knaue, you are like to haue

em the worse done.   80

Neu. Your wit is most actiue, I cal'd him knaue in

regard of his long stay Sir, not his worke.

Abra. But de'e heare Maist. *Neuill,* did you bespeake

a Vizard with a most terrible countenance for me?

Neu. A verie Diuels face, I feare nothing but that it   85

wil fright the weomen.

Abra. I would it would, and a huge Mustachios?

Neu. A verie Turkes.

Abra. Excellent.

Count. But do you thinke he will come at all?   90

Om. Oh, there he is.   ⌈*Scudmore*⌉ *speakes within.*

By your leaue, stand backe, by your leaue.
    Enter Scudmore like a Vizard-maker.
ᶦ*Scud.*ᴵ Nothing can be done to night, if I enter not.
2 Ser. Stand backe there, or Ile burne you.   95
Scud. T'were but a whoorish tricke Sir.
3 Ser. Oh Sir ist you, Hart you'le be kild.
Scud. Marry God forbid Sir.
Neu. Pray forbeare, let me speake to him,
Oh you vse vs verie well.   100
Scud. In good Faith, I haue beene so troubled about
this Gentlemans scuruie face (I take it) tis wonderfull.
Abra. Well, are you fitted now?
Neu. Fitted at all points.
Count. Where are the Caps?   105
Scud. Heere Sir.
Pen. Let me see mine.
Count. Come helpe me on with mine.
Abra. This a rare face to fright the Maids i'th Coun-
trey, heere now Ile pin my purse, come helpe me on.   110
Neu. So, so, away, mine being on Ile follow you.   H3
Om. Pray make hast.
                Exeunt S. Iohn, Count, Pen., S. Abra.
Neu. So that doores fast, and they are busied
About their charge: on with this Robe of mine,   115
This Vizard and this Cap; helpe me a litle.
                    Change habit.
Scud. At first Change I must tell her who I am?
Neu. Right, tis agree'd, I (leading of the Maske,)
Should dance with *Bellafront.*   120
 Scud. And at the second,
I come away with her and leaue them dancing,
And shall finde you at the backe doore.
Neu. The rest
That followes, is digested in my breast.   125

Ser. What would you do? Stand backe,
Vnlesse you can eate Torches.

Enter Count, Pend:, Sir Abrahm in their Masking robes.
Count. Come, come, away for shame.
Scud. Tis such a tedious rascall. So ha we'e.   130
                              Exeunt Maskers.
World. Thou hast wel fitted em, though thou mad'st
em stay.
Neu. I forbid any man to mend em Sir, good night
your worship.   135
World. Wilt not stay?
Neu. Alas Sir, I haue another to set foorth
This very night: By your leaue my Maisters.
                         Exit Neuill through them.
2 Ser. By your leaue, by your leaue, you'l let a man   140
go out?
World. Now go with me, and let all in that will.
Exit Sir Iohn with them, & run in three or foure.

[Actus quintus, Scena secunda.]

Enter 2. or 3. setting 3. or 4. Chaires, & 4. or 5. stooles.
Loud Musicke, in which time, enter Sir Iohn Worldly, Sir In-
nocent, Bellafront, Lucida, Kate, my Lady Ninnie, Mrs.
Wagtaile: they seate themselues, Lady Ninnie offers at two
or three Chaires; at last finds the great one: they point at
her, and laugh. As soone, as she is set, she drinkes of hir
bottle, the Musicke playes, and they enter.   7
                                                   [H3ᵛ]
After one straine of the Musicke, Scudmore takes Bellafront,
who seemes vnwilling to dance, Count takes Lucida, Pen-

dant Kate, Sir Abraham Mistris Wagtaile; Scudmore as
they stand, the other Courting too, whispers as followes.

Scud. I am your *Scudmore.*   *Soft Musicke.*
Bell. Ha?
Scud. By heauen I am,   15
Be rul'd by me in all things.
Bell. Euen to death.
Abra. Sfut did you not know me by my purse?
Wag. I should ne're haue knowne you by that, for you
weare it on your head, and other folkes in their pockets.   20
La. Nin. Which is my Lord I pray?
World. The second man;
Young *Neuill* leads.
Inno. And where's Sir *Abraham*?
World. He with the terrible visage.   25
La. Nin. Now out vpon him to disfigure himselfe so,
And t'were not for my bottle, I should swound.
Musicke, & they dance, the second strain; in which Scudm:
                    goes away with her.
Om. Spect. Good verie good.   30
 The other foure dance, another straine, honor and end.
Count. But where's the Bride and *Neuill*?
Om. Ha.
Abra. Ware trickes.
World. Oh, there they come, it was their parts to do   35
 so.
Enter Scudmore vnvizarded, Bellafront with Pistols,
                    and the right Parson.
Count. This *Neuill*, this is *Scudmore.*
Om. How?   40
Count. But heere's my Ladie,
Scud. No my Gentlewoman.
Abra. Zoones Treason, I smell powder.

Bell. In short know,

That I am married to this Gentleman,   45

To whom I was contracted long ago: [H4ʳ]

This Priest the inuiolable knot hath ty'de,

What ease I finde being vn-Ladifyed.

    Count. What Riddle's this?

    Inno. Ware the last Statute of two Husbands.   50

    Scud., Bell. Pish.

    Count. This is the verie Priest that married me,

Is it not Sister?

    Neu. No.

           Enter Neuill like the Parson too.   55

    Abra. Lord Blesse vs, heere is coniuring,

Lend me your Aqua-vitæ bottle good Mother.

    World. Hoy-day, the worldes turn'd vp side downe, I

haue heard and seene two or

Three Benifices to one Priest, or more,   60

But two Priests to one Benefice, ne're before.

    Pen. Married not you the Earle?

    Par. Bona fide, no.

    World. You did then?

    Neu. Yes.   65

    Count. I haue the Priuiledge then.

    World. Right, you were married first.

    Scud. Sir Iohn you doate,

This is a Deuill in a Parsons coate.

Neuill puts off the Priests Weeds, & has a Diuels robe vnder.

    Om. A prettie Emblem.   71

    Neu. Who married her, or would haue caus'd hir

    marry

To any man but this, no better was,

Let circumstances be examined,   75

Yet heere's one more, and now I hope you all,

Perceiue my marrying not Cannonicall.

Slips off his Diuels weedes.

Om.   *Neuill,* whoop.

Count.   Hart, what a deale a Knauery a Priests cloake   80
can hide, if it be not one of the honestest friendliest
Coozenages that ere I saw, I am no Lord.

Kate.   Life, I am not married then in earnest.

Neu.   So Mistris *Kate,* I kept you for my selfe.   [H4ᵛ]

World.   It boots not to be angry.   85

Inno., La. Nin.   No faith Sir *Iohn.*

     Enter Strange with Powts on his backe.

2 Ser.   Whether will you go with your Calfe on your
backe Sir?

World.   Now more knauerie yet.   90

Stra.   Prethee forbeare, or I shall do thee mischiefe:
By your leaue, heere's some sad to your merriment: know
you this Captaine?

Om.   Yes verie well.

Kate.   Oh Sister, heere's the Villaine slander'd me.   95

Stra.   You see he cannot stand to't.

Abra.   Is he hurt in the arme too?

Stra.   Yes.

Abra.   Why then by Gods-lid thou art a base Rogue, I
knew I should liue to tell thee so.   100

La. Nin.   Sir *Abraham* I say.

Om.   Heauen is iust.

Cap.   What a Rogue are you, is this the Surgeon you
would carry me to?

Stra.   Confesse your slander, and I will I sweare.   105

Cap.   Nay tis no matter, Ile crie quittance with you,
Forgiue me Mistris *Kate,* and know all people
I li'de not with her, but beli'de her once,
And to my recantation, that same Souldier
Enforc'd my hand.   *They all looke on the Paper.*   110

Stra.   Yes, heere tis Mistris *Kate.*

Cap. I see now how I am cheated, loue him well,
He has redeem'd your honor with his sword.
   World. But where is *Strange* my Sonne, oh were he
     heer   115
He should be married new to make all sure.
   Kate. Oh my Diuining Spirit, hee's gone to Sea.
   Cap. This cunning in her is exceeding good,
Your Sonne, your husband, *Strange* is murther'd.
   Om. How?   120
   Stra. Peace, peace, for Heauens sake peace,
Come Sir, Ile carrie you to a Surgeon,
Heer's Gold to stop thy throat, for God-sake peace.
   Cap. Sirra, you haue brought mee to a Surgeon
alreadie, Ile be euen with you.   I
   Kate. Of all men liuing I could marrie thee,
Were not my heart giuen to another man,
Sir you did speake of *Strange.*
   Cap. These women are as craftie as the Diuell,
Yes, I did speake of him, Sir *Iohn,* my Lord,   130
Know *Strange* is murther'd by that Villaines hand,
And by his wifes consent.
   Om. How?
   World. God forbid.
   Cap. Search presently the Closset and the Vault,   135
There you shall finde his bodie, tis too true,
The reason all may gesse, her husband wanting
Spirit to do on me what he hath done,
In hope to marrie her, he hath murther'd him.
   Kate. To marrie me, no villaine I do hate him   140
On this report, worse then I do thy selfe,
And may the plagues and Tortures of a Land
Ceize me, if this be not an Innocent hand.
   World. Fore-God tis most like truth, son *Scudmore*
     pray   145

Looke to this fellow, Gentlemen assist,
Torches, some Torches, Ile go search my selfe.

  Inno. I will assist you.

  Count. But I pray Sir how came you vnto this knowl-
    edge?   150

  Cap. From his mouth.

  Stra. Ile saue your labor, and discouer all:
Thou periur'd villaine, didst not sweare thou wouldst not
discouer me?

  Cap. I but swore in iest.   155

  Stra. Nay but remember thou didst wish *Strange* liuing
If euer thou didst tell, Sir all is true,
And would my punishment would ease my Conscience.

  World. To New-gate with him hence, take her along,
Out Murtherers, whoore thou art no child of mine,   160
Fetch Constable and Officers, Away.

  Stra. Sir do but heare me speake.

  World. Fetch Officers.

  Cap. Go fetch a Surgeon.

  Stra. Sir, you are then too violent, I will baile her.   165

  Kate. Oh my deere *Strange.*   *Discouers himselfe.* [I1ᵛ]

  World. My Sonne.

  Scud., Luci., Bell. Brother.

  Om. Yong *Strange.*

  Cap. Hart, I was neuer sicke before, helpe me now to 170
a Surgeon, or I shall swoon instantly.

                     As 2. leads him he speakes.
Thou wer't borne a woman-Citizen, fare thee well,
And farewell loue, and weomen, ye diseases,
My horse and sword shall be my Mistresses,   175
My Horse Ile court, my sword shall lye with me.   *Exit.*

  Stra. The way to cure lust, is to bleed I see.

  Count. Tell him al *Scudmore,* whilst I go a woing
again, Sir *Iohn* will you go along, and my two worshipful

Elders, I pray be you wit-　⌈*Neu., Scud., Bell., Stra.,*　180
nesses, Priest goe not you　│ *Kate Whispers in one*
away, Hart I haue so rumi-　│ *part, Pend., Sir Abra.,*
nated on a Wife, that I must　⌊ *& Wag. in another.*
haue one this night, or I shal run proud. Mistris *Lucida,*
you did once loue mee, if you doo still, no more words, but　185
giue me your hand, why are ye doubtfull?

Abra. Nere looke vpon me M. *Lucida,* Time was,
Time is, and Times past, Ile none of you now, I am otherwise prouided.

Pen. Well spoken Brazen head, now or neuer Sir　190
Abraham.

Abra. Then first as dutie binds, I craue consent
Of my two parents deere: If I, say so;
If not, Ile ha her, whether you will or no.

Inno. How, how.　　　195

La. Nin. I hope you wil not.

Abra. Mam, I am resolu'd, you haue a humour of your
Aqua-vitæ bottle, why shoulde not I haue a humour in a
wife?

World. An old man were a fitter match for her,　200
He would make much of her.

Abra. Much on her, I know not what ye call much
making on her, I am sure I haue made two on her.

Pen. And that an old man cannot do I hope.

Neu. Oh thou beyond *Lawrence* of *Lancashire.*　205

Inno. Come, come, you shall not.　　　I2

Abra. Speake not in vaine, I am to sure to change,
For hand and heart are sure, *Ecce signum,*
And this haue I done, and neuer lay with hir.

World. Nay, then tis too late,　　　210
Tis sure, Tis vaine to crosse the will of Fate.

Inno., La. Nin. Wel, wel, God blesse you.

　　　　　　　　　　　Ab. & Wag. kneel.

Abra. Thankes reuerend couple, and God blesse with-
    all   215
The little *Ninnie* that heerein doth spraule,
Parson you shall dispatch vs presently:
Lord how soberly you stand.
    Par. Now truly I could nere stand drunke in my life.
    Stra. Strange and most fortunate, wee must haue a new 220
Tucke then.
    Count. Is it a match?
    Luci. Tis done.
    Count. Then *Bacchus* squeeze Grapes with a plenteous
    hand.   225
Parson you'le take some paines with vs to night;
Come Brothers come, flye Willow to the woods,
And like the Sea, for healths let's drinke whole floods.
    Stra. I consecrate my deed vnto the Cittie,
And hope to liue my selfe, to see the day,   230
It shall be shewne to people in a play.
    Scud. And may all true loue haue like happie end,
Women forgiue me; Men, admire my Friend.
    World. On Parson on, and Boy out-voice the Musicke,
Ne're was so much (what cannot heauenly powers,) 235
Done and vndone, and done in twelue short howers.
                                      Exeunt.

[12ᵛ]

FINIS.

III. AMENDS FOR LADIES

III. AMENDS FOR LADIES

1. INTRODUCTION

i. Date and Performance

Amends for Ladies was not entered in the *Stationers' Register,* but evidence both internal and external permits one to date the play considerably earlier than its first publication, in 1618. Writing no later than and presumably in 1612, Field invites any woman who can show she does not deserve the satire on woman in *Weather-cocke* to *"continue so, but till my next Play be printed, wherein she shall see what amendes I haue made to her, and all the sex."*[1] Thus *Amends* seems to have been certainly planned and probably written by the time of publication of *Weather-cocke,* 1612.[2] This evidence is confirmed by an allusion in Anthony Stafford's *Admonition to a Discontented Romanist,* in *Staffords Niobe, Dissolved into a Nilus,* which was entered in the *Stationers' Register* 10 October 1611: *"I* will never write an *Amends for Woman* till I see Woman Amended."[3] Thus one is able to infer that *Amends* was not only written but also well enough known to give point to an allusion to it, by 10 October 1611.[4] A date before 1612 affords no real difficulty in connection with Cervantes as a source in part of the play.[5] No anterior limit for the date of composition may be set between 1611 and the Christmas sea-

---

[1]*W*, To any Woman, 11ff.

[2]Chambers, III, 313. Brinkley states that in 1612 "Field was writing *Amends*" [p. 47]; she goes on, however, to accept the evidence of the Stafford allusion and dates the play "about 1611" and believes that *Amends* followed *Weather-cocke* "very closely" [pp. 47–49].

[3]Fleay, *BC*, I, 201; Collier, *HEDP*, III, 434.

[4]Another indication of early date, according to Chambers, may be the introduction of Moll Cutpurse in 2.1, which would point to *"c.* 1610–11" [III, 314].

[5]Several English dramatists made use of the *Curious Impertinent* story before Shelton's translation, 1612; and the translator states that he translated five or six years earlier. See Rosenbach, 179–184. For Field's indebtedness to Cervantes see below, ii, Sources.

son of 1609–10.[6] If Stafford's allusion may be relied upon, *Amends* must have had its initial performance before 10 October 1611,[7] doubtless by Field's company, the "Children of the Revells to the Queene," who were still established at the Whitefriars.[8]

When to date the performance referred to on the title-page, "at the *Blacke-Fryers*, both by the PRINCES Seruants, and the Lady ELIZABETHS," is a vexing question. It is generally conceded[9] that this performance was held, not in the Blackfriars of the King's men, but in Rosseter's Blackfriars. Even so, the production can not be dated precisely because the evidence is inconclusive. The complicated story of the building of Rosseter's Porter's Hall or Puddle-wharf playhouse in Blackfriars[10] and the differing opinions of scholars concerning it I outline elsewhere.[11] Here it will perhaps suffice to say that the evidence suggests that the production of *Amends* at Rosseter's Black-

[6]Most scholars date the play similarly: Fleay [*BC*, I, 201f.] and Verhasselt [p. 501] 1611, Chambers [III, 313] not later than 1611, Harbage [p. 82] 1611 but with suggested limits "*c.* 1610–1611." Nungezer [p. 138] probably by a slip dates it 1616; Lawrence [*2*, 50], about 1615.

[7]Verity says "somewhere about 1612" [p. 335]; Bentley, "before 1611" [p. 436]. Neither offers authority.

[8]With what I consider excess of caution Harbage [p. 83] lists the auspices of the premiere as "Unknown" because, as he states in a letter to me, "the title-page and Field's function as a member of the Queen's Revels composed evidence that seemed to neutralize each other." The title-page, however, refers to a later production; and when we remember the close connection of the Revels, Prince's, and Lady Elizabeth's men a little later, the evidence hardly seems contradictory. Harbage generously adds: "That *Amends* was a Queen's Revels production at Whitefriars in 1611 seems a pretty safe inference." The play can hardly have been written "for Lady Elizabeth's" [Bentley, 435], with which company Field had no connection until March 1613 [*ibid.*, 176; Fleay, *LS*, 186; Brinkley, 29].

[9]Thorndike [*Influence of Beaumont and Fletcher*, 86], Lawrence [*2*, 50], and, by inference, John C. Adams [*The Globe Playhouse, Its Design and Equipment* (Cambridge, Mass., 1942), 160] alone among modern scholars would locate it in the King's Blackfriars. Since King's can hardly be expected to have turned over their house to a rival company, and since Rosseter's Blackfriars was constructed especially for performances by the Queen's Revels and the two companies named on the title-page of *A* [*MSC*, I, 278], it is almost certain that the latter theatre housed this production.

[10]Chambers, II, 472–474; Adams, 342–347.

[11]See exp. n. to *A*, t.-p. 4.

friars may be dated, conjecturally, in the winter of 1616–1617.[12] Presentation "both by" the Prince's and Lady Elizabeth's men has been interpreted to mean alternative[13] as well as combined[14] playing by the loose amalgamation of these companies.[15] In view of the comparatively short time that Rosseter's Blackfriars is likely to have been available for performances, production by the combined companies seems the more likely. Knowing so little as we do of the theatre itself, we have no knowledge of the physical resources of the stage on which the performance was given. Whether *Amends* had been recently produced when in 1639 Walbancke brought out the second quarto we do not know.[16] If the play has been revived, no such production has been mentioned by theatre antiquaries.

ii. Sources

The sources of *Amends* have been treated by Fischer[17] and others,[18] but the reader of these discussions is likely to get an exaggerated view of Field's indebtedness in the play. Perspec-

[12]Adams implies [pp. 336, 346] a date between "about February, 1617" and the destruction of the theatre or its remodelling for non-dramatic use following the order of 27 January 1616/17. Chambers [III, 313], who is not consistent with respect to this question [cf. III, 272], Harbage [pp. 244, 246, 250], and Bentley [p. 201, n. 2] dissent; see exp. n., t.-p. 4. One seems necessarily to base his date of this performance on his view as to the obscure history of the theatre.

[13]Chambers, II, 259. But Chambers is inconsistent; cf. III, 313.

[14]Murray, I, 250; Chambers, III, 313; Brinkley, 49. Carefully Bentley says "the play was acted by both companies" [p. 176; cf. also p. 198].

[15]Chambers, II, 259. If this was a production by the combined companies, the amalgamation did not stop, as Bentley states [pp. 176, 198], with Henslowe's death.

[16]Reginald Clarence (H. J. Eldridge) [*The Stage Cyclopaedia* (London, 1909), 20] lists a Whitefriars performance in 1639; but then, he dates a Blackfriars performance 1618. These notices seem to derive from title-pages only.

[17]Fischer does little in the way of source study beyond collecting what had previously been written on the subject, without acknowledgment of his dependence on his predecessors. His discussions are frequently little more than translations into German of Collier's remarks; e. g., see the quotation from Collier in exp. n. to *A*, 5.2.49 and cf. Fischer, 39. Fischer follows Collier, via Hazlitt, even when Collier is in error; e.g., see quotation from Collier in exp. n. to 3.4.106f., and cf. Fischer, 37.

[18]Rosenbach, 182; Edwin B. Knowles, Jr., *Four Articles on Don Quixote in England* (New York, 1941), 6. See also Brinkley, 48f., 50f., 74ff.

tive may be preserved if we keep in mind the following motives
in *Amends* and, roughly, the number of lines devoted to each.

1.	Debate framework	60 lines
2.	Maid-Ingen plot	650
3.	Widow-Bold plot	650
4.	Wife-Husband plot	430
5.	Subplots, episodes	510
	Total	2,300

Field's debate between Maid, Wife, and Widow over the
merits of their respective states can be called his medieval
heritage only by a considerable extension of that term. It has
been suggested, rather, that Field is indebted in it to two contemporary contention dialogues. "Der Streit zwischen Jungfrau, Ehefrau, und Witwe," writes Fischer, after Ward,[19]

ist unserem Dichter ohne Zweifel eingegeben worden durch
Samuel Rowlands' "Tis Merry when Gossips Meet" und Sir
John Davies' "Contention betwixt a Wife, a Widow and a
Maid." Diese beiden in Gesprächform abgefassten Dichtungen,
von denen die erstgenannte sich wahrscheinlich wieder auf de
zweite gründet, wurden im Jahre 1602 veröffentlicht. Da sich
beide grosser Beliebtheit erfreuten, so ist mit Sicherheit anzu-
nehmen, dass sie auch Field bekannt waren.[20]

Examination of *Tis Merrie when Gossips meete*[21] and *A Contention betwixt a Wife, a Widdowe, and a Maide*[22] indicates
that Fischer overstates the case when he says "Field schliesst
sich bezüglich der Fabel sehr eng an die beiden Quellen an."[23]
After a long discussion of important differences between these
poems and Field's sixty-line debate, Fischer concludes:

Der Vergleich hat uns gezeigt, dass Field von den beiden
Dialogdichtungen . . . ohne Zweifel die Anregung zu dem
Streite zwischen Jungfrau, Ehefrau und Witwe im ersten Akte
seiner Komödie empfangen hat, und zwar wird ihm Rowlands'

---

[19]III, 50, n. 2. Cf. Fischer's positive statement with Ward's "It is
conceivable that the general idea of this triple tribute was suggested to
Field by . . .".
[20]P. 25.
[21]*The Complete Works of Samuel Rowlands*, ed. Edmund Gosse (Glas-
gow, 1880), I.
[22]*Davison's Poetical Rhapsody*, ed. Hyder Rollins (Cambridge, 1931–
1932), I, 247ff.
[23]P. 25.

"Tis Merry when Gossips Meet" in erster Linie als Vorbild gedient haben.[24]

It should be at once apparent to the reader of *Amends* and the two dialogues that the first of these conclusions is both too strong and lacking in support, and that the second is untrue. Only fifty-four of Rowlands' five hundred fifty-eight lines pertain to the merits of the estates of maid, wife, and widow. Rowlands' Widow alleges the superiority of maidenhood; Field's, of widowhood. Rowlands' Wife, though objecting slightly, concedes maids a limited superiority; Field's Wife claims that beside hers, the estates of Widow and Maid are miserable. In Field both the positions taken and the arguments offered are entirely different from those in Rowlands. In Rowlands, indeed, the debate element can not be said to be prominent.

Fischer would seem to admit[25] that Field was not indebted to Davies for the conduct of his debate. Any debt he might owe in sixty lines to a poem of two hundred forty lines would perhaps lie in the arguments advanced. After a painstaking analysis of these arguments, I find but one passage which I judge worthy of citation; but as I point out,[26] its content and figures are proverbial and need not have come to Field from Davies. Certainly Field's debt to *A Contention* has been exaggerated; yet *A Contention* is closer to Field than *Tis Merrie*. Field did not demonstrably borrow from, and did not necessarily know, either of these poems. If he needed any source for his debate beyond the proverbial lore of the trichotomy and the garment figure, he might have drawn on Thomas Campion's "Who is the happier of the two, A maid, or wife?" from his *Masque at the Marriage of Lord Hayes*, available after its publication in 1607.[27] It advances the argument that "A maid is free, a wife is tied,"[28] which lies behind *Amends* 1.1.22f. Field's Widow, moreover, employs some subtle rea-

[24]Pp. 27f.
[25]Pp. 26, 27, 44.
[26]See exp. n. to 1.1.55ff. and *SFQ*, I (1946), 6f.
[27]*Thomas Campion, Songs and Masques*, ed. A. H. Bullen (London, 1903), 143–175. According to Reyher [p. 130], this song is a "réminiscence" of Davies' poem.
[28]*Campion*, 155.

soning found in venerable popular literature of England and
the Continent.[29]

The Maid-Ingen plot has been said to have been taken over
from Shakespeare,[30] but this claim pays insufficient attention
to a long line of disguised pages such as Julia or Viola.[31] In
respect to this motive, to which more than one-fourth the play
is devoted, Fischer seems to be correct when he borrows from
Collier[32] as follows:

Fur den Teil der Handlung, der sich auf die Liebesaffaire
zwischen Ingen und Lady Honour bezieht, lässt sich kein Vorbild finden; dies ist vermutlich eigene Erfindung des Dichters.[33]

Collier is responsible, also, I think, for the notion that the
attempt upon the Widow by Bold had for its source "an incident apparently well known about the date when the play was
written, and referred to in it."[34] Fischer follows vaguely, "Der
Anschlag Bolds auf die Witwe entstammt einem Motive, das
anscheinend um diese Zeit beliebt war."[35] He goes on, however, to cite Creizenach on the Italian device of a lover's disguising himself as servant to obtain entry into the house of
the beloved. He might have added that this use of disguise
had become almost a tradition in English drama.[36] Verity, as
was his custom, blindly followed Collier: "Bold's attempt in
disguise on the Lady Bright is supposed to be taken from a
contemporary incident in real life.[37] It should be sufficient
to say here that apparently the only reason for believing tha.
this plot was taken from a contemporary event is a remark
by the Widow,[38] which she may have invented for the purposes of her argument.

The question as to Field's source in the Wife-Husband plot
is quite complicated. As early as 1691 it was stated that "The
Plot of *Subtles* tempting the married Wife . . . seems to be

[29]See exp. n. to 1.1.46–48.
[30]Brinkley, 78.
[31]Freeburg, 61–89.
[32]Dodsley⁴, XI, 90.
[33]P. 36.
[34]*A*, 3f.
[35]P. 36.
[36]See exp. n. to 1.1.189.
[37]P. 415.
[38]4.1.124f.

founded on *Don Quixote's* Novel of the *Curious Impertinent.*"[39]
This view has been accepted by all subsequent writers on the
subject.[40] An effort to describe and audit Field's indebtedness
to Cervantes, however, has been made only recently.[41] It now
appears that only nine elements are common to Cervantes'
Curious Impertinent story[42] and *Amends.* Five of them appear
also in the anonymous *The Second Maiden's Tragedy.*[43] Of
the nine, five are to be given little weight for one good reason
or another. The case for Field's direct indebtedness to Cervantes rests upon the explanation why the friend has absented
himself,[44] the husband's injunction to the wife to treat the
friend as himself,[45] the choice of the friend as wife-tester because he will likely remain silent,[46] and the misinterpretation
of another's egress from the house.[47] Of these the most convincing, the last, perhaps could have been borrowed from *The
Second Maiden's Tragedy.* In respect to none of these elements
are Field's passages sufficiently similar to those of Cervantes
to prove beyond doubt that Field used *Don Quixote* in original
or in translation. If he did, then he can be proved to be indebted to Cervantes in less than twenty-five of the four hundred
thirty lines that comprise this, the shortest, of his three main
plot strands. The story of Field's Wife resembles that of Cervantes chiefly in its outline. The presence of the three or four
attendant circumstances common exclusively, so far as we
know, to Field and Cervantes would be explained as well by
Field's having heard someone tell, as by his having read, *Don
Quixote.*

The remaining sources of *Amends* may be treated briefly.
Field may be indebted to Shakespeare for hints toward Feesimple's comic boasting,[48] for a sequence of comic lines,[49] and

[39]Langbaine, 198.
[40]e.g., Collier, *A*, 3; Fleay, *BC*, I, 202; Ward, III, 50, n. 2; Bayne, 251;
Schelling, I, 520, n. 2; Rosenbach, 182; Brinkley, 48.
[41]*Hispanic Review*, XIV (1946), 344–353.
[42]Chaps. 6–8, Book IV, *The History of Don Quixote of the Mancha*,
trans. Thomas Shelton (Tudor Translations; London, 1896), II, 61–113.
[43]Ed. W. W. Greg (Malone Society, 1909).
[44]See 1.1.432ff. and exp. n.
[45]See 1.1.447f. and exp. n.
[46]See 1.1.480ff. and exp. n.
[47]See 4.1.170ff. and exp. n.
[48]See 4.2.88ff. and exp. n.
[49]See 1.1.191ff. and exp. n.

Amends for Ladies.

A COMEDIE.

As it was acted at the *Blacke-Fryers,*
both by the PRINCES Seruants, and
the Lady ELIZABETHS.

By *Nat. Field.*

LONDON:
Printed by *G. Eld,* for *Math. Walbancke,* and are to be
sold at his Shop, at the new Gate of *Grayes-Inne,*
or at the old.   1618.

PLATE III—COMMON TITLE-PAGE OF *Amends for Ladies,* 1618,
FROM THE COPY IN THE FOLGER SHAKESPEARE LIBRARY

for the device of cataloguing a lady's suitors;[50] and he alludes to Faltaff's disquisition on honor.[51] Field has been thought to be indebted to Jonson for suggestions toward the characters of Feesimple and Welltried.[52] To Jonson, also, he may be indebted for a series of instructions on wooing.[53] To the authors of *The Scornful Lady* he may be indebted for a disguise stratagem.[54] One instance of self-repetition, of a device used in *Weather-cocke*, may, finally, be observed.[55] All in all, though *Amends* is a less independent creation than *Weather-cocke*, it is a good deal more independent than it has previously been thought.

iii. The Editions of 1618 and 1639

Amends for Ladies was given two editions in the seventeenth century: the quarto of 1618,[56] *STC* 10851, and the quarto of 1639,[57] *STC* 10853. The former has the following title-page:

[*Ornamental headpiece*] / Amends for Ladies. / A COMEDIE. / As it was acted at the *Blacke-Fryers*, / both by the PRINCES Seruants, and / the Lady ELIZABETHS. / [*rule*] / By *Nat. Field*. / [*rule*] / [*ornament*] / *LONDON:* / Printed by *G. Eld*, for *Math. Walbancke*, and are to be / sold at his Shop, at the new Gate of *Grayes-Inne*, / or at the old. 16I8.

[50]See 3.3.83ff. and exp. n. If Field here used Shakespeare, from the point of view of acted comedy he improved upon his original.

[51]See 4.3.24 and exp. n.

[52]See exp. nn. to dram. pers. 2, 9.

[53]See 3.1.11ff. and exp. n.

[54]See exp. n. to 2.3.76.

[55]See *A* 1.1.446 and exp. n.

[56]Copies seem to be somewhat more scarce than those of *Weathercocke* 1612. This edition was based upon a collation of six copies as follows: Folger, Huntington (2), and McGill University libraries, the British Museum, and the Dyce Collection, Victoria and Albert Museum. I used microfilm copies of all but the Folger and McGill quartos; of the latter I used a photostatic copy. Another copy is in the Pforzheimer collection.

[57]Copies are comparatively numerous and well distributed: e. g., British Museum, Victoria and Albert Museum, the Bodleian, and the Huntington, Newberry, Congressional, Folger, Harvard, and Yale libraries. I used the Yale copy.

This edition has the following collation:

4°; A–H⁴; 32 unnumbered leaves.

A1: *blank* (missing from most copies); A2ʳ: *title-page*; A2ᵛ: *blank*; A3ʳ: *head-title* AMENDS FOR / *LADIES.* / [*rule*] / A COMEDIE. / [*rule*] / *and text* (ornamental headpiece); A3ᵛ— H4ᵛ: *text.* Running title: *Amends for Ladies.*

Single rule separates acts on C1ᵛ, D3ᵛ, F1ʳ, and G3ʳ; scenes, on H1ʳ.

Catchwords: *B1* And, *C1* I, *D1* That, *E1* Which, *F1 Wid.*, *G1 Seld.*, *H1 Welt.*

Pollard and Redgrave list one copy of what they call another edition, *STC* 10852, in the Henry E. Huntington Library.[58] It is not, however, a separate edition but rather a new issue with a cancel title-page. Within rules, the words "WITH / THE HVMOVR / OF *RORING*" have been inserted between lines 2 and 3. The only other difference is the presence in the unique copy of a rule between lines 3 and 4. A comparison of the title-pages reveals sufficient evidence from slightly broken and worn type to establish that the unique and common title-pages, with these exceptions, were printed from the same setting of type. Although it represents corrected states of certain forms, the body of this volume contains no corrections not found in certain other copies of the 1618 edition. From the point of view of one wishing to establish Field's text, this copy, therefore, is on a par with other copies of *Amends* 1618.

The printer of *Amends* 1618 was, according to the title-page, George Eld.[59] In comparison with *Weather-cocke* 1612, *Amends*

---

[58]From the Hoe library, this copy has been regarded as unique. It is interesting to note that in 1911 it was sold for only ten dollars, many times less than other copies of the first quarto have brought [*American Book-Prices Current*, XVII (1911), 255]. There would seem to be little if any reason for questioning its genuineness [*The Carl H. Pforzheimer Library: English Literature 1475–1700* (New York, 1940), I, 350].

[59]See exp. n. to t.-p., 12.

Amends for Ladies.

WITH
THE HVMOVR
OF *RORING*.

A COMEDIE.

As it was acted at the *Blacke Fryers*,
both by the PRINCES Seruants, and
the Lady ELIZABETHS.

By *Nat. Field*.

LONDON:
Printed by *G. Eld*, for *Math. Walbancke*, and are to be
fold at his Shop, at the new Gate of *Grayes-Inne*,
or at the old. 1 6 1 8.

PLATE IV—CANCEL TITLE-PAGE OF THE UNIQUE COPY OF
Amends for Ladies, 1618, IN THE HUNTINGTON LIBRARY

is well printed. It contains no blanks, no misprints in signatures, no stage directions without characters' names when the identity of the character is unclear, no unassigned speeches, no transposed letters, and only four patent misspellings. It is marred by relatively few typographical errors: one confusion of *r* and *t*, four turned letters, five pairs of adjacent words printed without intervening space, and eleven instances of failure to punctuate because of lack of room at the end of the line. The initial letters of only two verse lines are without capitals, but there are a few capitals at points where lower-case letters would seem to be needed. There are a few other errors in punctuation. In Acts III and V no scene division is indicated though the lines call for four and two scenes respectively. The scene division of Act V is complicated by the existence of variants, all of them incorrect, among the different copies.[60] In Acts II and IV, only the first scene is indicated though the lines call for four scenes in each act. Four stage directions are confused.[61] One speech[62] is wrongly assigned. The text contains no serious corruptions. There is some evidence that the 1618 quarto was printed from a promptbook.[63]

One reason why *Amends* 1618 is a relatively correct text is that much effort was expended in correcting it while it was at press.[64] The copies I have studied exhibit sixty-one significant variants. Like those in the quarto of *Weather-cocke*, they seem not to have been known to previous editors of Field. They show clearly that eight[65] of the sixteen forms required to print this quarto exist in two, and one[66] in three or four, states of correctness. The variants follow:

[60]See text. nn. to 5.1 and 5.2 s. divs.
[61]1.1.409, 2.3.76, 4.4.83, 5.2.5., and text. nn.
[62]3.4.122 and text. n.
[63]See text. nn. to 1.1. after 184, 5.2.170f., and (possibly) text. n. to 4.3.2.
[64]*The Library*, 5th series, II (1947), 53–59.
[65]Outer A, E, and H and inner C, D, E, F, and G.
[66]Inner G. The presence of only one variant in the final state of this form leaves one unable to prove that it was corrected a third time .

PAGE	LINE	STATE X (UNCORRECTED)[67]	STATE Y (CORRECTED)[68]
OUTER A			
4ᵛ	1.1.100	midnight, must	midnight. Must
	106	telling of folkes	telling folkes
	109	finger:	finger,
	111	hee,	hee:
	113	Il'e	I'de
		but	put
	115	theses	these
	121	distre'str	distrest
INNER C			
1ᵛ	1.1.485	the	them
	486	eies,	eies
	509	hoped	hope
2ʳ	2.1.31	*Louall*	*Loue-all*
INNER D			
1ᵛ	2.3.6	in Lord.	in. Lord
	7	females, all,	females, all?
	9	writes:	writes?
OUTER E			
1ʳ	3.2.60	to	two
2ᵛ	3.79	errant	arrant
3ʳ	101	gyues	gyns
4ᵛ	4.93	Dame me	Dam mee
	94	Dame me	Dam mee
	100	Dame me	Dam mee
	101	Dame me	Dam mee
	104f.	healths? wee'le	healths Master *Weltrid?* wee'le
	113	Dame me	Dam mee
	116	Lord	Lord,
	122	Dame me	Dam mee
	123	Dame me	Dam mee
	129	*Wel-trii'd*	*Wel-tri'd*
INNER E			
1ᵛ	3.2.95	loue,	loue:
2ʳ	3.46f.	fumbler, I	fumbler I
	47	perceiue	perceiue:
3ᵛ	4.24	Sarazan	Sarazin
	33	rogne	rogue
4ʳ	40	Gent	Gent.
	64	you outbraue	you, outbraue
	69	*Wel-tri'd* if	*Wel-tri'd,* if
	70	fight?	fight,
	83	Leeherie	Lecherie
INNER F			
3ᵛ	4.2.14	conuerssion	conuersion
OUTER H			
1ʳ	5.2.s. div.	*quarti*	*quinti*

[67]Represented as follows: *Outer A:* Folger, McGill; *Inner C:* British Museum, Dyce, Folger, Huntington (unique title-page), McGill; *Inner D:* British Museum, Dyce, Huntington (u. t.-p.); *Outer E:* Dyce, Folger, Huntington (2), McGill; *Inner E:* Dyce, Huntington (u. t.-p.); *Inner F:* Huntington (c. t.-p.); *Outer H:* Huntington (c. t.-p.).

[68]Represented as follows: *Outer A:* British Museum, Dyce, Huntington (2); *Inner C:* Huntington (c. t.-p.); *Inner D:* Folger, Huntington (c. t.-p.), McGill; *Outer E:* British Museum; *Inner E:* British Museum, Folger, Huntington (c. t.-p.), McGill; *Inner F:* British Museum, Dyce, Folger, Huntington (u. t.-p.), McGill; *Outer H:* same as Inner F.

PAGE	LINE	STATE M[69]	STATE N[70]	STATE O[71]	STATE P[72]

INNER G

PAGE	LINE	STATE M	STATE N	STATE O	STATE P
1ᵛ	4.3.39f.	foote-boy, t'is / by	foote-boy, t'is / by	foot-boy, / T'is by	foot-boy, / T'is by
	41	baile, or / pay	baile, or / pay	baile / or pay	baile / or pay
	4.7	And	And	In	In
	9	all	all	al	al
		spirit	spirit	spirit's	spirit's
2ʳ	40	And. . . men	And. . . men	And. . . men	And (. . . men)
	44	cut what by they list	cut what by they list	cut the waues that tost	cut the waues that tost
	67	It had this to	It had this to	'T had this, to	'T had this, to
3ᵛ	5.1.6	i'le	i'le	il'd	il'd
	9	friend it would good at	friend it would good at	friend would good e'ne at	friend would good e'ne at
	15	youj est	you jest	you jest	you jest
	41	A. . . conceit.	A. . . conceit.	(A. . . conceit.)	(A. . . conceit.)
4ʳ	48	lowzie	lowzy	lowzy	lowzy
	50	On I pray	On I pray	On pray	On pray
	57	readines	readines	artillerie	artillerie
	65	*nesct*	*nescit*	*nescit*	*nescit*
	73	wife. I	wife.—I	wife.—I	wife.—I
	82	seruan	seruan	seruant	seruant
	86	Conscence	Conscience	Conscience	Conscience

The second edition of *Amends for Ladies* was published in 1639, with the following title-page:

AMENDS FOR / LADIES. / With the merry prankes of Moll Cut- / Purse: Or, the humour / of roaring: / A Comedy full of honest / mirth and wit. / As it was Acted at the *Blacke-Fryers,* / both by the PRINCES Servants, and / the Lady ELIZA-BETHS. / [*rule*] / By *Nath. Field.* / [*rule*] / LONDON, / Printed by *Io. Okes,* for *Math. Walbancke,* and are to / be sold at his Shop, at *Grayes-Inne* Gate 1639.

[69]Uncorrected state, represented by the Dyce and Huntington (u. t.-p.) copies.

[70]Partially corrected state, represented by British Museum and McGill copies.

[71]More fully corrected state, represented by the Folger copy.

[72]Most fully corrected state, represented by the Huntington (c. t.-p.) copy.

AMENDS FOR
LADIES.

With the merry prankes of Moll Cut-
Purſe: Or, the humour
of roaring:

A Comedy full of honeſt
mirth and wit.

As it was Acted at the *Blacke-Fryers*,
both by the PRINCES Servants, and
the Lady ELIZABETHS.

By *Nath. Field.*

LONDON,

Printed by *Io. Okes*, for *Math. Walbancke*, and are to
be ſold at his Shop, at *Grayes-Inne* Gate 1639.

PLATE V—TITLE-PAGE OF *Amends for Ladies*, 1639, FROM THE
COPY IN THE HUNTINGTON LIBRARY

A page-for-page reprint of the 1618 edition, the 1639 quarto has the same collation as the quarto of 1618.[73]

Published a score of years after Field's death, and containing no evidence of having been corrected from his manuscript or personally-corrected first quarto, the second quarto of *Amends* is strictly without authority. Its variant readings are such as one usually finds in reprints: some represent "improvement,"[74] some deterioration.[75] To record all its variants would be wasteful in an edition attempting to "approach as closely as the extant material allows" to the author's fair copy. Though a complete collation has been made, only the more significant variants are included in the textual notes to this edition.

The printer of the 1639 edition was, according to the title-page, John Okes.[76] The book appears to have been set up from one or more copies of the first edition. From its readings in the forms that were corrected, we may be sure that the second quarto was not printed from any single copy studied for this edition.[77]

[73]Q2 lacks the catchword "I" on C1 and corrects the somewhat irregular catchword "I," on G3, to "*Husb.*"

[74]Alterations toward uniformity capable of being made without reference to a manuscript or corrected quarto. They include modernizing and normalizing typography, spelling, and punctuation and the correction of obvious misprints.

[75]It introduces new typographical errors, interferes with metre by omitting necessary and adding superfluous syllables, and makes other careless blunders.

[76]A printer in Little St. Bartholomew's, near Smithfield, from 1636 to 1644. See Henry R. Plomer, *Dictionary of Booksellers and Printers . . . 1641 to 1667* (London, 1907), 141.

[77]Q2 was printed from a copy or copies representing the following states and forms: corrected state of outer A, Inner D, Outer E, Inner E, and Outer H; partially corrected state of Inner G; and uncorrected state of Inner C. It is impossible to determine what state was represented in Inner F since the only variant there, an error in spelling and its correction, would likely have been eliminated in Q2 regardless of the state of the form.

[Ornament]

Amends for Ladies.

A Comedie.

As it was acted at the *Blacke-Fryers,*
both by the Princes Seruants, and   5
the Lady Elizabeths.

By *Nat. Field.*

[Ornament]   **10**

LONDON:

Printed by *G. Eld,* for *Math. Walbancke,* and are to be
sold at his Shop, at the new Gate of *Grayes-Inne,*
or at the old. 1618.   [A2ʳ]

[Dramatis personæ

Count Fee-simple.	Maid, *or* Lady Honor.
Lord Fee-simple.	Wife, *or* Lady Perfect.
Lord Proudly.	Widow, *or* Lady Bright.
Husband.	Grace Seldome.
Subtle.	Mall Cut-purse. 5
Ingen.	*A* Page.
Brother *to Ingen, or* Franck.	*A* Drawer.
Bould.	*A* Parson.
Well-tri'd.	*A* Boy.
Seldome.	*A* Seruant. 10
Roarers:	Serieants.]
Whore-bang.	
Botts.	
Teare-chops.	
Spil-bloud.	15

AMENDS FOR
LADIES.

A Comedie.

Actus primus, Scæna prima.

Enter Maid, Wife, Widow.

Maid. A Wife the happiest state? It cannot be.
Wife. Yes, such a wife as I, that haue a man
As if my selfe had made him: such a one
As I may iustly say, I am the rib   5
Belonging to his brest. Widow and Maide,
Your liues compar'd to mine are miserable,
Though wealth and beautie meete in each of you.
Poore virgin, all thy sport is thought of loue,
And meditation of a man, the time   10
And circumstance ere thou canst fixe thy thoughts
On one thy fancy will approue.
Maid. That trouble
Already may be past.
Wife. Why if it be,   15
The doubt, hee will not hold his brittle faith,
That he is not a competible choise,
And so your noble friends will crosse the match,
Doth make your happinesse vncertaine still: A3

Or say you marryed him, what hee would proue.   20
Can you compare your state then to a Wife?
   Maid. Nay, all the freedome that a virgin hath
Is much to be preferr'd. Who would endure
The humours of so insolent a Thing
As is a husband? Which of all the Heard   25
Runs not possessed with some notorious vice,
Drinking or whoring, fighting, Iealousie,
Euen of a Page at twelue, or of a Groome,
That rubs horse-heeles? Is it not daily seene,
Men take wiues, but to dresse their meate, to wash   30
And starch their linnen: for the other matter
Of lying with them, that's but when they please:
And whatsoere the ioy be of the bed,
The pangs that follow procreation
Are hideous, or you wiues haue guld your husbands   35
With your loud shrikings, and your deathfull throes.
A Wife or Widow to a Virgins life?
   Widow. Why should the best of you thinke yee inioy
The rest and rule, that a free widow doth?
I am mine owne commander, and the blisse   40
Of wooers, and of each varietie
Frequents me, as I were a maide. No Brother
Haue I to dice my patrimony away, as you
My maiden Madame may. No husbands death
Stand I in doubt on: for thankes be to heauen   45
(If mine were good) the grieuous losse of him
Is not to come; if hee were bad, hee's gone,
And I no more embrace my iniury.
But be yours ill, you nightly claspe your hate;
Or good, why he may dye, or change his vertue.   50
And thou (though single) hast a bed-fellow
As bad as the worst husband, thought of one,
And what that is, men with their wiues do doe,

And long expectance till the deed be done.
"A wife is like a garment vsde and torne: 55
"A maide like one made vp, but neuer worne.   [A3ᵛ]
    Maid. "A widow is a garment worne thred-bare,
"Selling at second hand, like Brokers ware.
But let vs speake of things the present time
Make happy to vs, and see what is best.   60
I haue a seruant then the crowne of men,
The fountaine of Humanitie, the prize
Of euery vertue, Morall and Diuine;
Young, valiant, learned, well-borne, rich and shap'd
As if wise Nature when she fashioned him,   65
Had meant to giue him nothing but his forme,
Yet all additions are conferr'd on him,
That may delight a woman: this same youth
To me hath sacrific'd his heart, yet I
Haue checkt his suite, laught at his worthy seruice,   70
Made him the exercise of my crueltie,
Whilst constant as the Sunne, for all these clouds
His loue goes on.
                 Enter INGEN.
    Widow. Peace, here's the man you name.   75
    Wife, Widow. Wee'll stand aside.
    Ingen. Good morrow to the glory of ⎰ *Meeting the*
      our age,   ⎱ *Wife* & *Wid.*
The Lady *Perfect,* and the Lady *Bright,*
The vertuous wife and widow: but to you   80
The Lady *Honor,* and my Mistresse,
The happinesse of your wishes.
    Maid. By this light,
I neuer heard one speake so scuruily,
Vtter such stale wit, and pronounce so ill.   85
But to you,
My Lady *Honor,* and my Mistresse,

The happinesse of your wishes.

   Ingen. Stop your wit,

You would faine shew these Ladies what a hand   90

You hold ouer your seruant. T'shall not neede,

I will expresse your tyranny well enough.

I haue lou'd this Lady since I was a childe,

Since I could construe *Amo*: now she saies

I doe not loue her, 'cause I doe not weepe,   [A4ʳ]

Lay mine armes ore my heart, and weare no garters,

Walke with mine eyes in my hat, sigh, and make faces

For all the Poets in the towne to laugh at,

Poxe a this howling loue, ti's like a dogg

Shut out at midnight. Must loue needs be poudred,   100

Lie steept in brine; or will it not keepe sweet?

Is it like beefe in sommer?

   Maid. Did you euer

Heare one talke fustion like a Butcher thus?

                             ᴵ*Exeunt Wife, Wid.*ᴵ   105

   Ingen. T'is foolish, this same telling folkes we loue,

It needs no words, t'will show it selfe in deeds,

And did I take you for an entertainer,

A Lady that will wring one by the finger,

Whil'st on anothers toes shee treads, and cries   110

By Gad I loue but one, and you are hee:

Either of them thinking himselfe the man,

I'de tell you in your eare, put for the business,

Which graunted, or denied, Maddam God b'wee.

   Maid. Come these are daily slaunders that you raise,   115

On our infirme and vnresisting Sexe,

You neuer met I am sure with such a Lady.

   Ingen. Oh many by this light, I haue seene a Chamber

Frequented like an office of the Law,

Clients succeede at midnight one another: 120

Whilst the poore Maddam hath been so distrest,

Which of her Loues to show most Countenance to,
That hir dull Husband ha's perceiu'd her wiles.
   Maid. Nay perhaps taught her, many of those
      Husbands   125
Are base enough to liue vpon't.
   Ingen. I haue seene another of 'em
Cheat by this light at Cardes, and set her women,
To talke to the Gentlemen that plaid,
That so distracted they might ouer see.   130
   Maid. Oh fie vpon yee, I dare sweare you lie.
   Ingen. Doe not faire Mistresse, you will be forsworne.
   Maid. You men are all foule mouth'd, I warrant, you [A4ᵛ]
Talke thus of me and other Ladies here,
Because we keepe the Cittie.   135
   Ingen. Oh prophane.
That thought would damme me, will you marrie yet?
   Maid. No I will neuer marry.
   Ingen. Shall we then
Couple vnlawfully? for indeed this marrying   140
Is but proclaming what we meane to doe;
Which may be done priuatly, in ciuill sort
And none the wiser, and by this white hand Lady,
The wrack, Strapado, or the boiling boote,
Should neuer force me tell to wrong your honor.   145
   Maid. May I beleeue this?
   Ingen. Let it bee your Creed.
   Maid. But if you should proue false. Nay ne'er
      vnhang
Your sword, except you meane to hang your selfe: 150
Why where haue you beene drinking? 'sfoot you talke
Like one of these same rambling boies,
That raigne in *Turnebull-street.*
   Ingen. How doe you know?
   Maid. Indeed my knowledge, is but speculatiue   155

Not practique there, I haue it by Relation,
From such obseruers as your selfe deare Seruant,
I must professe, I did thinke well of thee,
But get thee from my sight, I neuer more
Will heare or see thee, but will hate thee deadly,   160
As a man enemy, or a woman turn'd.   { Enter Wid-
Ladies come forth, see Sir what Curtesie   { dow, Wife.
You haue done to mee, a strange praise of you
Had newly left my lips, iust, as you entred,
And how you haue deseru'd it, with your carriage?   165
Villain, thou hast hurt mine honor to these friends,
For what can they imagine but some ill
Hath past betwixt vs by thy broad discourse?
Were my case theirs, by Virgin Chastity,
I should condemne them: hence, depart my sight.   170
   Ingen. Madam, but here mee, oh that these were men,   B
And durst but say or thinke you ill, for this
I haue so good a cause vpon my side,
That I would cut their hearts out of their brests:
And the thoughts out of them that iniur'd you.   175
But I obay your hest, and for my pennance,
Will run a course neuer to see you more,
And now I loose you, may I loose the light:
Since in that beauty dwelt my day or night.   *Exit Ingen.*
   Widow. Is this the vertuous youth?   180
   Wife. Your happines?
   Widow. Wherein you thought your seat so far 'boue
     ours?
   Maid. If one man could be good, this had beene hee.
See here comes all your sutors, and your Husband,   185
And roome for Laughter, heer's the Lord *Feesimple,*
What Gentlewoman do's hee bring along?

Enter HVSBAND, *embracing* SVBTLE, *the Lord* FEESIMPLE, *with young* BOVLD *like a waiting Gentlewoman,* ⌐WEL-TRI'D⌐. WEL-TRI'D, HVSB:, SVBTLE *talke with* WIFE.   190

Fees. One and thirty good-morrows to the fairest, wisest, chastest, richest Widdow that euer conuersation coapt withall.

Widow. Three score and two vnto the wisest Lord, That euer was train'd in vniuersitie.   195

Fees. Oh Curteous, bounteous Widow, shee ha's out-bid me 3I. Good morrowes at a clap.

Welt. But my Lord *Feesimple* you forgot the busines impos'd on you.

Fees. Gentlewoman, I crie thee mercie, but ti's a fault   200 in all Lords, not in mee only, we doe vse to sweare by our Honors: and as we are Noble, to dispatch such a businesse for such a Gentleman; and wee are bound, euen by the same Honors wee sware by, to forget it in a quarter of an houre,   [B1ᵛ]   and looke as if wee had neuer   205 seene the Partie, when wee meete next, especially if none of our Gentlemen haue bin considered.

Welt. I, but all your's haue, for you keepe none my Lord: Besides though it stands with your Honor to forget mens businesses; yet it stands not with your Honor, if   210 you doe not doe a womans.

Fees. Why then Maddam, so it is that I request your Ladiship to accept into your seruice this Gentlewoman, for her truth & honestie I will be bound, I haue knowne her too long to be deceiu'd, this is the second time I haue   215 seene her.

Maid. Why how now my Lord: a preferrer of Gentle-women to seruice like an old knitting woman? where hath shee dwelt before?

Fees. Shee dwelt with young *Boulds* sister, hee that is   220

my Corriuall in your Loue, she requested me to aduance
her to you; for you are a dub'd Lady: so is not shee yet.

Welt. But now you talk of yong *Bould,* when did you
see him Lady?

Widow. Not this month Maister *Well-tri'd,*   225
I did coniure him to forbeare my sight:
Indeed swore if he came Il'd be denied.
But tis strange you should aske for him, yee two were
wont neuer to be asunder.

Welt. Faith Maddam we neuer were together but wee   230
differd on some argument or other,
And doubting least our discord might at length
Breed to some quarrell, I forbeare him to.

Fees. He quarrell? *Bould*: hang him, if he durst haue
quarrel'd, the world knowes hee's within a mile of an oke   235
ha's put him too't, and soundly; I neuer car'd for him in
my life, but to see his sister, hee's an asse, pox an arrant
asse, for doe you thinke any but an arrant asse, would
offer to come a wooing, where a Lord atempts? he quarrell: hee dares not quarrell.   240

Welt. But hee dares fight my Lord, vpon my knowl-
        edge,
And raile no more my Lord, behind his back,   B2
For if you doe my Lord bloud must insue.   *Drawes.*

Fees. Oh, oh my honor dies, I am dead.   ⌈*Swoons.*⌉ 245

Welt. Vd'slight whats the matter, wring him by the
nose.

Widow. A paire of riding spurs now were worth gold.

Maid. Pins are as good, prick him, prick him.

Fees. Oh, oh.   250

Wife. Hee's come againe, lift him vp.

Omnes. How fares your Lordship?

Fees. Oh friends, you haue wrong'd my spirit to call
it backe, I was ee'n in *Elizium* at rest.

Welt. But why sir did you sowne? 255

Fees. Well though I die Maister *Wel-tri'd* before all these I doe forgiue you, because you were ignorant of my infirmitie, oh sir, i'st not vp yet, I die againe, put vp now whil'st I winke, or I doe winke for euer.

Welt. Ti's vp my Lord, ope your eies, but I pray tell 260 mee, Is this antipathie twixt bright steele and you naturall, or how grew it?

Fees. Il'e tell you sir, any thing bright and edg'd, works thus strongly with me, your hilts now I can handle as boldlie, looke you else. 265

Husb. Nay, neuer blame my Lord, Maister *Well-tri'd,* for I know a great manie will sowne at the sight of a shoulder of mutton or a quarter of Lambe, my Lord may be excus'd then, for a naked sword.

Welt. This Lord, and this knight in dogge-collers 270 would make a fine brace of beagles.

Maid. But on my faith twas mightily ouerseene of your father, not to bring you vp to foyles, or if hee had bound you Prentise to a Cutler or an Ire-monger.

Fees. I a poxe, hang him old gouty foole, he neuer 275 brought me vp to any Lordly exercise, as fencing, dancing, tumbling, and such like: but forsooth I must write and reade, & speake languages, and such base qualities, fit for none but Gentlemen. Now sir would I tell him, Father you are a Count, I am a Lo: a poxe a writing and 280 reading, and languages, let mee be brought vp as I was borne. [B2ᵛ]

Subt. But how my Lord came you first not to indure the sight of steele?

Fees. Why I'le tell you Sir, when I was a child, an 285 infant, an Innocent.

Maid. T'was e'ne now.

Fees. I being in the kitchin, in my Lo: my fathers

house, the Cooke was making minc'd pyes: so sir, I standing by the Dresser, there lay a heape of plums. Here was   290
hee mincing; what did mee I sir, being a notable little
witty coxcombe, but popt my hand iust vnder his chop-
ping knife, to snatch some Reysins, and so was cut ore the
hand, and neuer since could I endure the sight of any
edge-toole.   295

Widow. Indeede they are not fit for you my Lord, and
now you are all so well satisfied in this matter, pray
Ladies how like you this my Gentlewoman?

Maid. In troth Maddam exceeding well I, if you be
prouided, pray let me haue her.   300

Wife. It should be my request, but that I am full.

Widow. What can you doe? What's her name my
Lord?

Fees. Her name? I know not. What's her name Mr.
Well-try'd?   305

Welt. Her name? slid, tell my Lady your name.

Bould. Mistrisse *Mary Princox* forsooth.

Widow. Mistrisse *Mary Princox*: she has wit, I perceiue that already. Mee thinkes she speakes as if she were
a my Lords brood.   310

Bould. Brood Maddame, 'tis well knowne I am a
Gentlewoman. My father was a man of 500. *per annum,*
and hee held something *in Capite* too.

Welt. So does my Lord, something.

Fees. Nay, by my troth, what I hold *in capite* is worth   315
little or nothing.

Bould. I haue had apt breeding, how euer my misfortune now makes me submit my selfe to seruice: but
there is no ebbe so low, but hath his tyde againe: when
our dayes are at worst, they will mend in spight of the   320
frowning Destinies, For wee cannot be lower then earth,
and the same   B3   blinde Dame that hath cast her

bleare eyes hitherto vpon my occasions, may turne her
wheele, and at last winde them vp with her white hand
to some pinnacle that prosperously may flourish in the   325
Sunne-shine of promotion.

Fees. Oh mouth, full of agilitie, I would giue 20.
Markes now to any person that could teach mee to conuey my tongue (sance stumbling) with such dexteritie to
such a period. For her truth and her honesty I am bound   330
before, but now I haue heard her talke, for her wit I will
be bound body and goods.

Widow. V'dslight, I will not leaue her for my hood.
I neuer met with one of these eloquent old Gentlewomen
before. What age are you Mistresse *Mary Princox?*   335

Bould. I will not lye Maddam, I haue numbred 57.
Summers, and iust so many winters haue I past.

Subt. But they haue not past you, they lye frozen in
your face.

Bould. Maddam, if it shall please you to entertaine   340
me, so: if not, I desire you not to misconstrue my good
will, there's no harme done, the doore's as big as it was,
and your Ladiships owne wishes crowne your beauty with
content. As for these frumping Gallants, let them doe
their worst: it is not in mans power to hurt mee: 'tis well   345
knowne I come not to be scoff'd. A woman may beare and
beare till her backe burst. I am a poore Gentlewoman,
and since vertue has now a dayes no other companion
but pouerty, I set the Hares head against the Goose gib-
lets, and what I want one way I hope I shall be inabled   350
to supply the other.

Fees. A'nt please God, that thou wert not past children.

Widow. Ist e'ne so my Lord? nay good *Princox* do
not crie, I doe entertaine you, how do you occupie? what   355
can you vse?

Bould. Any thing fit to be put into the hands of a
Gentlewoman.

Widow. What are your qualities?

Bould. I can sleepe on a low stoole, if your Lady-ship   360
be talking in the same roome with any Gentle-man, I can
reade   [B3ᵛ]   on a booke, sing loue songs, looke vp
at the loouer light, heare and be deafe, see and be blind,
be euer dumb to your secrets, sweare and equiuocate, and
whatsoeuer I spie, say the best.   365

Widow. Oh rare Croane? how art thou endu'd? but
why did Master *Boulds* sister put you away?

Bould. I beseech you Madame to neglect that desire,
though I know your Lady-ships vnderstanding to be sufficient to partake or take in the greatest secret can be   370
imparted: yet.————————

Widow. Nay prithie tell the cause, come heer's none
but freinds.

Bould. Faith Madame, heigh ho, I was (to confesse
truly) a little foolish in my last seruice, to beleeue mens   375
oaths, but I hope my example, though preiudiciall to my
selfe, will be beneficiall to other yong Gentle-women in
seruice, my mistresses brother (the Gentle-man you nam'd
e'now, master *Bould*) hauing often attempted my honor,
but finding it impregnable, vow'd loue, and marriage to   380
me, at the last, I, a yong thing and raw, being seduced,
set my minde vpon him, but friends contradicting the
match, I fell into a greiuous consumption, and vpon my
first recouerie, least the intended sacred ceremonies of
Nuptials should succede, his sister knowing this, thought   385
it fit in her iudgement, we should be farther a sunder,
and so put me out of her seruice.

Omnes. Ha, ha, ha.

Widow. God a mercie for this discouerie ifaith, Oh
man what art thou? when thy cock is vp? come wil your   390

lordship walke in? tis dinner ⎰ *Enter hastily M. Seldome*
time.   ⎱ *with papers on his arme.*

Omnes. Whose this? whose this?

Maid. This is our Land-lord, Master *Seldome,* an
exceeding wise Citizen, a very sufficient vnderstanding   395
man, and exceeding rich.

Omnes. Miracles are not ceasd.

Widow. Good morrow Land-lord, where haue you
beene sweating?

Seld. Good morrow to your Honors, thrift is indus-   400
trious, your Lady-ship knowes we will not stick to sweat
for our   [B4ʳ]   pleasures, how much more ought
wee to sweat for our profits? I am come from master
Ingen this morning who is married or to be married, and
though your Ladyships did not honor his Nuptials with   405
your presence, he hath by me sent each of you a paire of
gloues, and *Grace Seldome* my wife is not forgot.   *Exit.*

Omnes. God giue him ioy, God giue him ioy.   *Exeunt.*

Manent ᴵMAID,ᴵ HVSBAND, WIFE, SVBTLE.

Maid. Let all things most impossible change now.   410
Oh periur'd man! oathes are but words I see.
But wherefore should not we that thinke we loue
Vpon full merrit, that same worth once ceasing
Surcease our loue to, and find new desert?
Alas we cannot, loue's a pit, which, when   415
We fall into we ne're get out againe,
And this same horrid newes which me assaults
I would forget, loue blanches blackest faults:
Oh! what path shall I treade for remedie?
But darkest shades, where loue with death doth lie. *Exit.* 420

Wife. Sir I haue often heard my husband speake
Of your acquaintance.

Husb. Nay my vertuous wife,
Had it beene but acquaintance, this his absence
Had not appear'd so vncouth, but we two   425
Were Schoole-fellowes together, borne and nurs'd,
Brought vp, and liu'd since like the *Gemini,*
Had but one suck; the Tauerne or the Ordinarie,
Ere I was married, that saw one of vs
Without the other, said we walk't by halfes,   430
Where deere, deere friend haue you beene all this while?
    Subt. Oh most sweet friend the World's so vicious,
That had I with such familiaritie
Frequented you since you were married,
Possess'd and vs'd your fortunes as before,   435
As in like maner you commanded mine,
The deprau'd thoughts of men would haue proclaim'd
Some scandalous rumors from this loue of ours,   [B4ᵛ]
As saying, mine reflected on your Ladie,
And what a wound had that beene to our soules?   440
When only friend-ship should haue beene the ground
To hurt her Honor, and your confident peace,
Spight of mine owne approu'd integritie.
    Husb. Wife, kisse him, bid him welcome, pox o'th
        World,   445
Come, come you shall not part from me in hast,
I doe command thee vse this Gentle-man
In all things like my selfe, if I should die
I would bequeath him in my will to thee.
    Wife. Sir, you are most welcome, and let scandalous   450
        tongues
No more deterre you, I dare vse you Sir,
With all the right belonging to a friend,
And what I dare, I dare let all men see.
My conscience rather, then mens thoughts be free.   455
    Husb. Will you looke in? Wee'le follow *Exit Wife.*

you. Now friend
What thinke you of this Ladie?
    Subt. Why sweet friend,
That you are happie in her, shee is faire,   460
Wittie and vertuous, and was rich to you,
Can there be an addition to a wife?
    Husb. Yes, constancie, for t'is not chastitie
That liues remote from all attempters free,
But there, ti's strong and pure where all that wooe   465
It doth resist, and turnes them vertuous too;
Therefore deere friend, by this, loues masculine kisse,
By all our mutuall engagements past,
By all the hopes of amitie to come,
Be you the setler of my jealous thoughts,   470
And make me kill my fond suspect of her,
By assurance that shee is loyall, otherwise
That shee is false, and then, as shee's past cure,
My soule shall euer after be past care.
That you are fittest for this enterprize   475
You must needs vnderstand, since prooue shee true
(In this your tryall) you my dearest friend,
(Whom onely, rather than the World besides   C
I would haue satisfied of her vertue) shall be,
And best conceale my folly, prooue shee weake,   480
T'is better you should know't than any man,
Who can reforme her, and doe me no wrong;
Chimicall metals, and bright gold it selfe
By sight are not distinguisht, but by'th test;
Thought makes good wiues, but triall makes them best: 485
To the vnskilfull owners eies alike
The Bristow sparkles as the Diamond,
But by a Lapidarie the truth is found,
Come you shall not denie me.
    Subt. Doe not wrong   490

So faire a wife (friend) and so vertuous,
Whose good name is a theame vnto the World,
Make not a wound with searching where was none,
Misfortune still such projects doth pursue,
He makes a false wife, that suspects a true;   495
Yet since you so importune, giue me leaue
To ruminate a while, and I will straight
Follow and giue you an answer.
    Husb. You must do it.   *Exit.*
    Subt. Assure your selfe deere——Coxcombe, I will do't 500
Or strangely be denied, all's as I wisht,
This was my aime, although I haue seem'd strange.
I know this fellow now to be an Asse;
A most vnworthie husband though in view
He beare himselfe thus faire, shee knowes this too, 505
Therefore the stronger are my hopes to gaine her:
And my deere friend that will haue your wife trid'e,
I'le trie her first, then thrust her if I can,
And as you said most wisely I hope to be
Both Touch-stone to your wife and Lapidarie.   *Exit.* 510

Actus secundus, Scæna prima.

Enter SELDOME *and* GRACE *working as in their shop.*

    Grace. Husband, these gloues are not fit for my wear-
ing, I'le put 'em into the shop and sell 'em, you shall
giue me a plaine paire for them.   [C1ᵛ]
    Seld. This is wonderfull, wonderfull, this is thy sweet 5
care and iudgement in all things, this goodnesse is not

vsuall in our wiues, well *Grace Seldome,* that thou art
faire is nothing, that thou art well spoken is nothing,
that thou are wittie is nothing, that thou art a Citizens
wife is nothing; but *Grace,* that thou art faire, that thou   10
art well spoken, that thou art wittie, that thou art a
Citizens wife, and that thou art honest I say, and let any
man denie it that can, it is something, it is something,
I say, it is *Seldomes* something, and for all the Sunne-
shine of my joy mine eyes must raine vpon thee.   15
            Enter MALL *with a Letter.*
Mall. By your leaue Master *Seldome,* haue you done
the hangers I bespake for the Knight?
Seld. Yes marrie haue I Mistris *hic* & *haec,* i'le fetch
'em to you.   *Exit.*   20
Mall. Z'oones, does not your husband know my name,
if it had been some bodie else I would haue cal'd him
Cuckoldlie slaue.
Grace. If it had been some bodie else perhaps you
might.   25
Mall. Well I may be euen with him, all's cleere; pritie
rogue I haue long'd to know thee this twelue moneths,
and had no other meanes but this to speake with thee,
there's a letter to thee from the partie.
Grace. What partie?   30
Mall. The Knight Sir *Iohn Loue-all.*
Grace. Hence lewd impudent
I know not what to tearme thee man or woman,
For nature shaming to acknowledge thee
For either; hath produc'd thee to the World   35
Without a sexe, some say thou art a woman,
Others a man; and many thou art both
Woman and man, but I thinke rather neither
Or man and horse, as the old Centaures were faign'd.
Mall. Why how now Mistris what lack yee? are you so   40

so fine with a poxe? I haue seene a woman looke as
modestly as you, and speake as sinceerely, and follow the
Fryars as zealously, and shee has beene as sound a jumbler
as e're paid for 't, t'is true Mris. Fipenie; I haue sworne
to leaue this letter.   C2

Grace. D'ee heare, you sword and target (to speake
in your owne key) *Marie Vmbree, Long-Meg,*
Thou that in thy selfe (me think'st) alone
Look'st like a rogue and a whore vnder a hedge:
Bawd, take your letter with you and begone,   50
When next you come (my Husband's Constable)
And *Bridewell is* hard by, y'aue a good wit,
And can conceiue.   *Enter Seldome with hangers.*
Seld. Looke you, heere are the hangers.
Mall. Let's see them. Fie, fie, you haue mistooke me   55
   quite,
They are not for my turne (b'y mistris *Seldome*).   *Exit.*
               Enter Lord PROVDLIE.
Grace. Heere's my Lord *Proudlie.*
Proud. My Horse Laquey, is my sister *Honor* aboue?   60
Seld. I thinke her Ladiship, my Lord, is not well, and
keeps her Chamber.
Proud. Al's one, I must see her, haue the other Ladies
din'd?
Grace. I thinke not my Lord.   65
Proud. Then i'le take a pipe of Tobacco heere in your
shop if it be not offensiue, I would be loath to be thought
to come iust at dinner time. *Garsoon;* fill, sirrah.
          Enter PAGE *with a pipe of Tobacco.*
What said the Gold-smith for the money?   70
   SELDOME *hauing fetch a candle, walk's off at th'*
      other end of the shop; PROVD. *sits by his wife.*
Page. He said my Lord he would lend no man money
that he durst not arrest.

Proud. How got that wit into *Cheape-side* 'tro, hee is 75
a Cuckold. Saw you my Ladie to day, what saies shee?

Takes Tobacco.

Page. Marry my Lord, shee said her old husband had
a great payment to make this morning, and had not left
her so much as a jewell. 80

Proud. A poxe of her old Cats chops, the teeth shee
had, haue made a transmigration into haire, shee hath
a bigger beard than I by this light. [C2ᵛ]

Seld. This custome in vs Cittizens is good, ⎧ *Proud.*
Thus walking off when men talk with our ⎨ *whispers* 85
   wiues, ⎩ *to Grace.*
It shew's vs curteous, and mannerly,
Some count it basenesse, hee's a foole that does so,
It is the highest point of pollicie
Especiallie when we haue vertuous wiues. 90

Grace. Fie, fie, you talke vnciuillie my Lord.

Proud. Vnciuillie, mew, can a Lord talke vnciuilly? I
thinke you a finicall taffatae pipkin may be proud ile sit
so neare it, vnciuillie mew.

Grace. Your mothers Cat ha's kitten'd in your mouth 95
sure.

Proud. Prithee but note yon Felow, do's he not walke
& look as if hee did desire to be a Cuckold?

Grace. But you doe not looke as if you could make
him one, now they haue dind my Lord. 100

Enter Lord FEESIMPLE, *Maister* WEL-TRI'D.

Fees. God saue your Lordship.

Proud. How dost thou Coze, hast thou got any more
wit yet?

Fees. No by my troth I haue but litle money with that 105
little wit I haue, and the more wit euer the lesse money,
yet as litle as I haue of either: I would giue some thing
that I durst but quarrell, I would not be abused thus daily

as I am.

Welt. Saue you my Lord.   110

Proud. Good Maister *Wel-tri'd,* you can informe mee, pray how ended the quarrell betwixt yong *Bould,* and the other Gentleman?

Welt. Why very fairelie my Lord, on honorable tearmes, Young *Bould* was iniur'd and did challenge him,   115 fought in the field, and the other gaue him satisfaction vnder his hand, I was *Boulds* second, and can shew it heere.

Proud. T'is strange there was no hurt done, yet I hold the other Gentleman, farr the better Man.   120

Welt. So doe not I.

Proud. Besides they say the satisfaction that walks in the Ordinaries, is counter-feit.

Welt. He lies that saies so, and ile make it good,
And for I know my frend is out of towne,   C3
What Man soeuer wrongs him is my foe,
I say he had full satisfaction,
Nay that which wee may call submission:
That the other sought peace first, and who denies this,
Lord, Knight, or Gentleman, English, French, or Scot,   130
I'le fight and proue it on him with my sword.

Fees. No sweet Maister *Well-tri'd,* let's haue no fighting till (as you haue promis'd) you haue rid me from this foolish feare, and taught mee to endure to looke vppon a naked Sword.   135

Welt. Well and i'le be as good as my word.

Fees. But doe you heare Cozen *Proudly?* they say my old Father must marrie your sister *Honor,* and that hee will disinherit me, and intaile all his Lordships on her, and the heire he shall beget on her bodie, i'st true or not?   140

Proud. There is such a report.

Fees. Why then I pray God he may die an ould Cuck-

oldlie slaue,
Oh world what art thou? where is Parents loue?
Can he denie me for his naturall Child,   145
Yet see (oh fornicator) ould and stiffe,
Not where he should be, that's my comfort yet,
As for you my Lord: I will send to you as soone as I
dare fight and looke vppon steele, which Maister *Wel-*
tri'd I pray let be with all possible speede.   150
   Proud. What d'ee this afternoone?
   Fees. Faith I haue a great mind to see long-megg and
the ship at the Fortune.
   Proud. Nay afaith let's vp and haue a rest at Primero.
   Welt. Agreed my Lord, and toward the Euening il'e   155
carrie you to the Companie.
   Fees. Well no more words.
      Exeunt Lord Provdly, *Lord* Fees., Wel-tr.
   Grace. I wonder Sir you will walke so and let anie
bodie sit prating to your wife! were I a man Id'e thrust   160
'em out ot'h shop by the head and shoulders.
   Seld. There were no pollicie in that wife, so should
I loose their custome; let them talke them selues wearie,
and giue thee loue tokens still, I loose not by it.   [C3ᵛ]
Thy chastitie's impregnable, I know it,   165
Had I a dame whose eies did swallow youth,
Whose vnchast gulph together did take in
Masters, and Men, the Foot-boies and their Lords,
Making a Gally-moferie in her blood,
I would not walke thus then: but vertuous wife,   170
He that in chast eares poores his ribauld talke
Begets hate to himselfe, and not consent;
And euen as durt throwne hard against a wall
Rebounds and sparkles in the throwers eies,
So ill words vtter'd to a vertuous Dame,   175
Turne and defile the speaker with red shame.   *Exeunt.*

[*Actus secundus, Scæna secunda.*]

Enter HVSBAND *and* WIFE.

Husb. Z'oones, you are a whore, though I entreat him
    faire
Before his face, in complement, or so,
I not esteeme him truly as this rush,   5
Ther's no such thing as friend-ship in the world,
And he that can not sweare, dissemble, lie,
Wants knowledge how to liue, and let him die.
Wife. Sir I did thinke you had esteem'd of him
As you made shew, therefore I vs'd him well,   10
And yet not so but that the strictest eie
I durst haue made a witnesse of my cariage.
Husb. Plague a your carriage, why he kist your hand,
Look't babies in your eies, and wink't and pink't,
You thought I had esteem'd him, S'blood you whore, 15
Doe not I know, that you doe know you lie,
When did'st thou heare me say and meane one thing?
Oh I could kick you now, and teare your face
And eate thy Breasts like vdders.
Wife. Sir you may,   20
But if I know what hath deseru'd al this
I am no woman; 'cause he kist my hand,
Vnwillingly.
Husb. A little lowder pray.
Wife. You are a base fellow, an vnworthie man   25
As e're poore Gentlewoman match't withall,

Why should you make such shew of loue to any
Without the truth, thy beastly minde is like
Some decai'd Tradseman that doth make his wife   [C4ʳ]
Entertaine those for gaine he not endures,   30
Pish, swell and burst, I had rather with thy sword
Be hew'd to peeces, then lead such a life,
Out with it valiant sir, I hold you for
A drawer vpon women, not on men,
I will no more conceale your hollow heart,   35
But e'ne report you as you are in truth.
    Husb. This is cal'd marriage, stop your mouth you
      whore.
    Wife. Thy mother was a whore if I be one.
                Enter SVBTLE.   40
    Husb. You know ther's companie in the house: sweet
      friend
What haue you writ your letter?
    Subt. T'is done, deere friend, I haue made you stay
      too long: 45
I feare you'll be benighted.
    Husb. Fie, no, no,
Madame and sweetest wife farewell, God blesse vs,
Make much of master *Subtle* heere my friend   *Kisse her.*
Till my returne, which may be ee'n as't happens,   50
According as my businesse hath successe.   *Exit.*
    Subt. How will you passe the time, now fairest Mis-
      tresse?
    Wife. In troth I know not, wiues without their hus-
      bands   55
Methinks are lowring daies.
    Subt. Indeed some wiues
Are like dead bodies in their Husbands absence.
    Wife. If any Wife be, I must needs be so

That haue a Husband farre aboue all men,   60
Vntainted with the humors others haue,
A perfect man, and one that loues you truly,
You see the charge he left of your good vsage.
    Subt. Push, hee's an Asse, I know him, a starke Asse,
Of a most barbarous condition,   65
False-hearted to his friend, rough vnto you,
A most desembling and perfideous fellow,
I care not if he heard me, this I know,
And will make good vpon him with my sword
Or any for him, for he will not fight.   70
    Wife. Fie seruant, you shew small ciuilitie
And lesse humanitie, d'ee requite   [C4ᵛ]
My husbands loue thus ill, or what d'ee thinke
Of mee, that you will vtter to my face
Such harsh, vnfriendly, slanderous iniuries   75
Euen of my Husband? Sir, forbeare I pray
My eares, or your owne tongue, I am no hous-wife
To heare my Husbands merrit thus deprau'd.
    Subt. His merrit is a halter by this light,
You thinke hee's out of Towne now, no such matter   80
But gone aside, and hath importun'd me
To trie your chastitie.
    Wife. It cannot be,
Alas he is as free from jealouzie,
And euer was as confidence it selfe,   85
I know he loues me to, too heartily
To be suspitious, or to proue my truth.
    Subt. If I doe faine in ought, ne're may I purchase
The grace I hope for, and faire Misteris
If you haue any spirit, or wit, or sence,   90
You will be euen with such a wretched slaue,
Heauen knowes I loue you, as the ayre I draw,

Thinke but how finely you may cuckold him,
And safely too, with me, who will report
To him, that you are most inuincible,   95
Your Chastitie not to be subdu'd by man.
    Wife. When you know, I'm a whore.
    Subt. A whore, fie, no,
That you haue beene kind, or so; your whore doth liue
In *Pict-hatch, Turnebole-streete.*   100
    Wife. Your whore liues there,
Well Seruant leaue me to my selfe a while,
Return a-none, but beare this hope away,
T'shall be with you, if I at all doe stray.   *Exit Subtle.*
Why heer's right wordly friendship, ye are well met;   105
Oh men! what are you? why is our poore sexe
Still made the disgrac't subiects, in these plaies?
For vices, follie, and inconstancie?
When were men look't into with such criticall eies
Of obseruation, many would be found   110
So full of grosse and base corruption,   D
That none (vnlesse the Diuell himselfe turn'd writer)
Could faine so badly, to expresse them truely;
Some wiues that had a husband now like mine,
Would yeeld their honors vp, to any man,   115
Farre be it from my thoughts, oh let me stand,
Thou God of marriage and chastitie,
An honor to my sexe, no iniurie
Compell the vertue of my breast to yeeld,
I'ts not reuenge for any wife, to staine   120
The nuptiall bed, although she be yok't ill,
Who fals, because her husband so hath done,
Cures not his wound, but in her selfe makes one. *Ex. Wife.*

[Actus secundus, Scæna tertia.]

Enter INGEN *reading a letter, sits downe in a Chaire
and stampes with his foote: to him a* SERVANT.

Ingen. Who brought this Letter?
Ser. A little Irish foot-boy, Sir, he staies without for
an answere.   5
Ingen. Bid him come in. Lord
What deepe dissemblers are these females, all?
How farre vnlike a friend, this Ladie vs'd me,
And heere, how like one mad in loue, she writes?
      Enter MAID *like an Irish foot-boy with a dart, and*   10
            gloues in hir pocket, and a handkercher.
So blesse me Heauen, but thou art the prettiest boy
That e're ran by a Horse, hast thou dwelt long
With thy faire Mistris?
Maid. I came but this morning, Sir.   15
Ingen. How fares thy Ladie, boy?
Maid. Like to a turtle, that hath lost her mate,
Drooping shee sits, her griefe Sir cannot speake,
Had it a voice articulate, we should know
How, and for what shee suffers; and perhaps,   20
(But t'is vnlikely) giue her Comfort Sir,
Weeping shee sits, and all the sound comes from her,
Is like the murmure of a siluer Brooke,
Which her teares truely, would make there about her,   [D1ᵛ]
Sate she in any hollow continent.   25
Ingen. Beleeue me boy, thou hast a passionate tong,

Liuely expression, or thy memorie
Hath carried thy lesson well away,
But wherefore mournes thy Ladie?
 Maid. Sir, you know,   30
And would to God I did not know my selfe.
 Ingen. Ah las, it cannot be for loue to me,
When last I saw her shee reuil'd me (boy)
With bitter'st words, and wish't me neuer more
To approch her sight, and for my marriage, now   35
I doe sustaine it, as a pennance, due
To the desert, that made her bannish me.
 Maid. Sir, I dare sweare, she did presume, no words
Nor dangers, had beene powerfull to restraine
Your comming to her, when she gaue the charge———   40
But are you married truely?
 Ingen. Why my Boy?
Dost think I mock my selfe, I sent her gloues.
 Maid. The gloues she ha's return'd you Sir by me,
And praies you giue them to some other Ladie   45
That you'll deceiue next, and be periur'd to.
Sure you haue wrong'd her Sir, she bad me tell you,
She ne're thought goodnesse dwelt in many men,
But what there was of goodnesse in the world,
Shee thought you had it all, but now shee sees   50
The jewell she esteem'd is counterfeit,
That you are but a common man, your selfe,
A traitor to her, and her vertuous loue;
That all men are betraiers and their breasts
As full of dangerous gulphes, as is the Sea,   55
Where any woman thinking to finde Harbor,
Shee and her honor are præcipitated,
And neuer to be brought with safetie off:
Ah las my haplesse Ladie, desolate,

Distrest, forsaken Virgin.   60
   Ingen. Sure this Boy
Is of an excellent nature, who so newly   D2
Tane to her seruice, feeles his Mistresse griefe,
As he and they were old familiar friends,
Why weep'st thou gentle Lad?   65
   Maid. Who hath one teare,
And would not sau't from all occasions,
From Brothers slaughters, and from mothers deaths
To spend it heere, for my distressed Ladie;
But Sir my Ladie did commaund me begg   70
To see your wife, that I may bare to her
The sad report, what creature could make you
Vntie the hand-fast plighted vnto her.
   Ingen. Wife, wife, come forth-now Gentle boy, be
     iudge   75
Enter his BROTHER *like a woman maskt.* INGEN *kisses her.*
If such a face as this being paid with scorne
By her I did adore, had not full power
To make me marrie.
   Maid. By the God of Loue,   80
Shees a faire Creature, but faith should be fairer.
My Ladie, Gentle Mistresse, one that thought
Shee had some interest in this Gentleman,
(Who now is onelie yours) commaunded me
To kisse your white hand, and to sigh and weepe,   85
And wish you that content she should haue had
In the fruition of her Loue you hold,
She bad me say, *God giue you ioy,* to both;
Yet this withall (if ye were married)
No one, her foot steps euer more should meete,   90
Nor see her face, but in a winding sheete.

Bro. Ahlas poore Ladie, 'faith I pittie her,
And, but to be i'th same state, could forgoe
Anything I possesse, to ease her woe.

Maid. Loues blessing light vpon thy gentle soule,   95
Men raile at women Mistris, but t'is we
Are false and cruell, ten times more vnkind,
You are smoother farre, and of a softer mind:
Sir, I haue one request more.

Ingen. Gentle Lad,   100
It must be one of a strange qualitie
That I denie thee, both thy forme, and minde   [D2ᵛ]
Informe me that thy nurture hath beene better,
Than to betray thee to this present life.

Maid. T'is, that you would vouchsafe to entertaine me,   105
My feete do tremble vnder me, to beare
My bodie back vnto my vncouth Ladie,
To assure her griefe; what heart so hard, would owe
A tongue, to tell so sad a tale to her?
Ahlas, I dare not looke vpon her eyes,   110
Where wronged loue, sits like the Basilisque,
And sure would kill me for my dire report,
Or rather should not I appeare like death, ⌈ *Holding vp*
When euery word I speak shot through ⌊ *his dart.*
        her hart,   115
More mortallie than his vnsparing dart.

Bro. Let me speake for the Boy.

Ingen. To what end (loue?)
No, I will sue to him, to follow me,
Introth I loue thy sweet condition,   120
And may liue to informe thy Lady of thee;
Come in, drie, drie thine eies, respit thy woe:
The effects of causes, crowne, or ouerthrow.   ⌈*Exeunt.*⌉

⌐Actus secundus, Scæna quarta.⌐

Enter Lo. PROVD., *Lo.* FEES., WEL-TRI'D, *Ma.*
SELDOME, WIDOW, BOVLD *pinning in*
a Ruffe, WIFE.

Proud. S'light, what should be become of her, you
sweare she past not forth of dores, and i'th house she   5
is not?
Widow. Did you not see her *Princox*?
Proud. This same Bawd has brought her letters from
some yonger brother, and she is stole away.
Bould. Bawd, I defie you, indeed your Lordship   10
thinkes, you may make Bawds of whom you please, i'le
take my oath vpon a booke, since I met her in the neces-
sairie house i'th morning, I ne're set eye on her.
Grace. Shee went not out of dores.
Proud. Sure shee has an inuisible ring.   15
Fees. Marrie she's the honester woman, for some of
their rings are visible enough, the more shame for them,
still say I, let the pond at *Islington* be search't: goe to,
there's more   D3   haue drown'd themselues for loue
this yeare then you are aware of.   20
Proud. Pish, you are a foole.
Welt. S'hart call him foole againe.
Fees. By this light and I will, as soone as euer you
haue shew'd me the Swaggerers.
Wife. Her clothes are all yonder my Lord.   25
Grace. And euen those same she had on to day.
Proud. Madam where is your Husband?

Wife. Rid into the Countrie.

Fees. O' my conscience, rid into *France* with your
sister.   30

Omnes. Away, away for shame.

Fees. Why, I hope she is not the first Ladie that has
run away with other womens husbands.

Welt. It may be shee's stolne out to see a play.

Proud. Who should goe with her, man?   35

Widow. Vpon my life you'll heare on her at Master
Ingens house, some loue past betwixt them, and we heard
that he was married to day, to another.

Proud. S'hart, ile go see.   *Exit Proudly.*

Welt. Come to the Swaggerers.   40

Fees. Mercy vpon me, a man or a——Lord now?
                       Exeunt Fees., Welt.

Omnes. Heere's a quoile, with a Lord and his sister.

Widow. *Princox,* hast not thou pin'd in that Ruffe yet,
ah! how thou fumblest.   45

Bould. Troth, Madam, I was ne're brought vp to it,
t'is Chamber-maids work, and I haue euer liu'd Gentlewoman. And beene vs'd accordingly.   *Exeunt.*

Actus tertius, [*Scæna prima.*]

Enter HVSBAND *and* SVBTLE.

Subt. Shee's a rare wife beleeue it Sir, were all such,
Wee neuer should haue false inheritors.

Husb. Pish friend, there is no woman in the world
Can hould out in the end, if youth, shape, wit,   5

Met in one subiect, doe assault her aptlie;   [D3ᵛ]
For fayling once, you must not faint but trie
Another way, the path of womens minds
Are crooked, and diuerse, they haue by-waies
To leade you to the Pallace of their pleasures,   10
And you must wooe discreetely; first obserue
The disposition of her you attempt,
If she be sprightly, and heroicall,
Possesse her that you are valiant, and haue spirit,
Talke nothing but of beating euery man   15
That is your hinderance, though you doe not doe it,
Or dare not, t'is no matter. Be shee free
And of a liberall soule, giue bounteously
To all the seruants, let your angels flye
About the roome, although you borrow'd 'em.   20
If shee be wittie, so must your discourse
Get wit, what shift so'ere you make for it,
Though't cost you all your land, and then a song
Or two is not amisse, although you buy 'em,
There's many in the Towne will furnish you.   25
    Subt. But still I tell you, you must vse her roughly,
Beate her face black and blew, take all her cloth's
And giue them to some Punke, this will be ground
For me to worke vpon.
    Husb. All this I haue done.   30
I haue left her now, as bare, that should I die,
Her fortune (ô my conscience) would be
To marrie some Tobacco-man, shee has nothing
But an old black-woorke wastcote, which would serue
Exceeding wel to sit i'th shop and light   35
Pipes for the lowzie Footmen (and sweete friend)
First heere's a jewell to present her, then
Heere is a Sonnet writ against my selfe,
Which as thine owne thou shalt accost her with,

Farewell and happie successe attend thee.   *Exit.*   40
   Subt. Ha, ha, ha.   [*He reads.*

> *Fairest, still wilt thou be true*
> *To a man so false to thee?*
> *Did he lend a Husbands due,*   [D4^r]
> *Thou did'st owe him loyaltie;*   45
> *But will curses, wants and blowes*
> *Breed no change in thy white soule?*
> *Be not a foole to thy first vowes,*
> *Since his breach, doth thy faith controle,*
> *No beautie else, could be so chast,*   50
> *Thinke not thou honour'st women then,*
> *Since by thy conscience, all disgrac't,*
> *Are rob'd of the deare loues of men;*
> *Then grant me my desire that vow to proue*
> *A reall husband, his adulterate loue.*   55

Tooke euer man more paines to be a Cuckold?
Oh! monstrous age where men themselues we see,
Studie and pay for their owne infamie.   *Exit.*

[*Actus tertius, Scæna secunda.*]

Enter INGEN, MAID, PROVDLY, BROTHER
like a woman, swords drawen.

  Proud. Giue me my sister, Ile haue her forth thy heart.
   Ingen. No earthly Lord can pull her out of that,
Till he haue pluckt my heart first out, my Lord   5
Wer't not inhospitable, I could wrong you heere
In mine owne house, I am so full of woe,

For your lost sister, that by all my ioyes
Hop't for in her, my heart weepes teares of bloud,
A whiter virgine, and a worthier,   10
Had ne're creation: *Loeda's* Swan was black
To her virginitie, and immaculate thoughts.
    Proud. Where hast thou hid her? giue her me againe,
For by the God of vengeance, be she lost,
The female hate shall spring betwixt our names,   15
Shall neuer die, while one of either house
Suruiues, our children shall at seuen yeares olde
Strike kniues in one another.
    Ingen. Let Hell gape
And take me quick, if I know where she is,   20
But am so charg'd with sorrow for her losse,
Being the cause of it (as no doubt I am)
That I had rather fal vpon my sword   { *Offering to kill*
Then breath a minute longer.   { *himselfe.*
    Bro. Oh sir! hold.   [D4ᵛ]
    Proud. Thou shalt not neede, I haue a sword to bathe
In thy false blood, inhumane murderer.
    Maid. Good Sir be pacified, i'le goe, i'le run
Many a mile to finde your sister out;
Shee neuer was so desperate of grace,   30
By violence to rob her selfe of life,
And so her soule in danger; comfort Sir,
Shee's but retir'd somewhere on my life.
    Ingen. Preethee let me alone——— [*To his Brother.*
Doe I stand to defend that wretched life   35
That is in doubt of hers, heere worthy Lord,
Behold a breast, fram'd of thy sisters loue,
Hew it, for thou shalt strike but on a stock,
Since she is gone that was the cause it liu'd.
    Proud. Out false dissembler, art not married?   40

Ingen. No, behold, it is my yonger brother   { *Plucks*
    drest,   { *off his*
A man, no woman, that hath guld the world,   { *headtire.*
Intended for a happier euent
Than this that follow'd, that she now is gone,   45
Oh fond experiments of simple man,
Foole to thy fate, since all thy project men't
But mirth, is now conuerted vnto death.
    Maid. Oh doe not burst me joy, that modestie   *Aside.*
Would let me show my selfe to finish all.   50
   Proud. Nay, then thou hast my sister somewhere
    villain,
T'is plaine now, thou wilt steale thy marriage,
Shee is no match for thee, assure thy selfe.
If all the law in *England,* or my friends   55
Can crosse it, t'shall not be.
   Ingen. Would t'were so well,
And that I knew the Ladie to be safe.
Giue me no ill words; Sir, this Boy and I
Will wander like two Pilgrimes, till we finde her: 60
If you doe loue her as you talke, doe so:
The loue or griefe that is exprest in words,
Is sleight and easie, t'is but shallow woe
That makes a noise, deep'st waters stillest goe;
I loue her better then thy parents did,   E
Which is beyond a Brother.
   Proud. Slaue, thou liest.
   Ingen. Z'oones.   [*About to strike.*
   Bro. Kill him.
   Maid. Oh hold; Sir, you dishonour much your brother,   70
To counsaile him 'gainst hospitalitie,
To strike in his owne house.
   Ingen. You, Lord insolent, I will fight with you,
Take this, as a challenge, and set your time.

Proud. To morrow morning *Ingen,*   75
T'is that I couet, and prouoke thee for.
  Bro. Wil you not strike him now?
  Ingen. No, my good Boy
Is both discreete and just in his aduise.
Thy glories are to last but for a day;   80
Giue me thy hand,
To morrow morning thou shalt be no Lord.
  Proud. To morrow noone, thou shalt not be at all.
  Ingen. Pish, why should you thinke so, haue not I
    armes,   85
A soule as bold as yours, a sword as true:
I doe not thinke your Honor in the field
Without your Lordships liueries will haue oddes.
  Proud. Farewell, and lets haue no excuses, pray. *Exit.*
  Ingen. I warrant you, pray say your prayers to night,   90
And bring no ink-horne w'ee, to set your hand to
A satisfactorie recantation.   *Exeunt Ingen, Brother.*
  Maid. Oh wretched Maid, whose sword can I pray for?
But by the others losse, I must find death,
Oh odious brother, if he kill my loue: 95
Oh Bloodie Loue, if he should kill my brother;
Dispaire on both sides of my discontent,
Tel's me no safetie rests but to preuent.   *Exit.*

[Actus tertius, Scæna tertia.]

Enter WIDDOW *and* BOVLD *like* Princox.

Widow. What's a clock *Princox?*
Bould. Bed-time an't please you Madame.
Widow. Come, vndresse me, would God had made me

a man.   5

Bould. Why, Madame?

Widow. Because I would haue beene in bed as soone
as they, wee are so long vnpinning and vnlacing.

Bould. Yet many of vs Madame are quickly vndone
sometime, but heerein we haue the aduantage of men,   10
though [E1ᵛ] they can be a bed sooner than we, i'ts
a great while when they are a bed e're they can get vp.

Widow. Indeed if they be well laid *Princox,* one cannot get them vp againe in hast.

Bould. Oh God Madame, how meane you that, I hope   15
you know, ill things taken into a Gentlewomans eares,
are the quick corrupters of maiden modestie, I would be
loath to continue in any seruice vnfit for my virgin
estate, or where the world should take any notice of
light behauiour in the Ladie I follow: for Madame, the   20
maine point of chastitie in a Ladie, is to build the rock
of a good opinion amongst the people by circumstances,
and a faire shew she must make, *Si non caste, tamen
caute* Madame, and though wit be a wanton Madame: yet
I beseech your Lady-ship for your owne credit and mine, 25
let the bridle of judgement be alwaies in the chaps of
it to giue it head, or restraine it, according as time and
place shall be conuenient.

Widow. Precise and learned *Princox,* dost not thou
goe to *Black-fryers.*   30

Bould. Most frequently Madame, vnworthy vessell
that I am to partake or retaine any of the delicious dew,
that is there distilled.

Widow. But why shouldst thou aske me what I meant
e'ne now, I tell thee there's nothing vtter'd that carries a   35
double sence, one good, one bad, but if the hearer applie
it to the worst, the fault lies in his or her corrupt vnderstanding, not in the speaker, for to answere your lattine:

prauis omnia praua, beleiue me wench, if ill come into
my fancie, I will purge it by speech, the lesse will remaine   40
within: a pox of these nise mouth'd creatures, I haue seen
a norrow paire of lips vtter as broad a taile, as can be
bought for money; Indeed an ill tale vnutter'd, is like a
maggot in a nut, it spoiles the whitest kernell.

Bould. You speake most intellegently Madame.   45

Widow. Ha'st not done yet? thou art an old fumbler
I perceiue: me thinkes thou doest not do things like a
woman.

Bould. Madame, I doe my endeauour, and the best can
doe no more, they that could doe better, it may be would   E2
not, and then t'were all one, but rather then be a burthen to your Lady-ship, I protest sincerely, I would beg
my bread, therefore I beseech you Madame to hold me
excus'd, and let my good will stand for the action.

Widow. Let thy good will stand for the action? If   55
good will would doe it, there's many a Ladie in this Land
would be content with her old Lord, and thou canst not
be a burthen to me, without thou lie vpon me, and that
were preposterous in thy sexe; take no exceptions at what
I say, remember you said stand e'ne-now, there was a   60
word for one of your coate indeede.

Bould. I sweare Madame, you are verie merrie, God
send you good luck, ha's your Ladyship no waters, that
you vse at bed-time?

Widow. No introth, *Princox.*   65

Bould. No Complexion?

Widow. None but mine own I sweare, did'st thou euer
vse any?

Bould. No indeede Madame: now and then a peace of

scarlet, or so; a little white and red Cerusse; but in troth   70
Madame, I haue an excellent receipt for a night masque,
as euer you heard.

Widow. What is it?

Bould. Bores grease one ounce, Iordane Almonds
blanch't and ground a quarterne, red Rose-water, halfe a   75
pint, Mares vrine, newly couer'd, halfe a score drops.

Widow. Fough, no more of thy medicine, if thou
lou'st me; few of our Knights errant, when they meete a
faire Ladie arrant, in a morning, would thinke her face
had lien so plaster'd all night: thou hast had some   80
Apothecarie to thy sweet heart: but leauing this face
physick, for (by my troth) it may make others haue good
ones; but it makes me make a scuruie one. Which of all
the Gallants in the Towne would'st thou make a husband
of, if thou might'st haue him for thy chusing?   85

Bould. In troth Madame, I but you'll say I speake
blindly, but let my loue stand a side.

Widow. I think it not fit indeede your loue should
stand in the middle.

Bould. I say Master *Bould*; oh, do but marke him   90
Madame,   [E2ᵛ]   his leg, his hand, his bodie, & all his
members stand in print.

Widow. Out vpon thee *Princox*; no, me thinkes *Wel-*
tri'ds a handsome fellow, I like not these starch't Gallants: masculine faces, and masculine gestures please   95
me best.

Bould. How like you Master *Pert*?

Widow. Fie vpon him, when he is in his skarlet
clothes, he lookes like a man of waxe, and I had as leue
haue a dogge a waxe, I do not thinke but he lies in a case 100

a nights, he walkes as if he were made of gyns, as if
nature had wrought him in a frame; I haue seene him sit
discontented a whole play, because one of the purles of
his band was fallen (out of his reach) to order againe.

Bould. Why? *Bould* Madame is cleane contrarie.   105

Widow. I but that's as ill, each extreame, is a like
vitious; his carefull carelesnesse is his studie, he spends
as much time to make himselfe slouenly, as the other to
be spruse, his garters hang euer on the calues of his legs,
his dublet vnbutten'd, and his points vntrust, his haire   110
in's eyes like a drunkard, and his hat worne on his hinder
part of his head, as if he car'd more for his memorie, than
his wit: makes him looke as if he were distracted; *Princox,* I would haue you lie with me, I doe not loue to lie
alone.   115

Bould. With all by heart Madame.

Widow. Are you cleane skind?

Bould. Cleane skind Madame? there's a question, do
you thinke I haue the itch? I am an English-woman, I
protest, I scorne the motion.   120

Widow. Nay prithee *Princox* be not angrie, it's a
signe of honestie I can tell you.

Bould. Faith Madam I thinke ti's but simple honestie
that dwels at the signe of the scab.

Widow. Well, well, come to bed, and wee'le talke   125
further of all these matters.   *Exit.*

Bould. Fortune, I thanke thee, I will owe thee eies
For this good turne, now is shee mine indeede,
Thou hast giuen me that successe my project hop'd.
Of, false disguise that hast been true to me,   130
And now be *Bould,* that thou mai'st welcome be.   *Exit.* E3

[*Actus tertius, Scæna quarta.*]

Enter WHOORE-BANG, BOTTS, TEARE-CHOPS,
SPIL-BLOVD, *and* DRAWER: *seuerall
patches on their faces.*

Teare. Dam-me, we will haue more wine, sirrha, or
wee'l downe into the Seller, and drowne thee in a Butt   5
of Malmesey, and hew all the Hogs-heads in peeces.

Whore. Hang him rogue, shall he die as honorably as
the Duke of *Clarence*; by this flesh lets haue wine, or
I will cut thy head off, haue it rosted and eaten in *Pie-
corner* next Barthomew-tide.   10

Draw. Gentleman, I beseech you consider where you
are, *Turne-bole* streete, a ciuil place; do not disturbe a
number a poore Gentlewomen, Master *Whoore-bang,*
Ma: *Bots,* Ma: *Teare-chops,* and Ma: *Spill-bloud,* the
Watch are abroad.   15

Spilb. The Watch? why you rogue, are not we Kings
of *Turne-bole?*

Draw. Yes marrie are yee, Sir, for my part, if you'l
be quiet, ile haue a signe made of yee, and it shall be
cal'd the foure Kings of *Turne-bole.*   20

Botts. Will you fetch vs wine?

Whore. And a whoore (sirrah).

Draw. Why what d'ee thinke of me, am I an Infidell,
a Turke, a Pagan, a Sarazin; I haue beene at *Besse Turn-
ups,* and she sweares all the Gentlewomen went to see a   25
Play at the Fortune, and are not come in yet, and she
beleeues they sup with the Players.

Teare. Dam-me, we must kill all those rogues, we shall neuer keepe a whore honest for them.

Botts. Goe your waies, sirrha, wee'l haue but a gal-   30
lon a peice, and an ounce of Tobacco.

Draw. I beseech you, let it be but pottles.

Spilb. S'hart you rogue?   *Exit Draw.*

Enter WELL-TRI'D *and* FEE-SIMPLE.

Whore. Master *Well-tri'd,* welcome as my soule.   35

Enter DRAWER *with Wine, Plate, and Tobacco.*

Botts. Noble Lad, how do'st thou?

Spilb. As welcome, as the Tobacco and the Wine Boy.

Teare. Dam-me thou art.   [E3ᵛ]

Fees. Blesse me (saue you Gent.) They haue not one   40
face among 'em. I could wish my selfe well from them,
I would I had put out something vpon my returne, I had
as leue be at the *Barmuthoes.*

Welt. Pray welcome this Gentleman.

Spilb. Is he valiant?   45

Welt. Faith hee's a little faulty that way: somewhat
of a bashfull and backward nature, yet I haue brought
him amongst you, because he hath a great desire to be
flesh'd.

Fees. Yes faith Sir, I haue a great desire to be flesh'd: 50
now Mʳ. *Well-tri'd* said, hee would bring mee to the
onely flesh-mongers in the towne.

Welt. Sir, he cannot endure the sight of steele.

Whore. Not steele? zoones.   ⎧ *Claps his Sword ore*

Fees. Now I am going.   ⎨ *the Table.*   55

Botts. Here's to you sir, i'le fetch you again with a cup
of sack.

Fees. I pledge you sir, and begin to you in a cup of
Claret.

Welt. Harke you my Lo: what will you say, if I make   60
you beate all these out of the roome?

Fees. What will I say? why I say it is impossible, ti's
not in mortall man.

Welt. Well drinke apace, if any braue you, outbraue
him, Ile second you, they are a Companie of cowards be-   65
leeue me.

Fees. By this light I would they were els, if I thought
so, I would be vpon the Iack of one of 'em instantly,
that same litle Dam me. But M^r. *Wel-tri'd,* if they be not
verie valiant or dare not fight, how come they by such   70
Cuts and gashes, and such broken faces?

Welt. Why their whores strike 'em with Cans, and
glasses, and quart pots; if they haue nothing by 'em,
they strike 'em with the Poxe, and you know that will
lay ones nose as flat as a basket hilt Dagger.   75

Fees. Well let me alone.

Teare. This bullie dares not drink.

Fees. Dare I not Sir?

Welt. Well said, speake to him man.

Fees. You had best trie me Sir.   80

Spilb. Wee foure will drinke four healths to foure of
the seauen deadly sins, Pride, Drunkennesse, Wrath, &
Lecherie.

Fees. I'le pledge 'em, and I thanke you, I know 'em
all, heeres one.   [E4^r]

Whore. Which of the sinnes?

Fees. By my troth e'ne to Pride.

Welt. Why well said, and in this doe not you only
pledge your Mistris health, but all the womens in the
world.   90

Fees. So now, this little Cup to Wrath, because he and
I are strangers.

Teare. Braue boy, Dam mee he shall be a Rorer.

Fees. Dam mee, I will be a rorer, or't shall cost me a
fall.   95

Botts. The next place that falls, pray let him haue it.

Fees. Well, I haue two of my healths to drinke yet,
Lecherie and Drunkennesse which en'e shall goe together.

Welt. Why how now my Lord, a Morralist?

Botts. Dam mee, art thou a Lo: what vertues has thou?   100

Fees. Vertues? enough to keepe ere a Dam mee Company in *England,* me thinkes you should thinke it vertue
enough to be a Lord.

Whore. Will not you pledg these healths Master
Weltrid? wee'le haue no obseruers.   105

Welt. Why, *Mounser Whore-bang?* I am no play
maker, and for pledging your healths, I loue none of the
foure, you drank to so well.

Spilb. Zoones you shall pledge me this.

Welt. Shall I?   110

Fees. Whats the matter, do'st heere *Maister Wel-trid?*
vse thine owne discretion, if thou wilt not pledge him,
say so, and let me see, if er'e a Dam mee of 'em all,
will force thee.

Spilb. Puffe, will your Lordship take anie Tobacco?   115
you Lord, with the white face?

Botts. Heart he cannot put it through his nose.

Fees. Faith you haue neare a nose to put it through,
dee hear? blow your face sirra.

Teare. Youle pledge me Sir?   120

Welt. Indeede I will not.

Fees. Dam mee hee shall not then.

Teare. Lord, vse your owne words, Dam mee is mine,

I am knowne by it all the towne o're, d'ee heare?

 Fees. It is as free for mee as you, d'ee here Patch? 125

 Teare. I haue paid more for't.

 Welt. Nay Ile beare him witnesse in a truth, his soule
lies fort my Lord.

 Spilb. Wel-tri'd, you are growne proud since you got [E4ᵛ]
good Clothes, and haue follow'd your ⎰*Strikes,* & 130
Lord.   ⎱*they scuffle.*

 Whore. I haue knowne you lowzie, *Wel-trid.*

 Welt. Rorer you lie. ⎰*Draw and fight, throw*
 Draw. Oh Iesu.   ⎱*pots and stooles.*

 All Swaggerers. Zoones cleaue or be cleft: pell mell, 135
slash armes and legges.

 Fees. Hart let me alone with 'em. *Breake off.*

 Welt. Why now thou art a worthy ⌈*Exeunt Roarers.*⌉
wight, indeed a Lord a Lorne.

 Fees. I am a mad man, looke is not that one of their 140
heads?

 Welt. Fie no my Lord.

 Fees. Dam me but tis, I would not wish you to crosse
me a purpose, if you haue anie thing to say to me, so,
I am readie. 145

 Welt. Oh braue Lord, manie a rorer thus is made by
wine: come it is one of their heads my Lord.

 Fees. Why so then, I will haue my humour, if you loue
me, let's goe breake windowes somewhere.

 Welt. Drawer, take your plate, for the reckoning 150
there's some of their cloakes: I will be no shot-log to
such.

 Draw. Gods blessing o' your heart, for thus ridding
the house of them. *Exeunt.*

Actus quartus, Scæna prima.

Enter WIDOW *vndrest, a sword in her hand, and*
BOVLD *in his shirt, as started from bed.*

Widow. Vnciuill man, if I should take thy life,
It were not to be weigh'd with thy attempt:
Thou hast for euer lost mee.   5
Bould. Maddam, why?
Can loue beget losse? Doe I couet you
Vnlawfully? Am I an vnfit man
To make an husband of? Send for a Priest,
First consummate the match, and then to bed   10
Without more trouble.
Widow. No, I will not doe't.
Bould. Why you confest to mee as you'r Gentlewoman,
I was the man your heart did most affect:
That you did doate vpon my minde and body.   F
Widow. So, by the sacred and inuiolate knot
Of marriage, I doe, but will not wed thee.
Bould. Why yet inioy me now. Consider Lady,
That little, but blest time, I was in bed,
Although I lay as by my sisters side,   20
The world is apt to censure otherwise:
So 'tis necessitie that wee marry now.
Widow. Pish, I regard not (at a straw) the world:
Fame from the tongues of men doth iniury
Oftener then Iustice: and as conscience   25
Onely makes guilty persons, not report:
(For shew we cleare as springs vnto the world,
If our owne knowledge doe not make vs so,

That is no satisfaction to our selues.)
So stand wee ne're so leprous to mens eye, 30
It cannot hurt hart-knowne integritie.
You haue trusted to that fond opinion,
This is the way to haue a widdow-hood,
By getting to her bed: Ahlas young man,
Should'st thou thy selfe tell thy companions 35
Thou hadst dishonour'd mee (as you men haue tongues
Forked and venom'd 'gainst our subiect sexe)
It should not moue me, that know 'tis not so:
Therefore depart, Truth be my vertuous shield.
    Bould. Few widdowes would doe thus. 40
    Widow. All modest, would.
    Bould. To be in bed and in possession
Euen of the marke I aim'd at, and goe off
Foild and disgrac't, come, come, you'll laugh at me
Behind my back, publish I wanted spirit, 45
And mock me to the Ladies, call me childe,
Say you denide me but to trie the heate
And zeale of my affection toward you,
Then clap't vp with a rime, as for example.
      Hee coldly loues, retires, for one vaine triall, 50
      For wee are yeelding, when we make deniall.
    Widow. Seruant I make no question, from this time
You'll hold a more reuerent opinion [F1ᵛ]
Of some that weare long coates, and tis my pride,
To assure you that there are amongst vs good: 55
And with this continencie, if you goe away,
I'le be so farre from thinking it defect,
That I will hold you worthiest of men.
    Bould. S'hart, I am *Tantalus,* my long'd for fruit
Bobs at my lips, yet still it shrinks from me. 60
Haue not I that, which men say neuer failes
To o'recome any? oportunitie?

Come, come, I am too cold in my assault.
By all the vertues, that yet euer were
In man, or woman, I with reuerence   65
Doe loue thee Ladie, but will be no foole
To let occasion slip, her fore-top from me.
 Widow. You will faile this way to, vpon my knees
I doe desire thee to preserue thy vertues,
And with my teares my honor; t'is as bad   70
To loose our worths to them, or to deceaue
Who haue held worthy opinions of vs,
As to betray trust: all this I implore
For thine owne sake, not mine, as for my selfe,
If thou bee'st violent, by this stupid night,   75
And all the mischiefes her darke wombe hath bred,
I'le raise the house, I'le crie a rape.
 Bould. I hope
You will not hang me, that were murther Ladie,
A greater sinne, then lying with me sure.   80
 Widow. Come, flatter not your selfe with argument,
I will exclaime; the law hangs you, not I,
Or if I did, I had rather farre confound
The deerest bodie in the world to me,
Then that, that bodie, should confound my soule.   85
 Bould. Your soule, ahlas Mistresse, are you so fond
To thinke her generall destruction
Can be procur'd by such a naturall act,
Which beasts are borne to and haue priuiledge in?
Fie, fiie, if this could be, farre happier   90
Are sensitiue soules in their creation
Than man the prince of creatures, thinke you Heauen   F2
Regards such mortall deeds, or punisheth
Those acts, for which he hath ordained vs?
 Widow. You argue like an Atheist, man is neuer   95
The prince of creatures, as you call him now,

But in his reason, faile that, he is worse
Than Horse or Dog, or beasts of wildernesse,
And t'is that reason teacheth vs to doe
Our actions vnlike them: then that which you   100
Termed in them a priuiledge beyond vs,
The basenesse of their being doth expresse,
Compar'd to ours, Horses, Buls, and Swine,
Doe leape their Dams; because man does not so,
Shall we conclude his making happilesse?   105
    Bould. You put me downe, yet will not put me downe,
I am too gentle, some of you I haue heard,
Loue not these words but force, to haue it done
As they sing prick-song, e'ne at the first sight.
    Widow. Go too, keep off, by Heauen and Earth, i'le   110
       call else.
    Bould. How if no bodie heare you?
    Widow. If they doe not,
I'le kill you with mine owne hand, neuer stare,
Or failing that fall on this sword my selfe.   115
    Bould. Oh widdow wonderfull, if thou bee'st not
       honest.
Now God forgiue my mother and my sisters.
Thinke but how finely Madam vndiscouer'd
For euer you and I, might liue all day your Gentlewoman   120
To doe you seruice, but all night your man
To doe you seruice, newnesse of the trick,
If nothing else might stirre ye.
    Widow. T'is a stale one
And was done in the *Fleete* ten yeares agoe,   125
Will you begon? the doore is open for you.
    Bould. Let me but tarrie till the morning Madam,
To send for clothes, shall I goe naked home?
    Widow. T'is best time now, it is but one a clock,
And you may goe vnseene; I sweare by Heauen,   130

I would spend all the night to sit and talke w'ee,
If I durst trust you, I do loue you so,　　　　　　　　　[F2ᵛ]
My bloud forsakes my heart now you depart.

Bould. S'hart, will you marrie me heereafter then?

Widow. No, you are too yong, and I am much too old;　135
I and vnworthy, and the world will say,
We married not for loue, good morrow seruant.

　　　　　　　　　　　　　　　　　Exit Widow.

Bould. Why so? these women are the erranst Iuglers
in the World, the wry-leg'd fellow is an Asse to ⌠*Mu-*　140
'em. Well, I must haue this widdow, what e're ⌡*sique.*
come on't: Faith she has turn'd me out of her seruice verie
barely, harke, whats heere, musique.

Enter Svbtle *with a paper, and his* Boy *with a cloake.*

Subt. *Rise Ladie Mistresse, rise:*　　　　　　　　　145
　　The night hath tedious beene,
　　No sleepe hath fallen into my eies,
　　Nor slumbers made me sinne.
　　Is not she a Saint then say,
　　Thought of whom keepes sinne away?　　　　　　150
　　Rise Madame, rise and giue me light,
　　Whom darkenesse still will couer,
　　And ignorance darker than night,
　　Till thou smile on thy louer;
　　All want day till thy beautie rise,　　　　　　　155
　　For the graie morne breakes from thine eies.

Now sing it sirrha.　　　　[*The* Song *sung by the* Boy.

Subt. S'foote, who's this? yong Master *Bould?* God
saue you, you are an earely stirrer.

Bould. You say true Master *Subtle,* I haue been earely　160
vp, but as God helpe me, I was neuer the neere.

Subt. Where haue you beene Sir?

Bould. What's that to you Sir? at a womans labour.

Subt. Very good: I neare tooke you for a man Mid-
wife before.   165

Bould. The troth is, I haue beene vp all night at dice,
& lost my clothes, good morrow Master *Subtle,* pray
God the Watch be broke vp: I thanke you for my
Musique.   *Exit.*

Subt. Tis palpable by this aire, her husband being   170
abroad, *Bould* has layen with her, and is now conuai'd
out of doores. Is this the Ladie *Perfect* with a poxe?
The truth is, her ver-   F3   tuous chastitie, began to
make me make a myracle of her, still holding out to me,
notwithstanding her husbands most barbarous vsage of   175
her, but now indeede t'is no maruaile since another possesses her. Well Madame, Ile go finde out your Cuckold,
Ile be reueng'd on you and tell a tale
Shall tickle him, this is a cheate in loue,
Not to be borne, another to beguile   180
Me of the game, I plaid for all this while.   *Exit.*

⸢*Actus quartus, Scæna secunda.*⸣

Enter Wel-tri'd *and* Bovld *putting on his doublet,*
Fee-simple *on a bed, as in* Bould's *chamber.*

Welt. You see, we made bould with your lodging,
indeed, I did assure my selfe, you were fast for this
night.   5

Bould. But how the Deuill came this foole in your
companie?

Welt. S'foote man, I carried him last night among the
Rorers, to flesh him, and by this light he got drunke, and

beate e'm all.   10

Bould. Why then he can endure the sight of a drawne
sword now?

Welt. Oh God Sir, I thinke in my conscience he will
eate steele shortlie, I know not how his conuersion will
hold after this sleepe, but in an houre or two (last night)   15
he was growne such a little dam-me, that I protest, I was
afraid of the spirit, that I my selfe had rais'd in him:
but this other matter of your expulsion thus mads me to
the heart; Were you in bed with her?

Bould. In bed by Heauen.   20

Welt. I'le be hang'd, if you were not busie to soone,
you should haue let her slept first.

Bould. Z'oones man, she put her hands to my breasts,
and swore I was no maid, now I being eager to proue her
words true, tooke that hint, and would violently haue   25
thrust her hand lower, when her thought being swifter
then my strength, made her no sooner imagine that she
was betrai'd, but she leapes out of the bed, whips me
downe a sword that hung by, and as, if fortitude and
justice had met to assist her, spight of all argument   30
faire or fowle she forc't me away.

Welt. But is't possible thou should'st haue no more
wit, would'st thou come away vpon any tearmes, but sure
ones,   [F3ᵛ]   hauing night, her chamber, and her selfe
naked in thine armes? By that light, if I had a sonne of   35
14 whom I had help't thus farre, that had seru'd me so,
I would breech him.

Bould. S'hart, what would you haue me done?

Welt. Haue done? done, done twice at least.

Bould. Haue plaid *Tarquin* and rauish't her?   40

Welt. Pish, *Tarquin* was a block-head, if he had had
any wit and could haue spoke, *Lucrece* had neuer been
rauished, she would haue yeelded, I warrant thee, & so

wil any woman.

Bould. I was such an erronious heretique to loue,   45
and women, as thou art, till now.

Welt. God's pretious, it makes me mad, when I thinke
on't: was there euer such an obsur'd trick? now will she
abuse thee horriblie, say thou art a faint-hearted fellow,
a milk-sop and I know not what, as indeede thou art.   50

Bould. Z'oones, would you had beene in my place.

Welt. Z'oones, I would I had, I would haue so jumbl'd
her honestie: would'st thou be held out at staues end
with words? dost not thou know a widdow's a weake
vessell, and is easily cast if you close.   55

Bould. Weltri'd, you deale vnfriendly.

Welt. By this light I shal blush to be seen in thy
companie.

Bould. Pray leaue my chamber.

Welt. Poxe vpon your chamber,   60
I care not for your chamber, nor your selfe
More than you care for me.

Bould. S'blood I as little for you.

Welt. Why fare you well.

Bould. Why, fare-well you. *Weltri'd,* I prithee stay,   65
Thou know'st I loue thee.

Welt. S'hart, I loue you as well; but for my spleene,
or choller I thinke, I haue as much as you.

Bould. Well friend,
This is the businesse you must doe for me,   70
Repaire vnto the widdow, where giue out,
To morrow morne, I shall be married,
Inuite her to the wedding, I haue a trick,
To put vpon this Lord to, whom I made
My instrument to preferre me.   75

  Welt. What shall follow,   [F4ʳ]
I will not aske, because I meane to see't.

The iars 'twixt friends, still keeps their friendship
    sweet.   *Exit.*

Fees. Why *Weltri'd,* you rogue, whats that a vision? 80

Bould. Why how now my Lord? who do you call
rogue? the Gentleman you name is my friend, if you were
wise I should be angrie.

Fees. Angrie with me? why dam me Sir, and you be;
Out with your sword, it is not with me I tell you as 85
it was yesterday, I am flesht man, I. Haue you any thing
to say to me?

Bould. Nothing but this, how many doe you thinke,
you haue slaine last night?

Fees. Why fiue, I neuer kill lesse. 90

Bould. There was but foure: my Lord, you had best
prouide your selfe and begon, three you haue slaine starke
dead.

Fees. You jest.

Bould. T'is most true, *Weltri'd* is fled. 95

Fees. Why let the Rorers meddle with me another
time, as for flying, I scorne it, I kild 'em like a man; when
did you euer see a Lord hang for any thing? we may kill
whom we list, marry my conscience pricks me; ah plague
a this drinke, what things it makes vs doe, I doe no more 100
remember this now than a puppie-dogge.
Oh bloodie Lord that art bedawb'd with gore,
Vaine world adiew, for I will rore no more.

Bould. Nay stay my Lord, I did but trie the tender-
nesse of your conscience, all this is nothing so, but to 105
sweeten the tale (I haue for you) I foretold you this
fain'd mischance.

Fees. Is it a tale belonging to the Widdow?

Bould. I thinke you are a witch.

Fees. My grand-mother was suspected. 110

Bould. The Widdow has desired you by me to meete

her to morrow morning at Church in some vnknowne disguise, least any suspect it, for quoth she,
Long hath he held me fast in his moist hand,
Therefore I will be his in nuptiall band   115
    Fees. *Bould,* I haue euer taken you to be my friend,
I am very wise now, and valiant, if this be not true,
dam-me Sir,   [F4ᵛ]   you are the sonne of a whore,
and you lie, and I will make it good with my sword.
    Bould. I am, what e're you please Sir, if it be not 120
true; I will goe with you to the Church my selfe, your
disguise I haue thought on; the Widdow is your owne.
Come, leaue your fooling.
    Fees. If this be true, thou little Boy, *Bould,*   *Cant.*
So true, as thou tel'st to me,   125
To morrow morne when I haue the Widdow,
My deare friend shalt thou be.   *Exeunt.*

ᵣ*Actus quartus, Scæna tertia.*ᴶ

Enter MAID *like the foote-boy:* SELDOME *with a*
couple of SERIEANTS.

    Maid. Sir, t'is most true and in this shall you be
Vnlike to other Citizens that arrest
To vndoe Gentlemen: your clemencie heere   5
Perchance saues two liues, one from the others sword,
The other from the Lawes; this morne they fight,
And though your debtor be a Lord, yet should he
Miscarrie, certainely your debt were lost.
    Seld. Do'st thou serue the Lord *Proudly?*   10

Maid. Sir, I do.

Seld. Well, such a Boy as thou, is worth more money
Then thy Lord owes me, t'is not for the debt
I doe arrest him, but to end this strife,
Which both may loose my money and his life.   15

      Enter Lord Provdly *with a riding rod.*

Proud. My Horse there, Z'oones I would not for the
   world
He should alight before me in the field,
My name and honor were for euer lost.   20

Seld. Good morrow to your Honor, I doe heare
Your Lordship this faire morning is to fight,
And for your honor: Did you neuer see
The Play, where the fat Knight hight *Old-castle,*
Did tell you truly what this honor was?   25

Proud. Why, how now good man flat-cap, what d'ee
   lack?
Who doe you talke to, sirrha?

I. Serj. We arrest you.

Proud. Arrest me, rogue? I am a Lord ye curs,   30
A Parliament man.

2. Serj. Sir, we arest you though.

Proud. At whose suit?   G

Seld. At mine, Sir.

Proud. Why thou base rogue, did not I set thee vp,   35
Hauing no stock, but thy faire shop and wife?

Seld. Into my house with him.

Maid. Away with him, away with him.

Proud. A plot, a trick by Heauen. See *Ingens* foot-boy,
T'is by his Masters meanes, oh coward, slaue;   40
I'le put in baile, or pay the debt.

Seld. I, I, I, wee'll talke with you within—thrust
him in.   *Ex.*

[Actus quartus, Scæna quarta.]

Enter INGEN *looking on his sword and bending it,*
his BROTHER *like a Man.*

Ingen. If I miscarrie *Franck,* I prithee see
All my debts paid, about fiue hundred pounds
Will fully satisfie all men, and my land   5
And what I else possesse, by natures right
In thy descent, *Franck,* I make freely thine.
    Bro. I know, you doe not thinke I wish you dead
For all the benefit: besides, your spirit's
So opposite to counsaile, to auert   10
Your resolution, that I saue my breath,
Which would be lost in vaine, to expire and spend
Vpon your foe, if you fall vnder him.
    Ingen. *Franck,* I protest you shall doe iniurie
Vnto my foe, and much disturbance to   15
Vnto my soule departing, die I heere
Fairely, and on my single enemies sword,
If you should not let him go off vntouch't.
Now by the Master of thy life and mine,
I loue thee Boy, beyond any example,   20
As well as thou do'st me, but should I goe
Thy second to the field, as thou dost mine,
And if thine enemie kild thee like a man,
I would desire, neuer to see him more,
But he should beare himselfe off with those wounds   25
He had receau'd from thee, for that time safe,
And without persecution by the Law,
For what hap is our foes, might be our owne,

And no mans iudgement, sits in Iustice place,   [G1ᵛ]
But weighing other mens as his owne case.   30
    Bro. He has the aduantage of you being a Lord,
For should you kill him, you are sure to die,
And by some Lawyer with a golden tongue,
That cries for right, ten angels on his side;
Your daring meete him, cal'd presumption: 35
But kill he you, hee, and his noble friends
Haue such a golden snaffle for the jawes
Of man-deuouring Pithagorean Law,
Thei'le reyne her stubborne chaps, e'ne to her taile:
And (though she haue yron teeth to meaner men)   40
So master her, that who displeasd her most,
She shall lie vnder like a tired jade,
For small boates on rough seas are quickly lost,
But ships ride safe, and cut the waues that tost.
    Ingen. Follow what may, I am resolu'd deare Brother,   45
This monster vallor, that doth feed on men,
Groanes in me for my reputation.
This charge I giue thee to, If I doe die,
Neuer to part from the yong Boy, which late
I entertain'd, but loue him for my sake: 50
And for my Mistresse the Ladie *Honor,*
Whom to deceiue, I haue deceiu'd my selfe,
If she be dead, pray God I may giue vp
My life a sacrifice on her brothers sword;
But if thou liu'st to see her gentle brother,   55
If I be slaine, tell her I dy'de because
I had transgrest against her worthy loue.
This sword is not well mounted, lets see thine.
        Enter MAID *like a foote-boy.*
    Maid. Your staying Sir, is in vaine, for my Lord   60
      Proudly,
Iust at his taking horse to meete you heere,

At *Seldomes* suit the Citizen, was arrested
Vpon an action of two hundred pounds,
I saw it Sir, t'is true.　　　　　　　　　65
　　Ingen. Oh, scuruie Lord,
'T had beene a cleanlier shift then this, to haue had
It hinder'd by command, he being a Lord,　　G2
But I will finde him.　　　*Enter Lord Proudly.*
　　Proud. You see, valiant Sir, I haue got loose　70
For all your stratagem, oh rogue are you there.
　　　　　　　　　Proud. stabs his sister.
　　Ingen. Most ignoble Lord.　⎰*Ingen stabs Proud.*
　　Proud. Coward thou did'st this ⎱*in the left arme.*
That I might be disabled for the fight,　　　75
Or that thou mightst haue some excuse to shun me,
But t'is my left arme, thou hast lighted on.
I haue no second; heere are three of you,
If all doe murther me, your consciences
Will more then hang you, damn you; come prepare.　80
　　Ingen. Brother walk off, and take the boy away,
Is he hurt much?
　　Bro. Nothing or very little. *Bro. thrusts the Boy out.*
　　Ingen. I'le bind your wound vp first, your losse of
　　blood　　　　　　　　　85
May sooner make you faint.
　　Proud. Ingen, thou art
A worthy Gentleman, for this curtesie,
Go-too i'le saue thy life, come on Sir: hay,　⎰*A passe*
I'le cut your codpeice point Sir, with this thrust,⎱*or two.* 90
And then downe goes your breeches.
　　Ingen. Your Lordships merrie,　　*Passe.*
I had like to haue spoild your cut-worke band.
　　Enter MAID *like a foote-boy running,* BROTHER
　　　after him; MAID *kneeles betwixt 'em.*　95
　　Maid. Oh Master, hold your hand, my Lord hold

yours,

Or let your swords meete in this wretched breast,

Yet you are both well, what blood you haue lost

Giue it as for the iniurie you did,   100

And now be friends.

    Proud. S'hart, t'is a louing rogue.

    Ingen. Kind Boy, stand vp, t'is for thy wound he

    bleeds,

My wrong is yet vnsatisfied.   105

    Proud. Hence away,

It is a Sisters losse that whets my sword.

    Maid. Oh stay, my Lord, behold your sis- ⎰*Discouers*

    ter heere ⎱*her selfe.*

Bleeding by your hand. Seruant see your mistresse   110

Turn'd to thy seruant running by thy Horse,

Whose means it was to haue preuented this,

But all in vaine.

    Bro. Oh noble Ladie.

    Ingen. Most worthie patterne of all women kind.   115

    Proud. Ingen, I am satisfied, put vp your sword.   [G2ᵛ]

Sister, you must with me, I haue a husband

The Lord *Fee-simple's* father, old, but rich:

This Gentleman is no match for you; kneele not,

That portion of yours, I haue consum'd,   120

Thus marrying, you shall neuer come to want.

    Maid. Oh! sweet my Lord, my brother do not force me,

To breake my faith or to a loathed bed.

    Ingen. Force you, he shall not, brother beare her

    hence,   125

Shee is my wife, and thou shalt finde my cause

Ten times improu'd now.

    Proud. Oh, haue at you Sir.

    Maid. Hold, hold for heauens sake, was e're wretched

    Lady   130

Put to this hazard? Sir, let me speake
But one word with him, and i'le goe with you,
And vndergoe, what euer you command.
   Proud. Doo't quickly, for I loue no whispering,
T'is strange to see you Madame with a sword,   135
You should haue come hither in your Ladies cloathes.
   Maid. Well, as you please my Lord, you are witnesse,
whatsoe're before
Hath past be twixt vs: thus I doe vndoe.
Were not I mad, to thinke thou could'st loue me   140
That would'st haue slain my Brother?
   Proud. Sai'st true sister.
   Ingen. Oh thou faire creature! wilt thou be as false
As other Ladies?
   Maid. Thou art my example,   145
Ile kisse thee once, farewell for euer, come
My Lord, now match me, with whom you please, a
     tumbler.
I must doe this, else had they fought againe.
   Proud. Mine own best Sister, farewel Master *Ingen.*   150
                          Ex. Proud. & Maid.
   Bro. Oh antient truth to be denied of no man,
An Eele by'th taile's held surer than a woman.   *Exeunt.*

Actus quintus, *[Scæna prima.]*

        Enter SVBTLE *with* HVSBAND.

   Subt. Shee is not to be cast.
   Husb. It cannot be:
Had you a wife, and I were in your case,   G3

I would be hang'd euen at the chamber doore   5
Where I attempted, but il'd lay her flat.

Subt. Why tell me truely, would it please you best,
To haue her remaine chast, or conquered.

Husb. Oh friend twould do me good e'ne at the heart
To haue her ouercome, shee do's so brag   10
And stand vpon her chastitie forsooth.

Subt. Why then in plaine termes Sir, the fort is mine,
Your wife has yeelded, vp-tailes is her song,
The deed is done, come, now, be merrie man.

Husb. Is the deed done indeed? come, come, you jest,   15
Has my wife yeelded? is vptailes her song?
Faith come, in prose, how got you to the matter first, ha?
Pish, you are so bashfull now.

Subt. Why, by my troth i'le tell you, because you are
my friend, otherwise you must note it is a great hurt to   20
the art of whooremasterie to discouer, besides the skill
was neuer mine o' th price.

Husb. Very good, on sir.

Subt. At the first she was horrible stiffe against me,
then Sir I tooke her by the hand, which I kiss'd.   25

Husb. Good Sir.

Subt. And I cal'd her pretie Rogue, and I thrust my
finger betwixt her breasts, and I made lips; at last, I
pul'd her by the chin to me, and I kist her.

Husb. Hum, very good.   30

Subt. So at the first, she kist very strangely, close,
& vntoward; then said I to her, thinke but vpon the
wrongs, the intollerable wrongs, the rogue your Husband
does you.

Husb. I that was very good, what said she to you   35
then sir?

Subt. Nay, I went on. First quoth I, thinke how he
hath vs'd you, left you no meanes, giuen all your clothes

to his Punckes, struck you, turn'd your gray eies into
black ones, but yet——   40

Husb. (A pretie conceit.)

Subt. Quoth I, these things are nothing in the Rascoll, thinke but what a base Whoore-master, the Rascoll is.

Husb. Did you call me Rascoll so often are you sure.   45

Subt. Yes, and oftner, for said I, none comes amisse
to   [G3ᵛ]   the rogue, I haue knowne him quoth I, do
three lowzy beggars vnder hedges in the riding of ten
mile, and I swore this to.

Husb. Twas verie well, but you did lie. On pray.   50

Subt. Pish, one must lie a little, now sir by this time
shee began to kisse some what more openly, and famil-
iarlie, her resistance began to slacken, and my assault
began to stiffen, the more her Bulwarke decai'd, the
more my batterie fortified, at last sir, a little fumbling   55
being past to make the Conquest more difficult, shee
perceauing my artillerie mounted, fals me flat vpon her
backe, cries mee out aloud

Ahlas I yeeld, vse me not roughly friend,

My fort, that like *Troy* towne, ten yeares hath stood   60

Beseig'd and shot at did remaine vnwon:

But now tis conquer'd. So the deede was done.

Husb. Then came the hottest seruice. Forward with
your tale sir.

Subt. Nay *Caetera, quis nescit? lassi requieuimus ambo:*   65
Proueniant medii sic mihi saepe dies.

Husb. Which is as much to say: I am a Cuckold, in all
Languages, but sure tis not so, It is impossible my wife
should yeeld.

Subt. Hoyday, ene now, it was impossible she should   70
hold out, and now it is impossible she should yeeld,
stay you but heere & be an eare witnes to what followes,

Ile fetch your wife.—— I know he will not stay.   *Exit.*
Husb. Good faith Sir but he will.
I doe suspect some knauerie in this.   75
Here will I hide my selfe, when thought as gone,
If they doe ought vnfitting I will call
Witnesse, and straight way sue a diuorce.   *Exit.*
               Enter WIFE *and* SVBTILL.
   Subt. I knew hee would not stay. Now noble Mistrisse,   80
I claime your promise.
   Wife. What was that good seruant?
   Subt. That you would lie with me.
   Wife. If with anie man,
But prithee first consider with thy selfe   85
If I should yeeld to thee, what a load thy Conscience   [G4ʳ]
Would beare about it, for I wish quick thunder
May strike me, if I yet haue lost the truth,
Or whitenesse of the hand I gaue in Church,
And twill not be, thy happinesse (as thou think'st)   90
That thou alone should'st make a woman fall,
That did resist all else, but to thy soule
A bitter Corasiue, that thou didst staine,
Vertue that else had stood immaculate,
Nor speake I this, as yeelding vnto thee,   95
For tis not in thy power, wert thou the sweet'st
Of natures Children, and the happiest,
To conquer me, nor in mine owne to yeeld,
And thus it is with euery pious wife.
Thy daylie railing at my absent Husband   100
Makes me indure thee worse, for let him doe
The most preposterous ill relishing things
To me, they seeme good, since my Husband does 'em,
Nor am I to reuenge or gouerne him,
And thus it should be with all vertuous Wiues.   105
   Subt. Poxe a this vertue and this chastetie,

Doe you know faire Mistresse, a young Gentleman
About this towne cald *Bould,* where did he lie
Last night, sweet Mistris, oh oh, are you catch'd,
I saw him slip out of the house this morne,   110
As naked as this truth, and for this cause
I haue tould your Husband that you yeelded to me,
And he I warrant you, will blaze it thoroughly;
As good doe now then as bee thought to doe.
   Wife. No, twill not be yet, thou iniurious man,   115
How wilt thou right me in my Husbands thoughts,
That on a false surmise, and spight has tould,
A tale to breed vncurable discontent?
Bould was that ould wench that did serue the Widdow,
And thinking by this way to gaine her loue   120
Mist of his purpose, and was thus cashier'd,
Nor cares shee to proclame it to the world.
   Subt. Zoons, I haue wrong'd you Mistris. On my
     knees   *Kneels.*
I aske you pardon, and will neuer more,   [G4ᵛ]
Attempt your puritie, but neglect all things
Till that foule wrong I haue bred in your Knight
I haue expeld, and set your loues aright.   ⌜*Enter Husb.*⌝
   Husb. Which now is done alreadie Madame, wife,
                    Kneeles. 130
Vpon my knees, with weeping eies, heau'd hands,
I aske thy pardon, oh sweet vertuous creature,
I prithee breake my head.
   Wife. Rise, rise, Sir pray:
You haue done no wrong to me, at least I thinke so;   135
Heauen hath preuented all my iniurie,
I doe forgiue and marrie you a new.
Come, we are all inuited to the weddings,
The Ladie *Honor* to the old rich *Count,*
Yong *Bould* vnto another Gentlewoman,   140

We and the Widdow are inuited thither,
Embrace and loue, henceforth more really,
Not so like worldlings.
 Husb. Heere then ends all strife.
Thus false friends are made true, by a true wife. *Exeunt.*   145

Actus quintus, Scæna secunda.

 Enter old COVNT *wrapt in furs, the* MAID *drest
like a Bride, the* Lord PROVD., WEL-TRI'D, BOVLD,
leading* FEE-SIMPLE *like a Ladie masqu'd,* HVSBAND,
WIFE, SVBTLE, WIDDOW; *to them*
BROTHER, *with a letter,* SELDOM, *and* GRACE.   5

 Bro. Health and all joy vnto this faire assemblie,
My brother, who last tide is gone for *France,*
A branch of willow feathering his hat,
Bad me salute you Ladie, and present you
With this same letter written in his blood,   10
He prayes no man, for his sake euermore
To credit woman, nor no Ladie euer
To beleiue man, so either sexe shall rest
Vniniur'd by the other, this is all,
And this I haue deliuer'd.   15
 Proud. I and well,
You pronounce rarely, did you neuer play?
 Bro. Yes, that I haue, the foole, as some Lords doe.
 Welt. Set forward there.
 Count. Oh, oh, oh, a pox a this cold.   H
 Welt. A cold a this poxe you might say, I am a feard.
 Maid. How full of ghastly wounds this letter shewes,
 oh, oh.   *Swoones.*

Proud. Looke to my sister.

Bould. S'hart the Ladie swoons.   25

Wife. Strong-water there.

Fees. If strong breath would recouer her, I am for her.

Count. Ahlas good Ladie, hum, hum, hum.

                              Coughs perpetually.

Subt. He has fet her againe with coughing.   30

Maid. Conuey me to my bed, send for a Priest

And a Physition, your Bride I feare,

In stead of *Epithalamions* shall neede

A Dirge, or Epitaph, oh lead me in,

My bodie dies for my soules periur'd sinne.   35

        Exit MAID, GRACE, WIFE, HVSB., SVBTLE.

Bould. Hymen comes towards vs in a mourning robe.

Welt. I hope friend, we shall haue the better day.

Proud. I'le fetch the Parson and Physition. *Exit Proud.*

Bro. They are both readie for you.   *Exit Bro.*   40

Welt. Madam, this is the Gentlewoman,

Who something bashful does desire your pardon,

That shee does not vnmasque.

Widow. Good Master *Wel-tri'd*, I would not buie her

face, and for her manners if they were worse, they shall   45

not displease me.

Welt. I thanke your Ladyship.

Fees. Looke, how the old Asse my father stands, he

looks like the Beare in the play, he has kil'd the Ladie

with his verie sight as God helpe me, I haue the most to   50

do to forbeare vnmasquing me, that I might tell him his

owne, as can be.

Bould. Fie, by no meanes. The Widdow comes

towards you.

Count. Oh, oh, oh, oh.   55

Widow. Seruant, God giue you joy, and Gentlewoman,

Or Ladie as full joy, I wish to you,

Nor doubt that I will hinder you, your loue,
But heere am come to doe all curtesie
To your faire selfe, and husband that shall be.   60
 Fees. I thank you heartilie.
 Welt. S'hart, speak smaller man.
 Fees. I thanke you heartilie.   [H1ᵛ]
 Count. You're going to this geere to Mʳ. *Bould,* vm,
vm, vm.   65
 Bould. Not to your couching geere my Lord, though
I be not so olde, or rich as your Lordship, yet I loue a
yong wench as well.
 Welt. As well, as my Lord, nay by my faith, that you
do not, loue a yong wench as well as he, I wonder you   70
will be vnmannerly to say so.
 Count. Faith Master *Wel-tri'd,* troth is I loue them
well, but they loue not me, vm, vm, vm, you see, what
ill luck, I haue with them, vmp, vmp, vmp, a poxe a this
cold still say I.   75
 Welt. Where got you this cold my Lord? it can get in
no where that I can see, but at your nostrels, or eies,
all the other parts are so barricado'd with furre.
 Fees. It got in at his eies, and made that birdlime
there where *Cupids* wings doe hang intangled.   80
 Count. Is this your wife, that (vm, vm, vm) shall be,
Ma. *Bould,* i'le be so bould as kisse her.
  WIDOW *and* BOVLD *whisper aside.*
  COVNT *sits in a chaire and fals a sleepe.*
 Fees. Sir, forbeare, I haue one bould enough to kisse   85
my lips, oh olde coxcombe, kisse thine owne naturall
sonne, t'is worse then a Iustices lying with his own
daughter, but Mʳ. *Wel-tri'd* when will the Widdow
breake this matter to me?
 Welt. Not till the very close of all, she dissembles   90
it yet, because my Lord your Father is heere, and her

other suitor *Bould.*

   Fees. That's all one, he's o'th plot a my side.

   Widow. T'is needlesse Master *Bould,* but I will doe

Any thing you require to satisfie you, 95

Why should you doubt, I will forbid the banes,

For so your friend, heere tould me? I should rather

Doubt that you will not marrie.

   Bould. Madam by heauen,

As fully I am resolu'd to marry now, 100

And will to, if you doe not hinder it,

As euer louer was, only because

The World has taken notice of some passage

Twixt you and me, and then to satisfie

My sweetheart heere, who poore soule is a feard, 105

To haue some publike disgrace put vpon her, H2

I doe require some small thing at your hands.

   Widow. Well, I will doe it, and this professe besides,

Married, you shall as welcome be to mee

As mine owne brother, and your selfe faire Ladie, 110

Euen as my selfe, both to my boord, and bed.

   Welt. Ah, ah, how like you that?

   Fees. Now she begins,

Abundant thanks vnto your widdow-hood.

Z'oones my Fathers a sleepe on's wedding day. 115

I wonder'd where his cough was all this while.

   Enter INGEN *like a Doctor:* A PARSON, BROTHER,
      PROVDLY, SELDOME, GRACE, HVS-
        BAND, WIFE, *and* SVBTLE.

   Ingen. I pray forbeare the chamber, noise does hurt 120
   her.

Her sickenesse I ghesse rather of the minde

Than of her bodie, for her pulse beates well,

Her vitall functions not decaid a whit,

But haue their naturall life and operation. 125

My Lord, be cheer'd, I haue an ingredient
About me, shall make her well I doubt not.
In Master Parson, it shall be yours I pray,
The soules Physition should haue still the way.

      [Exit Ingen; Parson shuts the doore. 130
Widow. How cheeres she pray?
Wife. In troth exceeding ill.
Grace. A verie weake woman indeed she is, and surely
I thinke cannot scape it.
Husb. Did you marke how she ey'de the Physition? 135
Wife. Oh God I, she is very loath to die.
Grace. I that's n'ere the better signe, I can tell you.
Subt. And when the Parson came to her, she turn'd
away, and still let the Physition hold her by the hand.
Proud. But see what thought the Bride-groome takes, 140
my conscience knowes now, this is a most præposterous
match, yet for the commoditie, we winck at all incon-
ueniencie. My Lord, my Lord.
Count. Vmp, vmp, vmp, I beshrow you for waking
of me, now shall I haue such a fit of coughing, hum, 145
hum ——
Bould. Oh haplesse wife, that shall haue thee, that
either [H2ᵛ]   must let thee sleepe continually, or be
kept waking her selfe by the cough.
Widow. You haue a proper Gentleman to your sonne, 150
my Lord, he were fitter for this yong Ladie than you.
Welt. D'ee marke that againe?
Fees. Oh sweet widdow.
Count. He a wife, he a fooles head of his owne.
Fees. No, of my Fathers. 155
Count. What should he doe with a vmp, vmp?
Wife. What with a cough? why he would spit, and
that's more than you can doe.
Proud. Your bride my Lord is dead.

Count. Marrie, e'ne God be with her, griefe will 160
not helpe it, vmp, vmp, vmp.

Bro. A most excellent spouse.

Proud. How fares she M^r. Doctor? Z'oons, ⎧*Looks in*
   whats here?   ⎨*at the*
Bould, Widow, Welt., Fees. Hoy-day.   ⎩*window.* 165
Husb., Wife, Seld., Grace, Subt. How now?

Fees. Looke, looke, the Parson joynes the Doctors hand
& hers; now the Do. kisses her by this light. [*Omnes whoop.*
Now goes his gowne off, hoy-day, he has read breeches
on: Z'oones, the Physition is got o'th top of her, be like 170
it is the mother she has, harke the bed creakes.

Proud. S'hart, the doores fast, break 'em open, we
are betrai'd.

Bro. No breaking open doores, he that stirs ⎧*Draws &*
   first   ⎨*holds out* 175
I'le pop a leaden pill into his guts   ⎩*a pistoll.*
Shall purge him quite away, no hast good friends,
When they haue done (whats fit) you shall not neede
To breake the door, thei'll open it them selues.

A curtaine drawne, a bed discouer'd, INGEN *with his sword* 180
   in his hand, and a Pistoll, the LADIE *in a peti-*
            coate, the PARSON.

Proud. Thy blood base villain shal ⎧*The Bros. set*
   answere this,   ⎨*back to back.*
I'le dye thy nuptiall bed in thy hearts gore. 185

Ingen. Come, come, my Lord, t'is not so easily done,
You know it is not. For this my attempt
Vpon your sister, before God and man   H3
She was my wife, and n'ere a bed-rid gowt
Shall haue my wench, to get diseases on.   190

Proud. Well mai'st thou tearme her so that has con-

sented,
Euen with her will to be dishonor'd.
   Ingen. Not so, yet haue I lyen with her.
   Maid. But first (witnesse this Priest) we both were   195
      married.
   Parson. True it is Domine.
Their contract's run into a marriage,
And that my Lord into a carriage.
   Proud. I will vndoe thee Priest.   200
   Parson. 'Tis to late,
I'm vndone alreadie, wine and Tobacco; I defie thee
Thou temporall Lord, *perdy* thou neuer shalt
Keepe me in jayle, and hence springs my reason,
My act is neither Felonie nor Treason.   205
   Fees. I Sir, but you do not know, what kindred she
may haue.
   Omnes. Come, come, there is no remedie.
   Wife. And weigh't right
In my opinion my honor'd Lord,   210
And euery bodies else, this is a match,
Fitter ten thousand times, than your intent.
   Omnes. Most certaine t'is.
   Widow. Besides, this Gentleman
Your brother in law well parted, and faire mean'd,   215
And all this come about (you must conceiue)
By your owne sisters wit as well as his.
   Ingen. Come, come, t'is but getting of me knighted
my Lord, and I shall become your Brother well enough.
   Proud. Brother your hand, Lords may haue projects   220
      still,
But there's a greater Lord, will haue his will.
   Bould. This is dispatcht. Now Madam is the time,
For I long to be at it, your hand sweet heart.
   Fees. Now, boyes.   225

Widow. My Lord, and Gentlemen, I craue your wit-
nesse
To what I now shall vtter. 'Twixt this Gentleman
There has been some loue passages and my selfe,
Which heere I free him, and take this Ladie.   230
Welt. Law ye, and take this Ladie.
Widow. Which with a mothers loue, I giue to him,
And wish all joy may crowne their marriage.   [H3ᵛ]
Bould. Nay Madame, yet she is not satisfied.
BOVLD *giues her a ring, and she puts it on her thumb.*   235
Widow. Further, before yee all I take this ring
As an assumpsit, by the vertue of which
I bind my selfe in all my lands and goods,
That in his choice, i'le be no hinderance:
Or by forbidding banes, or claiming him   240
My selfe for mine, but let the match goe on
Without my check, which he intendeth now.
And once again I say, I bind my selfe.
Bould. Then once again, I say, widdow thou 'rt mine:
Priest marrie vs, this match I did intend,   245
Yee are all witnesses, if thou hinder it,
Widdow your lands and goods are forfeit mine.
Widow. Ha, nay take me to, since there's no remedie,
Your Widdow (without goods) sels scuruilie.
Omnes. Whoop, God giue you joy.   250
Count. S'light, I am cozend of all sides, I had good
hope of the Widdow my selfe, but now I see euerie bodie
leaues me sauing vm, vm, vm.
Bould. 'Troth my Lord, & that will sticke by you I
warrant.   255
Widow. But how Sir, shall we salue this Gentle-
woman?
Bould. Hang her whoore.
Welt. Fie, you are too vnciuill.

Fees. Whoore in thy face, I doe defie thy taunts.   260
Bould. Nay hold faire Ladie, now I thinke vpon't.
The old *Count* has no wife, lets make a match.
Omnes. If he be so contented.
Count. With al my heart.
Bould. Then kisse your Spouse.   265
Count. S'foot she has a beard: how now, my sonne?
Omnes. T'is the Lord *Fee-simple.* [*Fees. vnmasques.*
Fees. Father, lend me your sword, you and I are made
a couple of fine fooles, are we not? If I were not valiant
now, and meant to beate 'em all, heere would lie a   270
simple disgrace vpon vs, a *Fee-simple* one indeed, marke
now what i'le say to 'em, d'ee heare my Masters, Dam-me,
yee are all the sonne of a whoore, and ye lie, and I
will make it good with my sword, this is cal'd Roaring
Father .   275
Subt. I'le not meddle with you Sir.   [H4r1
Proud. You are my blood.
Welt. And I flesht you, you know.
Bould. And I haue a charge comming, I must not fight
now.   280
Fees. Has either of you any thing to say to me?
Husb. Not we Sir.
Fees. Then haue I something to say to you. Haue you
any thing to say to me?
Bro. Yes marrie haue I Sir.   285
Fees. Then I haue nothing to say to you, for that's
the fashion, Father if you will come away with your
cough, doe. Let me see how many challenges must I get
writ: You shall heere on me beleiue it.
Proud. Nay, wee'le not now part angrie, stay the   290
Feasts
That must attend the weddings, you shall stay.
Fees. Why, then all friends, I thought you would not

haue had the manners to bid vs stay dinner neither.

    Husb. Then all are friends, and Ladie, wife, I crowne   295
Thy vertues with this wreath, that 'tmay be said,
There's a good wife.

    Bould. A Widdow.   ⌠*They set Girlonds*
    Ingen. And a Maid.   ⌡*on their heads.*

    Wife. Yet mine is now approu'd the happiest life,   300
Since each of you hath chang'd to be a wife.   *Exeunt.*

FINIS.

IV. EXPLANATORY NOTES

IV. EXPLANATORY NOTES

1. WEATHER-COCKE

Title-page

1–3.] A proverb to the popularity of which Field's use of it as title here may have contributed; see *SFQ*, X (1946), 11. Throughout these notes Field's proverbs and proverbial lore are identified by numbers assigned them in the *SFQ* article, thus: "(Field, 54)." See that article for references to the standard works on the proverb, parallel passages, and further comment. Of this proverb, Apperson (703f.) lists no example prior to 1633; but if *Against Women Unconstant* be Chaucer's, Chaucer had applied the weathercock metaphor to the fickleness of women [*Works*, ed. F. N. Robinson (Boston, 1933), 636], as had Henryson [*Poems*, ed. G. Gregory Smith (Edinburgh, 1908), III, 23], Greene [*Works*, ed. A. B. Grosart (London, 1881–1883), VI, 76], and Middleton [*Works*, ed. A. H. Bullen (London, 1885–1886), *The Family of Love* (1602), 1.2.58f. and 2.4.30f.].

6. *White-Hall*] "You must no more call it York Place. That's past," we are told in *Henry VIII* (1613),

> For since the Cardinal fell that title's lost.
> 'Tis now the King's, and call'd Whitehall.   (4.1.95ff.)

James I's London palace, also called Westminster.

8. *White-Friers*] The Whitefriars theatre was located in the precinct of the dissolved monastery of the White or Carmelite Friars, which until 1608 was, like the nearby Blackfriars, a liberty. The theatre was remodeled from the Great Hall of the house which Michael Drayton and Thomas Woodford had leased from Robert, Lord Buckhurst, for the unlucky King's Revels company (Adams, 311f.). Adams (p. 312) estimates the size of the playhouse as "approximately thirty-five feet in width and eighty-five feet in length." The theatre was occupied during 1607–1609 by the Children of the King's Revels (Hillebrand, 221), during 1609–1613 by Rosseter's, or the Second, Queen's Revels children (Chambers, II, 516).

8f. *Children of her Maiesties Reuels*] On the history of this, the second company of that name, see Murray, I, 357–360; Chambers, II, 56–61, and Hillebrand, 237–252. According to the actor-list to *Epicoene*, the company included Field, William Barksted, Giles Carey, William Penn, Hugh Attawell, Richard Allen, John Smith, and John Blaney; according to that to *The Coxcomb*, also Joseph Taylor, Emanuel Read, and Robert Benfield.

13.] Juvenal *Sat.* i. 79.

14.] McKerrow 283 [*Printers' & Publishers' Devices in England and Scotland 1485–1640* (London, 1913), 110]. The motto, *Heb Ddieu heb ddim*, "Without God, without anything," is part of a Welch proverb. McKerrow, who lists no use of this device between 1610 when it appeared in Elyot's *The Castle of Health* and 1615 when Jaggard used it in *This World's Folly*, states that its intermediate history is obscure. Greg, however, states without elaboration that the printer of *Weather-cocke* 1612 "appears from the device to have been William Jaggard" (*Bibl. Dram.*, 438). In the question of who printed *Weather-cocke*, one should give little weight to the evidence of the device until its ownership in 1612 is established. The device is of further interest because of its use in the 1619 quartos of Shakespeare and the quartos of that year misdated 1600 and 1608; see W. J. Neidig, *MP*, VIII (1910), 145–163.

15. *Budge*] From 1606 till his death in 1625, John Budge was a bookseller specializing in theological literature. From 1609 to 1615 he sold at the locations here specified; see McKerrow, *A Dictionary of Printers & Booksellers . . . 1557–1640* (London, 1910), 54.

16. *Paules*] The churchyard of the old St. Paul's Cathedral was once headquarters of the book trade; see Stow, *A Survey of London* [ed. Charles L. Kingsford (Oxford, 1908)] I, 338. "I could now fetch you about noone," writes Dekker, ". . . and carry you with mee into *Paules Church-yard*; where planting your selfe in a Stationers shop, many instructions are to bee giuen you, what bookes to call for, how to censure of new bookes, how to mew at the old. . ." [*Guls Horne-booke, Non-Dramatic Works*, ed. A. B. Grosart (London, 1884–1886), II, 265].

16f. *Brittaines Bursse*] i. e., the New Exchange in the Strand, opened by James I 10 April 1609; see *SE*, II, 176.

Dramatis personae

1. *Bellafront*] The name had been used for the title character of Dekker and Middleton's *I The Honest Whore* (1604) and *II The Honest Whore* (1605) [Dekker, *Dramatic Works*, ed. R. H. Shepherd (London, 1873)]. Despite the fact that the original Bellafront is reclaimed, Field may have gained satirical point by calling the chief woman of *Weather-cocke* Bellafront.

2. *Worldly*] Following the morality tradition and Jonson, Field gives many of his characters characterizing names. He seems to have reversed the reasoning of this character, "*Worldly's* my Name, *Worldly* must be my deeds" (1.2.319).

3. *Lucida*] cf. Latin *lux*. Not until a considerably later date was *Lucida* used in astronomy to refer to the brightest star in a constellation; *NED*, *s. v. Luce* is the name of the rich and beautiful woman loved by Humphrey in *Knight of the Burning Pestle* (1607), in which Field probably played Humphrey.

4. *Scudmore*] cf. *Scudamour*, the shield of love, in *The Faerie Queene*, Book IV.

Lady Ninnie] Abraham is not "the one and onely *Ninnie*" (1.2.167) of this house. Sir Innocent and his lady, too, are characterized by their surname, i. e., *simpleton* or *fool*.

5. *Strange*] Unlike most citizens, whom "the Playes flout still" (2.1. 276), Strange not only hopes to live to see the day his story will be shown to people in a play (5.2.230f.) but shows himself something of a playwright in withholding the explanation of his "other course" (3.1.23), in disguising himself as his "murderer" (3.4 and 4.2) for the purpose of proving Pouts a liar, and by extracting the utmost theatrical value from his disguise by prolonging his "guilt" to such an extent that one questions his motivation (5.2.157f. and exp. n.). Here Field seems to be violating character for the sake of theatrical values.

Wagtayle] A common seventeenth-century nickname for courtesan. Cf. *Michaelmas Term* (1606), 3.1.211 and *A Trick to Catch the Old One* (1605), 2.1.84.

6. *Pendant*] An obviously appropriate name for him who lives "vpon commending my Lord" (2.2.91).

7. *Powts*] A characterizing name for a sullen, vindictive captain of *miles gloriosus* descent. In Pouts, Field has been thought "to have had Master Stephen of *Every Man in His Humour* in mind" (Brinkley, 74).

Page] One of Field's most effective characters. He had appeared frequently in Italian comedy, in Lyly, and in various later plays for boy companies. And "even companies composed of adult actors," as Creizenach says (p. 310), "were only too ready to seize upon so telling a contrast as that, for instance, between the great mountain of flesh, Falstaff, and his tiny shield-bearer."

8. *Innocent*] The father of the Ninny family is a fool by both names.

9. *Sir Abraham*] This given name, too, probably suggested idiocy; cf. the discharged bedlamites, Abraham-men, described by Dekker in *The Belman of London* (*Non-Dramatic Works*, III, 101f.). In Sir Abraham Field presents his most noteworthy satirical portrait of the new nobility. Part of the effect is due to Abraham's use of proverbs and proverbial phrases; see exp. n. to 2.1.331ff. Sir Abraham, as Brinkley (p. 74) points out, "is a queer combination of Sir Amorous La-Foole and Master Matthew."

To any Woman

1f. *to any Body*] Field was preceded in the witticism of this epistle by Marston, who had dedicated *Antonio and Mellida* (1599) "to the onely rewarder, and most just *poiser of vertuous merits, the most honor*ably renowned No-body . . ." [*Plays*, ed. H. Harvey Wood (Edinburgh and London, 1934–1938), I, 2] and by John Day, who had dedicated *Humour Out of Breath* (1608) to "Signior No-body" [ed. Arthur Symons, in *Nero and Other Plays*], p. 271.

2. *forty shillings*] This passage has been used as evidence that this sum was an author's usual reward for a dedication; Malone Var., III, 163f., n. 1; Phoebe Sheavyn, *The Literary Profession in the Age of Elizabeth* (Manchester, 1909), 26, n. 1.

11. *my next Play*] i.e., *Amends*. Whether or not he so intended, Field has here asked woman to be constant for six years, *Amends* having been first printed in 1618.

13f. *without a Latine sentence*] Assuming an amused and amusing contempt for learning which he may have felt appropriate from a dashing young actor, Field here probably does not express his true attitude toward Latin. As Verity pointed out, Field "seems to have rather piqued himself on his knowledge of Latin" (p. 338, n. 3). See To the Reader, 14 and *W* 2.2.49f. and exp. nn. Dean Brinkley observes in a letter: "It is an interesting note of satire on woman" that in this dedication "To any Woman" there is no Latin, while in that "To the Reader" Juvenal is quoted. Speaking of Field's knowledge of Latin, Verhasselt (p. 494) reports that Field employs "many Latin stage directions." Except in the opening of *W*, I find comparatively few.

To the Reader

1. *the Sale-man*] One of comparatively few references to the promotional aspect of Renaissance publishing.

5. *as I could then make*] This evidence reinforces the dating of the play three years before its publication. See above, *W* Intro., i. In 1609 Field was not over twenty-two years old.

8f. *Mirrour of mens liues and actions*] With good Renaissance critical doctrine Field comes to the rescue of plays and players. Later he was to defend the quality against Sutton. The fact that the mirror figure occurs in a number of other places renders not at all sure the claim that here Field is paralleling *Hamlet* 3.2.22ff. (McGinn, 160).

11. *Quales . . . Cluuienus*] Juvenal *Sat.* i. 80. Cluvienus was probably a poetaster of Juvenal's day.

14. *had enough in him*] As a pupil of Mulcaster's school, Field was doubtless introduced to Latin early. The extent of his reading, beyond selections from Horace and Martial (*Ben Jonson*, I, 137), is not known.

15. *vexed with vile playes my selfe*] In 1612, the probable date of composition of this epistle, Field had been an actor for twelve or thirteen of his twenty-five years. For a list of plays in which he had probably acted, see above, Gen. Intro., 1. It is not unlikely that he had heard many plays, also, of other companies than his own.

19. *for a yeare or two*] Chambers follows Verity in understanding from this passage that Field "did not mean to spend his life as a player" (III, 313). This was a satisfactory explanation when we still had to account for an early retirement from the stage. Verhasselt thinks (p. 501) that Field may be referring to his joining the Lady Elizabeth's men, March 1613. Adams' suggestion that "Possibly this reflects the failure of the managers [of the Whitefriars] to renew the lease" (p. 342, n. 1), which was to expire in 1614, may provide an explanation.

To his Loued Sonne

Sonne] Following contemporary custom (Malone Var., VIII, 314, n. 8), Chapman addresses Field as his son— a fact of possible significance to the relative influence of Chapman and Jonson upon Field (see *SAB*, XXI (1946), 84f. and above, Gen. Intro., 2). Jonson said that Field was his scholar, but not his son; Field was never sealed of Ben's tribe. The only person whom we know Field to have addressed as Father was Henslowe (Greg, *HP*, 84).

1. *many formes*] Fleay [*ES*, XIII (1889), 31] takes this line as an indication that by 1612 Field had written other works than comedy. The only other known works by that year are the commendatory verses to *Volpone* and *The Faithful Shepherdess*. Olliphant [*The Plays of Beaumont and Fletcher* (New Haven, 1927), 119] without giving evidence says that Field "would seem to have written tragedy, as well as comedy, by that date." It is more likely, I think, that Chapman here refers to Field's acting many types of roles or to his versatility in being both actor and playwright.

4. *Addition*] Mark of distinction.

Homers Sea-man] Probably Proteus, but possibly Odysseus himself.

1.1

Perhaps opens on the lower inner stage, with Scudmore going to the outer at 129, leaving Nevill the inner for his reading.

This scene has been thought to resemble *Every Man in His Humour*, 1.5 (Brinkley, 75) but is closer to the opening scene of *The Widow's Tears* (1605), in which Field probably had acted; see *SP*, XLIII (1946), 495. Paul V. Kreider [*Elizabethan Comic Character Conventions* (Ann Arbor, 1935), 12f.] describes "Direct Self-Characterization," here used by Scudmore, in the comedies of Chapman.

2. *ready*] Dressed.

15. Cf. Dorigen's vow in *Four Plays in One* (1612) and Martius' quotation of it (*Beaumont and Fletcher*, X, 304, 306).

Element of Fire] Bellafront seeks examples of remote contingencies in the medieval, remotely classical, doctrine of the four elements. High above the world were concentric zones of the purer elements, water, air, and—nearest the spheres of the planets and fixed stars—the zone of fire; see *Medieval Contributions to Modern Civilization*, ed. F. J. C. Hearnshaw (New York, 1922), 132–136. Bellafront, and indeed Field, seem unaware that "the Element of Fire is quite put out" [*Poems of John Donne*, ed. H. J. C. Grierson (Oxford, 1912), I, 237].

16. *Pyramids*] Referring to the aspiring shape of flames [cf. Milton's "Pyramid of fire," *Paradise Lost* II, 1013; *Works*, gen. ed. F. A. Patterson (New York, 1931)], Bellafront may mean "Sooner will flames burn downward instead of upward." More probably, however, she means "Sooner will the most aspiring element take the place of the least aspiring."

20. *exhalation*] Bellafront's final example of remote possibility is based upon the cosmological theory of the fixed stars; Hearnshaw, *op. cit.*, 136. She seems to mean, "Sooner shall stars, testimony of the order in the universe, fall like meteors, testimony of its disorder, than I be false."

22. *ought ne're*] i. e., *anything near*. It is possible that *ought* is the past tense of *owe, possess*, with inversion of sense, *belonged; NED, s.* ought v. A, I, i, b; if so, take the second *ne're* for a double negative.

44f.] One of many passages in Field reflecting his interest in the theatre. Noticing Scudmore's letter, Nevill paraphrases lines from an important scene in *The Spanish Tragedy:*

> Whats heere? a letter? tush, it is not so:
> A letter written to *Hieronimo.*
> *Works of Thomas Kyd*, ed. F. S. Boas (Oxford, 1901), 3.2.24f.

For another allusion by Field to this play see *W* 1.2.340ff. and exp. n. This is not the place to collect the many instances of imitation and burlesque of *The Spanish Tragedy* in Jacobean drama; for a few references see Kyd, *Works*, lxxxiii–xcvi.

56. *importance.*] I take as an interrupted rather than completed speech. See text. n.

68f. *friendship play with mine*] Cf. Ferdinand to Gerrard in *Four Plays in One* (1612): "or doth thy friendship play / (In this antipathous extreme) with mine" (*Beaumont and Fletcher*, X, 317).

75. *farewell worthy friend*] Nevill's pretenses of going and Scudmore's promptings to stay are repeated in *Amends*, 1.1.446 and *Four Plays in One* (*Beaumont and Fletcher*, X, 318).

90. *other*] i. e., *others'*.

passages] acts, happenings.

94. *reading*] H glosses as *advice*, but the word may be used generally for *a portion to be read.*

94f.] "nec te quaesiveris extra," Persius *Sat.* i. 7.

101. *Fayries Treasure*] This has been called a "rather rare figure" and the "only rare figure that Field uses" (Brinkley, 90, 64). Actually Nevill alludes to a tabu of folk literature, that against speaking while searching for treasure; see Stith Thompson, *Motif-Index of Folk Literature* (Bloomington, 1932–1936), C401.3. Brinkley notes the recurrence of the figure in *The Fatal Dowry* (1619), 4.1.197; and see Lockert's n. to that line.

104. *Continent*] That which contains. Cf. "Heart, once be stronger than thy continent," *Antony and Cleopatra* (1607), 4.14.40, and "you have over-charg'd my brest / With grace beyond my continence," *Four Plays in One* (*Beaumont and Fletcher*, X, 316).

109. *keepe thy secret*] Ferdinand similarly says to Gerrard: "thy bosom bindes some secret, / Which do not trust me with" (*Beaumont and Fletcher*, X, 318).

120. *waues*] figurative for *veins?* Mitford in the Folger copy of the play has underlined *waues* and written *veins* above.

121. *exhausted*] In the Latin sense, *drawn out*. Semen was thought to be drawn from the blood.

123. *two brethren*] the Gemini, Castor and Pollux.

126. *Cautelous*] *Deceitful*, a frequent meaning, is not the meaning here. Read *circumspect* or *heedful*.

127. *doubt, on likelyhoods*] doubt regarding the probable.

128. *exquire*] search out.

139ff.] This passage makes use of the folk beliefs that certain animals may be tamed by the beauty, royalty, or virginity of a lady; cf. Una and the lion. On the beliefs see Thompson, *Motif Index*, B771; E. Kölbing, *ES*, XVI (1892), 454ff.; and Arthur Dickson, *Valentine and Orson: A Study in Late Medieval Romance* (New York, 1929), 198, n. 86.

172. *spoake my heart in twaine*] This popular expression (cf. *Hamlet*, 3.4.156f. and *Widow's Tears*, 5.2.33) Field here uses seriously. He seems to ridicule it, however, in *W* 4.3.50f.

175. *the red burning Zone*] the sphere in which the sun moves; cf. "Singeing his pate against the burning zone," *Hamlet*, 5.1.305.

179. *the Temple*] The privileged district in southwest London containing the Inner, Middle, and Outer Temples, Inns of Court, "a whole Universitie, as it were, of students, practisers or pleaders and Iudges of the lawes of this realme" (Stow, *Survey*, I, 76).

181.] "Additional suggestions as to what the characters are to do upon the stage are given within the lines," Brinkley points out, citing this and the following line (p. 69).

191.] Note Field's use of proverbial matter for its epigrammatic value (Field. 13), and cf. *A*, 4.4.153.

1.2

Outer stage. Although the Count, Pouts, and Pendant comment on the approach of the Ninnies (139f.), nothing suggests that the guests are on a different stage. When the wedding music plays at the end of the act, perhaps all go in at the curtained center opening, but either side door would also serve.

The Fatal Dowry, 4.1 has been called "almost a replica" of this scene; Brinkley, 84.

1. *trussing*] tying the laces which fastened breeches to doublet.

15. *in print*] Proverbial (Field, 45). Frequently encountered in the early seventeenth century, in reference to the pleats of the ruff, the phrase usually means *perfectly*. Cf. *A* 3.3.92.

16. *the Pickadell*] "a wired or stiffened support of an erected band or broad collar worn in England from 1590 until about 1630" (Linthicum, 164).

18. *S. Georges sute*] a suit to wear at the splendid festival of St. George, 23 April; cf. modern *Easter bonnet*.

26.] The exit of the Tailor without protest involves a *reductio ad absurdum* of scenes in other plays treating the reluctance of gallants to pay tailors' bills; Creizenach, 142 and n. 3.

48. *vouchsafe reflection*] deign to glance at them.

52f.] Field here seems to be echoing Shakespeare's *Sonnet* XX: "Nature as she wrought thee fell a-doting."

55. *of a little man*] "Pendant has to flatter the Count by pretending that women always admire little men" (V, n.). The construction of *of* seems idiomatic.

61. *proud for her loue*] In the seventeenth century, *sexually excited*, used chiefly of female animals.

64. *wastcoate*] Among women, only strumpets appeared in waistcoats; Linthicum, 214.

67. *Pict-hatch*] A disreputable tavern in Turnmill Street, Clerkenwell, often referred to in literature of the period; see *The Alchemist* (1610), 2.1.62; *Merry Wives* (1600), 2.2.19, and Partridge, *s. v.* Cf. *Amends*, 2.2.100.

68f.] Cf. "Lest thou deare Lord (*Narcissus*-like) should doate / Vpon thyselfe, and dye" (*Fatal Dowry*, 4.1.72f.; cited by Brinkley, 90). Ovid *Meta.* iii 402ff.

71. *all one*] usually *all the same*, but here probably with double entendre in reference to the unity of Narcissus and his love.

77. *man of wax*] a "proper" man; cf. *Romeo and Juliet*, 1.3.76. Field uses the expression again in *A*, 3.3.99.

79. *Commendations*] "I do liue vpon commending my Lord" (2.2.90).

86. *commend*] A reference to the practice of ordering verses from a hack writer. To *commend* was apparently confused or blended with *to command* (*NED, s.* commend, v.), but this is certainly an unusual form of the past tense.

95. *pudding*] See Partridge, *s. v.*, 2. Verity (n.) glosses "a kind of sausage," after *H*, who had added (n.) "but here it seems to have an indelicate sense, which may be readily conjectured." In the face of so many possibilities, I must admit that the bawdy captain's exact meaning eludes me unless we admit that the imagery is much confused.

97. *case*] usually the *vulva;* but cf. the predicament of Lawrence of Lancashire, who by witchcraft was done "out of a doing case it seemes" [Thomas Heywood, *Dramatic Works*, ed. Pearson (London, 1874), IV, 232].

118. *a Bucket on's head*] with reference to the elaborate ruffs worn in England in Elizabethan and Jacobean times; Linthicum, 157ff. Since the ruff had been introduced from France, the reference to the *Italian* Taylour" here is not entirely clear. Collier notes that "nothing on the point is to be found in R. Armin's *Italian Taylor and his Boy*, 1609."

123. *cast*] dismissed. References to cast captains are frequent in Jacobean plays; but *cast* here, despite Maxwell, 21, does not indicate a military discharge. Pouts is dismissed by Kate and her father. *Cast* is apparently from *cassed*, past participle of *cass; NED, s.* cass, v., 2.

123f.] This mention of the disputes over the succession of Cleves, a duchy in Germany, furnishes us an anterior limit of date for *Weather-cocke*; see above, *W* Intro., i. "Would I had gone for *Cleeueland*" would seem to indicate that the English had left for participation in the war and that the war was still going on. See also *W*, 1.2.313.

135. *Law*] An exclamation giving emphasis to a following statement.

141. *Guesse*] An acceptable seventeenth-century plural for *guest*.

143.] Note the practical stagecraft in Field's method of introducing characters on their first entrance; cf. *Amends* 1.1.185ff. and *Four Plays in One* (*Beaumont and Fletcher*, X, 339). For Field's practice in this matter see *SP*, XLIII (1946), 492, n. 59.

149f. *like a Needle in a Bottle of Hay*] Proverbial (Field, 38) expression applied to a hopeless search. *Bottle* means *bundle*.

151.] Is this proverb (Field, 40) a suggestion also for Lady Ninny's make-up?

154. *backside*] Usually *back yard*, but possibly *the posteriors*.

Aqua-vitae] Any hard liquor, such as whisky or brandy.

165. *haue got him Knighted*] A satirical thrust at the lavish and indiscriminate creation of knights by James I. Within six weeks after he left Scotland to become England's king, James is said to have conferred knighthood on two hundred thirty-seven persons [John H. Jesse, *Memoirs of the Court of England during the Reign of the Stuarts* (London, 1855), I, 39; W. Kennett, *A Complete History of England* (London, 1706), I, 665]. Cf. *W* 3.4.13ff. and *A* 5.2.218f. Other satirical references in the drama may be found in *The Alchemist* (1610) 2.2.86ff. and *Epicoene* (1609) 1.4.60; *The Phoenix* (1604) 1.6.150f., *A Mad World My Masters* (1606) 1.1.64f., and *Michaelmas Term* (1606) 1.1.191ff. and 3.1.48ff.; *Bussy D'Ambois* (1604) 1.2.124, *Monsieur D'Olive* (1604) 1.1.264ff. and 4.2.76ff., and *Widow's Tears* (1605) 4.1.28; and elsewhere. James' making of knights in the early years of his reign is not to be confused with the sale of the Baronetcies in 1611 and after, to raise funds for the support of the army in Ireland (Gardiner, *op. cit.*, II, 111f.).

167. *run at Ring*] Innocent's choosing the pageant rather than combat field for his son's forthcoming exploits probably adds to the humor.

172. *how.*] Probably an exclamation rather than, like 1.1.56, an interrupted speech.

194. *Venison*] Then used for any wild animal killed in hunting, and regarded as choice meat.

195. *such Venison as a Beare is*] A further allusion to Lady Ninny's size? "Bears are very fat in the fall of the leaf, at which time they are excellent venison" (Josselyn, *New English Rarities* (London, 1672), 48; cited by *NED*, s. venison 1).

196. *Hart*] Buc, who licensed this play, often expunged "Sheart" and "Heart" in enforcement of James' statute of 1606 prohibiting the use in plays of the name of the Deity; see Virginia C. Gildersleeve, *Government Regulation of the Elizabethan Drama* (New York, 1908), 90, 111f. Neither

Weather-cocke nor *Amends* shows signs of having been shorn of oathes, which occur in Field frequently but I think without the variety which has been reported (Brinkley, 55).

Bumbard] A liquor jug or bottle; figuratively, the person who habitually employs such a jug.

201f.] In letting Sir Abraham furnish his pedigree, Field not only makes him out a fool but also satirizes pretenders to pedigree and the nobility generally; his ancestors were gentlemen all, and, according to Field, fools. Cf. *ninnyhammer, yellow-hammer, woodcock, gull,* and other bird names applied in this sense. Satire on pedigree and mock genealogies occur frequently in the drama; see *Every Man in His Humour* [1616], 1.4.10f., *Epicoene,* 1.4.37ff.; *An Humorous Day's Mirth,* Sc. 5, 88f., *The Gentleman Usher,* 1.1.152. Baskervill points out [*English Elements in Jonson's Early Comedy* (Austin, 1911), p. 132, n. 2] that Cob's mock genealogy has, besides classic, English precedents in *James IV, Dr. Faustus, Mucedorus,* and other plays.

203. *Knocker*] probably a double entendre. *Knocker* follows *Hammer* but also means "A (notable or frequent) performer of the sexual act" (Partridge, *s. v.*).

212. *the treason*] The celebrated Gunpowder Plot of 5 November 1605; see Gardiner, *op. cit.,* I, 234–264.

218ff.] Field enhances his satirical characterization of Sir Abraham by having him combine here two proverbial expressions (Field, 34 and 43).

226. *be couer'd*] One remained more than momentarily uncovered only at Court and in the presence of royalty; hats were worn at church and at meals; see *SE,* II, 109.

233. *with a Willow*] The willow was "worne of forlorne Paramours" (*Faerie Queene,* I, 1, 9:3); for a general account see John W. Draper, *The Funeral Elegy and the Rise of English Romanticism* (New York, 1929), 335–337. The willow is worn or referred to in *All Fools* (1604), 1.1.40, *3 Henry VI* (1591), 3.3.228, *Othello* (1604), 4.3.41ff., *The Maid's Tragedy* [*Beaumont and Fletcher,* I, 17] and *Amends,* 5.2.8. See also *W* 2.1.68.

240. *and I*] Unable to complete his rhyme, Abraham breaks off his verse and attempts to salvage his wit by the proverbial (Field, 46) juxtaposition of *rhyme* and *reason* in prose. Cf. *As You Like It* (1599), 3.2.416ff.

256–272.] This passage has been cited as an illustration of Field's "broken lines and rough, changing metre" (Brinkley, 61). ". . . The irregularity in metre often causes the verse to be very rough. It is necessary to do violence to the pronunciation of words in order to scan the line; often it is essential to slur several syllables" *(ibid.).* Three of the lines quoted, however (259, 261, 262), are lines which resulted from alterations in lineation by modern editors; and they account in part for the roughness charged. Field's metrics, which have not been studied in a critical edition, may be of some importance in the study of Field as a collaborator.

258.] Kate's forthrightness elsewhere leads me to reject the interpretation of H and V that this speech is an aside.

272. *Tumbler*] In cant, a decoy for swindlers or card-sharpers.

Coney] In calling Kate this, and Strange a tumbler, Worldly was being facetious.

273. *old fellow*] used contemptuously, of persons of little worth.

278. *no Soldiers*] Those who pretended to be veterans were common in Elizabethan life and literature; Malone Var., XVII, 80, n. 3. Cf. *W*, 1.2.286.

284. *standing*] standing-room.

287. *Whose standings pay for them*] probably *who live on their names as soldiers*.

288. *Pedler*] an incompetent.

289. *Pot-gun*] a braggart.

290. *Iron Tale*] Used in relation to a threatened kicking?

298. *change*] The old, as distinguished from the new, Royal Exchange; see exp. n. to *W* t.–p., 16f.

300. *or*] The conservative editor can hardly emend (see text. n.) since the lines are explicable. Pouts has threatened Strange, who replies, elliptically, "You will make good that threat as quickly as you would kiss a firing cannon or do anything else you talk about doing." The transition is from particular to general.

306. *disposition*] mental constitution.

313. *Cleeueland*] The Duchy of Cleves; cf. *W* 1.2.123f. and exp. n. The allusion here seems to mean that Pouts is expected to serve in the war but has not yet done so. Perhaps Kate would not want her words interpreted literally; very likely she means only that Pouts as a professional soldier will frequently be off fighting somewhere.

314. *hot shots*] those who shoot "hotly"; cf. "trigger-happy."

340ff.] A clever parody on some famous lines. See Thomas Watson, *'Ekatompathia: or Passionate Centurie of Loue* (Manchester, 1869), *Sonnet* 47, 5f.; *The Spanish Tragedy*, 2.1.9f.; *Poetaster*, 3.4.215–222. The device of having a character recognize quoted verses has been attributed to Jonson (Brinkley, 75). Kate detects Abraham's plagiarism of Kyd (323), but no one detects Field's of Jonson. A list of attractions, mentioning eyes, chin, cheek, body, and leg, similar to Abraham's here, appears also in *Four Plays in One* [X, 300]. Field enhances the humorous effect of this parody by having the Count, Pendant, Strange, Worldly, and even Lucida herself join in the fun (344–352). This device makes possible, too, what may be satire on Kyd's Senecan stichomythia.

367f. *round Breeches*] Trunk or French breeches, fashionable ca. 1558 and by the date of *W* becoming unfashionable; Linthicum, 205f.

368. *sound*] swoon, faint.

250   THE PLAYS OF NATHAN FIELD

371. *Plum-tree*] In reference to its crooked shape; cf. *Duchess of Malfi*, 1.1.30f. [*Works*, ed. F. L. Lucas (Boston, 1928)].

380. *Vniuersitie*] "The subsequent reference to Babram" (391), if the name of that village was not inserted for the rhyme, "points to Cambridge" (*V*, n.). On early football see *SE*, II, 462f.

381. *Verse vaine*] i.e., his speaking in verse, 339ff., *passim*.

383. *off Garters blew*] Abraham here rejects the color language by which the servant conversed with his lady; Linthicum, 24–29, 263. Abraham's behavior and some of his ideas here are repeated in *The Queen of Corinth* (1617), VI, 50 (noted by Brinkley, 112).

387. *greene Shoo-strings*] One of the conventional insignia of lovers; Linthicum, 32.

390. *Thankes gentle Dublet*] Apparently a suggestion in the lines of the actor's vaudeville-like business.

391. *Babram*] Parish and village six and one-half miles southeast of Cambridge.

2.1

Nevill walks before the church doors, which with theatrical propriety could well have been the curtained aperture between outer and inner stages. This position would give most prominence to the two most theatrical pieces of business in the scene, Scudmore's challenging of Bellafront (140f.) as she enters the church and Pouts' slander of Kate (236ff.) as she leaves. It would afford sufficient room, too, I think, for the wedding processional (116ff.) and recessional (222ff.).

7ff.] This passage has been cited in illustration of Field's use of "very awkward parenthetical exposition or an explanatory aside, instead of revising what has already been written" (Brinkley, 62f.). But see exp. n. to *A*, 4.4.149.

23f.] Despite his use of proverbial lore (Field, 12) to win credence, this passage is evidence that Field, when pressed, cared less for consistency of characterization than for theatrical effect. Nevill's whole plan (2–22), outside the theatre, is somewhat unconvincing. A true friend would more likely have shared his plans with the troubled lover. But by the ruse here explained, Field is able to make Nevill's disguise work double deception—on the wedding party and on Scudmore. This soliloquy carefully outlines the plan to the audience at the outset; for Field that much, at any rate, can be said.

25. *in Tawny*] conventionally worn by the rejected lover; Linthicum, 26, 47—but line 26 here glosses 25.

46.] An interrupted speech was sometimes so punctuated; cf. *W* 1.1.164.

57. *word*] A seventeenth-century variant of *world*; cf. *A* 2.2.105.

58. *loose my selfe*] Perhaps this statement is sufficient evidence that the sense of 56f. was intended to be left incomplete.

60.] Descriptive of Nevill's business during Scudmore's long speech.

80. *contracted*] i.e., by the institution of pre-contract; Powell, 16–18

89. *faire pull on't*] Irony for the purpose of satirizing law.

92. *Pancridge Parson*] A contemptuous term for convenient clergyman; cf. *A Fair Quarrel*, 5.1.374. Sir Hugh in Jonson's *Tale of a Tub* is *"Vicar of* Pancrace." *Pancridge* is a corruption of *St. Pancras*, an unsavory suburb south of Cheapside and east of St. Paul's.

96.] Probably an aside.

116ff.] For stage purposes Field departs from the typical wedding procession of his day in that the brides here accompany the grooms rather than meet them at the church porch, and that the bride's father here leads the procession rather than follows the bride and attendants at some distance; see J. C. Jeaffreson, *Brides and Bridals* (London, 1872), I, 88ff. The full but unliterary stage direction here, with its apparent breaking of the procession into groups for the stage picture, seems to be descriptive of actual performance and may have bearing on the nature of the copy furnished the printer of *W* 1612.

119. *W. P.*] Probably *Worldly* and *Parson* rather than *Waits Playing*, as C conjectured; or *Wedding Party*, which Verity adopted as his reading; or *William Penn*, the proposal of W. J. Lawrence (*TLS*, 12 July 1928, 520); see *TLS*, 16 February 1946, 84.

136.] Neither Bullen [*Lyrics from the Dramatists of the Elizabethan Age* (London, 1901), 173] nor Edward Bliss Reed [*Songs from the British Drama* (New Haven, 1925), 122] notes the inappropriateness of this song to the marriages of the Worldly daughters (cf. 123f.) though at least Reed attempts to furnish some context.

160. *in Posse*] *in possible being*, a legal term usually applied to a child not yet born.

166f. *one . . . the other*] i. e., *law* and *conscience*.

167. *wilde Virginia*] Besides its role as "Earth's onely Paradise" [Drayton, *Works*, ed. J. William Hebel (Oxford, 1931–1941), II, 363] Virginia, often mentioned in Jacobean literature, like other distant lands stood for "hardship, for everything knotty, objectionable, unattainable" [R. R. Cawley, *Unpathed Waters: Studies in the Influence of the Voyagers on Elizabethan Literature* (Princeton, 1940), 161].

179. *Intrant Templum*] That is, as Collier notes, all go in except Kate, Strange, and Scudmore.

189. *tis so*] Hazlitt and Verity take as an answer to Strange's line, "'Tis such a forward child" (180), rather than to Scudmore's speech (181–188), which Hazlitt regards as an aside. This interpretation is not necessarily the correct one, however; for when the others have passed into the church, Scudmore might naturally continue his appeal; and an offer of sympathy from Kate would be no less appropriate than that from Strange (190f.). Neither Kate nor Strange had joined in the previous opposition to Scudmore (140–154, 162–164, 171–175).

208. *Buzzes*] Seeding heads of the dandelion, milkweed, or other plant whose seed is scattered by wind.

212. *you*] Following Verity, Brinkley quotes *you* as *ye*, which she offers in illustration of "a striking confusion of pronouns" (p. 62) that she finds characteristic of Field's style.

216. *still giuen*] A crux; see text. n. *Still*, usually *always*, with *giuen* might by only a little extension mean *promiscuously*. *Still* may, however, mean *secretly*. Scudmore seems to refer to women's hands' being privily or indiscriminately given to men.

222ff.] This full but unliterary stage direction, which seems to be descriptive of performance, is of the sort I think one would expect from the author who is also an actor.

228. *rellish*] i. e., *give a relish to*.

230. *no rub checkes our course*] In bowls, a rub is an obstacle to a bowl's pursuing its proper course.

235.] Field and the captain seem here to be burlesquing the preacher, but in a gentle way. Field professed to "reverence the feete of those that bring glad tidings of the Gospell" (Halliwell-Phillipps, *Illustrations*, 115). In Pouts' slander some may see a reflection of *Much Ado*, 4.1.

275ff.] Besides such eulogies of citizens as *The Shoemakers' Holiday* and Heywood's *The Four 'Prentices of London*, the early drama contains diatribes against citizens for their servility, gluttony, selfishness, and cuckoldry, and against their wives for social climbing; see Creizenach, 136–140, 142–145. Here, later in *W* (2.2.97ff.), and in *A* (2.2.29ff.) Field takes the common position; but he says also some words on the other side of the question (*A* 2.1.5–15).

308. *Wittall*] contented cuckold.

312. *on the backe of Law*] Field repeats the beast metaphor in *A* 4.4. 37ff. and, if Field is the author of *The Triumph of Love*, in *Four Plays in One* (X, 331). "The corrupt state of law and of religion are major subjects for Field's satire" (Brinkley, 59).

328.] As Abraham says, this is a proverb (Field, 47) and an old one.

331ff.] In this thrust Field combines satire on the unworthy courtier with the disapproval of the proverb which was inchoate in his time. Abraham uses seven proverbs or proverbial expressions, which contribute to his characterization; see *SFQ*, X (1946), 13f.

338. Cf. "What averse star rul'd my Nativity?" in *Four Plays in One* (X, 326).

352. *hit all right*] i.e., *if all hit right*, *hit* meaning *come to a desired end*.

2.2

Outer stage. The Page may have concealed himself (lf.) behind the curtain dividing outer from inner stage, any other hanging accessible to the outer stage, or one of the doorposts. Dramatic effectiveness for his pert comments, no doubt, would be enhanced if he spoke in full view of the audience but more or less hidden from Wagtail. He would seem to go to her after his line, "By this light I haue heard enough" (35).

5. *haulke*] The representation of nausea on the Jacobean stage was not uncommon. The use of the device here has been connected, I think inappropriately, with the parson in *Epicoene*; Brinkley, 76.

9f. this . . . me] Possibly a direct address to the audience.

11. *pepper'd*] done for, finished.

20. *Casting Bottle*] Literally, a *vinaigrette*; the figurative sense is clear.

34f.] Note the suggestion of Wagtail's business during the foregoing passage.

38. *Mutton*] Seventeenth-century slang for *prostitute*.

41. *Dosser*] Basket, usually carried on the back. Thus C's note: ". . . here used very inappropriately with reference to the burden Mrs. Wagtail carries before her."

44. *the Plague*] The opening years of the century were relatively free from plague, but after the great infection of 1603, for five years the plague became endemic, "generally showing itself from July to November and reaching its maximum in September or October" (Chambers, I, 329). Although the plague of 1609 was the heaviest since 1603 (*ibid.*, IV, 351), the vagueness of this allusion would make it seem unsafe as evidence of date. After 1609, "plague did not again become a serious factor in London life until 1625" (*ibid.*, I, 329f.).

49f. *Ex nihilo*] A proverb of considerable antiquity (Field, 39). Cf. the Page's attitude toward learning here with Field's own in the epistles "To Any Woman," 13f. and "To the Reader," 14, and exp. nn.

50. *Duello*] The use of the term is indicative of the contemporary popular interest in duelling and duelling codes.

63. *Within*] Probably a stage direction before *Will, Will*; see text. n.

98. *base slaue*] Dramatists frequently bring this charge against shopkeepers for their mercenary use of their wives and sometimes allow the merchants to defend themselves; see *The Family of Love* (1602), 2.1.1–23; *Dutch Courtesan* (1604), II, 107; *Michaelmas Term* (1606), 2.3.35ff. Depending upon his immediate purpose, Field takes either side of the question. The shopkeeper Seldom in *A* does not think it base to employ his wife as lure; but then, he had very special reasons (*A* 2.1.5–15). Similar passages which may be Field's occur in *The Honest Man's Fortune* (1613) [X, 234, 258]. See also Charles W. Camp, *The Artisan in Elizabethan Literature* (New York, 1923), 102–115.

103. *Chameleon vpon the ayre*] Proverbial (Field, 5). Sir Thomas Browne refutes this belief; *Works*, ed. Geoffrey Keynes (London, 1928–1931), II, 257ff.

113. *casts a sute euerie quarter*] cf. "they skip into my Lords cast skins some twice a yeere," *The Fatal Dowry*, 2.2.104 (noted by Brinkley, 88).

118. *as the play saies*] Possibly a reference to Beaumont and Fletcher, *The Woman-Hater* (1606), in which a prostitute marries a mercer.

3.1

This threshold scene (Chambers, III, 60) offers interesting use of both lower and upper levels. Strange enters the lower at one door, probably one of the proscenium doors at right or left, possibly crosses the stage, and knocks at the other proscenium door (1) as if the stage were a street and he were knocking at a house. Pouts' servant appears and goes in to deliver Strange's message, whereupon Pouts enters "aboue" (17), i. e., at a window [see another Whitefriars play, Marston's *Insatiate Countess*, III, 36], or on a small balcony, over the proscenium door. It was probably not, I think, a large balcony over the inner stage such as must have been common in the public theatres somewhat earlier; see Chambers, III, 153, or what John C. Adams calls the chamber (upper inner stage).

16. *shift himselfe . . . ouer*] to slip unobserved across the Channel to the Continent. Cf. *1 Henry VI*, 5.3.167.

21. *Mazard*] head.

3.2

Outer stage. The entrances and exits of Scudmore (56, 68) are confusing. I take it that his first entrance is by one of the proscenium doors. The wedding guests go out, leaving Scudmore to follow the way to Bellafront pointed out by Worldly (63). From the direction at 68ff. we are to understand, according to Lawrence, "that after Scudmore's exit by one of the regular doors, the rear-stage curtains draw, revealing Bellafront asleep, and that he reënters by the middle door" [*The Physical Conditions of the Elizabethan Public Playhouse* (Cambridge, 1927), 19f.], which Lawrence places "at the back of the rear stage, or inner room, otherwise the curtained space between the two commonly-used doors" [*ibid.*, 16f.]. Creizenach (p. 373) places the third door not in the upstage wall of the inner stage but immediately behind the downstage curtains. On first consideration, *passeth* might seem to mean *walks by without going through*, but Lawrence's explanation seems the more plausible. Scudmore need not have entered the door in the upstage wall of the inner stage, however, for other doors or at least entrance-ways seem to have been available; Chambers, III, 83–85, 134. Although the nature of the canopy on the Elizabethan stage is controversial [cf. Wallace, 48, n. 4 and Chambers, II, 557], the *Taffata Canopie* here probably refers to an overhead covering for the chair, not, as more commonly, to a set of stage curtains (Lawrence, *Physical Conditions*, 46–49). The remainder of this closet scene is, of course, on the lower inner stage.

2. *Enter with Table Napkins*] The usual way of indicating, in the drama, that a meal has been or will be served; cf. *A Woman Killed with Kindness* (Heywood, *Works*, II, 117) and *The Shoemakers' Holiday*, (Dekker, *Dramatic Works*, I, 71).

17. *topshackeld*] inebriated. Nautical?

21f. *peace and Coram*] a type of justice of the peace; cf. *Merry Wives*, 1.1.6. *Coram*, in the presence of, was often confused with *quorum*.

28f. *naturall begotten Mother*] Cf. "my true-begotten father," *Merchant of Venice*, 2.2.36f.

34. *Primero*] A Spanish card game very popular among fashionable gamblers in the sixteenth and seventeenth centuries; see *SE*, II, 472–474. Middleton describes cheating at primero in *Your Five Gallants* (1607), 1.1.147–162. Field probably acted in this play.

40. *Bowles*] This sport, frequently mentioned in the drama, furnished writers with a number of metaphors; cf. *W* 2.1.230 and exp. n. On the sport see *SE*, II, 463–465.

59. *Lucie*] Not, I think, a short form of *Lucida* but another young lady who does not appear in the play. Scudmore would hardly pretend to be the servant of Lucida when attempting by that disguise to obtain admission to Lucida's own house. Field's choice of name is unfortunate; it facilitated the incorrect identification of Lucie with Lucida by previous editors and resulted in the erroneous assignment of speeches at 31, 43, 46, and 50. See text. nn. to those lines.

71ff.] Scudmore's encounter with Bellafront here has been said to show the influence of the Closet Scene in *Hamlet*; Koeppel, 76; McGinn, 108. Proposed parallels are cited in the nn. below.

83ff.] The figure is proverbial (Field, 49). Field uses it again in *The Fatal Dowry*, 2.1.83f. (noted by Brinkley, 88). The proverbs in this tense, melodramatic scene illustrate Field's use of proverbial lore to win audience support in a serious argument by appealing, as it were, to authority—that of the ancient wisdom of the race; see *SFQ*, X (1946), 14f.

86. *in Hectors Tent*] In the *Iliad* (Bk. XXII) Pallas in disguise appears to Hector and treacherously persuades him to stand against the onslaught of Achilles. The interview takes place, however, on the battlefield, not in Hector's tent.

89. *enforcst*] From the following line I take these as Bellafront's words to Scudmore while she is dreaming. "Ha," marking her surprise on waking and finding an apparently strange man present, and the following line, seem to be addressed to Scudmore as Lucie's servant. *Enforcst* is glossed by 135ff., but see exp. n. to those lines.

96.] Here Bellafront recognizes the intruder as Scudmore.

Basiliske] The existence of the basilisk, frequently mentioned by Elizabethan and Jacobean writers, according to Sir Thomas Browne we can not safely deny; *Works*, II, 199. See also *W* 3.4.9f. and exp. n. to 10, and *Four Plays in One* (X, 307), where Field may again have used it, much as here.

109ff.] Cf. "Oh Hamlet, speak no more! / Thou turn'st mine eyes into my very soul," *Hamlet*, 3.4.88f. (Koeppel, 76). McGinn (p. 108) I think rightly treats this and other similarities as contributing to an imitation of scene rather than as constituting separate verbal parallels.

125.] Cf. "These words like daggers enter in mine ears," *Hamlet*, 3.4.95 (Koeppel, *ibid.*).

135ff. *I was enforst*] These lines illustrate one of Field's limitations as a dramatist. Up to this point he has given us no indication that Bellafront was under any compulsion to accept Count Frederick's hand. Though at the opening of the play Bellafront subscribed her letter to Scudmore, *"Yours through the world, and to the end of Time,"* we first see her on the arm of the Count in her wedding procession; and her first words to Scudmore (2.1.142f.) are rude. Before her father and friends she denies Scudmore, calling him "insolent, nay strangely sawcie" (2.1.162). After the ceremony in which so far as she knows she has become a Countess, she concludes that the unpleasant encounter with Scudmore gave zest to her wedding (2.1.228). Not until the present passage does Field give us the extenuating circumstances, which the reader may want to call, with Scudmore, "painted causes" (140). Our experience of Worldly does not permit us to believe him "a seuere Father"; his control over Bellafront or her fortunes has not been demonstrated; and no neglect on Scudmore's part, or loose speech regarding Bellafront (138f.) has been established. Occasionally Field sacrifices truth, or sincerity in character portrayal, to his avowed thesis, that woman is a weathercock. One may ask whether a writer can portray inconsistency consistently. In this play at least I think not; for had Field given Bellafront true rather than painted causes, his play might have been more credible but as a manifesto in the war between the sexes less clever and appealing.

140. *painted*] artificial.

146f.] Scudmore is using proberbially untrustworthy objects (Field, 14, 20).

149ff.] Another of Field's numerous passages on the theatre. Any attempt at identifying the play spoken of would be hazardous.

155.] A difficult line. Previous editors have taken *so* with *retaine*, but they did not know of the corrections during impression. *So*, however, may and probably should be construed with *heare mee*, see text. n.

160. *Antipodes*] Separated from civilized portions of the earth by equatorial fire and the terrors of the equatorial ocean, according to Crates of Mallos, are inhabited regions exactly opposite ours; see John Kirtland Wright, *The Geographical Lore of the Time of the Crusades* (New York, 1925), 19. According to Crates, Scudmore could not have made his threatened journey since the antipodal regions are absolutely inaccessible to us.

163. *iust*] i. e., *exactly*, as the word *Antipodes* perhaps implies.

175f.] Cf. *Hamlet* 3.4.88f., quoted in exp. n. to *W*, 3.2.109ff. (Koeppel, 76).

188.] Aphoristic and perhaps proverbial (Field, 33).

193] Field sometimes packs his rhythmical line full. If this sort of dialogue is spoken, as it probably was, with sufficient bravado, it is rhetorically effective.

197. *woe*] i. e., *woo*.

200. *Monkies*] The lustfulness of monkeys is proverbial (Field, 36).

207. *Begot by Drunkards*] According to a proverbial notion (Field, 17), the offspring of inebriates are visited for their father's sins in various ways. Beaumont and Fletcher in *The Woman-Hater* connect a drunken father with inconstant daughters (X, 85).

212. *deceitfull as are Crocodiles*] The false tears of crocodiles, who are alleged to weep with feigned pity either before or while devouring men, are proverbial (Field, 8) and frequently mentioned in literature . According to Bullokar (*English Expositor*, 1616; quoted in Malone Var., IX, 427), a nine-foot crocodile, dead "but in perfect forme," was exhibited in England about this time.

228. *Lucretiaes knife*] The knife with which Lucretia stabbed herself after having been ravished by Sextus Tarquinius. The subject had been treated in English by Chaucer, *Legend of Good Women*; Painter, *The Palace of Pleasure*; and Shakespeare, *The Rape of Lucrece*; but it must have been widely known to schoolboys from Ovid. Field refers to Tarquin in *A*, 4.2.40.

3.3

Outer stage. Sir Abraham (1) and Pendant (14), both of whom had been bowling, probably enter at the same door, presumably that by which the party had gone out to the bowling alley in the previous scene. I suspect that Abraham and Pendant leave (126 and 133) by the proscenium door at the opposite side of the stage.

5.] *Rub* and *flye* are the cries of the bowlers offstage, as we know from 6.

12. *Boy*] Cupid.

vaile my Bonnet] acknowledge myself overcome. Cf. Lyly: "hee will vaile bonet to beautie" [*Works*, ed. R. W. Bond (Oxford, 1902); *Endymion*, 3.3.83].

13ff.] "Like Master Matthew in *Every Man in His Humour* and Daw in *Epicoene*, Sir Abraham composes verses; but whereas Jonson's characters only read their verses to us, Sir Abraham composes his in our presence" (Brinkley, 76).

27. *Newington conceit*] C puns when he calls 26 "probably a hit at the sort of '*worsted* conceits' " to be found in plays at the theatre at Newington Butts. *Crewel* is a kind of worsted goods. Chambers (II, 405) calls this "a bad pun," but it appears also in the "cruel garters" of *Lear* (2.4.7). Field may have heard it in the "cruel Nightcap" of *The Scornful Lady* (1613; perhaps written ca. 1610) [I, 247]. The history of the theatre at Newington Butts Chambers terms "very obscure" (II, 404). According to *Henslowe's Diary* (I, 17ff.), in 1594 and after, many well known plays, including a *Hamlet*, and *Tamburlaine* (1587), *The Jew of Malta* (1589), *Doctor Faustus* (1592), and *Titus Andronicus* (1594), were there acted, as was *Long Meg of Westminster* (1595), a lost play probably referred to in *A* 2.1.152 as then being produced "at the Fortune." "Apparently in Field's time," V notes, "the theatre was not in good repute." When Field made this reference to Newington, however, the theatre had

probably been out of use for ten years; Chambers, II, 405 and n. 3; Harbage, 249.

34. *frump*] flout.

47. *knacking of the tongues*] i. e., the sounding of the tongs, the rustic musical instrument called for by Bottom (*Midsummer Night's Dream*, 4.1.31). The choice of instrumental accompaniment doubtless indicates Pendant's low opinion of Sir Abraham's poem.

61. *fitter for my turne*] As Pendant is quick to acknowledge, Abraham puns on *bauble*, a trifling piece of finery, and the truncheon of the fool.

80. *stand to it*] submit to trial upon it. Note the pun on *stand* in *stood*, 81, and cf. 1.2.287 and *A*, 3.3.61 and exp. nn.

91. *puld an olde house ouer my heade*] A proverbial expression (Field, 26) meaning "to get oneself into trouble."

95. *all one*] cf. *W* 1.2.71 and exp. n.

96. *Roaring Boyes*] "Swaggerers" (*A* 2.4.24), riotous fellows of Elizabethan and Jacobean times frequently mentioned in literature. For the character of the roarer see Webster, *Works*, IV, 31f. In Middleton and Rowley's *A Fair Quarrel* (1617) Chough and Trimtram provide satire on roaring by attending a school—not, as Collier says (*A*, 50) setting up such a school—offering instruction in the "mathematical science" of roaring in several languages: "Sclavonian, Parthamenian, Barmeothian, Tyburnian, Wappinganian" (4.1.35f.). Field introduces excellent satire on the practice in *A* 3.4. For a cursory view of the subject see Burton Milligan, *SAB*, XV (1940), 184–190; and a reply, *SAB*, XXIII (1948), 12–16 and 78–86.

97.] A suggestion of the actor's business in the lines (91ff.)?

107. *the Pond at Islington*] The fields and ponds of Islington, in the seventeenth century a country village considered remote from London, were long the popular Sunday resort of London citizens. By Field Islington was regarded as a suitable location for drownings; see *A* 2.4.18. On the later rich associations of Islington see Wheatley, II, 266–270.

116. *That goes by fate*] Proverbial (Field, 31).

124. *Fates aboue all*] A proverbial apothegm (Field, 21).

3.4

Though the scene doubtless represents Pouts' lodgings, nothing in it suggests the use of the upper level or the inner stage. It may or may not have been played before the door at which Strange knocked in 3.1.

3ff.] Probably a Wellerism (Field, 15).

10. *the death ont*] The drama frequently mentions the allegedly fatal glance of the basilisk; see *W* 3.2.96 and exp. n. The reference here, however, is to the doctrine of "priority of aspection"; see *The Explicator*, IV (1946), No. 43. In resolving to flee, Pouts has said that law resembles the basilisk in that he who jumps the gun has the advantage. Perhaps the figure is not very apt, but its interpretation does not require an emendation; see text. n.

14f. *poor knights*] Cf. 1.2.164f. and exp. n. to 165, *A* 5.2.218.

16. *like a Souldier*] This disguise plot is the "other course" for which Strange left us in 3.1.23.

23. *Fortunatus his pouch*] The purse from which Fortunatus could at any time produce ten pieces of gold. The German folk tale, which was dramatized by Hans Sachs in 1553, served as the basis of a *Fortunatus* (1590) and of Dekker's *Old Fortunatus* (1599); Chambers, III, 291.

35. *the Beare*] The Bear at the Bridge Foot, a celebrated tavern outside the Great Gate at the Southwark end of old London Bridge. Suckling's letter, "The Wine-drinkers to the Water-drinkers" [*Works*, ed. A. Hamilton Thompson (London, 1910), 315], mentions and was dated from the Bear. For a collection of allusions to the tavern see Wheatley, I, 135f.

36. *Graues-end*] The boundary port on the Thames about twenty-five miles east of London. In the parish church of St. George there, Pocahontas is buried.

4.1

Outer stage. Neville and Scudmore probably leave (120) by the door opposite that by which Pouts and Strange enter at the opening of the next scene.

10f. *women, which do alwaies shun /Their louers*] Proverbial (Field, 22).

39. *in a possibility*] "*i. e.*, Her treachery was not absolutely completed" (V, n.). Cf. *Bartholomew Fair* 1.3.59f.: "she is in possibility to be your daughter in law." Cf. *in Posse, W* 2.1.160.

69. *disease*] cause of distress.

71.] A crux; see text. n. The word *vnder-borne* may be the participle of *underbear,* to endure; if so, the passage may mean, "We see those [who are] happiest in best parts and [who have] endured fortunes beneath their merit, grow. . ."

76ff.] Note the "hard" variety of cultural primitivism here; Arthur O. Lovejoy and George Boas, *Primitivism and Related Ideas in Antiquity* (Baltimore, 1935), 10f.

81. *capitulate*] to draw up in chapters, to specify.

94. *Rather to loose a soule*] Proverbial (Field, 28).

95. *wit*] Probably "wisdom, good judgment, discretion, prudence" as in 102. The series in 80 seems to rule out several possible meanings. In 106 the meaning of *wit* may have shifted to "apt association of thought and expression."

116. *a prodigious wight*] One may not accept V's gloss for *wight, fool. Wight* was used for superhuman as well as human beings. Perhaps Nevill means no more than, "Even though tomorrow morning I may seem to have done the superhuman, I'll give. . ."

118. *Enginer*] strategist, plotter. Cf. *Catiline,* 3.760.

4.2

Outer stage. The technique of scene identification exhibited in 2 reminds one of the suave radio playwright of the twentieth century.

2. *Lambeth fields*] This marshy royal hunting ground east of Westminster Bridge, frequented if at all by prostitutes and cutpurses, was an appropriate setting for the present encounter.

14. *enforc'd marriages*] A popular literary theme; cf. *The London Prodigal* (1604) and *The Miseries of Enforced Marriage* (1607) though both these plays fail to make their point (Powell, 199); see also Louis B. Wright, *Middle-Class Culture in Elizabethan England* (Chapel Hill, 1935), 209. Why the captain should regard Kate's marriage to Strange as enforced is not perfectly clear; for though Strange's wealth has been mentioned as a factor (1.2.124f.), the captain himself has admitted, "Mistris *Kate* likes me not" (1.2.93).

20. *(For so my Name is)*] "Not an addition, as it would probably be in Massinger, nor a subordinated element, as it would probably be in Massinger, but the clear sign of slovenly thinking," writes Marianne Brock (ed., *The Knight of Malta*, unpublished Ph. D. dissertation, Bryn Mawr, 1944, ciii)—being, I think, a little hard on Field.

21ff.] If we are to believe contemporary accounts such as that of Henry Bullinger, *The Christen state of Matrimonye*, the wedding feast here described was little more riotous than some which occurred; see Powell, 26f.

51. *necessarie vault*] a privy. This instance and that in *A* 2.4.12f. are the earliest cited by the *NED*.

61. *no Maide*] Cf. 2.1.237f.

67-71.] In a whimsical manner Strange later makes the captain rue this oath; see 5.2.156ff.

68. *Strapadoes*] Instruments of torture by which victims, hands lashed crosswise behind their backs, were hoisted into the air. In the half strappado, after cooling their heels, they were let down again; in the full strappado, they were let fall with a jerk which dislocated their shoulders. Field mentions the strappado also in *A* 1.1.144.

69. *Roman Yoke*] A symbol of servitude rather than an instrument of torture.

Scotch Boote] An instrument formerly used for persuading confessions from prisoners in Scotland; for a description see Dodsley[3], IV, 53. C (n. to *A*, 1.1.144) equated with the "boiling boote" there mentioned, the Scotch boot obtaining its effect by wedges which applied pressure to the bones; the boiling boot, by hot oil or water which scalded the flesh. Under Mary, Elizabeth, and James the Privy Council could and did order offenders against the state to be put to such tortures as these; see James Spedding, *The Letters and Life of Francis Bacon* (London, 1861-1874), V, 92f. and n.

82. *Why*] Previous editors take interjectionally; see text. n. But may we not understand *because*?

85. *Thou*] Note that in his invective Strange employs the form which, ironically, to an equal was an admission of intimacy and to an inferior was a rude expression of contempt.

86. *foist*] "A diver with two fingers, a pickpocket," Moll Cutpurse in *The Roaring Girl*, 5.1.290.

87. *Slops*] wide bagging breeches; for the various types see Linthicum, 209f.

Cat a Mountaines] wildcat's. Cf. *The Custom of the Country* (*Beaumont and Fletcher*, I, 307).

88. *blather*] an early variant of *bladder*.

robustious] blustering. Not an evidence for Field's addiction to "somewhat unusual forms of expression" (Brinkley, 70); the word was "in common use during the 17th century" (*NED*, s. v., a., 2) and is current today, though chiefly in a humorous sense.

92. *snapst*] goes shares with thieves; cf. *The Roaring Girl*, 5.1.294f.

106. *the Noble science of Defence*] Louis B. Wright takes this line as Field's acknowledgment of an actor's skill at fencing [*MLR*, XXII (1927), 272]; but though the match may have been well fought, the line need not be so taken. Possibly it refers only to the fashionable society or school of self-defense which gave exhibitions before Henry VIII and Elizabeth and offered degrees comparable to academic degrees. Tarlton and Robert Greene are reported to have attained the master's degree in the noble science. See Malone Var. VIII, 30f., n. 8 and Horace S. Craig, *University of California Publications in English*, IX (1940), p. 5, n. 11. That the skill should be called a science is perhaps a reflection of the Renaissance emphasis on the study of fencing.

109. *I vnderstand you*] Not even in defeat can the captain refrain from a pun, which is not new. This to us perhaps inappropriate foolery may have been suggested to Field by the thorough going-over Speed and Launce give these words in *Two Gentlemen of Verona*, 2.5.21–34. Perhaps the lack of serious tone helps us to know that "al shalbe wel" (116).

120. *Moore-fields*] Perhaps these fields north of the City, laid out in 1606 and soon after serving as the haunt of thieves, beggars, and outcasts, ultimately redeemed themselves by providing an open-air preaching ground for Wesley and a playground for young John Keats; see Wheatley, II, 560, 562. Disguised as an old soldier—but not, as C stated, "upon a wooden leg" (*W*, 60, n.)—Brainworm sold Master Stephen a sword there. On a close parallel between this speech by Pouts and one by Golding in *Eastward Ho!*, (Chapman, *Plays and Poems*, 1.1.134–138) see *MLN*, LXII (1947), 131f.

4.3

Though Wagtail is supposed to be "in the Gallery" (3.3.121), we are not, I think, to infer that this scene was acted on the upper level. When Sir Abraham prevents Wagtail's attempt at "suicide" (96) and gives her a ring, their proximity seems to be implied.

3f. *Sprindge to catch a Wood-cocke*] Proverbial (Field, 56), in reference to the bird's alleged simplicity. Cf. *Hamlet* 1.3.115 and 5.2.317.

7. *throw the house out at window*] Proverbial (Field, 27), for "to make a great disturbance in a house."

14. *call me Cut*] a proverbial (Field, 10) term of abuse; cf. Falstaff, "call me horse," *1 Henry IV*, 2.4.215.

23. *Caroch*] a sumptuous coach; cf. the third madman in *The Duchess of Malfi*, 4.2.104ff.: "Woe to the Caroach, that brought home my wife from the Masque, at three a clocke in the morning, it had a large Feather-bed in it."

26. *stealing*] "Furtively" (H, n.).

31. *Knight-hoods Mirror*] A reference to Diego Ortuñez de Calahorra, *The Mirrour of Princely deedes and Knighthood*, of which the popularity is attested by its having had ten publications between 1578 and 1601 [Arundell Esdaile, *A List of English Tales and Prose Romances* (London, 1912), 105f.].

34.] References to the romance, *Sir Beves of Hamtoun*; John Edwin Wells, *Manual of the Writings in Middle English* (New Haven, 1916——), I, [13]. Arundell was Bevis' famed horse; Morglay, his sword.

43. *Poles*] i.e., Paul's Walk, which Earle, who gives us its character, calls "the Lands Epitome, or you may call it the lesser Ile of Great Brittaine" [*Micro-Cosmographie*, ed. Edward Arber (London, 1868), 73]. Dekker gives instructions "How a Gallant should behaue himselfe" there (*Non-Dramatic Works*, II, 228–237). See also exp. n. to *W* t.–p. 16.

49. *Law ye*] An exclamation; cf. exp. n. to *W* 1.2.135.

51. *cleaues my heart in twaine*] See *W* 1.1.172 and exp. n. In this context, however, Field seems to be ridiculing the expression.

56. *Pinkanies*] A term of endearment, probably originating in child's language (*NED*, s. Pinkeny, 1 and 2), first applied to the eyes and then to the whole person. C takes as a "reference to the redness of Sir Abraham's eyes from soreness" (n.), but the lines (59f.) make clear that the running of his eyes was not from that cause.

76f. *child begot in a Dreame*] in allusion to folk belief; Thompson, *Motif Index*, F 611.1.13 and T 516.

88. *whipping.*] An interrupted speech; cf. *W* 1.1.56 and text. n.

109. *Maske*] See below, 5.2.7–31.

5.1

Outer stage. Perhaps one proscenium door, by which Nevill and party enter (64ff.), represents a passage to the interior of the house; the other, by which Scudmore enters (93), one to the street. John C. Adams (*The Globe Playhouse*, 152f.) evidently thinks that Nevill locks the door at the rear of the inner stage before 114. Nevill doubtless goes out (139) the door by which Scudmore had come in.

20.] The difficulty of concealing love is proverbial (Field, 7).

30. *happier much then ours*] Field opens *A* with a debate on which is the happiest state, that of maid, wife, or widow. His conclusion in *A* is different from that reached here; see *A* 5.2.300f.

47. *Graues-end*] See above, exp. n. to 3.4.36.

49. *Torches*] Torchbearers were conventional in the mask; see Reyher, 463.

70. *the case is alter'd*] "The title of one of Jonson's plays is incorporated in Abraham Ninny's remark" (Brinkley, 57); but the expression was proverbial (Field, 3).

95.] The threats resorted to by this servant seem to have been not untypical of doorkeepers at Renaissance masks; cf. Reyher, 37f.

97. *you'le be kild*] Possibly in warning to Scudmore that he will be abused for having been so late with the wigs, or, perhaps, indicative that the third servant now recognizes Scudmore's disguise—though the latter might be hard to convey to the audience.

118ff.] "A very skilful bit of dialogue" (Brinkley, 53).

Change] i. e., of partners in the dance; see Chambers, I, 198.

137. *set foorth*] provide with masks—an interesting glimpse into the trade of the vizard-maker.

5.2

This typical "hall scene" (Chambers, III, 63–65) was manifestly played on the outer stage. The dance of the mask itself may begin in, and even remain on, the inner stage though there seems little reason why such a strong element visually should have been impaired by restriction to that area, which by some is thought to have "proved too dark and too cramped for the convenient handling of chamber scenes" (*ibid.*, 120). Field himself specifies much of the actual business in this scene. The play ends with a survival in modified form of what has been called the custom of the early private theatres, a valedictory song (234).

1ff.] Note the full non-literary stage directions, which seem to be descriptive of a performance.

4. *offers at*] tries to sit in.

13–17.] Field has Scudmore and Bellafront converse, as they dance, with praiseworthy economy of dialogue.

28. *strain*] Like *Change* above, another technical term from masking; Chambers, I, 198.

29. *away with her*] In the early seventeenth century the inclusion in plays of masks or features of the mask was quite popular; Schelling, II, 128f. and nn. Middleton uses a mask to untangle the plot of *Your Five Gallants* (1607), in which Field probably had acted; but the situations are hardly similar. I take it that the use of a mask here is not "another evidence of Jonson's influence" (Kerr, *op. cit.*, 57) since Jonson preferred "to keep his masques and comedies separate" (Thorndike, 185). The mask for abduction here is paralleled in *The Maid in the Mill* (1623) [*Beaumont and Fletcher*, VII, 22–25].

264   THE PLAYS OF NATHAN FIELD

31. *honor*] "a ceremonial reverence to the company" (Chambers, I, 198). Elyot carefully defines the term, *The Boke Named The Gouernour* [ed. H. H. S. Croft (London, 1880), I, 241f.]. Here the honor, however, does not as there precede the other movements. Chambers points out that the term is still traditional in folk dances (I, 198, n. 2).

50. *last Statute of two Husbands*] I. Jac. I. C. 11, "An Acte to restrayne all persons from Marriage until their former Wyues and former Husbandes be deade," 1603–4 [*The Statutes of the Realm* (London, 1810–1822), IV, 1028]. This act made bigamy a felony.

60f.] This passage is cited by C. Van Der Spek in his survey, *The Church and Churchman in English Dramatic Literature before 1642* (Amsterdam, 1930), 132. Field's satire on the clergy seems written for amusement rather than correction. See also *W* 2.1.235 and exp. n.

74. Supply, "than a devil."

78.] A previous example of double disguise (Freeburg, 26, and n. 21) is found in Heywood's *The Wise Woman of Hogsden* (1604). Nevill's wearing of the Devil's weeds here exists for its "wit" (cf. 80f.).

81f.] Count Frederick, it has been justly objected, here "is not hurt at all" (Brinkley, 60). Yet if we are to have a happy ending—and remember that "al shalbe wel" (4.2.116)—what can the playwright do but make Frederick regard as lightly as possible the loss of his rich, beautiful wife? Not having been convinced of any very compelling quality about his love for Bellafront, the audience probably had small reason to be sorry for Frederick. The playwright helps all he can with Worldly's line (85), itself out of character if we are to accept the speaker's behavior later (159ff.). Field, it has been stated, "is not sympathetic with these creatures that he portrays and is concerned with their actions rather than their emotions. The characters themselves are very carefree and take both their traits and their affairs in a matter-of-fact way" (Brinkley, 60). Perhaps this casualness on Field's part does as has been said *(ibid.)* contribute to Field's sprightliness of style; it probably derives, however, from what seems to be a characteristic of the lesser journalistic playwrights of Field's day and ours, a willingness to sacrifice integrity of character for the sake of plot or theatrical effect.

84. *I kept you for my selfe*] If this is not said jokingly, I do not know what it means. Doubtless from this line Brinkley concludes (pp. 50, 52) that Kate is to marry Nevill. Two other lines, however, "Were not my heart giuen to another man" [i. e., Strange] (127) and "Oh my deere Strange" (166), supported as they are by the strongly united family front of Worldly, Scudmore, Lucida, and Bellafront when Strange reveals himself, as well as the absence of any solution for a problem which would arise if Kate were intended to live happily ever after with Nevill, are strong evidence that she remains steadfast in her love for her merchant Strange. Cf. Frederick S. Boas, *An Introduction to Stuart Drama* (London, 1946), p. 331.

96. *stand to 't*] Note the double entendre.

117. *Oh my Diuining Spirit*] The citation of this line (McGinn, 160) as an allusion to or echo of *Hamlet* 1.5.40, "O my prophetic soul!" hardly seems justified. Hamlet's exclamation is an admission, I take it, that by intuition he has already experienced the conviction that his father's death was not a natural one. Kate's is a lame effort to make reasonable the statement she is about to utter, that Strange has gone to sea—an untruth, and a matter of which she could hardly have known had it been true. As such, Kate's words serve Field as well as any, no doubt, and that, without reference to Shakespeare, may have seemed sufficient reason for using them.

123.] Strange's motivation in this attempt to silence Pouts does not convince. Knowing the facts in the case, Strange would have had small reason for being so aroused as Field lets him be. Perhaps this is another instance in which Field's knowledge of theatrical values and evident fondness for making full theatrical use of a situation stand between him and an authentic reading of life; see above, Gen. Intro., 3.

138. *he*] i. e., Strange "like a Souldier."

153. *periur'd villaine*] Technically correct, of course, as witness 4.2.67–71. Strange, however, is being whimsical in reminding Pouts of his oath before clearing himself and the woman he loves, or, rather, before clearing up the mystery. For Strange acts like a playwright rather than a lover, apparently so that Field may squeeze every drop of value out of this situation. Strange's postponement of his self-discovery might be very fitting if life were, as has been said, a play.

157f.] Like 123, again a response which seems out of character and the basis for a charge against Field for lack of integrity in portraying character. Giving the lines to someone else (see text. n.) will not help. The passage may argue that Field applied a special significance to the merchant's surname; see above, Gen. Intro., 3.

167f.] What an admirable united front this happy family at once sets up! The episode is repeated in *Four Plays in One* (X, 333; noted by Brinkley, 103).

184. *proud*] See exp. n. to *W* 1.2.61.

187f. *Time was, Time is, and Times past*] The words spoken by Friar Bacon's Brazen Head to the servant Miles; see *The Famous Historie of Fryer Bacon* [*Early English Prose Romances*, ed. William J. Thoms (London, 1906), 299f.] and *The Honorable Historie of Frier Bacon and Frier Bungay* (1589) [Greene, *Works*, XIII, 79f].

203.] For the sake of a play on words, Field allows Abraham to contradict himself; cf. *W* 3.3.77–80.

205. *Lawrence of Lancashire*] Collier identified (n.) with a clownish character in *The Late Lancashire Witches*, and it is unfortunate that he can not be correct since Lawrence in that play is bewitched in a way that would make him relevant here; see Heywood, *Dramatic Works*, IV, 232. Since that play deals with a trial of 1633, however, the allusion here must be to another work, probably the ballad "*Lustye* LAWRENCE," entered

SR 14 June 1594 [II, 653] and continued in *"the Second parte of Lusty LA[W]RRANCE,"* entered 15 November 1596 [III, 74]. The hero of this apparently bawdy and popular ballad is said by Gayton in *Wit Revived,* 1656, to be one who "may be thought to have been the greatest wencher of an English man" and in *A Brown Dozen of Drunkards,* 1648, is called "a stallion that neighs after every female Filly"; quoted from Hyder E. Rollins, *An Analytical Index to the Ballad-Entries* (Chapel Hill, 1924), 140. See also Robert B. Sharpe, *The Real War of the Theatres* (Boston, 1935), 57 and n. 31.

208. *Ecce signum*] Holding up her hand to show on it his ring? Cf. 4.3.108.

221. *Tucke*] Genial, convenient Friar Tuck, confessor to Robin Hood.

223.] Field seems to have made inadequate preparation for Lucida's acceptance of the Count.

229ff. *I . . . play*] Though many dramatic portraits of citizens are uncomplimentary (cf. exp. n. to 2.1.275ff.), Strange actually wants to see himself in a play.

234. *Boy out-voice the Musicke*] Lawrence points out that this speech knits the song to the action of the play in a manner not usual; *1,* 83.

235f.] It has been said that Field not only "strictly observes unity of time in both plays" but here "even calls our attention to the time element" (Brinkley, 73). Field does not, however, observe the unity of time in *A*; see *SP,* XLIII (1946), 491, n. 55. Langbaine (p. 199) notes the emphasis upon the unity of time here.

2. AMENDS

Title-page

4. *Blacke-Fryers*] Not the first Blackfriars (Adams, 91–110), or the second Blackfriars (*ibid*., 182–233), in which Field had lived and acted, but evidently Rosseter's Blackfriars, called also Porter's Hall or the Puddle-Wharf theatre; *ibid*., 342–347, Chambers, II, 472–474; and see above, *A* Intro., i. The history of this theatre, about which scholars hold differing opinions, is both complicated and obscure. On 31 May 1615 was issued a Signet Bill which resulted in the Patent of 3 June 1615 authorizing Rosseter and others to build a theatre in the suburbs of London (*MSC*, I, 278). By 26 September 1615 a complaint had been filed with the Privy Council, stating that Rosseter and the rest "are nowe erectinge a Newe Playhouse" in the Blackfriars "to the great p'iudice and inconvenience of the Gouerment" of London (*MSC*, I, 373). Yielding to pressure from the residents (see Hillebrand, 246), and taking advantage of a legal point made by Sir Edward Coke, the Lord Chief Justice—that Blackfriars having been made a part of the city by charter in 1608, the new theatre was not being built where authorized—on 26 September 1615 the Council ordered the Lord Mayor to forbid Rosseter "to proceede in the makeinge, and convertinge the said Buildinge into a Play house" (*MSC*, I, 373). On 28 September there is record of a payment for money "disbursed about the restraint" of this project (Hillebrand, 244, n. 26). Rosseter may not have waited, as has been thought (Gildersleeve, *op. cit.*, 199f.), until Coke was removed from office, 15 November 1616 (*DNB*, XI, 235; Spedding, *op. cit.*, VI, 97), but since Coke's fall was expected, may have resumed building some months before. If the performance described on the title-page of the 1616 quarto of *The Scornful Lady* was given in Rosseter's Blackfriars (as Chambers says, III, 230), the theatre may have been sufficiently complete to use for performances by 19 March 1616, when *The Scornful Lady* was entered *SR* [III, 585]. It was said to be "almost if not fully finished" on 27 January 1616–1617 (Malone Var., III, 494; *MSC*, I, 374; Chambers, II, 473), when the Council wrote the Lord Mayor again, declaring that it was His Majesty's pleasure that they pull down and make unfit for playing the building "lately erected and made fitt" (*MSC*, I, 374). Note that this order refers to certain persons "that goe about to sett vp a Play howse" *(ibid.)*, perhaps indicating that the establishment of a company there was not yet completed. One of the scholarly problems about this theatre arose because of the misdating of this order 26 January 1616 by Mrs. C. C. Stopes [*Shakespeare Jahrbuch*, XLVIII (1912), 105]. Following Stopes, Hillebrand (p. 247) concludes that we have no evidence of a second Blackfriars theatre after 1616. When Rosseter's Blackfriars was used for performances is a problem rendered perhaps insoluble, on the basis of existing evidence, by the facts that a build-

ing may be used some time before it is officially completed and that we
do not know when the order of 27 January 1616–1617 was fully carried
out. In 1623 Travis speaks of "stay to be made" in building the theatre;
he does not say that it had been torn down (Hillebrand, 246). Chambers
from the title-page of *A* places its Blackfriars performance "c. 1615–16"
(III, 313). Earlier, however, he states that Daborne's *The Poor Man's
Comfort* (1617) may allude to "attempts to preserve the Porter's Hall
theatre from destruction" (III, 272) in that year. The theatre itself
Chambers dates "1615–17" (III, 230). Adams, however, on the basis of
an undated letter (Greg, *HP*, 93) which we may date in this winter,
states that the theatre "seems to have been ready for the actors about
the first of January, 1617" (p. 346). From this date Bentley (p. 201,
n. 2) dissents, in part because he finds no reason for assuming that the
undated letter, which he dates "probably . . . in the winter of 1616–17"
(pp. 200f.), preceded the order of 27 January 1616–1617. Though I think
it probably did, it need not have done so for Adams' argument to hold;
for as has been said, we have no evidence as to when the final order was
carried out. Harbage says that Rosseter's Blackfriars "was used for a
time in 1615 by Lady Elizabeth's and Prince's Men (in coalition with
the disbanded Queen's Revels)" (p. 250). Under his discussions of the
first two of these companies, however, Harbage queries his remarks (pp.
246, 244). In a letter to me he states: "I agree that 1615 may be too
early but I don't see how we can plump for 1617 in particular. . . . I
should put '1616 (?).'" Though *The Scornful Lady* may have been produced at the Puddle-Wharf as early as March 1616, it is true that the
later one puts conjectural dates for the functioning period of this theatre,
up to 27 January 1616–1617, the more likelihood there is that they may
be correct. This consideration and the evidence from Field's biography
lead me tentatively to favor the winter of 1616–1617.

5. *Princes Seruants*] The company under the patronage of Charles,
Duke of York, who became Prince of Wales in November, 1616. On the
company see Murray, I, 229–242; Chambers, II, 241–246; and Bentley,
198–217.

6. *the Lady Elizabeths*] The company under the patronage of the
Lady Elizabeth, who became Queen of Bohemia; Murray, I, 243–264;
Chambers, II, 246–260; Bentley, 176–197. In 1613 they were united with
members of the Second Queen's Revels and, after March 1614, played
under the management of Field.

12. *G. Eld*] An important London printer from 1604 to 1624; he issued
Stow's *Annals* and Camden's *Remains*. Eld was one of many printers of
the day who married into the business. He died of plague in 1624. McKerrow, *Dictionary of Printers & Booksellers*, 98.

Math. Walbancke] A publisher and bookseller, 1618–1667, having law
books for his specialty. In 1628 he was one of the dealers in "old libraries"
required to send their catalogues to the Archbishop of Canterbury. For

him Okes printed the second quarto of *A*. Walbancke published the early news sheet, *The Exact Diary*. Plomer, *op. cit.*, 186.

13. *new Gate of Grayes-Inne*] A "fayre Gate" of red brick which, with "a Gatehouse for a more conuenient, and more honourable passage into the high streete of Holborne" the Gentlemen of Gray's Inn erected at the end of the sixteenth century; Stowe and Howes, *Annales* (London, 1631), 1073. See also Cecil Headlam, *The Inns of Court* (London, 1909), 143f.; Wheatley, II, 142f.

Dramatis personae

1. *Maid*] In this character, according to Boas (*op. cit.*, p. 333), "Field reproduces with a less delicate touch an exquisite Beaumont and Fletcher model."

2. *Lord Fee-simple*] Attention has been called to some resemblance between Feesimple and Kastril in *The Alchemist* (1610), likewise taught to quarrel (Brinkley, 76f.). With the Feesimples here cf. the Ninnies of *W*.

3. *Widow*] The conquest of a widow by a bold young man is presented also in Barry's *Ram Alley* (1608) and Cooke's *Greenes Tu Quoque* (1611).

4. *Husband*] Perpetuating an incorrect identification made by C, all who have referred to this character have called him Sir John Loveall, a personage mentioned in the play (2.1.31) but distinct from the Husband, who is not named; see *NQ*, CLXXXIX (1945), 192. The Husband is not, as has been charged (Brinkley, 74), a profligate. Throughout the play his difficulty is his ungrounded excessive concern over his wife's constancy.

5. *Subtle*] Jonson had given this name to the title character of *The Alchemist* (1610). Perhaps to the seventeenth-century audience it had a higher appropriateness here than to the reader of the twentieth, who is likely to find Subtle's testing of the Wife less crafty than bluntly unscrupulous.

Mall Cut-purse] One of the most fascinating underworld characters of the period and "a true Elizabethan in courage and flamboyancy of spirit" (*SE*, II, 501). Being born ca. 1584, dying in 1659, she lived a long and notorious life. She was the original of Dekker and Middleton's *The Roaring Girl, or Moll Cutpurse* (1610), on the title-page of the 1611 quarto of which her picture appears, with the notable inscription, "My case is alter'd, I must worke for my liuing." John Day is credited with writing her biography in *Mad Pranks of Merry Moll of the Bankside*, entered *SR* 7 August 1610 but not known to have been printed. An anonymous seventeenth-century biography is *The Life and Death of Mrs. Mary Frith*, London, 1662. An epitaph on her has been ascribed to Milton with, according to his recent editors, "some chance these verses are his" (*Works*, XVIII, 358, 590). By 1605 she had made a sensational stage appearance [Chambers, *RES*, I (1925), 78]. In 1611 she did penance at Paul's Cross; but having just finished drinking three quarts of sack, she was perhaps drunk at the time (Middleton, *Works*, IV, 4). Immediately before the

Restoration she left a bequest of twenty pounds so that on Charles' return
the conduit might run with wine (*ibid.*, 5). On occasions, for sufficient
incentive, she would help recover stolen goods as well as dispose of them
[see Margaret Dowling, *RES*, X (1934), 67–71]. Field, who brings her
on the stage for one brief scene quite without artistic justification, offers
a less attractive portrait of Moll than that in *The Roaring Girl*. The fea-
turing of her name on the 1639 title-page (see *A* Intro., iii) probably may
be charged to commercialism.

    6. *Ingen*] "In born," noble.

    8. *Bould*] In Bold's Princox, Field makes excellent use of the proverb
[*SFQ*, X (1946), 14] and brilliantly satirizes the Precisian.

    9. *Well-tri'd*] Suggestive, according to Brinkley (p. 74), of Jonson's
Wellbred.

    11. *Roarers*] "It is to be feared that Whorebang, Bots, Tearchaps, and
Spillblood were contemporary characters" (Brinkley, 54). They appear
only in 3.4. On roaring boys see exp. n. to *W* 3.3.96.

    Serieants] Why such minor characters, whose lines are headed *I. Serg.*
and *2. Serg.* and who are nowhere addressed by name, are given names in
the stage direction at 4.3.2 (see text. n.) I have no guess.

    13. *Botts*] From a disease of animals caused by maggots (Partridge,
s. v.), or possibly "a corruption of *pox*" (H, n.).

1.1

    Outer stage. In its hangings or in the curtains dividing it from the
inner stage, it no doubt offered sufficient concealment for the Wife and
Widow. At some point before the general exodus (408), Welltried, who
at 190 was with the group remaining, may join those leaving.

    1. *Maid, Wife, Widow*] A proverbial (Field, 32) trichotomy of woman-
kind. By making amends to representatives of these three estates, Field
makes amends, of a sort, to all womanhood.

    17. *compatible*] *suitable* rather than *legally competent*.

    22f.] The underlying argument that a maid's estate is superior because
she is free appears in *Campion*, 155; but a writer would hardly need a
source for it.

    32. *but when they please*] This view is repeated in *The Fatal Dowry*,
2.2.49f.

    42–44.] Perhaps a slight preparation for a development of some im-
portance in the plot. See 4.4.120 and exp. n.

    46–48.] Here the Widow employs a venerable argument of popular
literature; cf. *An Alphabet of Tales* [ed. M. M. Banks (London, 1894–
1895)], p. 379 and Johannes Pauli, *Schimpf und Ernst* [ed. Johannes Bolte
(Berlin, 1924)], I, 142; *Comparative Literature Studies*, XXI–XXII
(1946), 29.

    55ff.] Here Field may be indebted to Davies' *A Contention*, in which
the maid calls herself "The spotlesse garment that was neuer worne"
(*Davison's Poetical Rhapsody*, I, 254). The figurative connection between

a maid and a garment, however, was proverbial (Field, 24); and 55–57 are preceded in the copy-text by inverted commas—the normal method of calling attention to proverbs and moral maxims (Simpson, 101ff.). The garment figure is repeated in *The Knight of Malta* (1618) [*Beaumont and Fletcher*, VII, 154; noted by Brinkley, 130].

61. *seruant*] one devoted to a lady's service; a lover.

67. *additions*] marks of distinction; cf. *W* To his Loued Sonne 4.

95ff.] The distinguishing marks of a lover furnish Field comedy also in *W* 1.2.383ff.; see exp. n. to 383.

100. *poudred*] preserved, like meat, by salting or spicing.

104. *fustion*] here *jargon* rather than *inflated language*, if proper weight is given to *like a Butcher*.

130. *ouer see*] spy on the players.

144. *wrack, Strapado, or the boiling boote*] Under quite different circumstances Field refers to these instruments of torture in *W* 4.2.67–69; see exp. nn. to those lines.

148ff.] A suggestion in the lines of the business of the actor, who is about to swear upon his sword.

152. *rambling boies*] Roaring boys, mentioned in *W* 3.3.96 and presented on the stage in *A* 3.4. They are called *Swaggerers* in *A* 2.4.24.

153. *Turnebull-street*] Spelled variously, but properly Turnmill Street, between Clerkenwell Green and Cow Cross. In it was located Pict-hatch; see *W* 1.2.67 and exp. n., *A* 2.2.100. For collections of some of the many references to it see Malone Var., XVII, 136, n. 8; Dodsley³, IX, 208, nn. 47f.; and Wheatley, III, 411.

161. *turn'd*] Usually *changed, become indifferent*; but here possibly *cheated*.

189. *like a waiting Gentlewoman*] "Of all the disguise stratagems of lovers the one of gaining access to a lady protected by a female habit is . . . the most nearly crystallized into a dramatic tradition," writes Freeburg, who treats its origin and course in English drama and mentions this instance (pp. 191, 188–191).

191ff.] Here, I think, we have evidence of a bona fide borrowing from Shakespeare. The parallel between this passage and "Madam and mistress, a thousand good-morrows!" followed by "Sir Valentine and servant, to you two thousand" (*Two Gent. Verona*, 2.1.102, 106f.) might not of itself convince those who are skeptical of parallel passages. But Field seems to be taking Shakespeare's hint for comedy also in what follows; see 196f. and exp. n. In syndrome the two parallels are unlikely to have occurred fortuitously.

192f. *that euer conuersation coapt withall*] McGinn (p. 167) cites as a parallel the same phrase in *Hamlet* 3.2.60. Though the correspondence is as close as could be desired, whether much significance should be attached to it depends upon whether or not the expression had a contemporary vogue. I have not observed one with the aid of the usual tools. *Coapt* means *encountered*.

196f.] Cf. Speed in *Two Gentlemen of Verona*, 2.1.108f.: "He should give her interest, and she gives it him."

205f.] The courtier's holding it a point of policy not to recognize another courtier is dramatized in *Four Plays in One* (X, 289f.; noted by Brinkley, 103).

207. *considered*] bribed.

215f. *this . . . her*] an aside.

221. *Corriuall*] rival suitor.

235. *within a mile of an oke*] Apparently a proverbial expression (Field, 41) though not cited in standard authorities on the proverb. I find it spoken by that peddler of paroemiology, Nicholas Proverbs, in Porter's *Two Angry Women of Abingdon* (*Nero and Other Plays*, 177). Both examples concern combat. Here understand *hard put to it*.

245. *Swoons*] Feesimple's comic aversion to steel may have had special significance in Jacobean times. Cf. "Queen" James' own aversion to it. At the knighting of Sir Kenelm Digby, James is said to have turned away his face from the blade, and the Duke of Buckingham to have guided the sword to Digby's shoulder to prevent James from putting out Digby's eyes; Jesse, *op. cit.*, I, 79f.

258. *infirmitie*] Digby attributes James' aversion to steel to his mother's fright at the assassination of Rizzio, which occurred in her presence before James' birth; Jesse, *op. cit.*, I, 79.

272. *ouerseene of*] neglected by.

274. *Ire-monger*] iron-monger.

278. *base qualities*] The ignorance of James' courtiers was often satirized. Lethe in *Michaelmas Term* is "the better regarded" among courtiers for his lack of literacy, "for that's but a needy quality" (1.1.306f.).

287.] By modern standards this doesn't seem very sophisticated. That it may have been an aside has little to do with the question of its wit.

291. *did mee I*] The old double pronoun, logically superfluous but contributing to a lively colloquialism, is not unlike the ethical dative in Latin.

307. *Princox*] Cf. Latin praecox, "too soon ripe." Greene uses the name "Princockes" in *Menaphon* (*Works*, VI, 134). Since Bold's disguise is not revealed to the audience for some time (at 3.3.130f.), there is some question as to how broadly his role as woman should be played. Perhaps the audience was intended to identify him as a man from his first line; it could hardly have identified him as Bold, of whom there is much talk, until later.

313. *in Capite*] in chief, i. e., from the king. Note the pun in 314, 315f., where the phrase means *in the head*.

319f. *no ebbe so low*] Bold here combines allusions to two proverbial expressions (Field, 11, 48).

322. *blinde Dame*] Fortune.

336f. 57. *Summers*] In the light of 381, Princox's claim is ridiculous. Obviously Bold is more fully concerned with the humor of the situation

than with inventing a plausible story; he seems to have no fear at all of
being detected. Does this show the hand of a playwright who does not
care whether or not he is authentic so long as he gets his laughs?

342. *the doore's as big as it was*] Perhaps proverbial (Field, 16).

344. *frumping*] *jeering;* cf. *W* 3.3.34.

349f.] Proverbial (Field, 25), meaning "it's six of one to half a dozen
of the other."

362. *reade on a booke*] The most suitable book on such occasions was
Petrarch, which in them "does good offices" (*Monsieur D'Olive*, 5.1.195;
see also 190–200). The functions of a waiting-woman are mentioned in
All Fools (2.1.282ff.) and *Bussy D'Ambois* (2.2.58ff.); but though Field
probably had acted in all three of these plays, doubtless we should not
look here for a direct influence.

363. *loouer light*] An opening in the turret for the passage of smoke
or the admission of light. The *NED* cites this instance.

372f. *heer's none but freinds*] This expression is used similarly in
Middleton's *A Trick to Catch the Old One* (4.2.79), *Your Five Gallants*
(1.1.244), and *A Fair Quarrel* (5.1.246). Field probably had acted in the
former two plays, but the expression is not sufficiently distinctive to be
readily traceable.

381. *yong thing*] Cf. 336f. and exp. n.

397.] Proverbial (Field, 35).

407. *gloues*] The contemporary practice of giving gloves to wedding
guests is frequently mentioned in literature; e. g., *Epicoene* 3.6.70ff.,
where gloves are termed "ensignes of a wedding." "Betrothal gloves and
those given as favours to wedding guests," writes Linthicum, "were
obligatory" (p. 267) and very expensive (p. 268).

418. *loue blanches blackest faults*] Probably proverbial (Field, 30).

425. *we two*] Antonio in *The Coxcomb* (1609) says,

> Must we that have so long time been as one
> Seen Cities, Countreys, Kingdoms, and their wonders;
> Been bedfellows, and in our various journey
> Mixt all our observations, part . . . (VIII, 311).

Though Field may have played this role, since he is named first in the list
of principal actors, we should doubtless not regard this as an instance of
borrowing from Beaumont and Fletcher. Many such passages could, of
course, be found in plays with which Field had no connection. Renaissance friendship is studied by Laurens J. Mills in *One Soul in Bodies
Twain* (Bloomington, 1937). With this passage in *A* cf. Nevill and
Scudmore in *W* 1.1.53ff., 68ff. and Gerrard, speaking of Ferdinand, in
Four Plays in One (X, 319).

427. *Gemini*] Castor and Pollux, referred to also in *W* 1.1.123.

432ff.] Cf. *Don Quixote:* "deeming it (as it is reason that all discreet
men should) not so convenient to visit or haunt so often the house of his
friend after marriage, as he would, had he still remained a Batchelor.

For . . . a married mans honour is so delicate and tender a thing, as it seemes it may be sometimes impayred even by very brethren, and how much more by friends" (II, 62).

446. *part from me in hast*] An instance of self repetition in Field. In *W* 1.1 he obtains minor dramatic conflict within the scene by having Nevill start to leave and Scudmore induce him to remain (51–125). Evidently finding the device successful, he employs it again here, though not at such length, and in a collaborately written play; see exp. n. to *W* 1.1.75.

447f.] Cf. *Don Quixote:* "telling Camila at his departure, that whilest hee were absent, his friend Lothario would come and see to the affaires of his house, and to eate with her, and desired her therefore, to make as much of him, as she would doe of his owne person" (II, 80).

461. *was rich to you*] came to you well dowered.

463ff. *t'is not chastity . . . too*] This oppositional conception is suggestive of several proverbs (Field, 6). It appears in *The Second Maiden's Tragedy* (1611), 290–292 and 298–300; in *Don Quixote*, II, 65;. but also in what has been pointed out as Cervantes' source in *The Curious Impertinent* story, *Orlando Furioso;* see *Hispanic Review*, XIV (1946), 347f. Cf. Milton's doctrine of practiced rather than cloistered virtue (*Works*, IV, 311; XV, 114f.).

473f.] Proverbial (Field, 9).

479. *shall be*] supply *satisfied*. The construction is elliptical.

480ff.] In *Don Quixote*, Anselmo's reasons for entrusting the testing of Camila to Lothario are, first, that "if Camila be vanquished by thee, yet shall not the victory arrive to the last push and upshot;" second, if Camila prove weak, Anselmo's injury will be "concealed in the vertue of thy silence; for I know thy care to be such in matters concerning mee, as it shall be eternall like that of death" (II, 66).

487. *Bristow*] i. e., Bristol. Bristol diamonds are imitation gems made from Clifton limestone crystal formations.

488. *Lapidarie*] The use of this word, I believe, is insufficient reason for thinking that here Field had in mind the diamond figure used in *The Second Maiden's Tragedy* (315–319) and more elaborately in *Don Quixote* (II, 70). There is very little more in Field than in *Orlando Furioso;* see *Hispanic Review*, XIV (1946), 349.

493] Possibly proverbial (Field, 58).

495.] Sententious and possibly proverbial (Field, 53).

500. *Coxcombe*] This line has been taken as a possible indication "that Field had the Beaumont-Fletcher play in mind" (Brinkley, 48f.). To most readers the Husband here deserves the title without the justification of any literary borrowing or allusion. *A* bears only superficial resemblance to *The Coxcomb*, which is only slightly similar to the *Curious Impertinent*.

508. *thrust*] The bowdlerization of CHV, if it is that, is unfortunate since it would keep us from observing that here Field is punning on

rather than merely alluding to the proverbial expression (Field, 50), "try ere thou trust."

2.1

Probably Seldom's shop is revealed on the lower inner stage by the drawing of the curtains. If so, Seldom disappears by the door or one of the curtained openings on the inner stage to get the hangers for Moll (20), who presumably enters on the outer stage by one of the proscenium doors (16) and stands before rather than in the shop, or inner stage. The "aboue" of 60 is not necessarily a stage term, for one may represent a shop as being beneath a dwelling without showing the dwelling. No scene is located in the Maid's lodgings, and no one is shown descending from or ascending to them. Proudly's "here in your shop" (66f.) hardly argues that he ever goes on the inner stage proper, the necessary proximity to Grace being possible so long as she remains near the aperture between the two lower stages. A stool may well have been left before the shop by Seldom or Grace, or even brought on by Proudly's Page (69). In 71f. *"th' other end of the Shop"* can be either upstage or, if Grace and Proudly are at either left or right downstage, downstage at the opposite side from them. If as I think Feesimple and Welltried enter (101) by one of the proscenium doors on the outer stage, Grace and Seldom in the shop upstage of the group are out of the way so that we can attend to the conversation of the newcomers with Proudly. At the close of the scene the curtains dividing inner from outer stage may have been drawn to permit the unobserved removal of properties required by the shop scene.

7. *wiues*] See *W* 2.1.275ff. and 2.2.98 and exp. nn. thereto.

18. *hangers*] devices for buckling on the scabbard; Malone Var., VII, 498; Linthicum, 265.

19. *hic & haec*] Literally: *this*, masculine and feminine—referring, of course, to Moll's male garb and swagger.

29. *partie*] Not, as now, a vulgarism for *person*.

32. *impudent*] Probably not an exclamation (see text. n.) but a self-interrupted speech. Words momentarily fail Grace.

36. *some say*] Perhaps including Milton; see exp. n. to dram. pers., 5.

40. *Mistris what lack yee?*] A proverbial (Field, 52) phrase used as a contemptuous epithet for shopkeepers, based upon their cry.

42f. *follow the Fryars*] "an allusion to Blackfriars as a common residence of the Puritans" (C, n.). Cf. *The Alchemist* (1610), 1.1.128f.

43. *jumbler*] strumpet.

46. *sword and target*] Cf. *sword and buckler, 1 Hen. IV*, 1.3.230; but in these words we probably have a figure comparable to those of 19 and 49.

47. *Marie Vmbree*] An English heroine celebrated for her valor in assisting the Hollanders during the siege of Ghent, 1584. She is often mentioned in drama, e. g., in *Tale of a Tub*, 1.4.22, *Epicoene*, 4.2.123f.; and in *The Scornful Lady* (I, 298). A ballad on her may be seen in

Bishop Percy's Folio Manuscript [ed. John W. Hales and F. J. Furnivall (London, 1867–1868), I, 516–519].

Long-Meg] Another virago of great notoriety, whose stature was proverbial. Named after her were a cannon in Dover Castle and a flagstone in Westminster Abbey. She served as title-character of the lost play mentioned in *A* 2.1.152 and a leading character in Deloney's "Richard Casteler," in *The Gentle Craft*. For a discussion and collection of allusions see Frank W. Chandler, *The Literature of Roguery* (Boston, 1907), I, 144f.

52. *Bridewell*] a house of correction for strumpets, petty criminals, and vagabonds; see Wheatley, I, 241–244.

53. *conceiue*] comprehend.

55f. *mistooke me quite*] Moll may be referring to a special signification of hangers pointed out by Linthicum (p. 265) and observed in *Greenes Tu Quoque* (1611), in which fine hangers are recognized as gifts of ladies to their favorites (Dodsley[4], XI, 255).

66. *Tobacco*] Note that Field merely presents rather than ridicules (Brinkley, 59) the use of tobacco.

93. *taffatae pipkin*] Literally, a small French hat worn, after 1600, only by those with incomes too small to afford more fashionable headgear; Linthicum, 231. Here the use, however, may be figurative. With *finicall* perhaps *taffatae* means *fastidious* (*NED*, s. v., 2). Partridge glosses *pipkin* late in the century as "The female pudend" (*s. v.*).

95.] Grace refers to Proudly's frequent *mew*, a seventeenth-century equivalent of the modern American Bronx cheer.

152f. *long-megg and the ship*] There is doubt as to whether this passage refers to one title or to two. The lack of italics in the copy-text deprives us of what might have been slight typographical evidence. Chambers (II, 190) would seem to interpret it as a single title. Collier in his note leaves the matter open: "It is doubtful whether two plays . . . or only one with a double title are here intended to be spoken of" (n.). H silently revises C's note and prints: "It is tolerably evident that two plays . . . and not one with a double title, are here intended to be spoken of" (n.). V prints H's version of the note but signs it C. Using either H or V, modern scholars tend to agree that we have here two titles, though they have not always made independent investigations of the question; see Baskervill, *The Elizabethan Jig and Related Song Drama* (Chicago, 1929), 300; Gertrude M. Sibley, *The Lost Plays and Masques* (Ithaca, 1933), 94, 144; Lawrence, *Pre-Restoration Stage Studies* (Cambridge, 1927), 88; and Harbage, 58, 82. There is fair agreement that *long-megg* is probably the *long mege of westmester* performed by the Admiral's men at Newington in 1594 and probably for a long time afterwards; Greg, *HD*, I, 21–51, II, 174; Chambers, II, 190; Lawrence, *ibid.*, 88. Identification of *the ship* is more difficult. Baskervill (p. 300) takes it as one of "two titles that may belong to lost jigs" and reminds that "Field's play was written near the time when the Fortune attained its great notoriety in connection with jigs, and it is not improbable that 'The Ship' was a well-known jig of the period." Lawrence writes, "The reference here to two pieces shows undoubtedly that the second was a jig" (*ibid.*, 88). He takes *ship* as a misprint for *slip* and proposes that *The Slip* was "the accurate title of Phillips' jig" *The Slippers*. This is ingenious but seems farfetched. If *the ship* was an afterpiece, it is our only evidence, as Baskervill notes (p. 107, n. 2), that the title of a jig for a given occasion was announced in advance.

153. *the Fortune*] The famous theatre between Golding Lane and Whitecross Street built by Henslowe and Alleyn, probably in rivalry with the Globe. Of the details of its construction we know a good deal because the original builder's contract has been preserved (Greg, *HP*, 4–7). The home of the Admiral's men, who became the Prince's men, who became the Palsgrave's men, it was destroyed by fire at midnight 9 December 1621 and promptly rebuilt. See further Adams, 267–293; Greg, *HD*, II, 56–65; and Chambers, II, 435–443. I fail to see here the chaffing of this theatre seen by Chambers (III, 114).

154. *Primero*] See exp. n. to *W* 3.2.34.

162. *pollicie in that wife*] Because Seldom has a wife of unusual virtue (2.1.6ff.), his commercialism is perhaps less offensive than that of some shopkeepers (2.2.29f. and exp. n. to *W* 2.2.98). It reminds Verity (p. 437) of the courtier's of Song of the Citizen, *Fatal Dowry*, IV, ii, a scene Field may have written.

169. *Gally-moferie*] Literally, *hash*, but figuratively, as here, *a confused jumble.*

173ff.] Field seems to use a not dissimilar idea in *The Queen of Corinth* (1617), VI, 41, 60f. (noted by Brinkley, 118).

2.2

Outer stage. Another "threshold scene" (Chambers, III, 60).

14. *babies in your eies*] A figure common in seventeenth-century poetry. Cf. Herrick, *Hesperides*, Nos. 38, 297, 329, and 524 [*Herrick: The Hesperides & Noble Numbers*, ed. A. W. Pollard (London, 1898), I, 17, 151, 162, and 243]. An eye-baby is the image of the spectator seen in another's eye, but it seems to have connection with Latin *pupilla*, a little girl [J. W. Hebel and H. H. Hudson, *Poetry of the English Renaissance* (New York, 1938), 1012].

pink't] peered with half-closed eyes.

29ff. *decai'd Tradseman*] Cf. the behavior of Seldom in this play, and see *W* 2.2.98 and *A* 2.1.162 and exp. nn.

79. *His merrit is a halter*] Cf. the proverb, "An old thief deserves a new halter" (*Oxford Proverbs*, 43).

100. *Pict-hatch*] See exp. n. to *W* 1.2.67.

Turnebole-streete] Turnmill street; see exp. n. to *A* 1.1.153.

101.] With emphasis on *Your?*

105. *wordly*] *worldly;* see exp. n. to *W* 2.1.57.

107. *plaies*] More than those of most playwrights, I think, Field's characters like to talk about the theatre. Here probably no specific titles are in mind, although *W* is an example.

118f. *no iniurie / Compell*] Supply *let.*

2.3

Unless a chair was brought out for Ingen (1), this scene seems to have been performed on the lower inner stage. If so, a little less than five minutes was allowed for the removal of Seldom's shop and its properties—sufficient time, however, if one may judge from present-day scene shifts. If the outer stage was used, perhaps the opposite side from that used in 2.2 was employed; and Ingen's invitation to the Maid (122) may have been made to seem appropriate by his leading her out the other proscenium door or between the curtains into the inner stage.

4. *Irish foot-boy*] According to Freeburg (p. 95), this disguise is a borrowing from *The Coxcomb.* Collier, however, in a n. collects a number of examples of Irish footboys in plays of the time and remarks, "It seems to have been the custom to employ the Irish as lackies or footmen at this period."

10. *dart*] Apparently a conventional symbol for the Irish; see *A Fair Quarrel* (1617), 4.4.183f.

25. *continent*] i. e., container; cf. *W* 1.1.104 and exp. n.

31] Perhaps an aside.

43. *gloues*] See *A* 1.1.407 and exp. n.

57. *praecipitated*] Thrown headlong down, destroyed.

73. *hand-fast*] Marriage contract.

76. *like a woman*] Here Field may be repeating a disguise device from *The Scornful Lady,* in which the title character is made jealous by Welford disguised as a mistress of the Elder Loveless (I, 289).

107. *vncouth*] "In many examples . . . the exact sense is difficult to determine" (*NED, s. v.*).

111. *Basilisque*] See exp. nn. to *W* 3.2.96 and 3.4.10.

123. *crowne*] bless with success.

2.4

Probably the outer stage; the scene contains little that definitely fixes its staging.

12f. *necessarie house*] See exp. n. to *W* 4.2.51.

15. *inuisible ring*] A reference to the magic ring of folklore and romance; see Thompson, *Motif Index,* D 1361.17 and G. L. Kittredge, *Witchcraft in Old and New England* (Cambridge, 1929), 111, and 439f., nn. 49f.

17. *rings*] in slang, *vulvas.*

18. *Islington*] See exp. n. to *W* 3.3.107.

24. *Swaggerers*] See exp. n. to *W* 3.3.96.

34f.] Field frequently advertises the quality. In 35 we get "an interesting allusion to the necessity of a woman's having an escort when she attended a play" (Brinkley, 56).

43. *quoile*] stir, busyness.

46ff.] Note the weak but very naturalistic ending of the act.

3.1

Unlocated, but probably played on the outer stage. It may be regarded as a threshold scene outside the house of the Husband, who, leaving the stage (40), leaves the field to Subtle.

4ff.] The same cynical view of woman's virtue is expressed in Chapman's *May-Day* (1602), in which Field probably had acted, (e. g., at 1.1.151ff.), and in the plays of Beaumont and Fletcher. These lines, however, reflect a proverbial expression (Field, 54) found also in Lyly, Greene, Jonson, and Shakespeare.

11ff.] Similar instructions on the art of wooing are given by Truewit in *Epicoene* (4.1.94–125). I am inclined to see in this passage the influence of Jonson.

24. *buy 'em*] Field refers to this practice also in *W* 1.2.86.

34. *black-woorke*] black silk embroidery in 1611 no longer fashionable; Linthicum, 149.

wastcote] "A woman did not appear in waist-coat," we are told, "unless she were a strumpet" (Linthicum, 214).

46. *wants*] e. g., the loss of the Wife's clothes (27f., 33f.).

3.2

A threshold scene outside the house of Ingen, this would seem to have been played on the outer stage, possibly on the opposite side from that used in 3.1.

7ff. *I am so full . . . teares of bloud*] Much too common a figure, I think, to give it any value as evidence of Field's having been influenced by this as opposed to that playwright. It occurs, e. g., in *2 Tamburlaine* (1588), 5.3.161f., *Jew of Malta* (1589), 3.2.19 [*The Works and Life of Christopher Marlowe*, gen. ed. R. H. Case (London, 1930–1933)]; in *3 Henry VI* (1591), 5.6.63f., *Venus and Adonis*, 1054, and *The Winter's Tale* (1610), 5.2.96f.

11. *Loeda's Swan*] Zeus reputedly visited Leda in the likeness of a swan of immaculate dazzling whiteness in a meeting which has been frequently painted.

15. *female hate*] A difficult expression. None of the senses of *female* in the *NED* seems specific enough to be applicable here. Perhaps the meaning *pertaining to woman* is acceptable if with *hate* we can interpret it as *occasioned by woman* and remember such feuds as that between the Heatho-Bards and the Danes and that between the Frisians and the Danes, despite Freawara and Hildeburh, women meant for peace pledges.

41ff.] I find here little similarity to the unmasking of *Epicoene*; Frank's disguise, rather than "probably derived from *Epicoene*" (Brinkley, 76), may have been derived from *The Scornful Lady*; see exp. n. to *A* 2.3.76.

62ff.] A combination of two proverbial (Field, 29 and 51) expressions. Herrick, oddly, makes precisely the same combination in *Hesperides*, No. 38 (I, 17).

65–82.] This passage has been cited as evidence of Field's rough metre (Brinkley, 62). But 68f. are exclamations, which are commonly extra-metrical [*JEGP*, XXXVI (1937), 157] and which are perhaps more effective for breaking the measure.

67. *thou liest*] From early times "giving the lie," or *mentita*, has been the insult which invited an immediate challenge; F. R. Bryson, *The Sixteenth-Century Italian Duel* (Chicago, 1938), 3f., 6. Field uses it also in 3.4.133, 4.2.119, and 5.2.273.

72. *strike in his owne house*] Perhaps not a reference to the laws of the duello; I find nothing on the point in a number of Renaissance works or in F. T. Bowers, *JEGP*, XXXVI (1937), 40–65; H. S. Craig, *op. cit.*; Ruth Kelso, *The Doctrine of the English Gentleman in the Sixteenth Century* (Urbana, 1929); F. R. Bryson, *op. cit.*; and A. Forbes Sieveking, *SE*, II, 389–407. The offense here would have been, as the Maid says, one "'gainst hospitalitie" (71); it would, also, since Proudly is the challenged, have disregarded his right to name the place (Bryson, *op. cit.*, 27).

88. *liueries*] servants in livery.

89.] A further insult, to some extent excusing that in Ingen's next speech. According to the duelling code, an insult given between the challenge and the duel was a breach of honor; Bowers, *JEGP*, XXXVI (1937), p. 50 and n. 31.

91. *no*] The emendation by H (see text. n.) is dictated by a modern attitude. Ingen, the valiant, wants no recantation, but blood.

3.3

Though a chamber scene, this was not necessarily performed on the inner stage, which was at this time probably being set for the immediately following tavern scene, which requires a number of properties. The present scene requires virtually none; the Widow and Bold together could carry out the Widow's outer clothes, which Bold seems to remove (4, 46ff.); and Bold could take care of the disguise he removes at the end of the scene.

11.] The entire scene seems quite salacious. I do not attempt to gloss all the puns.

23f. *Si non caste, tamen caute*] Field may have remembered this Latin proverb from *The Malcontent* (1604), I, 186, he probably having acted in that play. But in English, too, the expression was proverbial (Field, 4).

29. *Precise*] i. e., like a Precisian, defined in one of the Overbury characters as "a demure creature, full of orall sanctity, and mentall impiety" [*Miscellaneous Works*, ed. Edward F. Rimbault (London, 1890), 102].

30. *Black-fryers*] the liberty; see exp. n. to *A* 2.1.42f.

32. *dew*] In view of the context, probably sermons rather than plays.

35. *that*] The line has occasioned misunderstanding; see text. n. The Widow says that not the speaker of double entendres, but the hearer of them who chooses the worse meaning, is at fault. The underlying idea is proverbial (Field, 57).

39. Cf. the Latin proverb (Field, 44), "Puris omnia pura." I have not found any other instance of this parody.

46. *done*] i. e., finished "vnpinning and vnlacing" the Widow. For *doe* in 49f. see exp. n. to 4.2.39. The theatrical effectiveness of this scene is understood to be great when we remember that Bold's being a man has not necessarily yet been revealed to the audience.

59. *preposterous*] unnatural.

61. *word*] That the word *stand* clearly had a pornographic significance in the Renaissance will be seen from 54–57, 60–62, and 87–89; one may be indicated in *W* 1.2.287. Yet no such sense is listed in the *NED,* and Partridge (*s. v.,* n. 2.) dates the usage within the nineteenth and twentieth centuries.

71. *receipt*] True-wit gives a similar description of woman's cosmetics in *Epicoene,* 2.2.136–139, but Field repeats none of the ingredients. Field may have mentioned cosmetics again in *The Knight of Malta* (1618), VII, 84 (noted by Brinkley, 125). For a collection of satirical references to cosmetics in this period see M. P. Tilley, *RES,* V (1929), 312–317. Tilley points out that satire on this subject is common and traceable to the early Christian fathers.

74. *Iordane Almonds*] A superior variety of almond grown chiefly in Malaga.

76. *newly couer'd*] i. e., the *mare.*

83ff.] In this catalogue of suitors Field has been said (Fischer, 38; Brinkley, 78) to owe a debt to Shakespeare; cf. *Merchant of Venice,* 1.2. The similarity between the scenes is limited to the basic element that in both a lady and her waiting-woman discuss the lady's suitors. Differences between the scenes are that in Field the waiting-woman is an impostor; that Field mentions three suitors to Shakespeare's six, in about 375 words to Shakespeare's approximately 675; that Field's scene closes with a major advance in the plot whereas Shakespeare's closes with the entrance of a servingman; and that Princox is not merely an interlocutor like Nerissa but decidedly a participating agent. Though in literary quality Shakespeare's scene may be superior to Field's, Field's is the more comic and has the additional merit of being integrated more closely with the advancing plot. From the point of view of the theatrical rather than the literary man, Field, if he is here borrowing from Shakespeare, improves upon Shakespeare.

92. *in print*] Proverbial (Field, 45). See exp. n. to *W,* 1.2.15.

99. *man of waxe*] Cf. *W*, 1.2.77 where, in the mouth of Pendant, the term is a compliment. For the connection of the term to wax figures see Malone Var., VI, 38, n. 9.

101. *gyns*] Machines, mechanical contrivances. Master Pert is said to walk like a robot. For the interesting history of this reading see text. n.

103f. *one . . . fallen*] "one of the purles of your band is (without all discipline falne) out of his ranke," *The Fatal Dowry*, 2.2.77f. (cited by *C*, n., and Brinkley, 89).

110. *vntrust*] Cf. *W* 1.2.1 and exp. n.

112. *memorie*] According to Elizabethan psychology, the faculty of common sense had its seat in the front, imagination in the center, and memory in the back of the head; cf. Lily B. Campbell, *Shakespeare's Tragic Heroes: Slaves of Passion* (Cambridge, 1930), 66. Thus Anthony Stafford speaks of the wastrel as having "eyes so hollow, that they runne back to salute his memory, least she should forget them" [*Staffords Niobe* (London, 1611), 40].

124. *dwels at the signe of the scab*] Cf. a number of similar colloquial expressions current in a later period; e. g., *to live at the sign of the cat's foot* was to be henpecked; *at the sign of the horn*, to be a cuckold (Partridge, *s.* sign). In view of the context, *scab* here seems more likely to imply venereal disease than itch.

127. *owe thee eies*] This remark, involving a proverbial notion (Field, 23), is paradoxical since Fortune is blind.

130f.] Here Princox probably unmasks, and we first are sure that she is Bold, whom we know from a good deal that has been said about him. His disguise is long sustained; but as Freeburg (pp. 12, 114, 117f.) has shown, the surprise disguise of this type had considerable vogue after *Epicoene* (1609). Field was probably familiar with it, also, from its earlier use by Lysander in *The Widow's Tears* (1605), in which play too he probably had acted.

3.4

Inner stage. The scene requires *"Wine, Plate, and Tobacco"* (36), a table (55), *"pots and stooles"* (134), and may have been set with something like a bar. One need not subscribe to the discredited alternationist theory of staging (see Chambers, III, 120f., and n. 2) to admit that a certain amount of time must have been required to remove these properties and clean up the debris from the fight. The curtains may have been drawn over the inner stage at the end of the scene.

This is the roaring scene to which attention was called in the cancel title-page of the 1618 quarto (see above, *A* Intro., iii) and for which we have been well prepared by numerous anticipatory references: 1.1.152f., 2.1.133ff., 148ff., 155f., 2.4.24, 40f. It has been said, on authority not furnished, that the scene "was probably drawn from a real model" (Brinkley, 54).

8. *Duke of Clarence*] Drowned, according to *The Mirror for Magistrates* [ed. Lily B. Campbell (Cambridge, 1938), 233f.], in a butt of Malmsey wine. Cf. also *Rich. III*, 1.4.161, 276.

9f. *Pie-corner*] A district in West Smithfield, famous for cooks, pastry shops, and broadsheet literature; Wheatley, III, 93f. On the roasting and eating of pigs there see *The Alchemist*, 1.1.25ff., *Bartholomew Fair*, 1.5.155, and Malone Var., XVII, 92f., n. 8.

10. *Barthomew-tide*] The festival of St. Bartholomew, 24 August; on the celebration see *Bartholomew Fair*.

12. *Turne-bole*] Turnmill Street; see exp. n. to *A* 1.1.153.

25f. *a Play*] There seems to be insufficient reason for identifying this with *The Roaring Girl* (Fleay, *BC*, I, 202).

28f.] If audiences have not changed more than we think, this hit, whether at rival actors or at all actors, by a leading actor of the day must have brought hearty laughter. Chambers argues from this passage and from 2.1.152f. as well as the introduction of Moll Cutpurse in 2.1, for a rivalry between *Amends* and *The Roaring Girl* (III, 314); and this is possible, I think, without taking "play" in 25f. to be *The Roaring Girl*. If the reference is to a specific company, *them* (29) probably refers to Prince Henry's men, a company which had played at the Fortune since its establishment (Chambers, II, 190). Fleay, I think without complete justification, takes "keepe a whore honest" as an allusion to *The Honest Whore* (*BC*, 1, 202).

32. *pottles*] half-gallons.

40f. *one face among 'em*] i. e., one *whole* face. They wear patches indicative at least of their having been in fights (71–74); and at least one of them, Botts, has lost his nose (75f., 118f.).

42. *put out something*] The practice of taking out insurance on one's safe return from a voyage is mentioned in *Every Man Out*, 2.3.245ff., *The Tempest*, 3.3.48, and elsewhere; see Malone Var., XV, 125f., n. 7.

43. *Barmuthoes*] Either the Bermudas, which had then a mixed reputation, or a noted London haunt of cheats and rascals, named for them. This line has been taken (V, n.) to refer to the district in London. Since Feesimple has deliberately chosen to go to such a place with Bold, however, it would seem as probable that he refers to the western islands.

68. *Iack*] "The *jack*, properly, is a coat of mail, but it here means a buff *jacket* or *jerkin* worn by soldiers or pretended soldiers" (C, n.) Perhaps so, but *to lay or be upon the jack* was slang for *to thrash or scold soundly* (Partridge, *s.* jack).

75. *basket hilt Dagger*] Despite Shakespeare's contemptuous use of the term (*2 Henry IV*, 2.4.141), a fine though old-fashioned weapon of which the handle and pommel bore a covering like basket-work; H. S. Craig, *op. cit.*, 24.

82. *seauen deadly sins*] The seven cardinal sins entailing spiritual death, as usually listed, were pride, envy, wrath, sloth, avarice, gluttony, and

lust. If we equate drunkenness with gluttony, Spillblood omits envy, sloth, and avarice. Note that only three healths are drunk.

101f. *Dam mee Company*] Throughout this scene the fellowship of roaring boys seems to claim the oath *Dam mee* as its exclusive property; cf. 122–128.

105. *obseruers*] "Whore-bang calls these play-makers [*sic*] 'observers,' as if suspecting that Welltried and Feesimple came among them for the purpose of making notes for a play" (C, n.).

106f. *play maker*] Welltried replies to the implied charge that he is an observer. "These words have reference, perhaps," C notes, "to Middleton and Rowley's curious old comedy of manners, *A Fair Quarrel*." What the connection is C does not state and Fleay (*BC*, I, 202) could not determine, nor can I.

125. *Patch*] Either *fool* or a reference, as C notes, "to the *patch* on the face of Tear-chaps," or both.

128. *lies*] lies in pawn, for swearing.

133.] Welltried gives Whorebang the occasion for a formal challenge (exp. n. to 3.2.67) despite the probable difference in their social positions.

139. *Lord a Lorne*] Field's knowledge of the ballad of this name (*Percy's Folio Manuscript*, I, 182–198) appears to have been inexact. Perhaps its young hero had shown cowardice in yielding his clothes and jewelry to the steward who was on the point of taking his life and who later had to crave mercy, but the lord's valiance is not stressed.

141. *heads*] A reference to the actor's business? Perhaps Feesimple here points to a round pot or other vessel.

149. *breake windowes*] "Lord Feesimple's suggestion . . . shows that the popularity of this sport had not waned since the day of Surrey" (Brinkley, 54).

151. *shot-log*] usually *shot-clog*, an unwelcome companion accepted because he pays the shot for the party.

4.1

Outer stage, perhaps the same side as that by which the Widow and Bold had left the stage at the end of 3.3. If Subtle and the Boy sing their serenade beneath a window, it might have been either the window above the opposite proscenium door, in which case they may have entered between the curtains dividing the inner from outer stage (144), or a curtained gallery over the inner stage. Subtle thinks that Bold has come from the house of the Wife (170f.); but since we do not know that a single area consistently represented that dwelling, I am unable to draw from his evidence conclusions clearly affecting the staging.

2. *shirt*] the usual bed-garment for men of the nobility; Linthicum, 215.

34. *getting to her bed*] Proverbial (Field, 1).

53.] With 116, Field's amends for ladies in the account of the Widow. For those in the accounts of the Maid and Wife see, respectively, 4.4.115

and 5.1.123ff. All three accounts are rendered again for reinforcement in 5.2.297–299.

67. *occasion slip, her fore-top*] The god Occasion, or Opportunity, was represented as bald except for a full forelock; whence the proverbial phrase (Field, 42), *to take occasion, opportunity,* or *time by the foretop* or *forelock.*

91. *sensitiue soules*] i. e., animals. Bold is referring to the classical and scholastic conception of the three souls, vegetative, sensitive, and rational or intellective; see *PQ,* XXV (1946), 382f. If man may be condemned, Bold says, for an act his by nature and to beasts permitted, then beasts are happier than men.

95ff.] Cf. St. Thomas: "Now in respect of the intellective soul we are said to be *men,* according to the sensitive soul *animals,* according to the nutritive soul *living*" [*Summa Contra Gentiles,* trans. English Dominican Fathers (London, 1923–1929), II, 142].

105. *making*] mating.

109. *prick-song*] Though sometimes a descant on a plain-song, here to be taken more generally as music sung from written notes rather than from memory; cf. *Romeo and Juliet,* 2.4.21f., *Bussy D'Ambois,* 1.2.88. On the pun see *Your Five Gallants,* 2.1.45f., in which Field probably had acted.

116.] Further amends to the Widow. This situation is not unlike those into which perhaps Field later puts Martius in *Four Plays in One* (X, 304, 310) and Miranda in *The Knight of Malta* (VII, 151–154); Brinkley, 122–124, commenting: "it is the remarkable inflexibility of the women that finally convinces the men that here at last is one woman who is not as 'insatiate as the grave.' "

124f.] I am unable to find record of any such incident. When he concluded that the Widow-Bold story is based upon an incident from real life, C, I suspect, was making far too much of these lines; see *A* Intro., ii. The Widow desperately needs an argument against Bold's suggestion that they continue to live together as lady and waiting-woman, but illicitly. When Bold says that she might be led into this arrangement out of delight in the newness of the trick, a very appropriate answer is that the trick is not new. The following line, on which the case of C seems to rest, may represent only enough invention of detail by the Widow to give credibility to her charge that the trick is stale.

125. *the Fleete*] After the abolition of the Star Chamber, Fleet Prison came to be used for debtors, bankrupts, etc. It is rich with literary associations since it was the temporary residence of, among many others, Surrey, Nashe, Donne, Lucius Carey, Prynne, and James Howell; Wheatley, II, 57ff.

135–137.] Seldom does Field achieve such warm, human characterization as in these lines.

139. *Iuglers*] tricksters.

140. *the wry-leg'd fellow*] I have been unable to track down this reference, which seems to be to a contemporary celebrity of some sort.

144. *with a cloake*] Field seems here to be trying to disguise a convention of the Jacobean stage, that songs should be sung by skilled boys introduced for that purpose rather than by actors. The true purpose of the boy is to sing. Writing on "extraneous song" in the drama of the period, Louis B. Wright uses the song at 145ff. as an illustration [*SP*, XXIV (1927), 270]. This song, however, is not extraneous from the point of view of dramaturgy since it makes a direct connection between two of the plot strands, Subtle's attack on the Wife and Bold's on the Widow.

145ff.] "Das an die Ehefrau gerichtete Lied, das Subtle in derselben Szene verliest, lehnt sich in seinem Schlusse an ein bekanntes lyrisches Gedicht dieser Zeit an" (Fischer, 39). If Fischer here had anything more definite in mind than the following n. by C, I have been unable to find it. C notes: "The concluding thought of this pretty song has been in request by many poets of all countries. . . ." It appears unlikely that Fischer would refer thus to the sonnet of Eustachio Manfredi which C goes on to mention. That the concluding figure is paralleled in *The Fatal Dowry* (ed. Lockert, p. 145) has been noticed (C, n.; Brinkley, 88).

161. *neuer the neere*] Proverbial (Field, 18).

163. *at a womans labour*] A stock "gag" useful on being stopped by the watch late at night and on other occasions; see *A Trick to Catch the Old One* (Middleton, *Works*, II, 351),*The Black Book* (*ibid.*, VIII, 35), and the Beaumont-Fletcher *Four Plays in One* (X, 347).

164f. *man Mid-wife*] That both Bold and Subtle had the watch in mind may perhaps be inferred from this reply; for *man-midwife* was a contemporary nickname for *sergeant*. Cf. *The Whore of Babylon* (Dekker, II, 213) and *The Roaring Girl* (3.3.198).

168f.] Bold takes as his the serenade which Subtle has arranged for the Wife. In *Don Quixote* Anselmo suggests that Lothario "bring musicke under her windowes by night" (II, 76); but this stratagem is not so uncommon among dashing young men that Field need have learned it of Cervantes.

170ff.] In *Don Quixote*, seeing the lover of Camila's maid leave the house at daybreak, Lothario falsely concludes that whoever left "at so unreasonable an houre, had not entred into it for Leonelas sake . . . but onely thought that as Camila was lightly gotten by him, so belike she was wonne by some other" (II, 91). In a jealous rage, therefore, he informs Anselmo that Camila is dishonest. Cf. also *The Second Maiden's Tragedy*, 928–978.

4.2

With the bed (2) not thrust out but discovered, and its location "Bould's *chamber*" (2) specified in both stage directions and lines (3, 59ff.), this scene, which does not require an upper level, was likely presented on the lower inner stage. If so, the curtains are probably drawn at the close of the scene.

39. *done*] A euphemism; cf. *NED*, *s*. do, v. 16b. Shakespeare employs the same expression in *Love's Labour's Lost*, 3.1.200 and *All's Well That Ends Well*, 2.3.246. Cf. the definition in Jonson's translation of a fragment from Petronius [*Poems*, ed. Bernard H. Newdigate (Oxford, 1936), 220].

40. *Tarquin*] See exp. n. to *W* 3.2.228.

50. *milk-sop*] sissy.

52. *jumbl'd*) known carnally.

55. *cast*] *brought around*, as of a ship.

80. *a vision*] With reference to the departing Bold.

88ff.] In Feesimple's comic boasting Field's further debt to Shakespeare has been seen by Fischer (p. 38) and Brinkley (p. 78), who calls this passage "the reverse of" *1 Henry IV*, 2.4.175ff., "where Falstaff tells of the robbery at Gads Hill."

98f. *we may kill whom we list*] Untrue, of course, but an exaggeration useful in Field's satire on the nobility. If we may judge by the words of the Maid in 4.3.5–7, and by 4.4.67 (see exp. n.), the nobility were not immune to this extent.

117. *if*] This word makes Feesimple out a coward and scoundrel who hides behind the "Lie Conditional." Touchstone glosses: "All these you may avoid but the Lie Direct, and you may avoid that too, with an If. . . . Your If is the only peacemaker. Much vertue in If" (*As You Like It*, 5.4.102ff.). See also H. S. Craig, *op. cit.*, 16, n. 55.

118. *sonne of a whore*] This and the following insults are more or less standard incitements to a challenge. Hazard in *The Gamester* (1633) [*Dramatic Works and Poems*, ed. Gifford and Dyce (London, 1833), III, 195] states that gentleman

> cannot quarrel
> About a glass of wine, but out flies straight,
> *Son of a whore!* Dead mothers must be torn
> Out of their graves, or living, have their names
> Poison'd by a prodigious breath . . .

Middleton and Rowley selected this charge as the Colonel's insult to Captain Ager in *A Fair Quarrel* (1617), 1.1.351, 368, where it is important to the plot. How bitter a charge it was is described in that play at 2.1.1ff. Its frequent use is one of the absurdities of roaring boys Field ridicules by having Feesimple repeat it in 5.2.273.

124ff.] These lines appear to have been written in imitation of or allusion to, rather than "taken from some song of 'Little Boy Blue'" (H, n.; cf. Fischer, 39).

4.3

The outer stage was probably used for this threshold scene near the house of Proudly. On the morning of his duel with Ingen he enters "*with*

a riding rod" (16) and calls for his offstage horse. Seldom and the ser-
geants arrest Proudly and thrust him into Seldom's house (37, 42f.), which
may have been represented by the opposite proscenium door.

17ff.] At least in Italy, the challenger rather than the challenged apparently was expected to arrive first in the field (Bryson, *op. cit.*, 38).

24. *Old-castle*] Another illustration of interest, on the part of Field
and his characters, in theatrical matters. All authorities, I think, take this
passage as a reference to Falstaff's catechism on honor in *1 Henry IV*
(1597), 5.1.130–143; e. g., Adams, *A Life of William Shakespeare* (Boston, 1923), 231; Chambers, *S*, I, 382; Koeppel, 76; Fischer, 38; Evelyn May
Albright, *Dramatic Publication in England, 1580–1640* (New York, 1927),
172. Field's evidence is said to have helped settle the controversy over the
original name given to the character of Falstaff; Malone Var., XVI, 193
and 410–419. Albright (p. 172) uses this allusion as evidence that *1 Henry
IV* was played at least once in uncensored form.

26. *flat-cap*] Like the proverbial *what lack yee?*, this was a contemptuous epithet for shopkeeper, evidently based upon the merchant's headgear.

29.] I see no significant resemblance between Seldom's arrest of Proudly
and the passage in *Westward Ho!* cited by Fischer (p. 37). The Maid
here induces Seldom to arrest Proudly so as to prevent the duel. Tenter-
hook is induced by his wife Moll for a less charitable reason.

36. *faire shop and wife*] From the use made of shopkeepers' wives in
the period, if we may judge from literature, it is not entirely inappropriate
to speak of a merchant's wife, along with his stock, as part of his assets.
Previous editors need not have troubled to emend; see text. n.

4.4

Outer stage, serving for if not representing the duelling field (62).
Verisimilitude is preserved by having Ingen order Frank to "walk off, and
take the boy away" (81); but the following stage direction is in the practical terminology of the theatre: *"Bro. thrusts the Boy out"* (83). The
contending factions may have left the scene by opposite proscenium doors
(151, 155).

2. *like a Man*] Here, I think, not "a servant," with H (n.); contrast
the stage directions on Frank's previous entrances (2.3.76, 3.2.1f.) in both
of which he was *like a woman*.

18. *vntouch't*] Although the origin of the duel remains an unsettled
question, because of its connections with the ordeal and trial by combat
the duellist's psychology was that of one invoking the god of battle to
decide a debated matter. Any effort on the part of either duellist or his
supporters to renew the conflict after the sign had been given was outside
the code of honor, indeed, a sort of blasphemy against the god of battle.
Moralists, moreover, argued that duelling was justified because it prevented
the adherents of those who had received affronts, from flying to arms and

thus embroiling the state in civil wars (Kelso, *op. cit.*, 103). In the following lines Ingen and Frank have an argument very good for dramatic purposes because a strong case can be made out on each side.

33ff.] Field has a similar attack on law in *W*, 2.1.310ff.; see exp. n. to 312.

37. *snaffle*] A bridle-bit with less restraining power than one provided with a curb *(NED, s. v.)*, and therefore the less objectionable to the "patient Asse" which Field calls law *(W, 2.1.313)*.

38. *Pithagorean*] Perhaps in allusion to the doctrine of transmigration of souls attributed to Pythagoras. If this is the proper connection to make, the word here means something like *shape-changing*.

43f.] Proverbial (Field, 2).

67. *cleanlier shift*] less ignoble ruse. Ingen has concluded that Proudly has turned coward and arranged to have himself arrested.

68. *by command*] Apprised of a forthcoming duel, on occasions the Privy Council would apprehend the duellists and charge them in His Majesty's name not to fight. In 1608 and 1610, for example, it prevented Lord Herbert of Cherbury from making good with the sword his quarrels with Captain Vaughan, one Boqhuan [Buchan?], and Sir John Ayres; see *Calendar of State Papers, Domestic, 1603–1610* [ed. Robert Lemon and Mary Anne E. Green (London, 1856–1872)], 583; Herbert, *Autobiography* [ed. Sidney Lee (2d ed.; London, 1907)], 50f., 73, 74. Common law for some time had held duelling illegal, but the many duels at the time of the war in Cleves and Juliers (see Herbert, *op. cit.*, 180) and the marked increase in duelling in 1613 (see Chamberlain's letter of 9 September, Spedding, *op. cit.*, IV, 396) led James and Bacon to take more vigorous action. In 1613 James prohibited duelling by edict, and Bacon prosecuted vigorously the case of Priest and Wright in the Star Chamber; Spedding, IV, 339–416. That the royal edict did not succeed in abolishing duelling literature of the Restoration and eighteenth century shows.

89. *hay*] *you have it!*, the cry when a thrust has found its mark; Malone Var., VI, 98, n. 2.

90. *codpeice point*] the lace whereby the codpiece was fastened to the hose.

93. *cut-worke band*] The necks of well-dressed Jacobeans were decked out with bands, of which purl-trimmed or open-work linen, called cut-work, were most fashionable and expensive; Linthicum, 156.

115.] Field's amends for ladies in the account of the Maid.

120. *portion of yours*] For this constraining circumstance Field has not adequately prepared. A slight degree of preparation, however, may have been intended by 1.1.42–44.

143f.] Despite his having made amends, Field makes occasion for a renewal of his attack on women as in *W*.

148. *tumbler*] acrobatic entertainer, or in cant, one who entices victims into the clutches of swindlers; either is suitable enough as an example of an undesirable husband.

149.] Another passage which has been adduced in support of the view that Field was careless about revising his work (Brinkley, 62f.; cf. exp. n. to *W*, 2.1.7ff.). This passage, however, appears to be an aside for the purpose of restoring audience sympathy, which was probably impaired by 137–141. One must in fairness ask how revision could have improved the technique here. To get the full effect from this scene, the audience must be troubled when the "Boy" is thrust out, hopeful on his return, relieved when the duel is stopped on her self-discovery, distressed when it is resumed despite her pleading, resentful when she turns from Ingen to obey Proudly, and highly gratified at her ingenuity in finally putting an end to the conflict. I do not insist upon precisely these emotions, but something of this range is surely involved. The same passage has been adduced in support of the view that "Field was a painstaking craftsman and carried his audience ahead of the action on the stage by means of forward-looking hints and inconspicuous bits of preparation. . . . For example, in . . . *Amends* Lady Honour pretends to consent to Lord Proudly's arrangement for her marriage with Count Feesimple, but she whispers with Ingen when she tells him good-bye and explains in an aside that she has to acquiesce to prevent the continuation of the duel" (p. 52).

153.] Note Field's use of proverbial matter (Field, 18) for its epigrammatic value at the end of the act. Cf. *W*, 1.1.185.·

5.1

The outer stage was likely used for this threshold scene before the house of the Husband. His concealment (76) may have been behind curtains between the inner and outer stages, behind other hangings, or behind a doorpost. He has thus only to step out (128) at the proper moment and lead his wife and friend happily back into the house, perhaps by the door from which all three had entered.

12. *fort is mine*] See 5.1.53 and exp. n.

13. *vp-tailes*] *Up-tail's* all was the name of an old song and its tune, but the reference here is also to Subtle's supposed victory.

42f. *Rascoll*] In Jacobean times the word lacked the levity which it possesses today.

47. *do*] Cf. exp. n. to 4.2.39.

53. *assault*] The use of figures from a military siege in describing the siege of a lady was frequent in Renaissance Europe, probably because it had come down from medieval allegory; see Roberta D. Cornelius, *The Figurative Castle* (Bryn Mawr, 1930). They were, in short, literary commonplaces; cf. Chapman, *May-Day*, 2.1.421ff., and *The Widow's Tears*, 1.1.127, 154f., 1.3.94f., to pick a few examples from but two plays of one author. Consequently it is hardly an argument for Field's authorship of "The Triumph of Death" in *Four Plays in One* that Gabriella there says

> or did this body
> Yield to your false embraces with less labour
> Then if you had carried some strong Town   (X, 335).

Such phrases as "to lay closer siege to that Fortresse" and others in *Don Quixote* (II, 84, 91) are not proof that Field used Shelton's translation of that work. Nor is "the Castle is but vpon yeilding yet, / tis not deliuered vp" (2027f.) satisfactory proof that Field was indebted to *The Second Maiden's Tragedy*.

57. *fals me*] Cf. *A* 1.1.291 and exp. n.

65f.] Ovid *Amores*. I. 5.

72. *witnes*] In both *Don Quixote* (II, 92) and *The Second Maiden's Tragedy* (335ff.) the husband overhears an interview between the tester and the wife. Since such eavesdropping is almost implicit in the wife-testing motif, this point in common is of little value in determining Field's sources.

73.] Note the occurrence here of the rather infrequent overheard aside.

81. *promise*] See 2.2.104.

93. *Corasiue*] Literally *a caustic drug*, the word was used figuratively for *sharp grief*.

109. *catch'd*] detected. Cf. *The Alchemist*, 5.3.75.

111. *naked as this truth*] A proverbial comparison (Field, 37).

114.] Bold has used the same argument unsuccessfully against the Widow, 4.1.18ff.

121. *cashier'd*] dismissed.

123ff.] This is Field's amends for ladies in the account of the Wife. "With the coming of the drama of sensibility, added stress falls upon the idea of man's reclamation by the unassailable virtue of woman. Such a scene is found in *Amends*," here (Brinkley, 79).

133.] Used in illustration of the "Inability to hold elevation of tone" which Brinkley employs as a test of Field's authorship (p. 85).

5.2

From the standpoint of staging, one of Field's most interesting scenes. A hall scene, it doubtless opens on the outer stage. A chair is evidently provided for Count Feesimple (84). By which of the proscenium doors the Maid enters (1) is uncertain, but she and those who attend her probably leave (36) by the aperture between outer and inner stages so as to establish the location of her sickroom, specifically called "the chamber" (120). For the staging of the latter part of the scene W. J. Lawrence would have us depart from the known facilities of the Whitefriars and other private houses and, indeed, of the public theatres. Lawrence takes the direction at 163ff. to require the presence of windows on the lower outer stage (2, 50). It is possible that the Whitefriars or Rosseter's Blackfriars had such a window or windows; but lovers of the simple explanation will doubtless prefer not to suppose, on so little evidence, something for these theatres afforded by no other playhouse. John C. Adams (*The Globe Playhouse*, 160f.) equates the window here with the prompter's wicket in one of the proscenium doors. Proudly may, however, simply have drawn back the curtain (163ff.) sufficiently for him to see into the inner stage. The misplacing of this stage direction by C makes the text seem to indicate that all the characters can see in at the window. According to the quarto, only Proudly and Feesimple can. A second problem, not mentioned by Lawrence, concerns the door leading into the bedroom. Ingen and the Parson seem to enter it by a practicable door which the Parson shuts (130). Later Proudly seems to try the door (172). Unless it were earlier established by the Parson's shutting one of the proscenium doors that it led to the bedroom, for Proudly to try either of the doors ordinarily available on the outer stage of a private theatre would appear psychologically wrong if he has been looking in at a window evidently nearer where his sister is; perhaps this consideration supports Adams. Frank's line, "thei'll open it them selues" (179), however, immediately followed by the opening of curtains, presumably those between outer and inner stages, perhaps supports the view that the curtains only represented a door and that Proudly pretended to try them. Difficulties lie in the way of assuming that the curtains at the beginning of this scene opened on a "built" wall containing both window and door; for unless the curtains were closed again during the scene, the wall could not readily be removed without our seeing it. If such a piece were used and were not removed, the opening of the curtain in 180 would have to be that of a curtain over a window. I find it hard to believe that Field would write so sensational a scene as this and not exhibit it more fully than would be possible through a window, even a large one. It seems more likely that Proudly would try the door or curtains and fail; and, in the case of the curtains, the lack of any physical obstacle is perhaps obviated by Frank's stopping Proudly with a levelled pistol (174ff.). If Proudly did, on the other hand, the psychologically ineffective thing—left the window and tried one of the proscenium doors—I suspect that this business was prepared for by having previous entrances to the bedroom accomplished through the same door. The least safe of these interpretations, I think, is that which requires our assuming the existence of a window on the lower level of the outer stage.

5. *letter*] Doubtless explaining the plan for her release, as we may guess from 22f.

8. *willow*] See exp. n. to *W*, 1.2.233.

15. *deliuer'd*] A hint as to Jacobean acting. As the following lines show, the Brother has been speaking in a manner recognizable as that of the contemporary professional actor.

26. *Strong-water*] alcoholic spirits.

30. *fet*] fetched, i. e., revived.

37.] Cf. "Doth *Hymen* wear black?" *Four Plays in One* (X, 323).

49. *the Beare*] Although a bear pursues Antigonus in *The Winter's Tale* (1610), 3.3.58, this line "refers, no doubt, to the opening of the old 'most pleasant comedie of *Macedorus*' [*sic*] when Amadine is pursued by

the bear" (C, n.; cf. Fischer, 39; Brinkley, 57). *Mucedorus,* it may be added, was at the time once again in public favor, having been given new additions in a quarto in 1610 and revived by the King's men (Chambers, IV, 35). Chambers conjectures that the bears in both plays "were inspired by the successful bear in Jonson's *Mask of Oberon* on 1 January 1611." On animals as actors see Louis B. Wright, *PMLA,* XLII (1927), 656–669.

62. *smaller*] So as not to betray his disguise.

64. *geere*] goings on; i. e., do you intend matrimony?

66. *couching*] reclining, but the word may have had sexual implications.

78. *barricado'd with furre*] in reference to the "barricade" of his costume.

79. *birdlime]* In this unpleasant allusion to the signs of his father's cold, Feesimple refers to the glutinous substance used in catching birds.

84.] This stage direction describes the sort of business indulged in by the practical playwright rather than the dramatist who accepts a responsibility to record or interpret life sincerely. It is good theatre.

117. *like a Doctor*] The lover disguised as a physician was a favorite device in the *commedia dell 'arte* (Creizenach, 220). In Middleton's *A Mad World, My Masters* (1606), Penitent Brothel in the disguise of a doctor gains a meeting with Mistress Harebrain (III, 2).

128.] This line, I think, describes pantomime in which Ingen offers to let the Parson precede him off; see text. n. I take the antecedent of *it* to be *the honor of going first,* indicated by a gesture from the actor. The Parson, however, seems not to accept the courtesy, as we see from 128, unless he precedes and shuts the door from within. See *NQ,* CXCI (1946), 55f.

152.] To Feesimple.

159.] Proudly has neither evidence that this report is true nor reason for making it—except to motivate the Count's humorously callous line which follows. A commercial playwright interested in pleasing his audience may resort to such devices; a dramatist intent on the revelation of character will likely reject them.

171. *mother*] Usually glossed as *hysteria,* but obviously a double entendre is indicated here; cf. *The Duchess of Malfi,* 2.1.118f. As Genest says, "this scene must not be particularly described" (*op. cit.,* X, 22).

187. *For*] i.e., *As for.*

189. *gowt*] Rather than *gout,* I think the modernization should be *goat,* which historically might have been spelled *gowt* in this period.

198.] If spousals, either *de futuro* or *de praesenti,* were followed by intercourse, the couple was regarded, both by church and state, as legally married; Powell, 3f. and Lucas' note to *Duchess of Malfi,* 1.1.548 (*Works,* II, 140). In having the Parson conduct a marriage service, implied by 195f., Ingen and the Maid were taking every precaution.

199. *carriage*] A pun is more than probable.

215. *well parted, and faire mean'd*] Probably *of good parts and means.* The last word, however, may be a seventeenth-century spelling from *mien,* and thus refer to *bearing, manner.*

218. *knighted*] Here probably not meant satirically, but see *W* 1.2.165 and exp. n.

228ff.] A difficult passage to account for though not to understand; see text. n. Perhaps the lines give a clue to the stage business, the Widow taking Feesimple's hand, as V suggests (n.), thus arousing audience excitement over his campaign to win her, and giving it to Bold, thus allaying that excitement.

231. *law ye*] See exp. n. to *W* 1.2.135.

235. *thumb*] As we know from portraiture, some English women of the period wore their wedding rings on the thumb; *SE*, II, 145. Without citing any authority, Powell (p. 23, n. 1) locates the ring on the third finger. The use of the thumb here may be significant as a means of keeping the Widow from at once suspecting Bold's intention, rings having long been regarded as binding symbols in legal ceremonies such as the assumpsit which follows.

237. *assumpsit*] "A promise or contract, oral or in writing not sealed, founded upon a consideration" *(NED, s. v.)*; cf. *The Alchemist*, 1.2.69. What consideration the Widow here receives I do not know unless the ring, as in Greene's *Philomela* (*Works*, XI, 186, and n. at 321), be accepted as one.

256. *salue*] *heal* (supply *the heart of*).

266.] The hoaxing of an old gentleman, coxcomb, or braggart with a boy bride is of classical origin and traceable to Plautus' *Casina*, where it is complete even to the line about the beard; Freeburg, 101–120. It occurred in *May-Day* (1602), in which Field probably had acted. There seems to be insufficient evidence, therefore, for believing that the device here "was probably derived from *Epicoene*" (Brinkley, 76) or that "Field improves on this type of scene when he has the old Count kiss his fiancée and find the beard of his son" *(ibid.)*. The duping of Count Feesimple has been regarded as an episode "wholly gratuitous," of "no direct connection with the plots," and "probably added" for its "popular appeal" *(ibid.*, 51). It seems to me that Field has related it, at least partially, to one of his three main plots, the Bold-Widow motive, by the disguised Lord Feesimple's role in Bold's campaign for the Widow, and has related it organically to one of the subplots, the fleshing of Feesimple. It is his chagrin at being so duped, and perhaps at his father's being so duped, that leads him to prove that he has been fleshed, as he at once proceeds to do (263–289). Field's portrait of Feesimple is considerably strengthened by the coxcomb's exhibition of his ability to roar.

291. *Feasts*] For a brief account of the feasts at English weddings of this period, and the accompanying evils, see Powell, 24–27.

298ff.] Here Field reinforces his amends for ladies in the accounts of maid, wife, and widow.

301.] The final lines, bringing us back to 1.1.2–58, neatly round off the play and reduce to a unity, perhaps specious, the three main plots.

V. TEXTUAL NOTES

V. TEXTUAL NOTES

1. *WEATHER-COCKE*

Key to Sigla

Early edition
QQ—the six copies collated of the 1612 quarto
  Qa: Folger Shakespeare Library
  Ob: Henry E. Huntington Library
  Qc: Congressional Library
  Qd: Harvard College Library
  Qe: The Rosenbach Company
  Qf: Dyce Collection, Victoria and Albert Museum

Later editions
  C—J. P. Collier, 1829
  H—W. Carew Hazlitt, 1875
  V—A. Wilson Verity, 1888

Title-page

13. *facit*] *faciat* QQ.
If Field wrote *faciat*, he marred the measure and departed from Juvenal's text both Renaissance and modern.
Indignatio] *Indagnatio* QQ.
versum] *versnm* QQ.
16. great] gteat QQ.
Paules] *Panles* QQ.

Dramatis personae

6. Parson] Priest QQ, which uniformly have *Parson* in speech headings.
8. Ninnie.] Ninnie QQ.
9. Ninny.] Ninny QQ.
After 9.] *V adds* SCENE—*The Neighbourhood of* LONDON.
To the Dramatis personae V supplies also descriptive phrases as follows: Fredericke] engaged to BELLAFRONT. Scudmore] in love with BELLAFRONT. Neuill] his Friend. Strange] a Merchant in love with KATHERINE. Pendant] a Sycophant of Count FREDERICK. Sir Abraham Ninny] his [i. e., Sir Innocent's] Son. Bellafront Katherine Lucida]

Daughters of Sir JOHN WORLDLY. Lady Ninnie] Wife of Sir INNOCENT. Wagtayle] her Gentlewoman.

To any Woman

1.] Initial and capital reduced, lines respaced.

To the Reader

1.] Initial and capital reduced, lines respaced.
2. too.] too, QQ.
9. actions:] actions QQ.
now] nor *HV*.
11. *Quales*] *Qualeis* QQ.
Cluuienus.] *Cluuienus*, QQ.

To his Loued Sonne

1.] Initial and capital reduced, lines respaced.

1.1

S. div. *Scena*] *scen.* QQ.
V adds SCUDMORE's *Bed-chamber*.
3.] Initial and capital reduced, lines respaced.
11f. (out . . . make)] In seventeenth-century printing parentheses

had functions they no longer possess; see Simpson, 87ff. Field's use of them has bearing on the correction during impression of *A*, 1618; see *The Library*, 5th s., II (1947), 57f.

22. ought ne're] aught, ne'er *C*: aught near *HV*.

26. *Scud.*] This repetition of a speech heading was common after songs or letters in the text. Although it has been interpreted as evidence that a quarto was reported, the phenomenon is not so readily explicable; see H. T. Price, *JEGP*, XXXVI (1927), 163. Speech headings are not similarly repeated elsewhere in Field's comedies.

Loqui,] *Loqui.* QQ.

34. sex,] sex. *QQ*: period may be broken comma.

41.] H and V follow C in making a new line with *with*, thus improving none of the three lines concerned (39, 41, 42). This alteration, typical of C's editorial policy regarding metrics, permitted further unfortunate tampering with the text, as we see from 42 .

42. Not thy] Not [e'en] thy *H* : Not e'en thy *V*.

48. To] to *QQ*.

56. importance.] Interrupted speeches are frequently punctuated in texts of this period by the full stop; see Simpson, 84.

78. visitation] visitation. *QQ*.

81. thinke it so] think so *CHV*.

82. in] by *CHV*.

90. other] others *C* : others' *HV*.

93. about.] about, *QQ*.

105. pierc't *Qf*] pierc t *Qabcde*.

116. it] It *QQ*.

123. loue] So read all editions. It is possible, however, that *love* may have been intended since, according to one form of the story, Zeus or Jove rewarded the friendship of the Dioscuri by transforming them into stars.

124. againe] together *HV*. The emendation expresses the probable meaning but hardly seems justified.

127. doubt, on] doubting *CHV*. Emendation is not necessary, the sense of the quarto being clear.

135ff. me thought . . . an obiect] The passage appears to be corrupt.

Show'd has no grammatical object, for 136–138 are parenthetical. Perhaps the construction begun in 135 was completed in the two missing iambs of 138.

144. swum] swam *CHV*.

148. toward] towatd *QQ*.

158. and] & *QQ*.

160. Which *Bellafront?* Rich Sir *CHV*] Which, *Bellafront Rich*, Sir *QQ*.

164. What] Whar *QQ*.

my] Texts of the period frequently print interrupted speeches without end punctuation; see Simpson, 98f.

176. shame] shame! *CHV*.

182. as] yes, *H*. The passage may be corrupt though the meaning is clear without emendation.

190. too't, for if] to't: if *CHV*.

1.2

S. div. CHV.]

V adds *A Room in* Sir JOHN WORLDLY's *House*.

5. yet?] yet. *QQ*.

9. Lord.] Lord *QQ*, where the line is crowded.

11, 14.] HV add [*Aside.*

15. sits] sets *CHV*.

18. for] For *QQ*.

19.] C attempts to improve the metre by making a new line with *Taylour*; HV, with *I*. Neither improvement can make regular verse out of passages from this scene, which varies freely between prose, verse, and prose.

21. true; their] true: / Their *CHV*.

28. clocke?] clocke. *QQ*.

35.] HV add [*Aside.*

38. Lord] Lotd *QQ*.

51.] HV add [*Aside.*

61. for] of *CHV*. The emendation would destroy the contemporary meaning; see exp. n. This may be bowdlerization.

67. *Pict-hatch*] Pict-hatch *QQ*.

68. selfe.] selfe, *QQ*.

84f.] H italicizes.

Morrow] morning *HV*.

86. commend] commanded *HV*.

90. day?] day. *QQ*.

93. *Cap.*] The speech is unassigned in QQ, but it obviously be-

longs, as Mitford has indicated mar-
ginally in Qa, to Pouts.
94. had a pudding] had pudding
CHV.
97. mee:] mee, *QQ*.
102. Lord?] Lord: *QQ*.
103. should not they] if they
should not *C* : should they not *HV*.
105. *Page* (second instance)] *Boy*
QQ.
Catchword: *Cou.* But] Perhaps
the irregular two words are here
used because *Cou.* alone is the catchword of the preceding page.
106. her sodain] her so sudden
CHV.
108. know?] know. *QQ*.
124. for] to *CHV*.
125. Daughter, Ile] Daughter, /
Ile *QQ*.
After 142.] *Catchword:* It.
144. Maister] M. *QQ*.
145. *La:*,] *La:* *QQ*.
147. him?] him. *QQ*.
158. rude, rude, &] rude, and
CHV.
160. Maister] M. *QQ*.
161. *Ninny.*] *Ninny* *QQ*.
169. cost vs] cost s *Qc*.
176. and] & *QQ*.
179. *Abraham*] Abraham *QQ*.
183f. needs / be] be needs *CHV*.
185. now, we] now we *Qc*.
186. well wife, wee'le] well:
wife, we'll *CHV*.
190. *Exit Inno.*] *Exeunt* Sir IN-
NOCENT *and Lady* CHV.
191. thinke, hast] think: / Haste
CHV.
192. thou of] thou / Of *CHV*.
193. Voyage, where] voyage, /
Where *CHV*.
197. *Exeunt Lady, Wag.*] *Exeunt*
Lady Wag. QQ : *Exit* MRS. WAG-
TAIL *CHV*.
C evidently mistook the reading
of QQ as an error in address for
Wagtail and let Wagtail exit here
alone. The present reading makes
the probable business clearer. The
remarks about Lady Ninny in 192–
197 are, if more obvious, also more
comic if made while she is still on
stage. As her waiting woman, Wagtail, moreover, would probably accompany her off. See *NQ*, CXCI
(1946), 54.
199. *Abra.?*] *Abra.* QQ.

209f. Gunpowder.] Gunpowder
QQ.
213. *Abraham*] Abraham *QQ*.
240. and I] and— / I *CHV*.
245. you do] do you *CHV*.
248. thousand. Good-morrow]
thousand. / Good *HV*.
249. Bride; but] bride; / But *HV*.
249f. shee must] she / Must *HV*.
Many of Worldly's lines in this
scene are prose. In QQ only 251–
254 are printed as verse. By a little
manipulation it is possible, as HV
show, to make what approximates
verse out of other lines. To do so,
however, is to ignore the evidence
of the copy-text, which contains
numerous verse passages introduced
by prose. Cf. *W* 1.2.23f., 317ff.;
2.2.94ff., 128f.; 5.1.26ff.; 5.2.60ff.;
173ff.; *A* 2.1.144ff., 165ff.; 4.1.178ff.;
4.2.102f., 114f.; 5.1.59ff.
258.] HV add [*Aside.*
259. Title; a] title: / A *CHV*.
261. Soldiers; But] soldiers; /
But *CHV*.
262. money, therefore] money;
/ Therefore *CHV*.
265. braue] btaue *QQ*.
268. monie; by that time] monie
by that time; *QQ*.
274. yes.] yes? *QQ*.
277. Captaines; so] captains, /
So *CHV*.
280. Cuckolds.] cuckolds— *CHV*.
290.] To avoid crowding, the compositor of QQ has turned the line
with *like*, which he capitalized as
if it were verse. Since most of the
encounter between Pouts and
Strange is clearly prose, and since
a line begun with *like* will not scan,
I print prose.
296f. withdraw, / this] withdraw: / This *CHV*.
300. or] as *CHV*.
315. puffing good Captaine] puffing, captain *CHV*.
Captaine; leaue] captain; / Leave
CHV.
320f. throat without] throat /
Without *CHV*.
322. Pyrate, but] pirate, / But
CHV.
323. do, a] do: / A *CHV*.
330. *Abraham*] Abraham *QQ*.
332. keepe him] keep / Him
CHV.

Companie] An instance in which
a catchword (panie, *C3ᵛ*) remedies
an omission from the text.
334. But what] But / What
CHV.
Abraham] Abraham *QQ.*
343. might she] she might *CHV.*
353. *Abraham*] Abraham *QQ.*
359. leaue] cease *CHV.*
364. Sir] Sit *QQ.*
378. Right] Righr *QQ.*
396. Bride] Btide *QQ.*

2.1

S. div. *Scena*] *Scen* QQ.
V adds *In front of a Church.*
2.] Initial and capital reduced,
lines respaced.
3. reasons] reason *HV.*
besides] beside *HV.*
14. match,] match. *QQ.*
43. proud] prou'd *QQ.*
47. too well] too, too well *C* :
too-too well *HV.*
51. receiue] c *or perhaps worn*
e *QQ.*
56. And] and *QQ.*
66. *Frederick*] *Erederick* QQ.
75. And] and *QQ.*
After 79.] Catchword missing.
QQ.
85. Should] should *QQ.*
87. know: the] know the *QQ.*
88. into] inro *QQ.*
89, 95. And] and *QQ.*
92. *Pancridge*] Pancridge *QQ.*
95. vs *CHV*] vp *QQ.* Emendation seems necessary.
95, 96.] HV add [*Aside.*
97. to] To *QQ.*
101. And] and *QQ.*
119. *W. P.* QQ, CH] *The* Wedding Party *walk* V. See exp. n. In
QQ (except Qc) *P* is broken at right
so as to resemble *F.*
123.] Initial and capital reduced,
lines respaced.
126. *Resolu'd to*] *Resolu'dto* QQ.
entire,] *entire.* QQ.
130. *thy burning*] *th yburning*
QQ.
143. body.] body, QQ.
144.] *Before* The *HV add* [*To*
the rest.
149. Sir?] Sir. *QQ.*
152. And] But *CHV.*
160. *in*] in *QQ.*

186, 188. And] and *QQ.*
188.] HV add [*Aside.*
190. friend, I] friend, / I *CHV.*
191. but] But *QQ.*
195. her; so,] her so! *CHV.*
202. rewarded women, women?]
rewarded?—women! women! *CHV.*
208. Are] are *QQ.*
212. you] ye *CHV.*
214. And] and *QQ.*
216. still giuen] H prints *stal-*
lion, with the note: "The word
substituted is not satisfactory, but it
is the most likely one which has
occurred to me, and the term is
employed by our old playwrights
rather more widely than at present."
V prints *stealthy,* with the note:
"Some change is obviously necessary, and 'stealthy' may pass." I
think it will not, but I have no
emendation to propose.
217. must I see] I will see *CHV.*
225. *Pendant;*] *Pendant,* QQ.
225f. *Pouts . . . em*] *CHV* omit,
thus avoiding the repetition of 231,
the t. n. to which see. It seems more
probable, however, that Field put
the direction here; for the position
of *Ent. Captaine* at left in 231 suggests that it may have been a book-
holder's marginal notation. See
NQ, CXCI (1946), 54.
229. rather] rarher *QQ.*
231. *Cap.*] *Ent. Captaine. Cap.*
QQ.
233f. you I] you, (*To* STRANGE)
I *V.*
237. lyen] lain *CHV.*
247. thou not] not thou *CHV.*
256. lye] be *CHV.* Bowdlerization?
266. face,] face. *QQ.*
270. And] and *QQ.*
271. discerne] diseerne *QQ.*
276. As] as *QQ.*
282, 286. And] and *QQ.*
290. sleepe, weepe] sleep, [but]
weep *H* : sleep, but weep *V.*
weepe till't] weep / Till *CHV.*
295. sure he] sure / He *CHV.*
298. her] het *QQ.*
300. name] a *turned in QQ.*
301. And] and *QQ.*
303.] *In QQ lead prints after*
That.
305. Good, saue] Good [people];
save *H* : Good people, save *V.*

Heauen Ile] heaven / I'll *CHV*.
doo't.] doo't *QQ*.
319. And] and *QQ*.
336. me, not before,] me? not
before? *CHV*.

2.2

S. div.] *CHV* continue the scene.
2.1 was located before a church. 2.2
is unlocated. Since for a moment
after 2.1.353 the stage is empty and
since the following lines introduce
a new group of characters concerned
with a new action, the following
lines meet my tests for scene (Gen.
Intro., 5) and apparently those applied by previous editors. Uniformity argues for a new scene.
7, 17.] HV add [*Coughs and
spits.*
23. *In primis*] *Inprimis QQ* :
imprimis CHV. The preposition
was spelled with an *m*, incorrectly,
when the words were written as
one. The reading of QQ, however,
may be simply a failure to divide
words, QQ providing other instances
of faulty division.
36.] HV add [*Comes forward.*
41. Dosser?] Dosser. *QQ*.
46. pray?] pray. *QQ*.
63. *Within*] *CHV* place before
Will, Will, as the stage direction it
probably is. It is possible, however,
that *Within* is a part of Pendant's
order to the Page. The use of
italics is not alone conclusive; for
5.1.92, likewise an offstage speech,
contains no proper name and is
italicized. In 3.3.5, however, *within*
seems to be a direction and not a
word to be spoken.
64. has] hath *CHV*.
65. ont;] ont, *QQ*.
68. extreamely.] extreamely, *QQ*.
72. Prettie] Prettis *QQ*.
76. matter?] matter. *QQ*.
78. a] turned in QQ.
83. This] Thus *CHV*.
86. And] and *QQ*.
92. of hoasts] ofhoasts *QQ*.
besides:] besides, *QQ*.
94. And] and *QQ*.
96. Till] Tlll *QQ*.
97. And] and *QQ*.
99. shop walke] shop-walk *HV*.
101. Rogue or] rogue / Or *CHV*.

111. How] How, *QQ*.
cloths?] cloths. *QQ*.
115. me.] me *QQ*.
118. saies?] saies. *QQ*.
120. you?] you. *QQ*.
122. him?] him. *QQ*.
123. too.] too, *QQ*.
127f. him, / Stand *CHV*] him,
stand *QQ*. One seems justified in setting off the rhymed couplet with
which the scene closes.

3.1

S. div. *tertius*] *3 QQ*.
Scena prima] *Scen. Prima QQ*.
V adds *Before* Captain POUTS'
House.
1. *Enter a Seruingman*] *CHV*
place between 2 and 3.
2.] Initial and capital reduced,
lines respaced.
4f. Gentleman / Would] Gentleman / would *CHV*.
19. or] ot *QQ*.

3.2

S. div. *CHV*] V adds *A Room in
Sir JOHN WORLDLY's House*.
2. *Napkins:*] *Napkins. QQ*.
31, 43. *Luci.*] *Luce. QQ* : NEV.
CHV, with some misgiving. There
seems insufficient reason for altering the speech assignment of QQ.
33. And] and *QQ*.
42. *London*] London *QQ*.
46. *Luci.*] *Luce. QQ* : ABRA.
CHV.
50. *Luci.*] ABRA. *CHV*.
69. *sits in*] *sits asleep in* HV.
70. Canopie.] Canopie, *QQ*.
71. *Before* Oh QQ repeat *Scud*.
75. losse.] losse, *QQ*.
80. And] and *QQ*.
81. hap;] hap, *QQ*.
could] couid *QQ*.
89. enforcst: Ha,] enforc'd. /
Ha! *CHV*.
104, 106. And] and *QQ*.
115. Which] which *QQ*.
123. opinion,] opinion; *QQ*.
138. liberall talking tongue
Qacdef, CHV] liberall tongue *Qb*.
142. intergritie] The *NED* does
not list this form, and the first *r*
may be a typographical error since
it is not justified etymologically.

151. my glad eies *Qacdef, CHV*]
glad my *Qb*.
153. conuented] couented *Qacdef* : contented *Qb* : convented *CHV*.
The reading illustrates that a correction may introduce a new error.
Intending "conuented," the corrector altered "contented" to "couented" by the transposition of similar letters.
154. The Mistris that I had free of *Qacdef, CHV*] I had a Mistris free of all *Qb*.
155. her, so deare *Qacdef*] her, deare *Qb* : her so! dear *CHV*. The alteration of CHV requires one to assume that the corrector saw the need of adding a monosyllable, *so*, but made a mistake in placing it after the comma—a possibility, but an unlikely one. See exp. n. Lead prints after *so* in Qdf.
161. And] and *QQ*.
168. redeeme me from *Qacdef, CHV*] redeeme from *Qb*.
171, 176. And] and *QQ*.
197. all can *Qacdef, CHV*] all that *Qb*.
209. As] as *QQ*.
212. deceitfull] deeeitfull *QQ*.
222. knees: thou] knees, Thou *C* : knees—[*Kneels*.] / Thou *HV*.
223.] First part of line blank in QQ. *HV* silently rearrange 222f. as indicated. Greg (*Bibl. Dram.*, I, 438) attributes the blank to the compositor's being unable, apparently, to read the copy. Errors in lineation elsewhere, however, suggest that this may illustrate an effort at metrical improvement.
224. And] and *QQ*.
After 225.] HV add [*Rises again*.].

3.3

S. div. CHV] V adds *A Garden adjoining a Bowling Alley*.
3. little] litrle *QQ*.
5. *Rub, rub, within*,] *Within: Rub, rub, CHV*.
19ff.] CH italicize Abraham's poem throughout.
20. good.] good, *QQ*.
22.] Hyphen doubtful in Qdf.
27. conceit, and] conceit / And *HV*.

30. *Abraham*] *Abra*. QQ.
34. *Abraham*] *Abra:* QQ.
35.] QQ place st. dir. opposite 34. After 36] V adds [*Reads*.
40.] There is a blank in QQ between *and* and *pittie*. Collier's explanation, reprinted by HV, is fanciful: "Perhaps the blank was left to shew that he [Abraham] could not fill it up to his satisfaction, not liking the line as it stood when he first committed it to paper." This disregards the fact that *W* was a play intended for performance and performed. Greg's explanation (*Bibl. Dram.*, I, 438) seems little better; for if the compositor had been "unable to read his copy," would he not likely have picked up the reading from 31? The change of *vnto* to *and* between the two versions suggests the improbability of the obvious explanation that two words have accidentally dropped out. Note that in QQ the line is the last on its page.
43. set too] :oo *or perhaps* too with broken t QQ : set it to *CHV*.
48. Worthy and right *Qacdef, CHV*] right Worthy and *Qb*.
52. *Abraham?*] *Abraham*. QQ.
58f. scornfully.] scornfully QQ, where the line is crowded and a lead prints.
67. Ifaith *Qacdef*] efaith *Qb*.
68. child?] child. QQ.
70. tis *Qacdef*] as *Qb*.
71. her;] her, QQ.
72. *England*] England QQ.
74. wrong:] wrong, QQ.
78. arrant] errant *CHV*.
80. *Wagtaile*] Wagtaile QQ.
84. Troth *Qacdef, CHV*] Truth *Qb*.
87. mine *Qacdef, CHV*] my *Qb*.
89. quarrell?] quarrell. QQ.
96.] HV add [*Aside*.
101. *Pendant*] *Peudant* QQ.
107. *Islington*] Islington QQ.
120. Girle?] Girle. QQ.
123. And] and *QQ*.

3.4

S. div.] CHV continue the scene. 3.3, however, has taken place, if not as V says, in "*A Garden adjoining a Bowling Alley*," at least in the vicinity of Worldly's home, as we know from hearing the cries of the bowlers, 5. The following interview between Pouts and his servant suggests once more the location of 3.1, clearly Pouts' lodgings. Strange would not likely go to the Worldly house after his vow in 2.1.347. His complaint in 3.4.17f. further argues that the scene is Pouts' lodgings. Since, moreover, all the characters of 3.3 leave the stage before the entrance of another group of characters, a new scene division seems called for.

10. ont:] ont *QQ*. CHV conjecture *on us* or *of us*, but to do so is to ignore the doctrine of "priority of aspection" in relation to the basilisk; see exp. n. and *Explicator*, IV (1946), No. 43.

This] this *QQ*.

night] night: *QQ*.

London] London *QQ*.

15. art] att *QQ*.

16. st. dir.] CHV place before Strange is addressed in 15.

28. shame;] shame *QQ*.

34. And] and *QQ*.

36. *Graues-end*] Graues-end *QQ*.

4.1

S. div. CHV] V adds *A Room in* NEVILL's *House*.

2.] Initial and capital reduced, lines respaced.

9ff.] There is confusion here in the assignment of lines to speakers in QQ. CHV give 9–12 to Scudmore, along with 13–27, here given to him. QQ give 7–47 to Nevill. CHV might have paraphrased the passage thus:

Nev. You were to blame to seek trouble. It finds us; we need not seek it.

Scud. I don't agree with that opinion. Like women, trouble shuns those who seek it and seeks those who shun it.

But 9–12 make good sense, also, if they are given as by QQ to Nevill. The present reassignment of lines is adopted as a more conservative solution to the problem than that of CHV.

14. And] and *QQ*.

15. then's] there's *H*.

19. As] as *QQ*.

25. liue,] liue. *QQ*.

30. nor sure] nor [is] sure *H* : nor is sure *V*.

32, 41. And] and *QQ*.

45. meanes;] meanes, *QQ*.

47, 52, 55, 64, 71. And] and *QQ*.

71. And vnder-borne fortunes vnder their merrits] And fortunes underborn unto their merits *H* : But under-born in fortune to their merits *V*. A compositor could not easily have derived the reading of QQ from that of H. V glosses his emendation, "Whose fortune does not equal their merits," and comments, "This is at least sense, which the old reading . . . can scarcely claim to be." I suspect that Field's elliptic style (Brinkley, 62) is responsible for the difficulty and therefore refrain from trying my hand at rewriting.

76. As] as *QQ*.

79. hunger] hnnger *QQ*.

82. And] and *QQ*.

84. braines] brain *CHV*.

93f.] Foul bawdry, or strong arguments against / Ourselves, and stark blindly hold it best *HV*. The lines hardly seem so unsatisfactory, however, as to justify a rearrangement.

102. wit *Qbcef, CHV*] it *Qad*.

all Qad] al *Qbcef*. An instance in which the cautious editor will not follow the usual principle, of accepting even those readings of a corrected form which may be open to question (McKerrow, *Bibl.*, 212). The spelling *al* is an alteration consequent to the alteration of *it* to *wit* and therefore may be presumed to be less close than *all* to the author's copy; see Greg, *EP*, xlix.

110, 114. As] as *QQ*.

115, 120. And] and *QQ*.

116. a] *H emends to* [no].

118. Enginer;] Enginer *QQ*.

4.2

S. div. CHV] V adds *Lambeth Fields*.

8. As] as *QQ*.

13. And] and *QQ*.

26. As] as QQ.
30. After] after QQ.
31. Twas Qbcef, CHV] Was Qad.
season, to] season. To QQ.
32. As] as QQ.
33. And] and QQ.
37. Assur'd] assur'd QQ.
38. then] tehn QQ.
43. mee, I] me: / I CHV.
53, 57. And] and QQ.
66. you,] comma dim in QQ.
69. Scotch] Scotch QQ.
72. to] ro QQ.
76. and] & QQ.
80. And] and QQ.
81. amends] amends! CHV.
82. Why I] Why, I CHV.
85. Souldier] i high in line in QQ.
86, 90. A] a QQ.
87. Cat a Mountaines] cat-a-mountain CHV.
face] f ce Qacf.
88. blather] bladder CHV.
94f. slanderer.] slanderer QQ.
96f. murderer.] murderer QQ.
100. taken] raken QQ.
110. better;] better, QQ.
115. sword.] sword QQ.
117f. first, / And] first, & QQ.
118. wench, Come] wench, / Come QQ.
120. Moore-fields] Moore-fields QQ.
After 124.] Catchword of G4r missing.

4.3

S. div.] CHV continue the scene. Abraham, however, has left to overhear Wagtail "in the Gallery" (3.4.121ff.). Consequently a new scene division seems indicated here.
24. thy] rhy QQ.
27.] QQ repeat speech heading Wag.
doost thou loue Qbcef, CHV] doost loue Qad.
28. sworn it neuer Qbcef, CHV] sworn neuer Qad.
29. thee:] thee QQ.
30. Because he is Qbcef, CHV] Because is Qad.
is it Qbcef, CHV] that is Qad.
34. Morglay Qbcef, CHV] Morgley Qad.

38. A] a QQ.
39. As] as QQ.
were] was CHV.
40. thy] the V.
43. Poles] Poles QQ.
54. smil'd Qab, CHV] laugh'd Qcdef. Though after laugh'd for ioy in 53 it seems anticlimactic, one is forced to read smil'd from the corrected state since this correction is not consequent upon another; see text. n. to W 4.1.102.
56. In Qab, CHV] His Qcdef.
Pinkanies] pinken-eyes CHV.
59. run, (first instance)] run QQ.
rheumatickly Qab, CHV] rheumaticke Qcdef.
68.] HV add [Aside.
71. withall] with all CHV.
74. Lay] Lie HV.
79.] HV add [Aside.
88. Of being] Ofbeing QQ.
89.] CHV add [Aside.
93. st. dir.] QQ place at right opposite 92.
100. Abraham] Abra: QQ.

5.1

S. div. quintus, Scena] Quintus. Scen. QQ.
V adds A Room in Sir JOHN WORDLY's House.
Catchword of H1v missing.
21. comes] come CHV.
24. Neuil's] Neuil's QQ.
25. come.] come QQ.
After 38. H2] G2 QQ.
40. me.] me, QQ.
46. And] and QQ.
47. Graues-end] Hyphen faint in QQ.
48. two] SERVANTS CHV.
50. there, Sirrha go Qab, CHV] there, go Qcdef : lead prints between a and g Qa.
53f. You . . . yet?] QQ give to Scud. : CHV give to World. C notes: "it belongs to Sir John Worldly. Scudmore is not on the stage."
54. st. dir.] QQ place in previous line.
74. Maister] M. QQ.
75. Neuill?] Neuill. QQ.
77. doing] do HV.
84. me?] me. QQ.

87. Mustachios] moustachio *H* : moustachios *CV*.
103. now?] now. *QQ*.
105. Caps?] Caps. *QQ*.
114. busied] busied. *QQ*.
120. Should *QQ, HV*] should *C* [prose].
121f. second, / I *HV*] second, I *QQ, C*.
122f. dancing, / And *HV*] dancing, & *QQ, C*.

5.2

S. div.] CHV.
1. *2. or 3.*] Servants *V, who omits also the other numerals in the passage.* I attach little importance to this permissive direction (Greg, *EP*, 36f.) and that which has just preceded (5.1.143), as evidence of the nature of the copy which underlies QQ; see *W*, Intro., iii.
4. *Wagtaile:*] *Wagtaile*, QQ.
22. man;] man *QQ*.
28. strain;] Qab] *strain*, Qcdef.
29. her] BELLAFRONT *CHV*.
36. so.] so *QQ*.
44f. know, / That *CHV*] know, that *QQ*.
45. Gentleman] Gent. *QQ*.
48.] HV add [*Aside.*
51. Pish] pish *QQ*.
58. Hoy-day, the] Heyday! / The *CHV*.
59. seene two] seen / Two *CHV*.
59f. or / Three] or three *QQ*.
87. *Strange with*] STRANGE *like a Soldier, with* V.
90. QQ place at right opposite 89.
92. merriment: know] merriment. / Know *CHV*.
102.] QQ place at right opposite 101.
103. you, is] you! / is *C* [*prose*] : you! / Is *HV* [*verse*].
107. Mistris] Mrs. *QQ*.
108. but] bur *QQ*.
114. were] was *V*.
122. carrie] carrre *QQ*.
128. did] do *V*.

134.]QQ place at right opposite 129.
149f. knowledge?] knowledge *QQ*.
153f. not / discouer] not / Discover *CHV*.
154. me?] me. *QQ*.
157f. Sir . . . Conscience] HV make new speech and assign to Pouts, H with acknowledgment and V with none. To make a new speech, however, would not help. If Pouts speaks these lines, *him* in Worldly's next line would refer to Pouts; there would be no motive for Strange's next speech; and his discovery would be less exciting—and that would not, I think, have been Field's way. It seems more likely that the quarto is correct. See exp. n., and the discussion of this passage in Gen. Intro., 3.
172. *leads*] *lead* CHV.
173. woman-Citizen *Qbce, CHV*] Roman-Citizen *Qadf*. At first glance the reading of *Qadf* is tempting. The reading chosen, however, probably represents the corrected state though the question must be decided if at all on this one variant. *Thou,* like *thee,* I take to refer to Strange, Pouts' undoer. *Woman,* therefore, seems the more appropriate adjective for the citizen, as in keeping with the condescension toward tradesmen elsewhere found in Field; cf. *W* 1.2.130f., 252f.; *A* 2.2.29f.; etc. If *Roman* were adopted, the line would have to be regarded as Pouts' address to himself—a very difficult interpretation.
180. you] your *CHV*.
181. *Whispers*] *whisper* CHV.
196.] QQ place at right opposite 195.
not.] not *QQ*.
208. *Ecce signum*] QQ place at left before 209.
209. And] and *QQ*.
hir.] hir *QQ*.
229. the] ths *QQ*.

2. AMENDS FOR LADIES

Key to Sigla

Early editions

QQ—the six copies collated of the 1618 quarto

    Qa: Folger Shakespeare Library
    Qb: Henry E. Huntington Library (common title-page)
    Qc: Henry E. Huntington Library (unique title-page)
    Qd: McGill University Library
    Qe: British Museum (11773. C. 3.)
    Qf: Dyce Collection, Victoria and Albert Museum

Q2—the quarto of 1639 (copy in the Yale University Library)

Later editions
    C—J. P. Collier, 1829
    H—W. Carew Hazlitt, 1875
    V—A. Wilson Verity, 1888

Title-page

10.] Outer ring of ornament broken at bottom right in QQ.

Dramatis personae

After 15.] *V adds* SCENE—LONDON.
CHV supply descriptive phrases as follows: Count Fee-simple] father of Lord Feesimple. Subtle] his [i. e., Husband's] friend. Ingen] in love with Lady Honor. Brother] his [i. e., Ingen's] younger brother. Bould] in love with Lady Bright. Well-tri'd] his [i.e., Bould's] friend. Seldome] a citizen.

1.1

S. div. *primus,*] *primi* QQ.
V adds *A Room in* Sir JOHN LOVEALL's *House.*
1. MAID, WIFE, WIDOW] *the Lady* HONOR, *the Lady* PERFECT, *the Lady* BRIGHT QQ. V uses QQ readings from this stage direction as speakers' names throughout the play. QQ are inconsistent as to the names of these characters, but most often they are referred to as *Maid, Wife,* and *Widow.* All of their speeches are so headed. In all other stage directions than this the Wife and Widow are called *Wife* and *Widow.* In one stage direction (5.2.1) the Maid is called *"the* Ladie HONOR." In the lines the trio are sometimes referred to as *Lady Honor, Lady Perfect,* and *Lady Bright.* I have not altered the lines; but for consistency I call these leading ladies what Field most often called them, *Maid, Wife,* and *Widow.*
2. *Maid.*] QQ center and place above 2.
Initial and capital reduced, lines respaced.
13f. trouble / Already *CHV*] trouble already *QQ.*
15. be,] be. *QQ.*
24. insolent] excellent *Q2.*
39. rest] roost *HV.* There seems to be insufficient ground for trying to connect this line, which makes satisfactory sense without change, with the proverbial "rule the roast" (*Oxford Proverbs,* 537).

58. "Selling] Selling, QQ.
60. Make] Makes CHV.
78. age,] age. QQ.
81. Mistresse,] Mistresse. QQ.
83f. light, / I, CHV] light, I QQ.
86f. But to you, / My] "But to you, my CHV.
100. midnight. Must Qbcef, Q2, CHV] midnight, must Qad.
105. st. dir.] The precise point at which the Wife and Widow go out is not indicated in the quartos. It must, however, fall after Ingen's long speech and probably after the Maid's question in 103f., which seem addressed to them. See NQ, CXCI (1946), 54f.
106. telling folkes Qbcef, Q2, CHV] telling of folkes Qad.
109. finger, Qbcef, Q2, CHV] finger: Qad.
111. hee: Qbcef] hee, Qad.
113. I'de Qbcef, Q2, CHV] Il'e Qad.
put Qbcef, Q2, CHV] but Qad. The reading of the uncorrected state is tempting but not allowable.
114. Maddam God b'wee.] "madam, God be w'ye." CHV.
115. these Qbcef] theses Qad.
121. distrest Qbcef] distre'str Qad.
126. enough to CHV] enough / To QQ.
143f. hand Lady, / The] hand La: / The QQ : hand, / The CHV.
152f. boies, / That] boys, that CHV.
153. Turnebull-street] Turnebull-street QQ.
162. forth, see] forth. [st. dir.] / See CHV.
182. seat so far 'boue] seate 'bove Q2.
183. ours?] ours, QQ.
After 184.] QQ print Enter Svb-tle, Hvsband, Feesimple, Wel-tri'd. This anticipation of the direction in 188 looks like a prompter's reminder to himself (Greg, EP, 38f.) and is evidence for the view that QQ was printed from a playhouse copy; see A Intro., iii.
185. comes] come CHV.
192. wisest, chastest, richest] wisest, richest CHV.
198. forgot] forget CHV. QQ.

203. Gentleman;] Gentleman QQ.
205. houre,] houre. QQ.
and] And QQ.
Here the readings of QQ probably resulted from the change of page.
216.] HV add [Aside.
219. shee] Shee QQ where the word begins the line.
before?] before. QQ.
222. to you] to / You QQ.
228. two were] two / Were CHV.
236. soundly;] soundly, QQ.
245. st. dir.] CHV.
247. nose.] nose QQ, where it is final in a crowded line.
248. gold.] gold, QQ.
249. him.] Period dim in QQ.
254. backe, I] back: / I CHV.
Elizium] Elizium QQ.
261. mee,] mee QQ, where it is final in a crowded line.
266. Husb. CHV] Knight. QQ. There seems little reason for doubting that the speaker is the Husband.
274. Ire-monger] Iron-monger Q2, CHV.
275. I a] Ha Q2, CHV.
286. Innocent.] innocent— CHV.
287.] HV add [Aside.
291. did mee I] did I V.
299. exceeding]exceedingly CHV.
310. a my] my CHV.
346. scoff'd] scoff d Qbcef.
348. has] hath CHV.
349. against] unto CHV.
352f. children.] children; QQ.
370. secret] secret; QQ.
378. seruice;] seruice, QQ.
390. vp? come] up? / Come CHV.
394. an] An QQ, where it begins a line.
397.] QQ place at right opposite 396.
405. Ladyships] ladyship CHV.
409. st. dir.] In QQ appears after 420. The st. dir. after 408, at which point most of the characters leave, does not provide speakers for the remainder of the scene. Even that at 420 in QQ does not provide for the Maid to remain for her speech; it provides, too late, for the other speakers. It seems best to move the QQ direction and make

the small emendation I have made.
See *NQ*, CXCI (1946), 55.

420. *Exit.*] [*Aside and exit.* V.
421f. speake / Of *CHV*] speake
of *QQ*.
427. *Gemini*] Gemins *QQ*. The
reference is to Castor and Pollux;
see *W* 1.1.123 and text. n. An un-
identified hand has written in Qc,
"Read 'Like the Gemini.'" As one
may see from an illustration in
Moxon's *Mechanick Exercises*, 1683
(reproduced in McKerrow, *Bibl.*,
9), the arrangement of the seventeenth-century type case for lower-
case type was such that the compartment for *s* was adjacent to and
immediately above that for *i*. Bibliography and metrics argue against
a plural in *s*.
428. suck;] suck, *QQ*.
Ordinarie.] Ordinarie. *QQ*.
449. him in my will to thee] C
suggests: "Ought we not rather to
read, 'I would bequeath *thee* in my
will to *him?*'" Not taking cognizance of Renaissance friendship,
such an emendation might color
the text with the attitude of later
times.
450. and] & *QQ*.
454. see.] see *QQ*.
456f. in? Wee'le . . . friend] in?
/ Wee'le . . . friend *QQ* : in?
We'll . . . / Now friend *HV*.
466. resist] consist *Q2*.
479. be] see *HV*. There is no
reason to emend; see exp. n.
482. wrong;] wrong, *QQ*.
484. distinguisht,] Comma dim
in Qbc.
test;] test, *QQ*.
485. them *Qb*] the *Qacdef, Q2,
CHV*. Whether to read *them* or *the*
must be decided not from the context alone but after consideration of
the other variants in this form; see
Greg, *EP*, xlvii.
486. eies *Qb*] eies, *Qacdef, Q2, C*.
487. sparkles as] sparkles are as
Q2.
499.] *QQ* place at right opposite
498.
508. thrust] trust *CHV*. Bowdlerization?
509. hope *Qb, CHV*] hoped
Qacdef, Q2.

2.1

S. div. *secundus*,] *secundi QQ*.
V adds *Inside* SELDOM's *Shop*.
1. *and* GRACE] *his* WIFE *QQ*.
That the possessive is not intended
is proved by the fact that both Seldom and his wife are present.
2.] Initial and capital reduced,
lines respaced.
8.] *V omits* that . . . nothing.
11. well spoken, that] well-
spoken, and that *V*.
wittie, that] wittie, and that *V*.
16. MALL] MOLL CUTPURSE
CHV.
23. Cuckoldlie] cuckoldy *CHV*.
31. *Loue-all* Qb, HV] *Louall*
Qacdef, Q2, C.
32. impudent] impudent! *CHV*.
Cf. *W* 1.1.159.
40. Mistris] Mistris, *QQ*.
40f. so so] so *CHV*.
44. Fipenie;] Fipenie, *QQ*.
52. *Bridewell*] Bridewell *QQ*.
53. st. dir.] QQ center on separate line.
55. them. Fie] them. / Fie *QQ*,
CHV.
57. *Seldome*).] *Seldome*) *QQ*.
63. Ladies] La. *QQ*.
68. before *Garsoon*] HV add [*To
his servant*.
sirrah.] sirrah, *QQ*.
72. PROVD] *Lord* QQ.
75. *Cheape-side*] Cheape-side *QQ*.
76. Cuckold. Saw *CHV*] Cuckold. / Saw *QQ*.
82. had, haue] had / Have *CHV*.
haire, shee] hair: / She *CHV*.
84. *Proud.*] *Lo: QQ*.
96. sure.] sure: *QQ*.
99. could] would *Q2*.
105. haue but] have / But *HV*.
106. haue, and] have, / And *HV*.
106f. money, / yet [*prose*]]
money; / Yet [*verse*] *HV*.
107. either: I] either, / I *CHV*.
108. quarrell, I] quarrell, / I
QQ, CHV.
115f. him, fought *CHV*] him, /
Fought *QQ*.
116f. satisfaction / vnder *CHV*]
satisfaction / Vnder *QQ*.
119f. hold / the] hold / The
CHV [*verse*].
142f. Cuckoldlie] cuckoldy *CHV*.

143f. slaue, / Oh *CHV*] slaue, oh *QQ*.
158. *Exeunt*] *Enter Q2*.
163. their] my *CHV*.
custome;] custome, *QQ*.
171. eares] cars *C*.

2.2

S. div. CHV] V adds *A Room in* Sir JOHN LOVEALL's *House*.
20f. may, / But *CHV*] may, but *QQ*.
22. woman;] woman, *QQ*.
22f. hand, / Vnwillingly.] hand, vnwillingly. *QQ* : Unwillingly? *CHV*.
41. house: sweet] house, sweet *QQ* : house. / *Enter* SUBTLE / Sweet *CHV*.
45. long:] long *QQ*.
48. and] & *QQ*.
49. *Kisse*] *Kisses* CHV.
52f. Mistresse?] Mistresse. *QQ*.
64. Push *QQ, C*] Pish *HV*. Asse,] Asse. *QQ*.
73. or] for *CHV*.
83. QQ place at right opposite 79.
86. to, too] too, too *C* : too-too *HV*.
90. spirit, or *Qdef*] spirit or *Qb* : Comma dim in Qa.
99. so;] so, *QQ*.
100. *Pict-hatch*] Pict-hatch *QQ*. *Turnbole-streete*] Turnbole-streete *QQ*.
101. HV add [*Aside*.
105. wordly *QQ, H*] worldly *CV*.
107. disgrac't] degraded *V*.
118. iniurie] iniurie, *QQ*.

2.3

S. div. CHV] V adds *A Room in* INGEN's *House*.
4. Sir, he] sir. / He *HV*.
6. in. Lord *Qabd, Q2, CHV*] in Lord. *Qcef*.
7. females, all? *Qabd*] females, all, *Qcef*.
9. mad] man *Q2*.
writes? *Qabd*] writes: *Qcef*.
20. what shee] what cause she *Q2, CHV*.
23. siluer Brooke] silvery Brook *V*.
51. counterfeit,] counterfeit *QQ*.
52. That] That, *QQ*.
73. plighted] pledged *HV*.

76. st. dir.] Follows 73 in QQ.
84. commaunded] Commaunded *QQ*.
100f. Lad, / It *CHV*] Lad, It *QQ*.
102. minde] minde. *QQ*.
105. T'is,] Comma dim in Qb.
114. speak] spake *CHV*.
122. in,] Comma dim in Qbdef.
123. causes] pauses *Q2*.

2.4

S. div. CHV] V *adds* Lady BRIGHT's *Lodgings*.
2. BOVLD *pinning*] BOLD *still disguised as a* Waiting-woman, *Pinning* V.
5. sweare she] swear / She *CHV*.
8. Bawd has] bawd / Has *CHV*.
9. brother, and] brother, / And *CHV*.
stole] stolne *Q2, CHV*.
10. you, indeed] you. / Indeed *HV*.
11. Bawds of] bawds / of *C* [*prose*] : bawds / Of *HV* [*verse*].
12. booke, since] book, / since *C* [*prose*] : book, / Since *HV* [*verse*].
13. morning, I] morning, / I *HV*.
18. *Islington*] Islington *QQ*.
29. *France*] France *QQ*.
33. run] ran *CHV*.
36. on] of *CHV*.
42. st. dir.] QQ place opposite 40.
45. ah!] ha! *CHV*.

3.1

S. div. *tertius*,] *tertius*. QQ. *V adds* SUBTLE's *Apartment*.
In QQ this act is not divided into scenes. For the sake of consistency and ease in line numbering, I make a new scene where one is required by my uniform policy; see Gen. Intro., 5. In this act my division does not differ from that of previous editors.
2.] Initial and capital reduced, lines respaced.
5. if *Q2*] If *QQ*.
6. aptlie;] aptlie, *QQ*.
7. must] mnst *QQ*.
8. path] paths *CHV*.
13. sprightly] sprightfull *Q2, C* : spriteful *HV*.

27. her face black] her black *V*.
43. *To a man*] *To man* CHV.
46. *wants and*] *wanton* H. Emendation seems unnecessary.
49. *his breach*] *his first breach* Q2, CHV.
51. *women*] *woman* CHV.

3.2

S. div. CHV] V adds *A Room in* INGEN's *House*.
7. mine] my *CHV*.
8. sister,] Comma dim in Qbd.
9. of bloud] ofbloud *QQ*.
24. *himselfe.*] QQ place in 23.
25.] QQ place at right opposite 24.
43. no] or *V*.
55. *England*] England *QQ*.
60. two *Qe, Q2*] to *Qabcdf*.
68.] QQ place at right opposite 67.
78.] QQ place at right opposite 77.
81f. hand, / Tomorrow *CHV*] hand, to morrow *QQ*.
82. Lord.] Lo. *QQ*.
83. noone] morning *V*.
89. *Exit.*] *Exit. Pr.* QQ.
90. you,] Comma dim in Qbf.
91. no] an *H*. The emendation reverses the proper sense of the passage, as V evidently saw; see exp. n. Here V did what for him was unusual: where his predecessor had departed from, he followed, QQ.
92. *Exeunt Ingen, Brother.*] *Exit.* QQ.
95. loue: *Qabde*] loue, *Qcf*.

3.3

S. div. CHV] *V adds* Lady BRIGHT's *Lodgings*.
7. Because I] Because / I *CHV*.
8. they, wee] they. / We *CHV*.
23. make] take Q2.
Si] *Si*, QQ.
27. according] accordiug *QQ*.
30. *Black - fryers*] Black - fryers *QQ*.
35. that] but *CHV*. C called the present reading "clearly a misprint," but it seems satisfactory; see exp. n.
46f. fumbler/ I *Qabde*] fumbler, I *Qcf*.
47. perceiue: *Qabde*] perceiue *Qcf*.

54. excus'd] Apostrophe doubtful because of proximity of long *s QQ*.
57. old] own *V*.
62. I sweare] Isweare *QQ*.
66.] QQ place at right opposite 65.
74. Almonds] Almouds *QQ*.
78. me;] me, *QQ*.
79. arrant *Qe*] errant *Qabcdf*.
83. me make a] me a *CHV*.
86. Madame, I but] Madame, but *Q2, CHV*.
92. stand in] standin *QQ*.
101. gyns *Qe, Q2*] gyues *Qab cdf* : gins *CHV*. Had CHV known of the correction of QQ during impression, they might have had less difficulty with this word. C follows Q2 and says that the first quarto reads *gyves*. C goes on to explain that "the Widow means that master Pert walks as if he were made of *wires*; and *gyves*, or fetters, are hardly so applicable as *gins*, which were usually composed of wire." H did not define *gins*, but V called a gin "a perpendicular wooden axle with projecting arms," apparently after Halliwell-Phillipps, *Dictionary of Archaic and Provincial Words* (London, 1831), *s. v.* 4. See exp. n.
103. discontented] disconteuted *QQ*.
109. euer on] ever upon *Q2* : over upon *CHV*.
111. on his] on the *HV*.
129. hop'd.] hop'd *QQ*.

3.4

S. div. CHV] V adds *Inside a Tavern*.
4. Dam-me] Though the spelling of this oath was systematically corrected from *Dame me* to *Dam mee* each of the seven times it occurs on E 4 v, one would not be justified in respelling here and in 28, 39, and 69 since those lines occur on E 3 v and thus in the same form, outer E. In 143, which falls on F 1 r, in a form that was not corrected, the oath is spelled *Dam me*.
7. honorably] honourable *Q2, CHV*.
8. *Clarence*] Clarence *QQ*.
9. off, haue] off & have *Q2* : off and have *CHV*.

9f. *Piecorner*] Piecorner *QQ*.
12. *Turne-bole*] Turne-bole *QQ*.
place;] place, *QQ*.
13. *Whoore-bang*⌋ *Whoore-band*
QQ.
17, 20. *Turne-bole*] Turne-bole
QQ.
22. sirrah).] sirrah) *QQ*.
24. Sarazin;] Sarazin *Qabde* :
Sarazan *Qcf*.
33. rogue *Qabde*] rogne *Qcf*.
40. Gent. *Qabde*] Gent *Qcf*.
45.] QQ place at right opposite
44.
45, 49, 53] HV add [*Aside*.
59. Claret.] Claret: *QQ*.
61, 63] HV add [*Aside*.
64. you, outbraue *Qabde*] you
outbraue *Qcf*.
66.] HV add [*Aside*.
69. *Wel-tri'd*, if *Qabde*] *Wel-
tri'd* if *Qcf*.
70. fight, *Qabde*] fight? *Qcf*.
71.] HV add [*Aside*.
73. pots;] pots, *QQ*.
75, 76.] HV add [*Aside*.
77.] QQ place at right opposite
76.
78. Sir?] Sir. *QQ*.
79.] QQ place at right opposite
78.
82. Wrath] wrath *QQ*.
83. Lecherie *Qabde*] Leeherie
Qcf.
87.] QQ place at right opposite
86.
93, 94, 101. Dam mee *Qe*] Dame
me *Qabcdf*.
102. *England*] England *QQ*.
104f. healths Master *Weltrid?*
wee'le *Qe, Q2, CHV*] healths?
wee'le *Qabcdf*.
110.] QQ place at right opposite
109.
113. so,] so? *QQ*.
Dam mee *Qe*] Dame me *Qabcdf*.
116. Lord, *Qe*] Lord *Qabcdf*.
121.] QQ place at right opposite
120.
122. *Fees.* CHV] *Tear.* QQ, Q2.
The context makes the assignment
of CHV appropriate. Opposite the
line in Qf someone has written in
ink, "*Fees.*"
Dam mee *Qe*] Dame me *Qabcdf*.
123. vse your] use not your *Q2*.
That C was printing from Q2 rather
than Q1 is further evidenced by his

note to this line: "In the reply of
Tear-chaps there is also an error:
he is made to say, 'Lord, use *not*
your own words. . . .' "
Dam mee *Qe*] Dame me *Qabcdf*.
129. *Wel-tri'd* Qe] *Wel-trii'd*
Qabcdf.
132. *Wel-trid.*] *Wel-trid*, QQ.
Hyphen not in Qacd.
150. reckoning] reckoniug *QQ*.

4.1

S. div. *quartus,*] *quarti* QQ.
V adds Lady BRIGHT's *Lodgings*.
3.] Initial and capital reduced,
lines respaced.
12.] QQ place at right opposite
11.
13. you'r Gentlewoman,] you'r
a Gentlewoman *Q2* : your gentlewoman *CHV*.
23. at] as *Q2*.
56. continencie, if] continency.
If *CHV*.
78f. hope / You *CHV*] hope you
QQ.
91. sensitiue] insensitive *HV*.
The emendation would destroy the
significance of the passage and is
not admissible; see exp. n.
98. beasts] beast *Q2, CHV*.
99. t'is] t is *Qbd*.
104. Dams;] Dams, QQ.
120. you and I] I *HV*, who apparently seek to reduce the line to
a pentameter. The emendation is
tempting also on the ground of syn-
tax since *you* should not logically
be part of the subject of *might liue*.
125. *Fleete*] Fleete QQ.
128. home?] home. *QQ*.
130. vnseene;] vnseene, QQ.
137. seruant] seruaut QQ.
141. widdow *Q2*] wddow QQ.
151ff.] CHV make new stanza.
161. vp, but] up, / But *HV*.
163. labour. *QQ, CV*] labour? *H*.
164f. a man Mid-wife] a Mid-
wife *Q2*.
169. Musique.] Musique: *QQ*.
177. her. Well Madame, Ile go]
her. / Well, Madam, I will go *HV*.
177f. Cuckold, / Ile CHV] Cuckold, ile QQ.

4.2

S. div. CHV] *V adds* BOLD's
Lodgings.

2. on] *asleep on* HV.
14. conuersion *Qacdef*] conuers-sion *Qb*.
23. breasts,] Comma dim in Qbcd.
39. done? done, done] done? done? *V*.
40. her?] her. *QQ*.
44. woman.] woman *QQ*, where the line is crowded.
63, 65, 69. *Bould*] *Botts* CH.
64.] QQ place at right opposite 63.
65. fare-well you.] fare well. *HV*.
Weltri'd] Yet, *Weltried* HV. To rewrite with HV lessens the effectiveness of Bold's reply to Well-tried. V is right that H's improvement "is less abrupt than the old reading." The abruptness, however, contributes to the comedy.
67. well; but] well; / But *HV*.
68. haue as] have / As *HV*.
69f. friend, / This *CHV*] friend, this *QQ*.
77. meane] meant *Q2*. Despite H's note, "Edits., *meant*," I have seen no copy of the first quarto which so reads.
80. after *Fees*.] HV add [*waking*.]
81. who] whom *CHV*.
85. you as *CHV*] you / As *QQ*.
86. I. Haue *CHV*] I. / Haue *QQ* [*prose*].
91. was] were *CHV*.
108. Is it] It is *CHV*.
112. to morrow morning at] to-morrow at *V*.
120. if] If *QQ*.
121. true;] true, *QQ*.
124. *Bould*,] *Bould. QQ*.

4.3

S. div. CHV] V adds *A Street*.
2. SERIEANTS] *servants* Q2. QQ add PITS, DONNER. If these are actors' names which have crept into the text, no such actors are listed by Nungezer or Bentley.
4. Vnlike] vnlike *QQ*.
6. Perchance] perchance *QQ*.
11.] QQ place at right opposite 10.
25. this] his *HV*.
28. Who] Whom *CHV*.

29.] QQ place at right opposite 28.
30f. curs, / A *CHV*] curs, a *QQ*.
33.] QQ place at right opposite 32.
36. faire shop and wife] shop and fair wife *HV*. The emendation seems to be dictated by a modern attitude. It is not easy to account bibliographically for the juxtaposition which must be assumed if it is to be admitted. The reading of the quartos, moreover, is good meter; of the emendation, bad. The meaning in QQ is satisfactory; see exp. n.
39f. foot-boy, / T'is Qab, *CHV*] foote-boy, t'is / by *Qcedf*, *Q2*.
40f. slaue; / I'le *CHV*] slaue; i'le *QQ*.
41. baile, or pay] baile / or pay *Qab* : baile, or / pay *Qcdef*, *Q2*.

4.4

S. div.] CHV continue the scene. The following dialogue presumably takes place in Ingen's house. The previous scene took place outside Seldom's house (35). All the characters of 4.3 leave the stage, and a new group of characters is introduced. A new scene seems indicated.
5. fully] Not in Q2.
7. In *Qab*] And *Qcdef*, *Q2*, *CHV*.
9. all *Qcdef*] al *Qab*.
spirit's *Qab*, *CHV*] spirit *Qcdef*, *Q2*. The change from *all* to *al* may be consequent upon the other change in the line. See text. n. to *W* 4.1.102.
15. Vnto] Upon *Q2*, *CHV*.
23. enemie] enemies *Q2*.
26. for] from *Q2*, *CHV*.
30. case] So read all QQ. C, however, said that the first quarto "reads *scale* for *case*." It has since been shown that Collier printed from a copy of Q2, revised in some readings according to QQ. See Texas Studies, 1947, 6–8. C must have been mistaken about the reading of QQ in this line.
38. man-deuouring *CHV*] man, devouring *QQ*.
40. And (. . . men) *Qb*] And . . . men, *Qacdef*, *Q2*.
These parentheses are the sole evidence that the inner form of

Signature G was probably corrected a third time while at press. See *The Library*, 5th. s., II (1947), 57f.

teeth] In Qace the top of the first *t* seems to have been broken off at the cross bar in such a way that it resembles an *r*, which in this font is often hard to distinguish from *t*. In QQ the type shoulder of the worn *t* prints very slightly at lower left so as to resemble the base of an *r*. Thus the evidence by which one distinguishes *t* from *r* is largely obliterated.

44. cut the waues that tost *Qab, CHV*] cut what by they list *Qcdef, Q2*.

48. to] too *Q2, CHV*.

52. selfe,] selfe. *QQ*.

54. her] her, *QQ*.

67. 'T had *Qab*] It had *Qcdef, Q2, CHV*.

this, to *Qab, C*] this to *Qcdef, Q2, HV*.

72. st. dir.] QQ bracket and place opposite 70f.

81. and] & *QQ*.

81f. away, / Is *CHV*] away, is *QQ*.

83. Bro. (second instance)] *Fr.* QQ : *Pr.* Q2 : PROUDLY CHV.

An interesting illustration of the development of an error. See *NQ*, CXC (1946), 11f., 86, and 173.

87f. art / A *CHV*] art a *QQ*.

89. Sir: hay,] sir! *CHV*.

95. *him*] *her* CHV.

100f. did, / And *CHV*] did, and *QQ*.

106f. away, / It *CHV*] away, it *QQ*.

110. hand.] hand *QQ*.

112. means] meaning *HV*.

112f. this, / But *CHV*] this, but *QQ*.

128.] QQ place at right opposite 127.

H adds [*Pass.* : V adds [*A Pass.*

138. whatsoe're] W h a t s o e ' e r *CHV* [*verse*].

140. mad,] Comma dim in Qcdf.

142.] QQ place at right opposite 141.

143f. false / As *CHV*] false as *QQ*.

146f. come/ My] come my *QQ*.

147. now match] now / Match *QQ*.

150. Master] M^r. *QQ*.

5.1

S. div.] CHV.

quintus,] *quintus.* QQ.

V adds *A Room in* Sir JOHN LOVE- ALL's *House.*

2.] Initial and capital reduced, lines respaced.

3f. be: / Had *CHV*] be: had *QQ*.

4. case,] case. *QQ*.

Catchword: I.

Before 5.] QQ repeat *Husb.*, incorrectly, probably owing to the line's beginning a new page (G3^v). That it was not intended is indicated by the irregular catchword, *I*, where we would expect *Husb.* if the intention had been to repeat the speech heading. The previous recto, of course, is on the outer printing form, G3^v on the inner. This sort of repetition in speakers' names is not to be confused with that following songs or letters in the text. Cf. Price, *JEGP*, XXXVI (1937), 161–163.

6. il'd *Qab*] i'le *Qcdef, Q2* : I'd *CHV*.

9. friend twould *C*] friend would *Qab* : friend it would *Qcdef, Q2, HV*.

good e'ne at *Qab, C*] good at *Qcdef, Q2, HV*.

After giving a reading from State *o* or *p* of QQ and from Q2, C by guesswork arrives at an emendation which the history of this, the inner form of Signature G, not known to him, bears out; see *A* Intro., iii, for the various states of correctness. In the second correction, which produced State *o*, *e'ne* was introduced. The intention, I think, must have been to elide *it*, but for some reason the word was dropped. Though *it* disappears through what may be regarded as an alteration consequent to another alteration, the reading adopted seems sufficiently conservative.

15. you jest *Qabde*] youj est *Qcf*.

17. in] to *HV*.

17f. ha? / Pish [*prose*]] ha? /
Pish *CHV* [*verse*].
30. QQ place at right after 29.
33. wrongs *(second instance)*]
wrong *Qd*.
41. (A . . . conceit.) *Qab*] *A*
. . . conceit. *Qcdef, Q2, CHV*.
48. lowzy *Qabde*] lowzie *Qcf* :
louzie *Q2*.
50. On pray *Qab, CHV*] On I
pray *Qcdef, Q2*.
57. artillerie *Qab, CHV*] readines *Qcdef, Q2*. The change from
readines to *artillerie* between States
m and *n* and State *o* of this form
may perhaps be explained as arising
from someone's yielding to the urge
to improve a figure. Another explanation, however, seems more
likely. In Elizabethan chirography
the two words might have looked
almost identical, particularly if
artillerie had been spelled with
one *l*.
59. yeeld,] Comma dim in Qde.
60. *Troy*] Troy *QQ*.
65. *nescit* Qabde] *nesct* Qcf.
67. much to] much as to *Q2,*
CHV.
73. wife.— I *Qabde,, C*] wife. I
Qcf, Q2. HV insert [*Aside.*] after
wife.
74f. will. / I *CHV*] will. I *QQ*.
78. sue a] sue for a *CV* : sue
[for] a *H*.
Exit] QQ place after 75. HV
preface with [*Aside*.
82. seruant?] seruant *Qab* :
seruan *Qcdef*.
86. Conscience *Qabde*] Con-
scence *Qcf*.
88. if] If *QQ*.
90. think'st] apostrophe dim in
or absent from *Qabcdf*.
98. mine owne] mineowne *QQ*.
102. things] things, *C* : things.
HV.
107. you know] you [not] know
H : you not know *V*.
113. thoroughly;] thoroughly, *QQ*.
120. And] and *QQ*.
131. my] y *dim in Qdf*.
weeping] *Second* e *dim in Qd*.
139. to] and *CHV*.
Count,] Count. QQ.
141. Widdow] Widowes *Q2*.
144.] QQ place at right opposite
143.

5.2

S. div. *quintus*] quinti Qacdef,
Q2 : quarti Qb.
secunda CHV] prima QQ.
V adds *A Room in Lord* PROUD-
LY's *House*.
1. MAID] *Ladie* HONOR *QQ*.
5. BROTHER, *with a letter* CHV]
SVBTLE *with a letter* QQ. C notes:
"the words have been misplaced,
and should have followed 'Brother,'
who delivers it to the Lady Honor."
and GRACE] *and his wife* QQ :
with his wife Q2, CHV.
6.] Initial and capital reduced,
lines respaced.
14f. all, / And *CHV*] all, and
QQ.
16f. well, / You *CHV*] well,
you *QQ*.
20.] QQ place at right opposite
19.
21. might] migt *QQ*.
25.] QQ place at right opposite
24.
31. bed,] bed *QQ*.
33. *Epithalamions* Q2] *Epitha-*
lamious QQ.
39. Physition.] Physition *QQ*.
41. Gentlewoman,] Gentlewoman. *QQ*.
42f. pardon, / That *CHV*] pardon, that *QQ*.
43. does] Does *QQ*.
44. *Wel-tri'd*, I] Welltried, / I
CHV.
45. manners if] manners, / If
CHV.
49. like the] like a *Q2*.
55.] QQ place at right opposite
54.
62.] QQ place at right opposite
61.
64. *Bould*, vm] Bold? / Um *HV*.
66. couching] coughing *H*, who
emends no doubt in response to C's
query, "Ought we not rather to
read '*coughing* gear'?" I know no
form of *couch* or *couching* which
has a counterpart among the forms
of *cough* or *coughing*. Though Count
Feesimple coughs, *couching* is entirely appropriate.
geere my] gear, my *C* [*prose*] :
gear, / My *HV* [*verse*].
67. rich as] rich / As *HV*.

69. faith, that] faith, / That *HV*.

80. there where] there, / Where *CHV*.

Cupids] cupids *QQ*.

83. WIDOW *and* BOVLD] *Wid. Bould QQ*.

st. dir.] QQ bracket and place at right opposite 82.

84.] CHV place after 89.

91. it] as *Q2*.

93. side.] side: *QQ*.

99f. heauen, / As *CHV*] heauen, as *QQ*.

113f. begins, / Abundant *CHV*] begins, abundant *QQ*.

117. PARSON] QQ are inconsistent in respect to this character's name. In stage directions (117, 130, 182) he is uniformly called *Parson*. In the lines he is four times called Parson (39, 128, 138, 167) and three times called *Priest* (195, 200, 245). His two speeches are headed *Priest*. I uniformly call him *Parson*.

118. GRACE] MRIS. SELD. *QQ*.

126f. ingredient / About me, shall *CHV*] ingredient about me, / Shall *QQ*.

128. I] to *HV*. Emendation is not required since the passage can be explained as it stands; see exp. n. To adopt H's emendation would create a difficulty of interpretation in 129, which is clear if we keep QQ.

132.] QQ place at right opposite 131.

139. away, and] away, / And *QQ* : Away *HV* [*verse*].

hold her] hold / Her *HV*.

141. my] My *HV* [*verse*].

is a] is / A *HV*.

142. commoditie, we] commodity, / We *HV*.

142f. incon-ueniencie. My] inconviency. / My *HV*.

164. here?] here *QQ*.

165. Hoy-day] hoy-day *QQ*.

166. How] how *QQ*.

168. *Omnes*] omnes QQ.

Before 169.] QQ repeat *Feesi*.

170f.] The marginal note, "*Pistols / for Bro.*," bracketed at right in QQ, looks like a bookkeeper's re-

minder that the Brother be provided with these hand properties. Why the note occurs here rather than opposite the Brother's entrance at 117 I can not say; it can hardly be said to be an anticipatory direction. It seems to have bearing on the question of the copy furnished the printer of *Amends*. I relegate it to the notes because it is more likely to have originated with the company than with the author; see Greg, *Dramatic Documents from the Elizabethan Playhouses* (Oxford, 1931), 209.

181. in a] in her CHV.

183. *Bros.*] *Bro. QQ*.

187. For] Forgive *H*. But the emendation is no improvement either metrically or logically, and it is not necessary to emend. The remainder of Ingen's speech shows that he is in no mood to ask forgiveness.

189. gowt] gout *CH* : goat *V*.

195. first (witnesse] first, / Witness *CHV*.

196. married.] married, *QQ*.

197, 201. *Parson*] *Priest QQ*.

201. 'Tis] It is *HV*.

201f. late, / I'm] late. I am *HV*. vndone alreadie, wine] undone / Already [by] wine *H* : Already by wine *V*.

202. Tobacco;] Tobacco, *QQ*.

209f. right, / In *CHV*] right in *QQ*.

214f. Gentleman / Your *CHV*] Gentleman your *QQ*.

215. law] law ['s] *H* : law's *V*.

215f. mean'd, / And *CHV*] mean'd, and *QQ*.

216f. conceiue) / By *CHV*] conceiue) by *QQ*.

223. dispatcht] despatch *CHV*.

228ff.] H alters to:

'Twixt this gentleman and
   myself
There have been some love-
   passages, from which
Here I do free him, and
   [he] take this lady—.

V alters to:

'Twixt this gentleman

And myself, there have been
   some love passages
Which here I free him, and
   take this lady—.

These rearrangements seem arbitrary and not too helpful. The problems are what to the modern reader seems the awkward separation of the two parts of the compound object of *'Twixt, Gentleman* and *my selfe,* and the construction of *take.* The words *and my selfe,* it would be easy to say, might have been written in the margin of the author's manuscript and been set by the printer in the wrong line; but such explanations are only guesswork.

The word *take* may be part of a compound with *free* or an independent imperative. See exp. n. for one interpretation.
229. has] have *CHV.*
231. and take] and pray him take *HV.*
246. are all] all are *CHV.*
259.] QQ place at right opposite 253.
264.] QQ place at right opposite 258.
272. heare my] hear me, my *CHV.*
288. doe.] doe? *QQ.*
   must I] I must *CHV.*
299.] QQ place at right opposite 293.

VI. BIBLIOGRAPHY

VI. BIBLIOGRAPHY

1. WORKS BY FIELD

i. Individual authorship

A Woman is a Weather-cocke. London, 1612.
Amends for Ladies. London, 1618.
Amends for Ladies: With the Humour of Roring. London, 1618.
Amends for Ladies. London, 1639.

Collier, John Payne (ed.). *A Woman Is a Weathercock.* London, 1829. *Amends for Ladies.* London, 1829.
———— *A Woman Is a Weathercock* and *Amends for Ladies.* In *The Old English Drama.* London, 1830. Vol. II. A reprint of the 1829 ed.
———— *A Woman Is a Weathercock* and *Amends for Ladies.* In *Five Old Plays Forming a Supplement to the Collection of Dodsley and Others.* London, 1833. Often bound as Vol. XIII, Dodsley[3]. Remainders of the 1829 ed.
Hazlitt, William Carew (ed.). *A Woman Is a Weathercock* and *Amends for Ladies.* [1875]. In *A Select Collection of Old English Plays: Originally Published by Robert Dodsley in the Year 1744,* 4th ed. London, 1874–1876. Vol. XI.
Verity, A. Wilson (ed.). *A Woman Is a Weathercock* and *Amends for Ladies.* In *Nero and Other Plays.* Edited by Herbert P. Horne *et al.* Mermaid Series. London, 1888.

"*To the worthiest Maister Ionson.*" 1607. Dedicatory verse to *Volpone.* In:
> *Ben: Ionson his Volpone Or The Foxe.* 1607. Greg No. 259aII only; *Bibl. Dram.,* I, 391.
> Simpson, Percy. "Field and Ben Jonson," *NQ,* 8th Series, VIII (1895), 301.
> Cf. Herford, C. H. and Percy Simpson (edd.). *Ben Jonson.* Oxford, 1925— Vol. V, pp. 5f.

"*To my lov'd friend M. John Fletcher, on his Pastorall.*" 1608. Dedicatory verse to *The Faithful Shepherdess.* In:
> *The Faithfull Shepheardesse.* London, [1609–1610], both issues. Reprinted in quartos of 1629, 1634, 1656, and 1665.

Glover, A. and A. R. Waller (edd.). *The Works of Francis Beaumont and John Fletcher.* Cambridge English Classics. Cambridge, 1905–1912. II, 519.

"*To his worthy beloued friend M*ʳ*. Ben Ionson.*" 1611.
Dedicatory verse to *Catiline.* In:
Catiline his Conspiracy. London, 1611. Also in the edition of 1635.
Harris, Lynn Harold (ed.). *Catiline His Conspiracy.* Yale Studies in English, LIII. New Haven, 1916. P. 217.

Letter to Philip Henslowe, beginning "Mʳ Dawborne and J." [1613].
Dulwich MS I, Article 100.
Malone Var., XXI, 395; J. P. Collier, *The Alleyn Papers* (London, 1843), 48; Greg, *HP,* 84.
Letter to Philip Henslowe, beginning "Father Hinchlow J am vnluckily taken." [1613].
Dulwich MS I, Article 69.
Malone Var., XXI, 404f.; Collier, *The Alleyn Papers,* 65; Greg, *HP,* 67.
Letter to Philip Henslowe, beginning "you vnderstand oʳ vnfortunate extremitie." [1613]. Postscripts by Daborne and Massinger.
Dulwich MS I, Article 68.
Malone Var., III, 337f.; Collier, *The Alleyn Papers,* 120; Greg, *HP,* 65f.
*Feild the Players Letter to M*ʳ *Sutton, Preacher att St. Mary Overs.* 1616.
Calendar of State Papers, Domestic, 1611–1618. Edited by Mary Anne E. Greene. London, 1858. P. 419.
Halliwell-Phillipps, J. O. (ed.). *The Remonstrance of Nathaniel Field.* London, 1865. Reprinted in his *Illustrations of the Life of Shakespeare.* London, 1874. Pp. 115–117.

ii. Collaborative authorship

1. *Acknowledged collaboration*

With Fletcher and Massinger:
The Jeweler of Amsterdam, or the Hague. 1617. Lost.
With Massinger:
The Fatal Dowry. 1619.
The Fatal Dowry. London, 1632.
Lockert, Jr., Charles Lacy (ed.). *The Fatal Dowry.* Lancaster, 1918.

2. Attributed collaboration

With Beaumont and Fletcher, et al.?

Four Plays, or Moral Representations, in One. 1612. In:
*Comedies and Tragedies Written by Francis Beaumont
and Iohn Fletcher Gentlemen.* London, 1647.
Glover, A. and A. R. Waller (edd.). *The Works of
Francis Beaumont and John Fletcher*, X, 287–364.

The Honest Man's Fortune. 1613. In:
Comedies and Tragedies, 1647.
The Works of Francis Beaumont and John Fletcher, X,
202–280.

The Queen of Corinth. 1617. In:
Comedies and Tragedies, 1647.
The Works of Francis Beaumont and John Fletcher, VI,
1–78.

The Knight of Malta. 1618. In:
Comedies and Tragedies, 1647.
The Works of Francis Beaumont and John Fletcher, VII,
78–163.

Brock, Marianne (ed.). *Knight of Malta.* Unpublished
Ph. D. dissertation, Bryn Mawr, 1944. Introduction
available on microfilm.

2. PRINCIPAL WORKS ABOUT FIELD

Baldwin, Thomas Whitfield. "Nathaniel and Nathan Field," *Times Literary Supplement*, 27 May 1926, p. 355.
——————— "Nathaniel Field and Robert Wilson," *Modern Language Notes*, XLI (1926), 32–34.
Beck, C. *Philip Massinger, "The Fatal Dowry," Einleitung zu einer neuen Ausgabe.* Bayreuth, 1906.
Bentley, Gerald Eades. *The Jacobean and Caroline Stage: Dramatic Companies and Players.* Oxford, 1941. Pp. 434–436.
Boas, Frederick S. *An Introduction to Stuart Drama.* London, 1946. Pp. 330–336.
Boyle, Ronald. "Beaumont, Fletcher and Massinger," *Englische Studien*, V (1882), 74–96; VII (1884), 66–87; VIII (1885), 39–61; IX (1886), 209–239; X (1887), 383–412.
——————— "Beaumont, Fletcher, and Massinger," *Transactions of the New Shakespeare Society*, Series I, 1 (1880–1886), 579–628.
Brinkley, Roberta Florence. "Nathan and Nathaniel Field," *Modern Language Notes*, XLII (1927), 10–15.
——————— *Nathan Field, the Actor-Playwright.* Yale Studies in English, LXXVII. New Haven, 1928. Based on a Yale Ph. D. dissertation, 1924, of the same title.

Chambers, Edmund K. *The Elizabethan Stage.* Oxford, 1923. II, 316–318 and III, 313–314.

—————— "Nathaniel Field and Joseph Taylor," *Modern Language Review*, IV (1908–1909), 395–396.

Chelli, Maurice. *Étude sur la Collaboration de Massinger avec Fletcher et son groupe.* Paris, 1926.

Collier, John Payne. *Memoirs of the Principal Actors in the Plays of Shakespeare.* London, 1846. Pp. 206–223.

Fenton, Frank L. "Authorship of Acts III and IV of 'The Queen of Corinth,'" *Modern Language Notes*, XLII (1927), 94–96.

Fischer, Heinrich. *Nathaniel Fields Komödie "Amends for Ladies," eine literarhistorische Untersuchung und Quellenstudie.* Kiel, 1907.

Fleay, Frederick Gard. "Annals of the Career of Nathaniel Field," *Englische Studien*, XIII (1889), 28–36.

Greg, Walter William. "Nathan Field and the Beaumont and Fletcher Folio of 1679," *Review of English Studies*, III (1927), 337–338.

—————— "Nathaniel and Nathan Field," *Times Literary Supplement*, 15 April 1926, p. 83; 3 June 1926, p. 374.

—————— Review of Brinkley, *Nathan Field, the Actor-Playwright; Review of English Studies*, V (1929), 108–110.

Hillebrand, Harold Newcomb. Review of Brinkley, *Nathan Field, the Actor-Playwright; Modern Language Notes*, XLIV (1929), 397.

Keller, Wolfgang. Review of Brinkley, *Nathan Field, the Actor-Playwright; Shakespeare Jahrbuch*, LIV (1929), 200–201.

Knight, Joseph. "Field, Nathaniel." *Dictionary of National Biography*, XVIII, 408–410.

Langbaine, Gerard. "Nathaniel Field," *An Account of the English Dramatick Poets.* Oxford, 1691. Pp. 198–199.

Lawrence, William John. "A Puzzling Point in 'A Woman Is a Weathercock,'" *Times Literary Supplement*, 12 July 1928, p. 520.

Lockert, Jr., Charles Lacy (ed.). *The Fatal Dowry.* Lancaster, 1918. Pp. 8–21.

Lüdeke, H. Review of Brinkley, *Nathan Field, the Actor-Playwright; Beiblatt zur Anglia*, XL (1929), 305–306.

Mabbott, Thomas Olive. "Who 'Thrusts the Boy Out' in Field's 'Amends for Ladies'?" *Notes and Queries*, CXC (1946), 86.

Nungezer, Edwin. *A Dictionary of Actors.* New Haven, 1929. Pp. 135–141.

Oliphant, E. H. C. "A Note," *Modern Language Notes*, XLIII (1928), 112–113.

—————— *The Plays of Beaumont and Fletcher.* New Haven, 1927.

—————— "The Plays of Beaumont and Fletcher: Some Additional Notes," *Philological Quarterly*, IX (1930), 7–22.

—————— "The Works of Beaumont and Fletcher," *Englische Studien*, XIV (1890), 53–94.

Peery, William. "A Latin Quotation in 'Wonder of Women' and 'Woman Is a Weathercock,'" *Notes and Queries*, CXCI (1946), 33f.

———— "A Woman Is a Weather-cocke," *Times Literary Supplement*, 16 February 1946, p. 84.

———— "*Eastward Ho!* and *Woman Is a Weathercock*," *Modern Language Notes*, LXII (1947), 131f.

———— "Field's *A Woman Is a Weathercock*, III, iii," *The Explicator*, IV (1945–46), No. 43.

———— "Four Misassigned Speeches in *A Woman Is a Weathercock*," *Notes and Queries*, CXCI (1946), 230f.

———— "Frank vs. Frater in *Amends for Ladies*," *Notes and Queries*, CXC (1946), 173.

———— "Lady Perfect and Sir John Loveall," *Notes and Queries*, CLXXXIX (1945), 192.

———— "Nathan and Nathaniel Field Again," *Notes and Queries*, CXC 1946), 121.

———— "Nathan Field's Dates," *Modern Language Review*, XLI (1946), 409–410.

———— "Nid Field Was Whose Scholar?" *Shakespeare Association Bulletin*, XXI (1946), 80–86.

———— "Nineteenth-Century Editorial Practice as Illustrated in the Descent of the Text of Nathan Field." U. of Texas *Studies in English*, 1947, 5–17.

———— "Note on a Commonplace: The Three Souls," *Philological Quarterly*, XXV (1946), 382f.

———— "Proverbs and Proverbial Lore in the Comedies of Nathan Field," *Southern Folklore Quarterly*, X (1946), 1–16.

———— "Rosseter's Blackfriars Theatre," *Theatre Notebook*, I (1946), 59.

———— "Six Confused Exits and Entrances in the Plays of Nathan Field," *Notes and Queries*, CXCI (1946), 53–56.

———— "The *Curious Impertinent* in *Amends for Ladies*," *Hispanic Review*, XIV (1946), 344–353.

———— "The Influence of Ben Jonson on Nathan Field," *Studies in Philology*, XLIII (1946), 482–497.

———— "The Portrayal of Woman in the Comedies of Nathan Field," *Shakespeare Association Bulletin*, XXI (1946), 129–141.

———— "The 1618 Quarto of *Amends for Ladies*," *The Library*, 5th series, II (1947), 53–59.

———— "The Quarto of Field's *Weather-cocke*," *The Library*, 5th series, I (1946), 62–64.

———— "The Roaring Boy Again," *Shakespeare Association Bulletin*, XXIII (1948), 12–16, 78–86.

———— "Three Contented Widows," *Comparative Literature Studies*, XXI and XXII (1946), 29.

——————— "Who 'Thrusts the Boy Out'?" *Notes and Queries*, CXC (1946), 11–12.

Richter, H. Review of Brinkley, *Nathan Field, the Actor-Playwright; Die Neuren Sprachen*, n. s., XXXIX (1929), 222.

Simpson, Percy. "Field and Ben Jonson," *Notes and Queries*, 8th series, VIII (1895), 301.

Sykes, H. Dugdale. *Sidelights on Elizabethan Drama*. London, 1924. Pp. 200–219. Reprints "Nathaniel Field's Work in the Beaumont and Fletcher Plays," *Notes and Queries*, 12th Series, VIII (1921), 141–3, 164–7, 183f., 204–6.

Times Literary Supplement. Review of Brinkley, *Nathan Field, the Actor-Playwright; TLS*, 7 February 1929, p. 95.

Verhasselt, Éliane. "A Biography of Nathan Field, Dramatist and Actor." *Revue belge de philologie et d'histoire*, XXV (1946–47), 485–508.

VII. ABBREVIATED REFERENCES

VII. ABBREVIATED REFERENCES

A—Nathan Field, *Amends for Ladies.*

Adams—Joseph Quincy Adams, *Shakespearean Playhouses* (Boston, 1917).

Baldwin—Thomas Whitfield Baldwin, *Organization and Personnel of the Shakespearean Company* (Princeton, 1927).

Bayne—Ronald Bayne, "Lesser Jacobean and Caroline Dramatists," *CHEL,* VI, 236–270.

BC—see Fleay.

Bentley—Gerald Eades Bentley, *The Jacobean and Caroline Stage: Dramatic Companies and Players* (Oxford, 1941).

Bibl.—see McKerrow.

Bibl. Dram.—see Greg.

Brinkley—Roberta Florence Brinkley, *Nathan Field, the Actor-Playwright* (New Haven, 1928).

C—John Payne Collier.

Chambers—E. K. Chambers, *The Elizabethan Stage*, 4 vols. (Oxford, 1923).

Chambers, *S*—E. K. Chambers, *William Shakespeare: A Study of Facts and Problems*, 2 vols. (Oxford, 1930).

CHEL—*The Cambridge History of English Literature*. Edited by A. W. Ward and A. R. Waller, 14 vols. (Cambridge, 1907–1916).

Collier, *W*—John Payne Collier (ed.), *A Woman Is a Weathercock* (London, 1829).

Collier, *A*—John Payne Collier (ed.), *Amends for Ladies* (London, 1829).

Collier, *HEDP*—John Payne Collier, *The History of English Dramatic Poetry to the Time of Shakespeare: and Annals of the Stage to the Restoration*, 3 vols. (2d ed.; London, 1879).

Collier, *MPA*—John Payne Collier, *Memoirs of the Principal Actors in the Plays of Shakespeare* (London, 1846).

Creizenach—Wilhelm Creizenach, *The English Drama in the Age of Shakespeare*. Translated from *Geschichte des neuren Dramas*, IV, by Cécile Hugon. Philadelphia, 1916.

DNB—*Dictionary of National Biography*. Edited by Leslie Stephen and Sidney Lee, 63 vols. (London, 1885–1901).

Dodsley[3]—Robert Dodsley, *A Select Collection of Old English Plays*, 3d edition. Edited by John Payne Collier, 12 vols. (London, 1825–1827).

Dodsley[4]—Robert Dodsley, *A Select Collection of Old English Plays*, 4th edition. Edited by W. Carew Hazlitt, 15 vols. (London, 1874–1876).

EP—see Greg.

ES—*Englische Studien*. Leipsig, 1887—.

Field (followed by a number)—*SFQ*, X (1946), 1–16.

Fischer—Heinrich Fischer, *National Fields Komödie "Amends for Ladies," eine literarhistorische Untersuchung und Quellenstudie* (Kiel, 1907).

Fleay, BC—Frederick Gard Fleay, *A Biographical Chronicle of the English Drama, 1559–1642*, 2 vols. (London, 1891).

Fleay, LS—Frederick Gard Fleay, *A Chronicle History of the London Stage, 1559–1642* (London, 1890).

Freeburg—Victor Oscar Freeburg, *Disguise Plots in Elizabethan Drama: a Study in Stage Tradition* (New York, 1915).

Greg, *Bibl. Dram.*—Walter William Greg, *A Bibliography of the English Printed Drama to the Restoration*, 1 vol. published (London, 1939–   ).

Greg, EP—Walter William Greg, *The Editorial Problem in Shakespeare: A Survey of the Foundations of the Text* (Oxford, 1942).

Greg, HD—Walter William Greg (ed.), *Henslowe's Diary*, 2 vols. (London, 1904–1908).

Greg, HP—Walter William Greg (ed.), *Henslowe Papers: Being Documents Supplementary to Henslowe's Diary* (London, 1907).

H—W. C. Hazlitt.

Harbage—Alfred Harbage, *Annals of English Drama 975–1700: An Analytical Record of All Plays, Extant or Lost, Chronologically Arranged and Indexed by Authors, Titles, Dramatic Companies, etc.* (Philadelphia, 1940).

Hazlitt—W. Carew Hazlitt (ed.), *A Woman Is a Weathercock* and *Amends for Ladies*. In Dodsley⁴, XI.

HD—see Greg.

HEDP—see Collier.

Hillebrand—Harold Newcomb Hillebrand, *The Child Actors* (Urbana, 1926).

HP—see Greg.

JEGP—*The Journal of English and Germanic Philology*. Bloomington and Urbana, 1897—. In progress.

Koeppel—E. Koeppel, *Studien über Shakespeare's Wirkung auf zeitgenössische Dramatiker.* (Louvain, 1905).

Langbaine—Gerard Langbaine, *An Account of the English Dramatick Poets* (Oxford, 1691).

Lawrence 1—William John Lawrence, *The Elizabethan Playhouse and Other Studies* (Stratford, 1912).

Lawrence 2—William John Lawrence, *The Elizabethan Playhouse and Other Studies, Second Series* (Stratford, 1913).

Linthicum—M. Channing Linthicum, *Costume in the Drama of Shakespeare and his Contemporaries* (Oxford, 1936).

LS—see Fleay.

Malone Var.—*The Plays and Poems of William Shakespeare.* Edited by Edmond Malone; revised by James Boswell; 21 vols. (London, 1821).

McGinn—D. J. McGinn, *Shakespeare's Influence on the Drama of his Age Studied in Hamlet* (New Brunswick, 1938).

McKerrow, *Bibl.*—Ronald B. McKerrow, *An Introduction to Bibliography for Literary Students* (Oxford, 1927).

MLN—*Modern Language Notes.* Baltimore, 1886—. In progress.

MLR—The Modern Language Review. Cambridge, 1905–6—. In progress.
MP—Modern Philology. Chicago, 1903—. In progress.
MPA—see Collier.
MSC—Malone Society Collections, 2 vols. General editor W. W. Greg. (London, 1907–1931).
Murray—John Tucker Murray, *English Dramatic Companies, 1558–1642,* 2 vols. (London, 1910).
NED—A New English Dictionary on Historical Principles. Edited by J. A. H. Murray and others, 10 vols. and suppl. (Oxford, 1888–1933).
NQ—Notes and Queries. London, 12th Series; 1849—. In progress.
Nungezer—Edwin Nungezer, *A Dictionary of Actors and of Other Persons Associated with the Public Representation of Plays in England before 1642* (New Haven, 1929).
Oxford Proverbs—The Oxford Dictionary of English Proverbs. Compiled by William George Smith (Oxford, 1935).
Partridge—Eric Partridge, *A Dictionary of Slang and Unconventional English* (New York, 1937).
PMLA—Publications of the Modern Language Association of America. New York, 1886—. In progress.
Powell—Chilton Latham Powell, *English Domestic Relations, 1487–1653. A Study of Matrimony and Family Life in Theory and Practice as Revealed by the Literature, Law and History of the Period* (New York, 1917).
PQ—Philological Quarterly. Iowa City, 1922—. In progress.
RES—The Review of English Studies. London, 1925—. In progress.
Reyher—Paul Reyher, *Les Masques Anglais: Étude Sur les Ballets et la Vie de Cour en Angleterre (1512–1640)* (Paris, 1909).
Rosenbach—A. S. W. Rosenbach, "The Curious-Impertinent in English Dramatic Literature before Shelton's Translation of Don Quixote," *MLN,* XVII (1902), 179–184.
SAB—Shakespeare Association Bulletin. New York, 1924—. In progress.
Schelling—Felix E. Schelling, *Elizabethan Drama 1558–1642,* 2 vols. (Boston, 1908).
SE—Shakespeare's England: An Account of the Life and Manners of his Age. Edited by Sidney Lee and C. T. Onions, 2 vols. (Oxford, 1916).
SFQ—Southern Folklore Quarterly. Gainesville, 1937—. In progress.
Simpson—Percy Simpson, *Shakespearean Punctuation* (Oxford, 1911).
SP—Studies in Philology. Chapel Hill, 1904—. In progress.
SR—Transcript of the Registers of the Company of Stationers, 1554–1640. Edited by Edward Arber, 5 vols. (London, 1875–1894).
STC—Short-Title Catalogue of Books Printed in England, Scotland and Ireland, and of English Books Printed Abroad 1475–1640. Compiled by A. W. Pollard and R. G. Redgrave. (London, 1926).
Steele—Mary Susan Steele, *Plays & Masques at Court During the Reigns of Elizabeth, James and Charles* (New Haven, 1926).
Thorndike—Ashley H. Thorndike, *English Comedy* (New York, 1929).

TLS—Times Literary Supplement. London, 1902—. In progress.

V—A. W. Verity.

Verhasselt—Éliane Verhasselt, "A Biography of Nathan Field, Dramatist and Actor," *Revue belge de philologie et d'histoire,* XXV (1946-47), 485-508.

Verity—A. W. Verity (ed.), *A Woman Is a Weathercock* and *Amends for Ladies.* In *Nero and Other Plays,* edited by Herbert P. Horne and others (London, 1888).

W—Nathan Field, *A Woman is a Weather-cocke.*

Wallace—Charles William Wallace, *The Children of the Chapel at Blackfriars 1597-1603* (Lincoln, 1908).

Ward—A. W. Ward, *A History of English Dramatic Literature to the Death of Queen Anne,* 3 vols. (2d ed.; London, 1899).

Wheatley—Henry B. Wheatley, *London Past and Present: Its History, Associations, and Traditions,* 3 vols. (London, 1891).

VIII. INDEX

VIII. INDEX

[Some very good editions are not indexed. A complete index to a book of this sort, indeed, is seldom practicable. To list all the references to W, A, C, H, V, Brinkley, and Chambers, for example, would be to list under each of these headings the numbers of most of the pages of commentary in this work. The index which follows—to the introductions and notes only—is planned to meet those of the reader's needs that are readily predictable: for indices to the proper names, subjects (including words glossed), editions of standard authors cited (marked "ed"), and bibliographical information for such authorities as do not appear in the Bibliography or Abbreviated References (marked "bibl"). Principal discussions of authorities are indexed; mere citations of them—like names of editors and of characters in literary works, and like variants in textual notes—are usually not. Titles are grouped alphabetically under authors' names. Wherever possible, the spelling is modern so that confusion and duplication may be avoided; but I confess to traditionalism about the title of Spenser's epic and of some other works.]